TREASURY OF
WOODWORKING
PROJECTS

by the editors of
Science & Mechanics magazine

ARCO PUBLISHING, INC.
NEW YORK

Published by Arco Publishing, Inc.
215 Park Avenue South, New York, N.Y. 10003

Library of Congress Cataloging in Publication Data
Main entry under title:

Treasury of Woodworking Projects.

1. Woodwork—Amateurs' manuals. I. Science & Mechanics.
TT185.T74   1985   684.1'042   84-20339
ISBN 0-668-06325-4 (Cloth Edition)

Printed in the United States of America

10 9 8 7 6 5 4 3 2 1

CONTENTS

PROJECTS AND TECHNIQUES BY CATEGORY

TABLES

CABINETRY

MULTI-PURPOSE STORAGE UNITS

WALL UNITS AND BUILT-INS

DESKS

MISCELLANEOUS PROJECTS

TOOLS AND TECHNIQUES

ABOUT THIS BOOK

Whether you know the pleasures of working with wood or simply wish to explore them, whether you already consider yourself an expert craftsperson or are aspiring to that honorable title, this book will prove to be a valuable friend.

The projects were carefully chosen to suit different levels of woodworking skill. The majority of them are the creations of John Capotosto, who is well known for being the dean of do-it-yourself furniture designers. When built, these projects will enhance the beauty and utility of your home at a fraction of the cost of such furniture on the retail market. We hope you will appreciate the richly varied projects, and we think you will spot several that you will want to tackle.

You also will learn how to use joinery techniques, how to use tools more effectively, and how to properly finish wood. More experienced woodworkers will discover many new tricks and shortcuts, along with special-purpose joints that have long been used in making fine furniture.

A word about the second table of contents, Projects and Techniques by Category, seems in order. Groupings were, inevitably, somewhat arbitrary. For example, if cabinet storage is at a premium in your home, consider the Multi-Purpose Storage Units as well as the projects under Cabinetry for your first project. Alternatives might even be the Wall Units and Built-ins or, under Desks, the Hideaway Home Office and Classic Rolltop Desk. These, too, are attractive and provide generous storage space.

When friends compliment you on your first or current creation at some Saturday night get-together, you will have that great feeling of satisfaction, knowing that you built it. Good building!

The Editors

Master Craftsmen's Joinery Methods

IN ROUGH CONSTRUCTION and in much carpentry you can put joints together with nails, but in furniture making the fastenings must be concealed. Doweling is an easy solution. Well made dowel joints are amply strong for most work. A typical use is in the corner of a frame, where the end of a rail butts against a stile edge, or where the rail combines with a cabinet leg or post, and again when two stretchers come together to form a tee. In the simplest assembly, dowels pass through the stile into the rail, a satisfactory fastening where the frame edge will be covered by other wood or by opaque paint. To bore holes, clamp the well-fitting pair in a vise being sure that the parts meet at right angles with the face sides in exact alignment. When one piece is thinner than the other shim it. Mark meeting parts A-A for the first joint, B-B for the second, and so on. Gauge a centered pencil line along the edge of the stile to be bored, and make cross-marks to indicate dowel centers. As a tight dowel might split the end of the stile, space the near hole down a little, say ⅝ in.; and the second hole ½ in. from the level of the inside edge of the rail. A third dowel would be centered between the others. For ¾ to 1 in. stock, dowels ⅜ in. in dia. are commonly used. If the wood has alternating hard and soft grain, punch a starting hole for the auger bit with a small nail set. For boring, sight along the rail to parallel the bit with the work; if you're inexperienced, press a short straightedge against the face of the joint to check the bit direction. Continue boring until the hole in the rail is 1¼ in. deep. A bit gauge is valuable here.

Cut dowel pins slightly underlength, lightly chamfering one end of each. Apply glue to pins and holes and assemble frame, driving pins in. Clamp enough to close the joints, saw off projecting dowels, and clamp tightly. Pad blocks under the clamp jaws not only prevent marring of the edges but allow for dowels that might protrude as the points are tightened. Test for squareness. If frame is twisted when taken from the clamps, sight

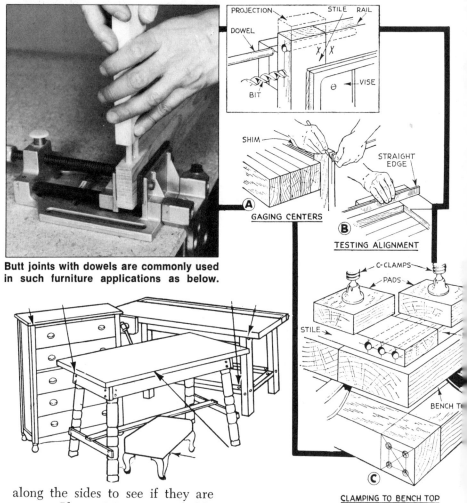

Butt joints with dowels are commonly used in such furniture applications as below.

A GAGING CENTERS
B TESTING ALIGNMENT
C CLAMPING TO BENCH TOP

To bore, clamp fitted pair in vise (A). Straightedge checks alignment (B). Crossmarks indicate the dowel centers in (C).

along the sides to see if they are sprung. If not, joints are probably cut out of true, a condition shown by laying a straightedge across each. Correct by sawing along the joints, fitting them more accurately, and doweling again.

Dress the joints with light planing and scraping, drawing scraper diagonally across to prevent tearing the wood. Sand as far as possible lengthwise of the grain. Secure work to the bench top with C-clamps for boring through dowel holes. If stock is nearly square, or thick, a better spread of dowels is possible by centering them on a diagonal. For greater strength, use four dowels. Through-doweling is featured in certain provincial furniture. The rail or apron is lapped over a leg and dowel holes are bored through. Square guide lines

across the rails, or in *splayed* work —legs spreading toward the floor— use a bevel square. Bore rail separately and use as a template for marking the legs. Often dowels are featured in furniture decoration being cut long enough to project as a rounded button, or, cut a little short to leave the hole unfilled to the top, a commercial button plugging the cavity. Sometimes pieces are screwed together, the screwhead being countersunk so that a button, glued in, hides the screw.

In blind, or hidden doweling, we must match up holes in the edges of the stiles with those bored in the rail ends, a situation much like that of doweling boards edge-to-edge. First, join frame corners. After the squared rail end has been fitted to the stile edge, set a marking gauge for half the thickness of the wood, and working from the face side, scribe a line on the joint edge of the stile and on the rail end. Square lines across the rail end to locate centers, punch them, and bore, taking every precaution to keep them square with the end. A doweling jig is a useful accessory. Mark dowel centers on the stile with the rail as a pattern; have the working faces of both to the same side and the working edges corresponding, usually the inside edges of the completed frame. Drill holes in a vertical position while pieces are held in the bench vise; in hard wood it

is easier to drill end grain horizontally.

Cut dowels ⅛ in. short so they will not hold the joints open, and to allow for air and glue imprisoned in the holes. Chamfer the ends slightly to keep them from tearing the wood as they are forced in. Test frame assembly for alignment, but don't enter dowels too far in the holes if they are very tight, as it might be impossible to pull them out. Whether the joint is flat when clamped can be tested without the dowels. A frame that will not lie flat after assembly will eventually twist, even though it has been brought flat in the clamps and while drying.

In some period tables and cabinets, aprons and rails are set flush with the legs or posts, and the doweling layout is the same as above.

When aprons or rails are set back ¼ to ⅜ in. from the faces of the legs, the marking gauge, after centerlining the rail ends, must be reset for the leg, allowing for the offset. That is, if T represents the thickness of the rail, set gauge for flush construction, as ½T, and use for marking legs and rails. For the offset, set gauge at 0—amount of offset plus ½T.

Most pieces of furniture require duplication in joints. For instance, a rectangular table has eight joints between apron and legs, requiring eight separate layouts for dowel holes. Some time is saved by clamping the rails together with working edges down and facing sides all to right or left, so that four ends at once can be marked with dividers by sliding one point along the bench top. A marking template of sheet metal, plastic or fiber, having a strip of wood nailed along the edge for a fence, and one at the end for a stop, locates dowel holes quickly and accurately. One set of pricks can be made for use

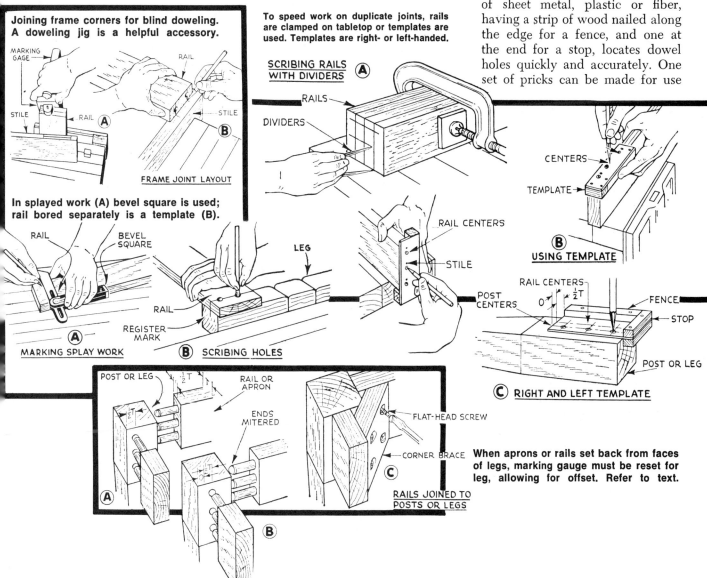

Joining frame corners for blind doweling. A doweling jig is a helpful accessory.

MARKING GAGE
RAIL
STILE
RAIL (A)
STILE
(B)
FRAME JOINT LAYOUT

In splayed work (A) bevel square is used; rail bored separately is a template (B).

RAIL
BEVEL SQUARE
RAIL
REGISTER MARK
(A) MARKING SPLAY WORK

LEG
(B) SCRIBING HOLES

To speed work on duplicate joints, rails are clamped on tabletop or templates are used. Templates are right- or left-handed.

SCRIBING RAILS WITH DIVIDERS (A)
RAILS
DIVIDERS

RAIL CENTERS
STILE

CENTERS
TEMPLATE
(B) USING TEMPLATE

RAIL CENTERS ½T
POST CENTERS 0
FENCE
STOP
POST OR LEG
(C) RIGHT AND LEFT TEMPLATE

POST OR LEG ½T
RAIL OR APRON
ENDS MITERED
FLAT-HEAD SCREW
CORNER BRACE
(C)
(A)
(B)
RAILS JOINED TO POSTS OR LEGS

When aprons or rails set back from faces of legs, marking gauge must be reset for leg, allowing for offset. Refer to text.

JOINERY METHODS

with a stile, where it is cut long to project some definite account, and another for the rail (which must be measured from the edge, and not from the stile projection). If stile is cut to net length, use the same set of pricks for both. Such a template is right-or-left-handed, and will work only on one end of a piece. To make it both right and left-handed, add guides on the upper sides, aligning them with those beneath. For marking offset legs, make a second row of pricks.

Legs of upholstered furniture are often doweled to the lower edges of nailed or doweled frames. A triangular block glued into each corner of a frame gives stock for boring ¾ in. dowel holes. The shaped legs are hard to gauge, but the dowel holes can be measured from the edges at the tops of the legs. Wrap the leg in a soft cloth and clamp lightly in a vise for boring. Incidentally, ready-shaped, carved and finished legs in many patterns can be purchased.

Tough joints for heavy jobs, such as workbenches are obtained by the use of drawbolts. They can be tightened when shrinkage or work strains have loosened them, and are easily disassembled for knocking down or packing. In accompanying drawing, the top rails of a bench are bolted to the legs. Square the joining members to fit snugly. Bore two centered bolt holes through each leg at right angles to each other, one enough above the other to miss it and both square with the faces; in 4x4 in. or heavier timber bore half-way in from opposite faces. While holes can be made slightly larger than the bolts for fitting ease, it isn't necessary in careful work and lessens the rigidity of the joint. Next, bore a hole from the inside face of each mating rail to receive the nut and washer. It must be large enough to allow free turning of the nut, with the edge about 1¼ in. from the end of the rail. The joint is stronger if the hole doesn't pass through the rail, although this may at times be a convenience, as the nut can then be tightened from either side by driving a nail set against the corners. Chisel a flat on the rail-end side to seat the washer. Bore the bolt hole

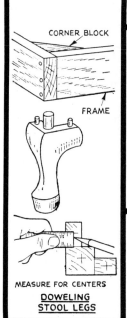

MEASURE FOR CENTERS
DOWELING STOOL LEGS

Legs of some furniture are doweled to frames. Holes can be bored into triangular corner block. Ready-shaped, finished legs are available in a variety of patterns. Wrap legs and lightly clamp the vise for drilling.

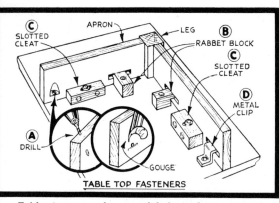

TABLE TOP FASTENERS

Table tops require special fastenings, several of which are seen here. Metal clips are common today.

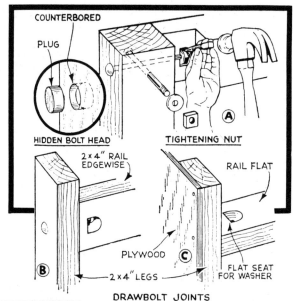

DRAWBOLT JOINTS

Joints for heavy jobs like workbenches are obtained by use of drawbolts, shown.

Grooving the end of a piece. Hands in safe positions steady and feed the work.

from the end into the nut hole. To assemble the joint, pass a carriage bolt through the leg and into the rail far enough to slip on a washer and nut, running up the nut with the fingers. Align the members before final tightening. Join posts and rails of rectangular section similarly by passing the bolt through the thickness of the leg and putting the rail in a vertical plane, or turning the rail to the horizontal, a better

plan if drawers are to be built under the bench. For trim, closed-in appearance cover the ends with ¼ in. plywood, recessed to fit over the bolt heads.

Table tops require special fastening to the understructure, but are often attached even in commercial furniture without much regard to requirements. A plywood top, which neither shrinks nor swells, can be fixed solidly with screws. Bore the hole at an angle from the top edge of the apron, coming out inside about 1¼ in. from the edge. Gouge out a clearance cavity with a flat bottom and enter a flat-head screw that will go about ½ in. into the table top. Position the top by laying it face down upon a pad, and set the leg structure upside down on it, sliding it around to equalize projection. Run a pencil

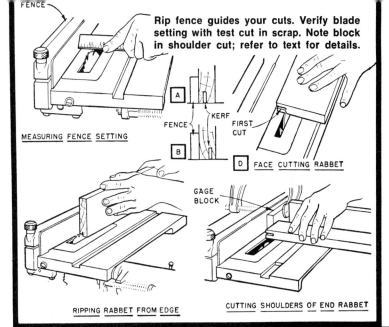

Rip fence guides your cuts. Verify blade setting with test cut in scrap. Note block in shoulder cut; refer to text for details.

MEASURING FENCE SETTING

FENCE   KERF   FIRST CUT

A

B

D   FACE CUTTING RABBET

GAGE BLOCK

RIPPING RABBET FROM EDGE

CUTTING SHOULDERS OF END RABBET

around the apron's outside for re-locating in case the frame should be shifted. An inexpensive fastening is cleats screwed to table top and aprons. Rabbeted hardwood blocks locking into apron grooves or metal clips are also satisfactory.

To secure a table top made from solid lumber, provide sliding holders. Such a top may increase in width ¾ in. during damp weather, shrinking correspondingly when dry. If solidly attached during damp seasons, the glue joints will break open or checks will appear when it shrinks during dry spells, unless the outer fasteners tear loose. If screwed tight in dry weather, swelling will buckle it. Fasteners allow movement when used as shown, being set away from the side aprons in dry-weather assembly and tight against them in wet times; clips are used in the same way. Slotted cleats with screws through washers into the table top, are satisfactory. Use a solid fastening at the middle of each end, which will overcome any tendency of the top to creep toward one edge or the other.

RABBETS, GROOVES AND DADOES

Even if you bungle with hand tools, you can make good furniture joints with your table saw. The rigid guidance from the fence and miter gauge demand only that you follow a few rules on setup and handling.

A practical way to rabbet the edge of a board, is to saw both sides. The table saw is unexcelled for edging rabbeted plywood cupboard doors. Remove the splitter and the guard, if it is mounted on the splitter. The operation is quite safe, for the saw is buried in the wood.

As in ripping, the rip fence guides the cuts. To cut into the edge, set the fence at the required distance from the blade, measuring from a tooth set toward the fence, if the thickness of the flange is critical, or from a tooth set away from it, if the rabbeted face is to slide against the fence. This puts the kerf in the waste wood. Set the blade projection above the table accurately, for if it is too high it

With dado head, rabbet is cut in one pass. Most heads can be built up to ¾-in. width. Arrange cutters as shown at near right. Molding head is also a good tool for rabbeting. Two types: the 3-blade type (A) far right, 2-blader (B) below it.

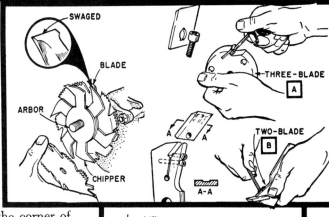

SWAGED

BLADE

ARBOR

CHIPPER

THREE-BLADE   A

TWO-BLADE   B

A-A

will score a crease in the corner of the rabbet, and if it is too low, the waste strip will have to be split out. Verify the setting with a test cut in a scrap piece.

Make the cut by feeding forward against the saw while pressing the board against the fence. Obviously, any rocking of the board against the the fence would result in an irregular cut. If the piece is wide, face the fence with a high board, preferably made of plywood to prevent warping, attaching it with bolts or screws. If no holes are present in the fence, screw wooden clips to the back to clasp the fence.

To saw the face cut, reset the fence and the saw projection, and run the edge against the fence. As always, observe safety rules, and use a push stick on short or narrow work. The sawed rabbet is usually smooth enough for ordinary joints, with a rip-saw making the roughest cut, a combination blade a little smoother, and the hollow-ground

Grooving with ordinary blade. Swath is as wide as throw of saw and depth is controlled by elevating or depressing table.

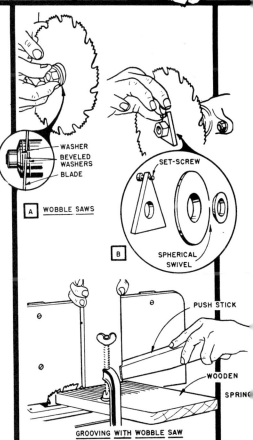

WASHER
BEVELED WASHERS
BLADE

A   WOBBLE SAWS

SET-SCREW

B

SPHERICAL SWIVEL

PUSH STICK

WOODEN SPRING

GROOVING WITH WOBBLE SAW

JOINERY METHODS

blade producing a rabbet ready for fine sanding. A rough rabbet can be dressed with a rabbet plane or with a cabinet scraper. When more than one rabbet is being sawed, save time by ripping all pieces with the first set-up, then changing over for the second cut. When ripping an end rabbet, as shown in photo, a high auxiliary fence is necessary to insure a vertical position for the piece. As shown, the shoulder of the rabbet is cross-cut, the distance from the end of the cut being ganged with a block clamped to the rip fence where it will engage the end before the start of the cut. The rod gauge can also be used. For a single rabbet it is usually sufficient to make a pencil mark on the forward edge of the piece.

With a dado head the rabbet is cut in one pass; if it is wide, two or more passes may be needed. When cutting a wide rabbet more than ½ in. deep, make more than one stroke. Most home workshop heads can be built up to a width of ¾ in. or ¹³⁄₁₆ in. Arrange the cutters as illustrated, with the swaged, or spread edges of the inside cutters (chippers) evenly spread and those next to the blades set in the openings between groups of teeth. The dado head is filed in a set, with the chippers cutting a little shallower than the blades, and the rabbets cut are a little uneven. This roughness is easily smoothed.

When using the dado head, the regular saw insert is replaced with another having a wider slot. To cut an edge rabbet the dado head must work to the edge of the board, or a little beyond. For this reason, an auxiliary fence is used, the projecting side of the dado head cutting into it. If the rabbet is too wide to make in one pass, cut the shoulder first and then shift to cut the

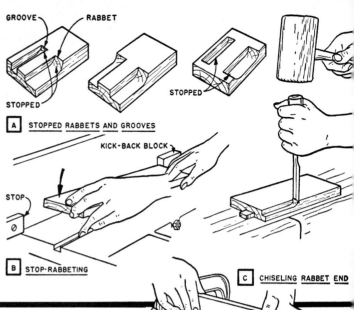

"Stopped" rabbets or grooves discontinued at a pre-set point. Stop block can be clamped to table as in (B). When both ends of rabbet are closed, clamp block to near end of table to prevent kickback (B and D). Chisel is used to trim groove or the rabbet square.

A STOPPED RABBETS AND GROOVES

B STOP-RABBETING

C CHISELING RABBET END

D EDGE STOP-GROOVING

remainder. In ordinary narrow rabbets the cut is made from the face or edge, depending on which is more convenient. If made from the edge, the flange can run between the fence and dado head, and no auxiliary fence will be needed.

A molding head is another fine tool for rabbeting. Two popular styles are available—a 3-bladed kind and a 2-bladed. The blades are locked in position with socket set-screws. To insure alignment, be sure that blades and seats are free from dirt.

As with the dado head, the ordinary rabbet is cut in one pass when the molding head is used. Handling of the work is almost the same for both. The cutters plane the rabbet smooth, leaving sharp corners. When rabbeting the end of a board it is best to saw the shoulder to avoid tearing as the blades cross the grain. A backing strip between the edge of the board and the miter gauge is advisable to prevent splintering of the edge. As in cross-cutting wide boards, the miter gauge can be turned end-for-end in the slot to seat it better when working wide boards.

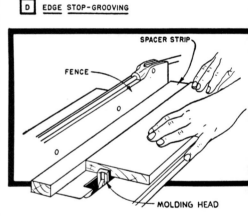

For two grooves, spacer between fence and work is used for the first pass. Remove spacer for cutting second groove.

Grooving can be done with an ordinary saw blade. Set the fence for ripping one side, and then the other. Practically all the waste is removed by making several cuts between. This is done on the *Shopsmith* by setting the saw by quill movement, moving the hand lever to advance the blade for successive cuts. Lock the quill for each cut.

A set-up for grooving by the wobble saw method is shown. The blade is mounted on the arbor in a tilted position and, upon turning, cuts a swath in the board as wide as the throw of the saw. The depth is controlled by elevating or depressing the arbor or table. The

For tapered rabbets or grooves, dado head (below) is used for clean shoulders. Pencil marks or rod gauge (right) can be employed to locate spacing of dadoes.

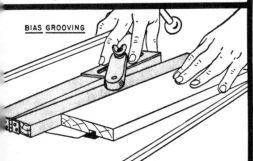

BIAS GROOVING

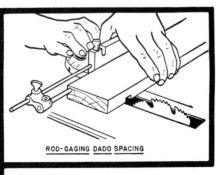

ROD-GAGING DADO SPACING

only accessory needed is a pair of wooden washers equally tapered in thickness. Place one behind the blade and the other in front, with tapers in opposite direction. When the nut is tightened the set-up is complete. Since centrifugal force springs the blade slightly to a more vertical position, it grooves a little narrower than is indicated by the tilt, and for this reason the machine should not be stopped or started while the blade is in the cut.

Commercial devices make a wobble set-up easy. The one shown has a washer swiveling on a spherical hub, to be placed behind the blade, where it adapts itself to any lean. A triangular plate located in front has a set-screw in one corner which, bearing against the blade, makes of the triangle a tapered washer giving the arbor nut full bearing. To set up, adjust the device to make a normal cut. With this as a centerline, set the fence half the groove width away, lean the top of the blade against it, and run out the set-screw to touch it. Tighten the arbor nut and turn by hand to see that it clears the insert slot. If a test cut proves the setting inaccurate, loosen the arbor nut and adjust the screw.

Edge and face grooving is largely a duplication of rabbeting, except that the fence is set back the

Simplest miter is face miter with ends of two boards cut at 45° angles to make square corner. Note tilt of blade here.

required amount to space the groove from the face or edge of the board.

The grooving of the end of a piece with a wobble saw is illustrated. The set-up with a wooden spring bearing against the lower end and a push stick propelling the piece is excellent for duplication, not only for grooving but for all end sawing. The wooden spring is made by sawing kerfs ³⁄₁₆ in. apart for a distance of 4 in. in a piece of hardwood having ends mitered 45° across the face. Set it close enough to the fence so that the work, in passing between, will spring the fingers out.

The dado head is a standard grooving tool. Using one blade, a ⅛ in. wide slot is made; two blades, ¼ in. Other widths, in jumps of ¹⁄₁₆ in. or ⅛ in. are obtainable by inserting chippers between the cutters, and fine adjustments are made by using paper or thin cardboard washers between. Set for depth of

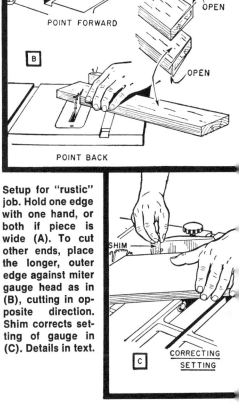

Setup for "rustic" job. Hold one edge with one hand, or both if piece is wide (A). To cut other ends, place the longer, outer edge against miter gauge head as in (B), cutting in opposite direction. Shim corrects setting of gauge in (C). Details in text.

Beat "creep" with brads or phono needles from toy (A), with sandpaper on extension (B) or with clamp on fence (C). Refer to the text for fuller explanation.

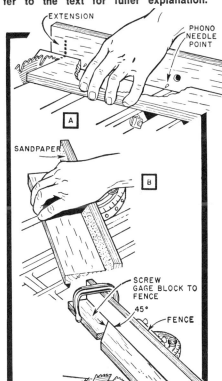

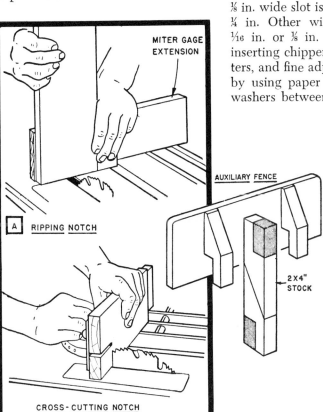

Accessory snap-on auxiliary fence is easily made, well worthwhile. Attach 2x4 stock to board with flathead screws countersunk flush. Protect it with a couple coats shellac.

JOINERY METHODS

cut and adjust the fence for locating the groove on the edge or face of the work.

By substituting the dado head with knives of proper width, smooth grooves can be cut rapidly. If more than one groove is to be made, move the fence to a new position. When several pieces are to be milled with two grooves, save time by inserting a wooden strip of proper width between the fence and work to space for one groove, removing it for cutting the second. This completes the grooving in a piece so that it can be piled back out of the way.

It often happens that a rabbet or groove must be "stopped" (discontinued a distance from one or both ends of the piece). If one end is to be open, advance the piece over the cutter until the end of the rabbet or groove, indicated by a pencil mark on the piece, is reached; or a stop block can be clamped to the table or fence where it will stop forward motion at the right time. Should both edges be rabbeted and stopped at the same end, forming a pair, work from one side of the fence and then the other.

When both ends of the rabbet are closed, clamp a block to the near end of the table or fence to prevent kickback. With the end of the piece bearing against this, slowly lower the forward end over the revolving cutter until full depth is reached, when it is fed forward. Stop at a pencil mark, or upon contacting a stop block forward.

Grooves and rabbets can be trimmed square with a chisel. Stop grooving of an edge is illustrated.

Tapered rabbets or grooves run bias with the length of the board, are handled in a tapering operation, using either the notched stick or adjustable tapering jig. To avoid splintering the arris of the side cut against the grain when using a molding head, feed slowly. With some work the use of the dado head is best, the saws cutting clean shoulders.

A *dado*, also called a *gain*, is a groove cut across the board. Support the edge of the piece against the miter gauge, as in cross-cutting, locating the spacing of the dadoes by means of pencil marks or by

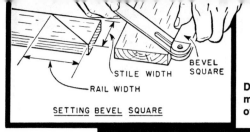

SETTING BEVEL SQUARE

Drawing diagonal on stile for door. In most doors, upper rail and stiles are of equal width with lower rail wider.

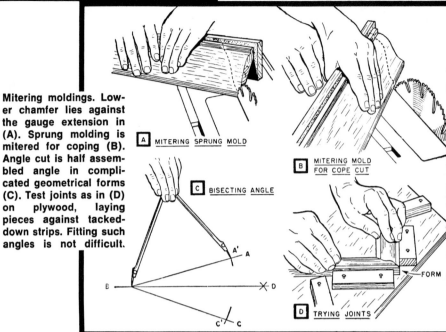

Mitering moldings. Lower chamfer lies against the gauge extension in (A). Sprung molding is mitered for coping (B). Angle cut is half assembled angle in complicated geometrical forms (C). Test joints as in (D) on plywood, laying pieces against tacked-down strips. Fitting such angles is not difficult.

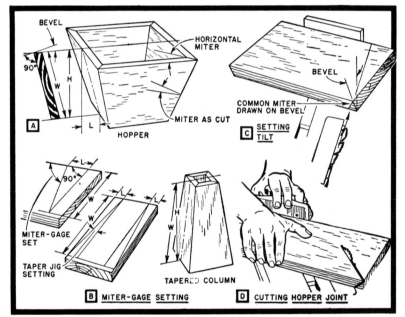

When sides of box slope, find gauge settings for side ends as in (A). See (B) for table tilt for hopper joints. Tilt saw until blade aligns with mark as in (D).

using the rod gauge. On long pieces use a miter gauge extension or auxiliary head, to which blocks can be clamped or screwed to determine dado positions. Multiple cutting with an ordinary blade, a wobble saw, or a dado head are effective for dadoing.

To cut small notches in the corner of a board, hold it upright against a deep miter-gauge auxiliary head to tip the side, then rest it on edge to cut the shoulder.

A hand accessory you can make yourself is a snap-on auxiliary fence. Saw the notched cleats from a single piece of 2 x 4 in. stock, notching the ends as shown and sawing the pieces apart with the tapered cut. Attach to the board

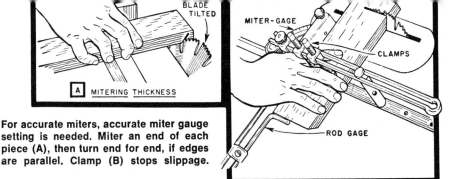

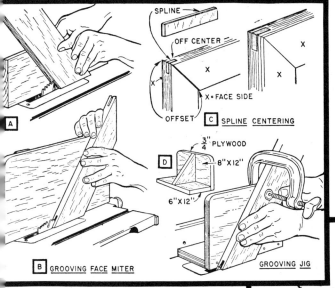

[A] MITERING THICKNESS

For accurate miters, accurate miter gauge setting is needed. Miter an end of each piece (A), then turn end for end, if edges are parallel. Clamp (B) stops slippage.

MITER-GAGE

CLAMPS

ROD GAGE

SPLINE

OFF CENTER

X = FACE SIDE

OFFSET

[C] SPLINE CENTERING

¾" PLYWOOD

[D] 8"X12"

6"X12"

[A]

[B] GROOVING FACE MITER

GROOVING JIG

Setup for grooving face miter is seen in (A) at left. Miter cut must rest fully on table. One cut will be against grain if same face side is held against fence (B). Sliding jig (D) contributes convenience and safety. Note triangular plywood brace between vertical, upright of the jig.

USING CLAMP NAIL

In thin wood of small boxes, clamp nails, right, are dandy, drawing joint together without glue. A short one, top and bottom, is suggested instead of long one.

with flathead wood screws countersunk flush. Protect with a couple of coats of shellac.

MITER AND HOPPER JOINTS

Probably the simplest miter joint is the face miter in which the ends of two boards are cut at an angle of 45° to make a square corner, such as in cabinet doors. If the joint is used in "rustic work," where the roughness of undressed lumber is displayed for textured effects, the ordinary combination blade will cut a satisfactory joint.

The setup for such a rough job is very simple. Elevate the saw blade above the table sufficiently for the teeth to project above the board, shift the rip fence out of the way, and set the miter-gauge to an angle of 45°. Hold one edge against the head of the gauge with one hand, or both if the piece is wide, with enough end projection beyond the blade for a full-width cut. Push the piece forward, holding it securely. On some saws this

can be done from either side, whichever is more convenient. If a four-sided frame is being made, cut one end of all pieces first so there won't be any variation.

To cut the other ends, measure the length on one, turn it end-for-end with the other face up, and cut. Since the outer edge is longer than the inner, it is advantageous to place that edge against the miter-gauge head, cutting the end in the opposite direction. Use the cut piece as a length pattern for the others.

Use a smooth-cutting saw, such as a hollow-ground blade or a fine-toothed crosscut for fine cabinet work. If you haven't such a blade,

dress cut ends with a plane to reduce roughness. Check the true angle of the miter-gauge with a test cut, for it may have been knocked out of true by a fall. Tightening the pivot pin corrects some miter-gauges, while others with round pins engaging holes or wedges entering notches may be true at some settings and slightly out at others. A shim of paper or a piece of tape stuck to the gauge head at the appropriate point may bring the angle back to a true 45°. Settings made by eye according to the scale are most likely to require test cuts. Place a test pair of corner pieces together in a square or form to check the fit. Once the setting is correct, cut the pieces. Aside from neat appearance, the fitting of a joint has much to do with its rigidity and durability, for if it is open at the center or a corner, only a small area of the jointing ends makes contact, and may crush under strain.

As the cut proceeds, the piece tends to creep toward the blade in an amount equal to the set of the teeth or hollowness of a planer blade at that side. It is hard to hold the work against the miter-gauge head solidly enough to prevent this. This causes the miter to be cut sharp if sawed from the outer corner, or blunt if it is cut from the inner corner. This peculiarity of the saw action can be overcome in various ways. One method is to clamp the piece to the miter-gauge. Two or three brads driven into the gauge extension and sharpened, or phonograph needles set in, will do the same thing, but the pricks mar the edge of the piece.

To gauge the length automatically, clamp or screw a block to the extension for the mitered end to stop against; and, since there's danger of crushing the sharp point and thereby altering the measurement, it is best to miter the gauge block to fit the mitered end of the piece.

In most doors the upper rail and stiles are of equal width while the lower rail is wider. This means that the lower stile ends must be cut to acute angles while the lower rail ends are correspondingly obtuse. On the rail measure back from a

JOINERY METHODS

squared end equal to the width of the stile, and draw the diagonal. On the stile set off the width of the rail, and draw the diagonal.

Occasionally a door panel is built up of four mitered pieces and assembled to run the grain around it. In the reverse of this assembly the grain radiates from the center. The cutting of the pieces is no different from that of making rails and stiles, except that usually the stock is wider and the pieces are triangular.

Moldings are mitered the same as flat pieces if they are within the capacity of the saw, as most solid moldings are. Sprung moldings, which are wide and made on the face of thin stock having the back chamfered at top and bottom to give bearing surfaces, must be cut with special care. One chamfer slides on the table, and the lower chamfer lies against the gauge extension. If the mold slips down ever so little, the joint will not be accurate. A sprung mold being mitered for coping is shown. The profile outlined by the cut is a guide for cutting the mold to fit against another piece in an inside corner.

Moldings fitted around complicated geometrical forms such as stars are more numerous but not much more difficult to fit. The angle to cut is half the assembled angle. A convenient way to test the joints is to draw the figure full-size on a piece of plywood, laying the pieces in place against strips tacked to the plywood, as shown.

Box and chest corners are often mitered. The end-beveling operation requires an accurate right-angle setting of the miter-gauge. Tilt the table or arbor, the angle depending on the number of sides. When using a tilt table, support the work on the low side, a position best served if the lower end butts against a stop block on the gauge extension. Miter one end of each piece; then turn end-for-end, if edges are parallel. Set the stop block for gauging the length, and cut the other end. If edges aren't parallel turn the gauge end-for-end to keep the head against the same

edge.

A miter-gauge clamp prevents slipping. The two clamp screws are positioned in a yoke held by means of a thumb nut at the head and a post screwed into the guide rod. Note use of rod gauge for determining the length.

In end mitering, try to flatten a warped board. If this isn't done, and the center bulges up, the end will curve outward slightly at the center, requiring correction by hand. If the hollow side is up, rock the board on the bulge, contacting the table with the part being sawed.

Column work requires that the staves be rip-mitered, a beveling job. This again calls for tilting of the arbor or table with the angle half that of the assembled joint. A planer blade will cut smoothly enough for gluing. A piece for a 3-sided column, being cut at 30°, is out of range of the saw tilt and must be held against the fence or an auxiliary fence for ripping from the edge. The guard is in the way of this operation.

When the sides of a box or column slope, the angle of cut, taken at right angles to the edge, is no longer 45° in the square assembly nor half of the normal corner for other numbers of sides. This introduces the hopper joint, which by regular methods involves rather difficult calculations. To find the miter-gauge setting for cutting the end of a side piece follow the procedure shown. The same principle works in the layout of tapered column joints. On the end of a side measure back for amount of lean and draw a line to the measured length of the stave, establishing the taper. Set a tapering jig to this slope.

To cut the other end swivel the gauge in the opposite direction, setting it by degrees read from the other setting, or with a bevel square. By turning the gauge end-for-end the head will bear against the same edge. A similar method applies to column mitering. Draw the common miter on the beveled end and align with the blade as the side bears against a tapering jig (described in preceding).

Mitered corners can be joined by

any of several methods. However, since the table saw is an excellent grooving tool, a slip tongue or spline glued into grooves is an easy-to-make reinforcement. A suitable spline for ¾ in. stock is a strip cut from ¼ in. plywood or a piece cut across the grain from hardwood. Set up a blade to cut slightly deeper than half the width of the strip. Make the groove by repeated cuts, by using a wobble saw, a couple of dado blades, or a molding head. In the first instance the waste is cleared by taking inside cuts, shifting the fence as necessary.

The setup for grooving a face miter is illustrated. The auxiliary fence supports the piece while the face side is slid against it. The miter cut must rest fully on the table, or the depth of groove will taper, causing interference when the joint is being assembled. It is evident that one cut must be made against the grain if the same face side is held against the fence. Feel the bite of the saw, and gauge the feed accordingly. If the lumber is uniform in thickness the opposite face can be placed against the fence, *providing the groove is exactly centered.* Failure in this makes assemblies like those shown, which require much surfacing of the joint and reduction of thickness.

Splines must enter mitered ends and edges at right angles. The closer the groove to the heel of the cut, the deeper it can be, as there's more stock. To cut the groove in an end miter on a tilt table place the edge against the miter-gauge, end miter down, on the upper side of the table, and use the rip fence for positioning. The position is similar if the arbor tilts. As the saw blades are buried under wood the operation is safe and the guard may be dispensed with.

In the thin wood used for small boxes a single saw kerf is wide enough to receive the thin spline needed. Clamp nails are excellent in such work. They are flat, finned nails that are driven into a No. 22-gauge saw cut, drawing the joint together and holding it without glue. Where possible, drive a short nail in the top and bottom, rather than using one long nail.

Classic China Cabinet

This elegant piece of furniture will be the center of attraction in any dining room. Neighbors and friends won't believe you made this beautiful project with your own two hands, but the step-by-step instructions and diagrams show you how.

The cabinet is actually two sections—upper and lower—built as seperate units and then assembled with screws.

THIS HANDSOME CHINA CABINET is made of common pine. Hardwood may be substituted but if the hardwood is thicker than the ¾-inch thickness of the pine, be sure to revise the dimensions accordingly.

The basic tools needed are a table saw, router and saber saw. A band saw and shaper are helpful but not essential.

The cabinet is made in two sections—upper and lower. These are built as separate units then assembled with four screws after it has been completed and moved to where it will be used.

The arched door and frieze above it are glued up from four pieces of stock with the grain in each piece running the length of the piece. The author has devised a unique method of gluing the pieces so that the joints are pulled tightly for a perfect glue line.

Other features are fluted pilasters, raised panels and a plywood grille which all add to the professional appearance of this fine piece.

Cut all parts to size as shown in the bill of materials. If you have a jointer make all pieces a trifle wider then dress down to the size shown in the materials list. To prevent cupping, the top, bottom and side members should be made by gluing narrow boards. Be sure to reverse the annular rings in alternate pieces as indicated.

Starting with the lower section rabbet the ends of the side pieces to take the top and bottom panels.

Make this rabbet ⅜" x ¾". The front edges of the side panels are also rabbeted but that rabbet is ¼" deep and ½" wide. The ¼" x ⅜" rabbets for the rear panel are also made at this time.

After the rabbets are cut, drill the two rows of holes to take the adjustable shelf brackets. These holes are made ¼" diameter and ⅜" deep. Layout the spacing as shown for the upper cabinet.

Set the pieces just cut aside and make up the front frame. Drill the holes in the upper rail to take the dummy drawer front screws. The ½" diameter holes are to allow clearance for the drawer pull screw heads. Dowel holes are also drilled at this time. A doweling jig is useful for this operation as it will assure perfectly aligned holes for the dowel pins. Use two dowels at each joint except for the center divider where only one hole is used. Before gluing these pieces, cut the groove at the back of the stiles. Make the groove ¼" wide by ¼" deep. Check the fit with the side member. If okay, you can glue up the front frame. Glue upper and lower rails to the divider first, then add the stiles. Use cauls under the clamp jaws to protect the edges of the stiles. The sides, top and bottom are now assembled using glue and screws. Be sure the assembly is square then set aside until the glue sets. The front frame can then be fastened to the case. Use glue at all joints and clamp securely.

The pilasters are cut from ½-inch stock. The grooves are made with a router or shaper. The shaper is

the easier to use as the piece is made to ride against the fence. Start and stop blocks are used to locate the grooves on the stock. If a router is used, it can be mounted on a board large enough so that similar stops can be utilized. The router is mounted so that the round end bit protrudes ¼". Use a movable side guide so the five grooves are cut as shown in the detail.

When the pilasters are finished, sand them smooth breaking all sharp edges, then fasten to the stiles as indicated. Place the nails so they will be hidden under the rosettes. Be careful with the glue. Keep it away from the edges as you do not want any squeeze-out to get onto the face of the stiles.

The lower doors are made with doweled joints (two dowels per joint). The rails and stiles are drilled for the dowels then as-

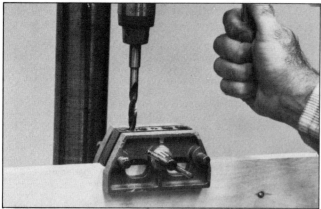

A doweling jig is always helpful when trying to locate proper position for dowels. Here it is being used on the edge of the stile. Two dowels are used at each joint.

The front frame is assembled with dowels. The center divider has already been glued. Spiraled dowels are used in all cases because they allow air to escape from hole.

Cauls are used under the clamps to protect the edge of the frame. Be sure the assembly is square, then set the piece aside until the glue sets. Then fasten to case.

A belt sander is used to true-up the glued side panels. A belt sander cuts fast, but a finishing sander must be used to obtain the desired smooth surface.

CLASSIC CHINA CABINET

sembled with glue and clamps. When the glue has set, cut the ⅜″ x ⅜″ rabbets on the inner and outer edges as shown in the sectional drawing.

The door panels are cut from a piece of ¾″ x 7″ x 14″ stock. Use the table saw to raise the panel. Elevate the blade 1¼″ and tilt it 15-degrees. Adjust the fence so that it is ¼″ away from the blade at the table surface. Holding the panel vertically, rest it against the fence and feed it slowly through the blade. Repeat this for all four sides When done, the waste will hang on lightly. Return the blade to the vertical position, lowering it so only ⅛″ projects from the table top. Set the fence 1¼″ away from the blade and recut each edge to remove the waste and to square off the angular cut left by the previous operation.

The inside corners of the rab-

beted door frame will have a radius left by the router bit. Use a chisel to square off the corners. The door panels should fit easily into the rabbeted area. If necessary, trim the panels slightly, especially at the sides as the wood will expand and contract during weather changes. If left too tight, some damage is bound to result. The panels are held by the use of panel retainers, six per door as shown.

The base ends, front and front blocks are now added. Assemble with glue and fasten with one-inch wire brads. The front blocks must be centered over the pilasters. Center the rosettes in the space provided and fasten with glue and one brad.

The moldings are now added to complete the base section. The stock is ⅝″ x ¾″ nose and cove molding. Each piece is cut and mitered to fit by taking measurements directly from the cabinet.

Thus, each piece is custom fit to allow for any discrepancies. The returns at the sides of the pilasters will require an inside and outside miter. These pieces are very short (about 1⅛″), so you must use care in making them. They can be made with a miter box, table saw, radial arm saw or cutoff saw. These pieces are held with glue alone. The longer moldings are fastened with glue and brads. Use glue sparingly as squeeze-out will cause finishing problems.

The upper section case is made with the same type of joints as used for the lower case. The front frame is different however. In order to save lumber, the crown section of the front frame is made as a separate unit which is later fastened to the stiles.

The crown piece is made by gluing up four 24-inch lengths of stock, measuring 5-17/32 inches wide. Use two dowels in each piece

Facing page. These drawings will help in the assemby of the project. Be sure to follow all of the measurements (even hole diameters) and positions of all pieces carefully. Also, note the detailed sections around the perimeter of the drawing which show specific areas.

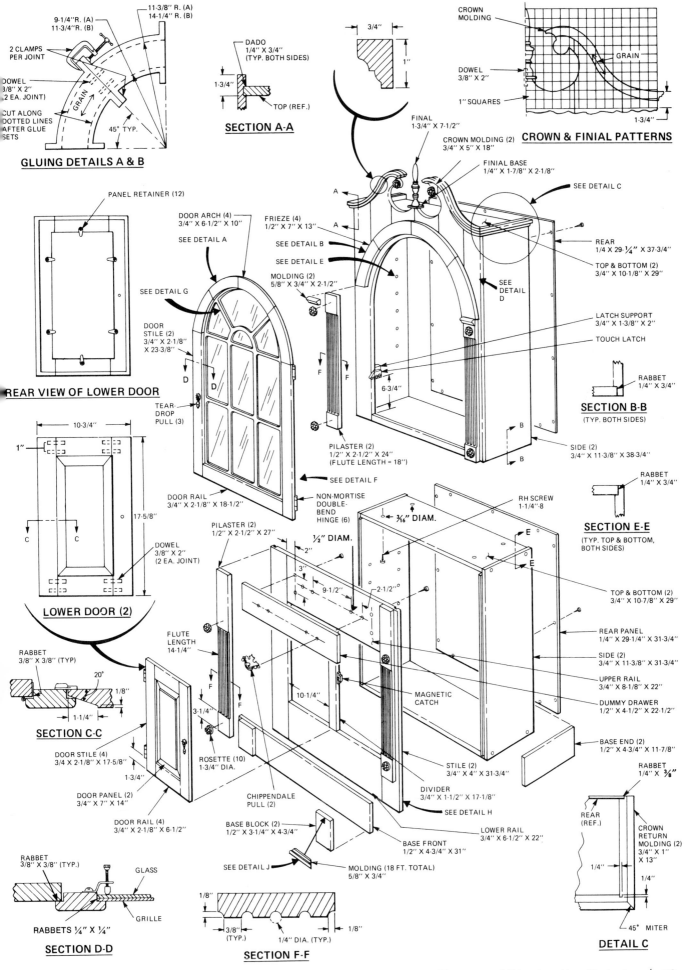

GLUING DETAILS A & B

2 CLAMPS PER JOINT

9-1/4"R. (A)
11-3/4"R. (B)

11-3/8" R. (A)
14-1/4" R. (B)

DOWEL 3/8" X 2"
(2 EA. JOINT)

GRAIN

CUT ALONG DOTTED LINES AFTER GLUE SETS

45° TYP.

SECTION A-A

DADO 1/4" X 3/4"
(TYP. BOTH SIDES)

1-3/4"

TOP (REF.)

3/4"

1"

CROWN MOLDING

DOWEL 3/8" X 2"

GRAIN

1" SQUARES

CROWN & FINIAL PATTERNS

1-3/4"

FINAL 1-3/4" X 7-1/2"

CROWN MOLDING (2) 3/4" X 5" X 18"

FINAL BASE 1/4" X 1-7/8" X 2-1/8"

SEE DETAIL C

A
A

FRIEZE (4) 1/2" X 7" X 13"

SEE DETAIL B
SEE DETAIL E

MOLDING (2) 5/8" X 3/4" X 2-1/2"

REAR 1/4 X 29-1/4" X 37-3/4"

TOP & BOTTOM (2) 3/4" X 10-1/8" X 29"

SEE DETAIL D

PANEL RETAINER (12)

DOOR ARCH (4) 3/4" X 6-1/2" X 10"
SEE DETAIL A

SEE DETAIL G

DOOR STILE (2) 3/4" X 2-1/8" X 23-3/8"

REAR VIEW OF LOWER DOOR

TEAR-DROP PULL (3)

LATCH SUPPORT 3/4" X 1-3/8" X 2"

TOUCH LATCH

6-3/4"

SECTION B-B
(TYP. BOTH SIDES)

RABBET 1/4" X 3/4"

SIDE (2) 3/4" X 11-3/8" X 38-3/4"

RABBET 1/4" X 3/4"

SECTION E-E
(TYP. TOP & BOTTOM, BOTH SIDES)

10-3/4"

1"

17-5/8"

DOWEL 3/8" X 2"
(2 EA. JOINT)

C   C

LOWER DOOR (2)

PILASTER (2) 1/2" X 2-1/2" X 24"
(FLUTE LENGTH = 18")

SEE DETAIL F

DOOR RAIL 3/4" X 2-1/8" X 18-1/2"

NON-MORTISE DOUBLE-BEND HINGE (6)

B
B

RABBET 3/8" X 3/8" (TYP)

20°

1/8"

1-1/4"

SECTION C-C

DOOR STILE (4) 3/4 X 2-1/8" X 17-5/8"

1-3/4"

DOOR PANEL (2) 3/4" X 7" X 14"

DOOR RAIL (4) 3/4" X 2-1/8" X 6-1/2"

RABBET 3/8" X 3/8" (TYP.)

GLASS

GRILLE

RABBETS 1/4" X 1/4"

SECTION D-D

PILASTER (2) 1/2" X 2-1/2" X 27"

FLUTE LENGTH 14-1/4"

F

3-1/4"

ROSETTE (10) 1-3/4" DIA.

CHIPPENDALE PULL (2)

BASE BLOCK (2) 1/2" X 3-1/4" X 4-3/4"

SEE DETAIL J

3/16" DIAM.

1/2" DIAM.

2"

3"

9-1/2"

2-1/2"

10-1/4"

RH SCREW 1-1/4"-8

E
E

MAGNETIC CATCH

STILE (2) 3/4" X 4" X 31-3/4"

DIVIDER 3/4" X 1-1/2" X 17-1/8"

SEE DETAIL H

LOWER RAIL 3/4" X 6-1/2" X 22"

BASE FRONT 1/2" X 4-3/4" X 31"

MOLDING (18 FT. TOTAL) 5/8" X 3/4"

TOP & BOTTOM (2) 3/4" X 10-7/8" X 29"

REAR PANEL 1/4" X 29-1/4" X 31-3/4"

SIDE (2) 3/4" X 11-3/8" X 31-3/4"

UPPER RAIL 3/4" X 8-1/8" X 22"

DUMMY DRAWER 1/2" X 4-1/2" X 22-1/2"

BASE END (2) 1/2" X 4-3/4" X 11-7/8"

RABBET 1/4" X 3/8"

REAR (REF.)

CROWN RETURN MOLDING (2) 3/4" X 1" X 13"

1/4"

1/4"

45° MITER

DETAIL C

1/8"

3/8" (TYP.)

1/4" DIA. (TYP.)

1/8"

SECTION F-F

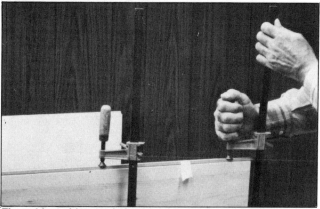

The cabinet sides are being glued to the front frame. The cauls have been taped to the sides to prevent any shifting. Be sure to clean away any excess glue from wood.

The top panel for the bottom section is fastened with glue and nails. Nails can be used here because when the cabinet is complete they will be hidden by top section.

Start and stop guides on the shaper fence are used to control the position of the flutes on the pilasters. This is very important if the flutes are to be uniform.

A marking gauge is used to position the pilaster on the stile. The pilasters were cut from ½″ stock and the flutes or grooves made with a router or a shaper.

CLASSIC CHINA CABINET

and locate them so they will not be cut away later when the arch and crown are cut. Determine this by lightly penciling the outline of the arch and crown from the pattern and measurements shown.

When glued up, the four pieces should total 22⅛ inches in width. Using dowels but no glue, fasten this center section to the two stiles then proceed to lay out the arch and crown cutting lines. Use a paper pattern made by enlarging the squared drawing. The curved arch should be trued up by using a beam compass made from a strip of wood about ⅛-inch thick and ½-inch wide. Place a pin through the strip near one end and drill a 1/16″ diameter hole 11-1/16 inches from the pin. This will give you the radius for the arch. Locate the center on some scrap wood placed on the table then scribe the arc. The

compass can be used later for the other arcs needed for the door and frieze.

After the cutting lines are laid out on the front frame, remove the stiles and cut the lines using a saber saw, jig saw or band saw. Set these pieces aside now and prepare to make the crown moldings.

Lay out the crown moldings on a piece of wood about 5 inches wide. Cut the lower edge only and be sure to extend the ends about 3 or 4 inches in a horizontal plane perpendicular to the imaginary vertical centerline of the crown. This is very important as it will provide a support for cutting the crown miter later. After the lower (or bottom) edge of the moldings are cut, the edge must be shaped with a router or on the shaper using a suitable cutter. Note: Two straight pieces for the returns, about 15″ long, should also be made at this time. After shaping, the upper edge

of the molding is cut. This should match the top edge of the crown which was previously cut. Using one-inch brads, temporarily fasten the moldings to the crown, then proceed to trim the ends to the shape shown, then remove the moldings.

The crown section can now be permanently fastened to the stiles with glue. Be sure the lower rail piece is installed at the same time. The front frame can now be glued to the case which was prepared earlier. Again, tack on the crown moldings then mark the mitering line on the left and right pieces. Support the moldings on the extended ends and miter carefully. The returns are mitered in the normal manner. These can now be fastened permanently. Apply glue sparingly then join securely with brads. You will have to rest the overhanging crown on a solid support when bradding as you will

Facing page. Note the positions of the glass holders in detail F on the rear of the upper door. If you are not confident enough to make the curved cut of the glass which goes in this door (it can be very tricky), it may be wise to have the cutting done by a professional.

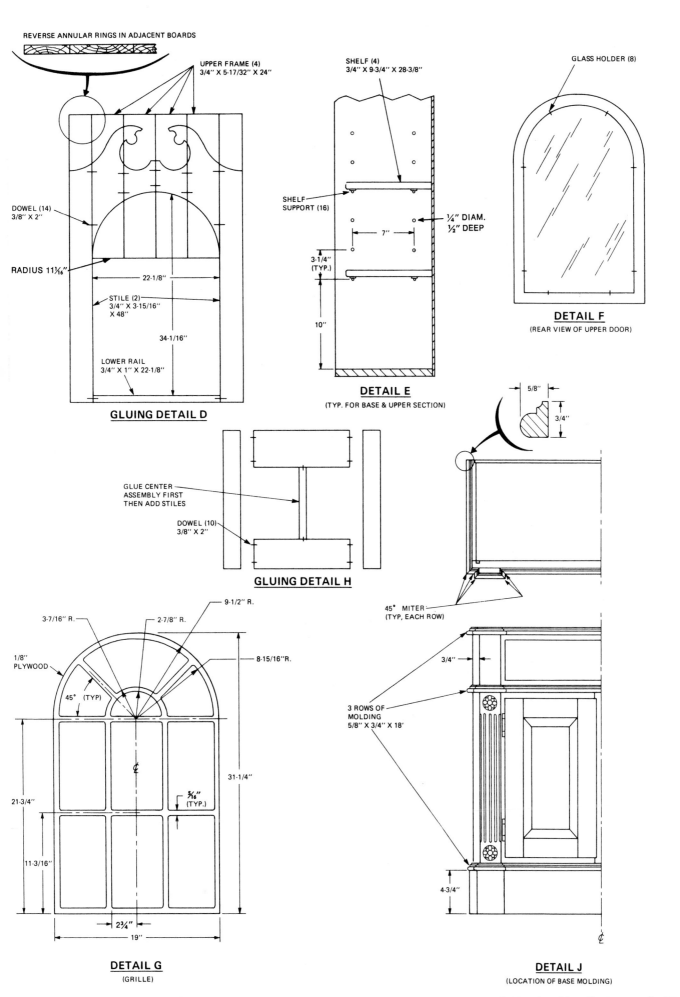

REVERSE ANNULAR RINGS IN ADJACENT BOARDS

UPPER FRAME (4)
3/4″ X 5-17/32″ X 24″

DOWEL (14)
3/8″ X 2″

RADIUS 11¹⁄₁₆″

22-1/8″

STILE (2)
3/4″ X 3-15/16″
X 48″

34-1/16″

LOWER RAIL
3/4″ X 1″ X 22-1/8″

GLUING DETAIL D

SHELF (4)
3/4″ X 9-3/4″ X 28-3/8″

SHELF
SUPPORT (16)

¼″ DIAM.
½″ DEEP

7″

3-1/4″
(TYP.)

10″

DETAIL E
(TYP. FOR BASE & UPPER SECTION)

GLASS HOLDER (8)

DETAIL F
(REAR VIEW OF UPPER DOOR)

GLUE CENTER
ASSEMBLY FIRST
THEN ADD STILES

DOWEL (10)
3/8″ X 2″

GLUING DETAIL H

5/8″

3/4″

45° MITER
(TYP, EACH ROW)

3-7/16″ R.

2-7/8″ R.

9-1/2″ R.

1/8″
PLYWOOD

8-15/16″R.

45° (TYP)

31-1/4″

21-3/4″

³⁄₁₆″
(TYP.)

11-3/16″

2¾″

19″

DETAIL G
(GRILLE)

3/4″

3 ROWS OF
MOLDING
5/8″ X 3/4″ X 18′

4-3/4″

DETAIL J
(LOCATION OF BASE MOLDING)

This rear view of the lower door shows how the panels are held in position by retainers. Non-mortise hinges used.

The lower edge of the crown molding is shaped with a router or shaper. Crown made of four 24″ lengths of stock.

After shaping the molding, it is trimmed to size on a band saw. This should match the top edge of crown.

MATERIALS LIST

All lumber used is pine, except for grille and rear panels which are plywood.

Name	Size	Amt. Required
PARTS FOR BASE SECTION		
Top & Bottom	¾x10⅞x29″	2
Side	¾x11⅜x31¾″	2
Lower Rail	¾x6½x22″	1
Upper Rail	¾x8⅛x22″	1
Stile	¾x4x31¾″	2
Divider	¾x1½x17⅛″	1
Rear Panel	¼x29¼x31¾ plywood	1
Base End	½x4¾x11⅞″	2
Base Front	½x4¾x31″	1
Base Block	½x3¼x4¾″	2
Pilaster	½x2½x27″	2
Dummy Drawer	½x4½x22½″	1
Door Stile	¾x2⅛x17⅝″	4
Door Rail	¾x2⅛x6½″	4
Door Panel	¾x7x14″	2
PARTS FOR UPPER SECTION		
Top & Bottom	¾x10⅛x29″	2
Side	¾x11⅜x38¾″	2
Lower Rail	¾x1x22⅛″	1
Stile	¾x3 15/16x38¾″	2
Upper Frame	¾x5 17/32x24″	4
Pilaster	½x2½x24″	2
Frieze	½x7x13″	4
Molding	⅝x¾x2½″	2
Crown Molding	¾x5x18″	2
Crown Return Molding	¾x1x13″	2
Finial	1¾x7½″	1
Finial Base	¼x1⅞x2⅛″	1
Door Stile	¾x2⅛x23⅜″	2
Door Rail	¾x2⅛x18½″	1
Door Arch	¾x6½x10″	4
Grille	⅛x19x31¼″	1
Rear	¼x29½x37¾″	1
Latch Support	¾x1⅜x2″	1
Shelf	¾x9¾x28⅜″	4
Rosette	1¾″ dia. (ROS)	10
Pull, Tear Drop	(TDP)	3
Pull, Chippendale	(CH)	2
Magnetic Catch	(MC)	2
Touch Latch	(TVC)	1
Panel Retainer	(PRB)	12
Glass Holder	(GH)	8
Molding	⅝x¾ (NC)	18 ft.
Shelf Support	(SHS)	16
Hinge, Non-Mortise	(FH)	6
Screw	1″–8 RH	6
Screw	⅝″–4 RH	24
Screw	1¼″–8 RH	18
Screw	4⅝″	20
Nail	2″ finishing	24
Brad	1″ #18	36
Dowel	⅜x2″ (SD)	59

CLASSIC CHINA CABINET

have trouble with the wood bouncing which will make nailing almost impossible. Have an assistant hold the case steady with just the crown resting on the workbench.

The arched parts of the door and frieze are made from small sections of glued up stock as shown. This will save stock, but more importantly, the grain will be running in the proper direction around the curve. Each segment is cut with tabs at the ends. These permit proper clamping of the joints. The tabs are cut away afterwards. Note that the segments are made oversize. This will permit accurate trimming to a compass-drawn line which is laid out after the segments are glued up.

The frieze will not require doweling but the door must have dowels for strength, two dowels per joint. The ends of each segment must be cut at 45-degree angles so that when joined, all four will make up a semi-circle. Note: When cutting the stiles for the doors, leave tabs at the top so that the stile can be clamped to the semi-circle easily. Glue the stiles to the lower rail then proceed to glue the segments as shown. After the glue sets, lay out the cutting lines using the beam compass, then trim with a saber saw or on the jig saw.

Rabbet the back of the door at the inner and outer edges. Use a chisel to square up the radius left by the router.

The grille is cut from a piece of ⅛-inch door skin. These are available at most lumber yards and are the same material used for facing hollow doors.

The frieze, pilasters and rosettes are fastened with glue and brads. The short lengths of molding atop the pilasters are cut square at the edges.

Cut the shelves, add the rear panels and install the finial at the top of the crown. Add hardware as shown then remove before applying finish.

If pine was used it need not be filled, but the grille door skin should be given a treatment of paste wood filler. The rear panels, too, if they are of open grain stock.

The entire cabinet should be given a thinned application of sealer so that staining will take evenly. (Do not use sealer straight as this will prevent stain from taking at all). Make tests on scrap wood beforehand to make sure that it will take stain to your liking.

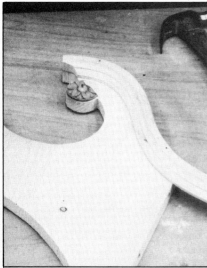

The molding is temporarily tacked to the crown with one-inch brads. Trim the ends and remove the molding.

A sanding attachment fastened to a jig saw simplifies sanding of the crown contour. Take time for good finish.

Arched part of door and frieze are made from small sections of glued-up stock with tabs at ends to permit clamping.

The final assembly of the glued segments form the arch. Each segment was cut at a precise 45-degree angle.

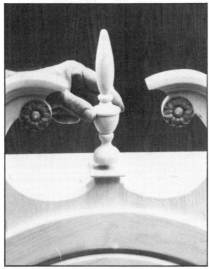

The finial slips over a 3/8″ dowel and is glued. Finials can be bought ready-made at home improvement centers.

The grille is cut very carefully with a jig saw. Using a fine blade here will produce the desired smooth edge.

Rosettes are added to the pilaster as an elegant decoration. Apply them with glue and a countersunk brad.

View of the assembled cabinet. Finish with stain of your choice and varnish. Then add all of the hardware.

Wall Unit with Foldaway Bed

Add an extra bed and handsome unit for your electronics hobby room—ideal for studios

COLOR TV, DISC PLAYERS and related electronic gear, a dilemma for both homeowner and apartment dweller. Although adding greatly to the enjoyment of our leisure and working hours, they are also gradually encroaching on our living quarters which, are being made smaller than ever before. In essence, we are cramped for living space.

That's where this hideaway bed/electronics storage unit comes in. The average twin bed occupies a floor space of about 30 square feet. If we can eliminate the bed we can gain that space. Of course we cannot eliminate the bed, but we can put it into the wall—and that's just what we have done. We placed the bed and all our favorite electronic equipment into the wall in a neat and orderly fashion. The "secret" making it possible is the Sico wall bed. This comes complete with box spring and mattress and requires only 18 inches stored.

The heart of the bed is the patented Power Pak unit. This is spring-loaded and requires only 12 lbs. of pressure to raise or lower bed, box spring and mattress. The bed is available in twin, double or queen sizes. All have an ingenious padded head rest which is slanted in the bed position and folds neatly to cradle the pillows in the stored position. The bottom panel, which is the frame of the bed, is designed to take a wood panel of your choice. This can be decorated with paper, paint, cork, or whatever meets your fancy. When stored it becomes a wall decoration.

Our wall system was designed to be compatible with the convertible wall bed, thus all units were made 18″ deep. The bed compartment size will vary in height and width depending on the bed size chosen, ranging from twin regular through Queen. Write to the company for details. Ours is a twin regular which requires a recess opening width of 41″ and a height of 83-½″.

Many readers interested in building this wall unit will have limited access to a woodworking shop, especially apartment dwellers. With this in mind, we have designed the system so that it can be built with nothing more than a hammer and square. Many lumberyards will cut your lumber to size if you furnish them will a bill of materials. The charge is nominal and with all the pieces pre-cut, the job is greatly eased. The reader with power tools can do the job equally well and save the cutting costs. A word of caution: Don't fall into the "boat in the basement" trap. These units are quite large and if built in the shop, be sure that you will be able to get them upstairs. We built ours in the garage.

Because of the 18″ depth, plywood panels are recommended because they eliminate gluing of narrow boards. We chose birch but other species such as oak, pine, etc. well serve equally well. If you plan to paint the cabinets as opposed to staining, you can use fir plywood and cut costs considerably.

As mentioned earlier, we have simplified the construction so that anyone can built the cabinets with ease. Butt joints, glue and nails are the technique. For the craftsman who would like more of a challenge, dadoed and rabbeted construction is recommended. See the optional detail drawing. If dadoes and rabbets are used, be sure to increase the horizontal width measurements accordingly.

For the strongest possible joints, we suggest that all edges to be glued should be glue-sized. Do this by thinning your glue with water about 25-percent. Mix thoroughly, then

Cabinet members are fastened with nails and glue. A spacer clamped to side panel assures accuracy during operation.

Throughout the assembly, it is important to check for squareness. A regular steel square is handy for corners.

Here, bed recess panel is checked for squareness after installation of rear panel. Panel is first primed with latex.

Veneer tape is one way to cover plywood edges. It bonds when heat is applied. Putting tape on roller makes it easier to use.

You can smooth edges of tape with sandpaper, but a hand held router works well. Check edges for smoothness with fingers.

Carriage bolts are used on baseplate. Draw them up tight with wrench. Later, the nuts and washers will be removed and replaced.

Wall Unit with Foldaway Bed

apply to the edges with a small brush. Allow to dry, then apply the glue in the usual manner. The sizing will seal the porous edges, resulting in a good strong joint which will not be starved for glue.

Another suggestion to consider is the use of galvanized finishing nails. These are similar to the regular finishing nail except that the surface is rough due to the galvanizing. This increases their holding power tremendously. (You can check holding power by driving one each of the nails into a piece of scrap wood. Leave the heads slightly extended. Then use the hammer claw to remove the nails. You will be surprised at how well the galvanized nail resists removal).

The spacing of the shelves was determined by the Radio Shack components we used: Computer TRS-80, Disc Player 16-301, Speakers-Nova 5, Color TV-16-230, Receiver STA-2290, Turntable LAB-395 and Cassette SCT-32. You should space the shelves to fit your equipment.

When installing the shelving, use spacers clamped as shown to assure accuracy and simplify installation. As each shelf is installed check if for squareness. When nailing is completed, sink nail heads and fill depressions.

The exposed front edges of the plywood can be covered in several ways. You can use solid lumber, wood tape or plastic shelf edging. If you plan to use the shelf edging you should slot the edges of all stock before assembling the boards.

We used heat-sensitive birch veneer tape, which is installed with an electric iron. The tape comes coated with a hot melt adhesive which becomes activated when the iron is applied. The tape veneer is available in many species and is easily applied. Non-adhesive veneer tape is also available; this type must be installed with contact cement. There are several methods of applying the tape. We found this method the most practical: Cut the horizontal (shelf) strips to exact size using a sharp single-edge razor blade. Apply these to the shelves and to the top and bottom members. After the horizontal strips are in place, follow with the long vertical sides. Butt the pieces tightly at each joint. Keep the iron moving to avoid scorching the wood. After all

Anchor bolts secure unit to masonry floor. Holes must be drilled for these; ordinary drill with masonry bit does the job.

This is Power Pak for bed before assembly. Heavy duty springs are in the tubes. The linkage in foreground operates headboard.

Here, left hinge frame member has been installed, bolted securely in place. The spring and the tube are shown at the left.

Braided cable will pass through the spring and ride over the cam. This will allow the bed to be raised and lowered very easily.

Level is used to check recess cabinet to insure it is square and plumb to the floor. If unit isn't square binding can result.

Bed frame is raised and checked for alignment with the edge of the recess. If necessary, shims can be used to bring unit square.

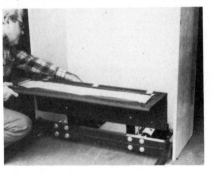

Headboard assembly installed. If done properly, it should fold into bottom corner when bed frame is in the raised position.

Two of the semi-completed units. Shelf arrangement is arbitrary. You should vary heights of shelves according to what you will house.

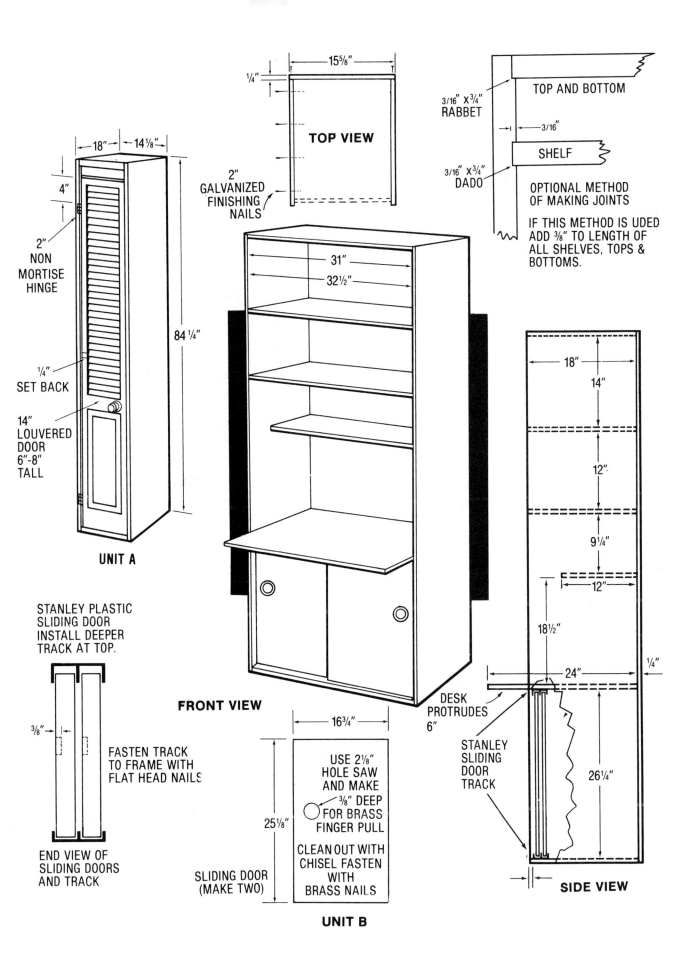

15⅝"

¼"

TOP VIEW

2" GALVANIZED FINISHING NAILS

3/16" X 3/4" RABBET

TOP AND BOTTOM

3/16"

3/16" X 3/4" DADO

SHELF

OPTIONAL METHOD OF MAKING JOINTS

IF THIS METHOD IS UDED ADD ⅜" TO LENGTH OF ALL SHELVES, TOPS & BOTTOMS.

18" 14⅛"

4"

2" NON MORTISE HINGE

¼" SET BACK

14" LOUVERED DOOR 6"-8" TALL

84¼"

31"

32½"

UNIT A

STANLEY PLASTIC SLIDING DOOR INSTALL DEEPER TRACK AT TOP.

⅜"

FASTEN TRACK TO FRAME WITH FLAT HEAD NAILS

END VIEW OF SLIDING DOORS AND TRACK

FRONT VIEW

16¾"

USE 2⅛" HOLE SAW AND MAKE ⅜" DEEP FOR BRASS FINGER PULL

CLEAN OUT WITH CHISEL FASTEN WITH BRASS NAILS

25⅛"

SLIDING DOOR (MAKE TWO)

UNIT B

DESK PROTRUDES 6"

STANLEY SLIDING DOOR TRACK

18"

14"

12"

9¼"

12"

18½"

24"

¼"

26¼"

SIDE VIEW

Wall Unit with Foldaway Bed

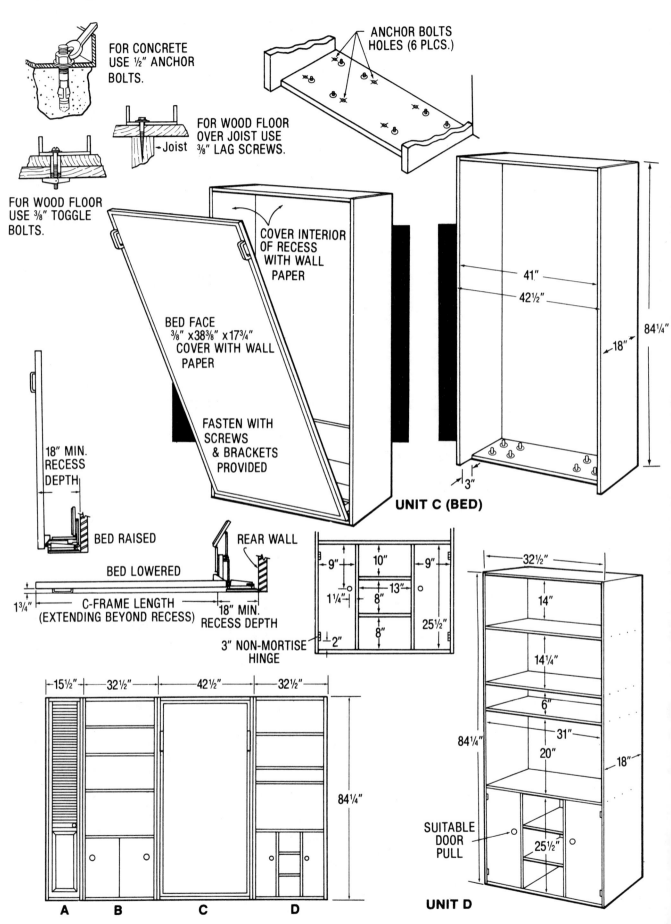

FOR CONCRETE USE ½" ANCHOR BOLTS.

FOR WOOD FLOOR OVER JOIST USE ⅜" LAG SCREWS.

— Joist

FOR WOOD FLOOR USE ⅜" TOGGLE BOLTS.

ANCHOR BOLTS HOLES (6 PLCS.)

COVER INTERIOR OF RECESS WITH WALL PAPER

BED FACE ⅜" x38⅜" x17¾" COVER WITH WALL PAPER

FASTEN WITH SCREWS & BRACKETS PROVIDED

41"

42½"

84¼"

18"

3"

UNIT C (BED)

18" MIN. RECESS DEPTH

BED RAISED

BED LOWERED

REAR WALL

1¾"

C-FRAME LENGTH (EXTENDING BEYOND RECESS)

18" MIN. RECESS DEPTH

3" NON-MORTISE HINGE

9"   10"   9"

1¼"   13"   8"

8"

2"

25½"

32½"

14"

14¼"

6"

31"

20"

84¼"

18"

SUITABLE DOOR PULL

25½"

UNIT D

15½"   32½"   42½"   32½"

84¼"

A   B   C   D

Danish oil finish being applied. After brushing keep wet for 30 minutes, then wipe. Wait sixty minutes then repeat the procedure.

Surface of bed can be finished as you like it. Wallpaper was used here. Small surface makes it easier to get material smooth.

Partial view of the completed unit. Even up close it does not look as if a bed is being hidden . . . indeed it looks more like a plain panel.

In the lowered position the headboard raises automatically. Note how the head of the bed opens away from the wall.

the strips are in place, sand the corners to break the sharp edges. Use 120 grit paper followed by 220.

The back of the cabinets consists of wall paneling fastened with paneling nails. Space all nails 6" apart at intermediate locations as well as around the perimeter. To simplify the application of stain and top finishing coats, do not apply the backs until these operations have been completed. We used Deftco Danish Oil Finish with excellent results. Simply brush it on, let it set 10 minutes, then wipe with a cloth. When dry follow with a clear topcoat.

The step-by-step instruction booklet accompanying the Sico In-Wall Bed is excellent. The instructions are easy to understand and well illustrated.

The bed is available with a baseplate or template. The baseplate has mounting bolts for the special hinges already installed. Anchor bolt holes are also drilled on the board. The front edge of the board is set back from the recessed sides; this allows the installation of a rug under the bed.

Regardless of the system used, the hinges must be installed with great care as they exert tremendous pressure counterbalancing the weight of the bed. The mounting plate for the springs is provided with slotted holes to permit adjustment of the bed frame within the recess.

If the bed is to be installed on a hard concrete slab floor, the baseplate should be anchored with the $\frac{1}{2}$" diameter expanding anchor bolts provided. The use of power-driven or non-expanding type anchors must not be used as they can work loose. For installation over wood floors, $\frac{3}{8}$" toggle bolts are used and, if over joists, $\frac{3}{8}$" lag screws are recommended.

The bed face material of your choice should be cut to fit the frame with 1/16" clearance all around. We used $\frac{3}{8}$" plywood faced with wallpaper. The board is fastened to the frame cross members using special clips and $\frac{3}{8}$ pan head screws provided.

When properly installed, the bed frame should center in the recess with a $\frac{1}{4}$" gap at the sides.

The bed frame is designed to take standard size mattress and box spring. These can be purchased with the frame or you can use your own if desired.

Bill of Materials

Note: All lumber is $\frac{3}{4}$" birch plywood except as noted. Backs are prefinished paneling. All measurements are in inches.

Unit A

Side	$\frac{3}{4}$ x 18 x 84$\frac{1}{4}$	2 req'd.
Top	$\frac{3}{4}$ x 18 x 14$\frac{1}{8}$	1 req'd.
Bottom	$\frac{3}{4}$ x 18 x 14$\frac{1}{8}$	1 req'd.
Back	$\frac{1}{4}$ x 15$\frac{5}{8}$ x 84$\frac{1}{4}$, plywood	1 req'd.
Header	$\frac{3}{4}$ x 2$\frac{1}{2}$ x 14$\frac{1}{8}$	1 req'd.
Door	1$\frac{3}{8}$ x 14 x 80	1 req'd.
Hinge, non-mortise 3"		2 req'd.
Door knob		1 req'd.
Wood tape veneer		17 ft.

Unit B

Side	$\frac{3}{4}$ x 18 x 84$\frac{1}{4}$	2 req'd.
Shelves	$\frac{3}{4}$ x 18 x 31	2 req'd.
Top	$\frac{3}{4}$ x 18 x 31	1 req'd.
Bottom	$\frac{3}{4}$ x 18 x 31	1 req'd.
Desk top	$\frac{3}{4}$ x 24 x 31	1 req'd.
Shelf	$\frac{3}{4}$ x 12 x 31	1 req'd.
Door	$\frac{3}{4}$ x 16$\frac{3}{4}$ x 25$\frac{1}{8}$	2 req'd.
Back	$\frac{1}{4}$ x 32$\frac{1}{2}$ x 84$\frac{1}{4}$, plywood	1 req'd.
Door track	Stanley, $\frac{3}{4}$"	1 set
Finger pull	2" dia.	2 req'd.
Wood tape veneer		32 ft.

Unit C

Side	$\frac{3}{4}$ x 18 x 84$\frac{1}{4}$	2 req'd.
Top	$\frac{3}{4}$ x 18 x 41	1 req'd.
Bottom	$\frac{3}{4}$ x 15 x 41	1 req'd.
Back	$\frac{1}{4}$ x 42$\frac{1}{2}$ x 84$\frac{1}{4}$, fir plywood	1 req'd.
Bed face	$\frac{3}{8}$ x 38$\frac{3}{8}$ x 79$\frac{3}{4}$	1 req'd.
Wallpaper,	double roll	2 req'd.
Wall bed	Sico 1900 Series	1 req'd.
Wood tape veneer		18 ft.

Unit D

Side	$\frac{3}{4}$ x 18 x 84$\frac{1}{4}$	2 req'd.
Top	$\frac{3}{4}$ x 18 x 31	1 req'd.
Bottom	$\frac{3}{4}$ x 18 x 31	1 req'd.
Shelf	$\frac{3}{4}$ x 18 x 31	4 req'd.
Divider	$\frac{3}{4}$ x 18 x 25$\frac{1}{2}$	2 req'd.
Shelf	$\frac{3}{4}$ x 13 x 18	2 req'd.
Door	$\frac{3}{4}$ x 8$\frac{7}{8}$ x 25$\frac{3}{8}$	2 req'd.
Back	$\frac{1}{4}$ x 32$\frac{1}{2}$ x 84$\frac{1}{4}$, plywood	1 req'd.
Hinge, non-mortise 2"		4 req'd.
Pull		2 req'd.
Wood tape veneer		32 ft.

Colonial Dry Sink

You can build this versatile and serviceable piece of Americana for less than $65

Early American furniture has retained its popularity from Colonial days right up to the present. The dry sink shown here is a typical piece of the furniture used by the early colonists. It was found in farm kitchens that lacked plumbing connections and was used for washing dishes, etc. Due to its recessed lined well, it is extremely serviceable and can be used as a bar, a buffet-server, a plant stand, or a simple storage cabinet.

A ready-made dry sink retails for several hundred dollars, but you can build your own for about one-fourth the price. (The price will vary depending on lumber prices in your area and the type of wood you use for construction.)

We recommend pine as it is easy to work with and the end grain poses no problem as it sands very smooth and takes paint or lacquer beautifully. Of course it can also be left natural or stained. There are many ways to finish the piece. Another excellent possibility is to antique it. Whatever your choice, you can bet that you'll have a great conversation piece when you're done with this one.

If you plan to paint the cabinet, you should choose lumber with a minimum of knots. To be sure of this, don't phone in your order, but go down to the lumber yard and personally pick out the best pieces available. You will undoubtedly end up with a few pieces with glaring knots, but you can place these where they won't show up, preferably the top or bottom panels. The top panel will be covered with plastic laminate and the bottom will be concealed by the doors.

To eliminate the need for gluing up boards, use 18-in. stock. These are glued up by the mill and the pieces are generally flat. Common pine can be had up to 24-in. wide.

Start the construction by building the main case which is really a large box. Cut the pieces to size then rabbet the rear edges to take the ¼-in. panel. Assemble the parts with glue and nails. Butt joints are used throughout. If you can temporarily install the rear panel, you can use this to square up the case.

The front frame is of doweled

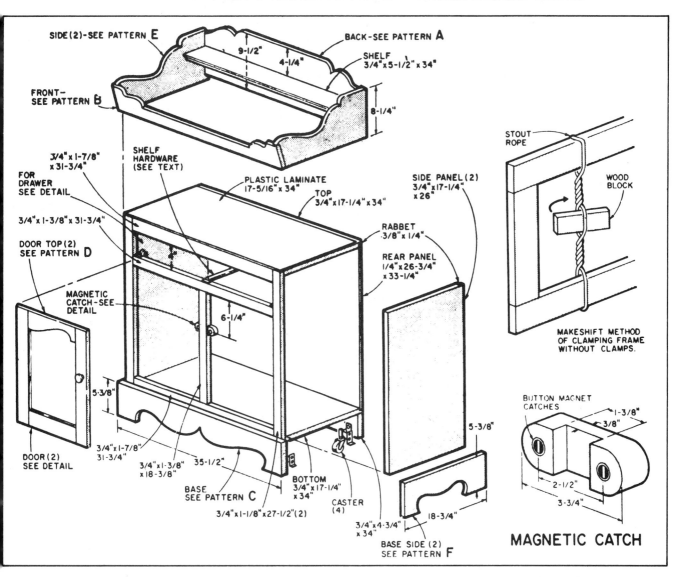

SIDE(2)-SEE PATTERN E

BACK-SEE PATTERN A

9-1/2"
4-1/4"

SHELF
3/4"x5-1/2"x34"

8-1/4"

FRONT-
SEE PATTERN B

3/4"x1-7/8"
x31-3/4"

SHELF
HARDWARE
(SEE TEXT)

PLASTIC LAMINATE
17-5/16"x34"

TOP
3/4"x17-1/4"x34"

SIDE PANEL(2)
3/4"x17-1/4"
x26"

FOR
DRAWER
SEE DETAIL

3/4"x1-3/8"x31-3/4"

RABBET
3/8"x1/4"

DOOR TOP(2)
SEE PATTERN D

REAR PANEL
1/4"x26-3/4"
x33-1/4"

MAGNETIC
CATCH-SEE
DETAIL

6-1/4"

5-3/8"

DOOR(2)
SEE DETAIL

3/4"x1-7/8"
31-3/4"

35-1/2"

5-3/8"

3/4"x1-3/8"
x18-3/8"

BASE
SEE PATTERN C

BOTTOM
3/4"x17-1/4"
x34"

CASTER
(4)

3/4"x1-1/8"x27-1/2"(2)

3/4"x1-3/4"
x34"

18-3/4"

BASE SIDE(2)
SEE PATTERN F

STOUT
ROPE

WOOD
BLOCK

MAKESHIFT METHOD
OF CLAMPING FRAME
WITHOUT CLAMPS.

BUTTON MAGNET
CATCHES

1-3/8"
3/8"

2-1/2"

3-3/4"

MAGNETIC CATCH

construction. The dowels assure that the frame will not separate and they add greatly to the strength of the cabinet. Follow the sequence shown to prevent difficulty in assembly. Glue up the center section first (shaped like the letter "H") then follow with the side pieces. Use spiral dowels or if not available, use regular dowels but crimp the surface with a pair of pliers to form grooves. Use a hammer and block of scrap wood to drive the sections home. If clamps are available, use them. Otherwise use the rope and turn-buckle system to tighten up on the joints. See illustration.

The base is installed next. Use a saber saw or jig saw to cut the scallops then round off the edge of the scallop with a router. Note that the sides and front base pieces are placed on the outside of the case

1. Cut cabinet case from 18" wide pine. Assemble with glue and finishing nails.

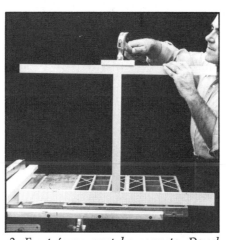
2. Front frame must be accurate. Dowel construction's used for added strength.

3. Assembled front frame. Close all sections using hammer, block of scrap wood.

Dry Sink

while the rear piece is positioned flush with the back of the cabinet.

The corner bracket casters are a good idea though not essential. They reinforce the corners and they automatically position themselves. No measuring is necessary. Just place them in the corner, drive in the screws, and the casters will protrude just the right amount. Mounted on casters, the dry sink will be easy to move about the room when cleaning or re-decorating.

The top section is assembled as a unit and then installed onto the cabinet using 2-in. finishing nails. Before assembling the top pieces, round off all top edges with the router. Be sure to stop short of the ends at the rear side of the front where it joins the sides.

The drawer is of simple construction. The front is ¾-in. pine, the sides and rear are of ½-in. pine. The bottom is ¼-in. plywood. Follow drawing details for construction. The center bottom drawer slide makes for quick and easy installation. These are available at hardware shops and lumber yards everywhere.

The recessed panel doors are easier to make than they seem. All pieces are cut to size then assembled with dowels. The scroll at the top of the doors is cut and sanded before assembly. The inside edge of the door (face side) is shaped with a router fitted with a small beading bit. The back side is done next with a square rabbeting bit to take the ¼-in. panel. The depth of the rabbet should be ⅜-in. to allow the panel to set below the surface about ⅛-in.

To operate efficiently, the magnetic catches should be placed as near as possible to the door pull. The button magnetic catches shown are ideal as they can be mounted on a small block of wood which fastens to the center divider.

The plastic laminated top is recommended as it will take plenty of wear and cleans easily. If you plan to spray the cabinet, mask the top surface of the laminate and install

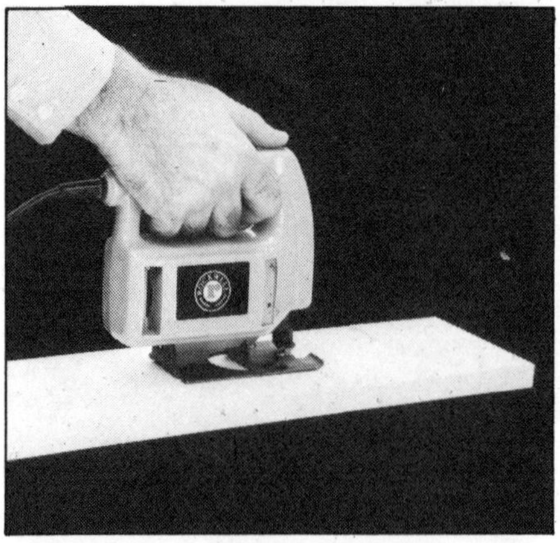

4. Saber saw is ideal for cutting various scallops. Use smooth cutting blade.

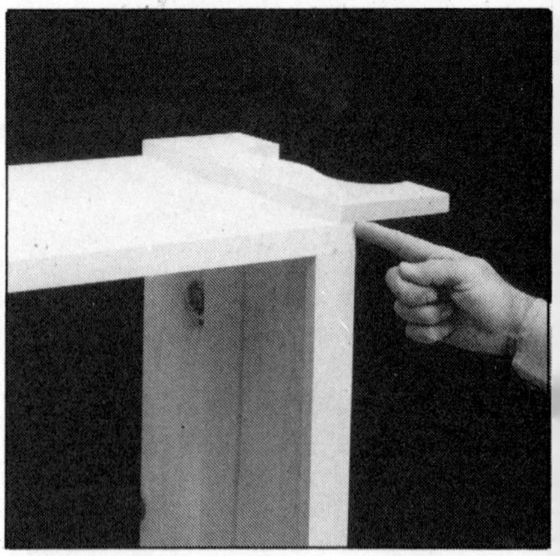

5. Base pieces are added to sides. Allow sufficient clearance for casters.

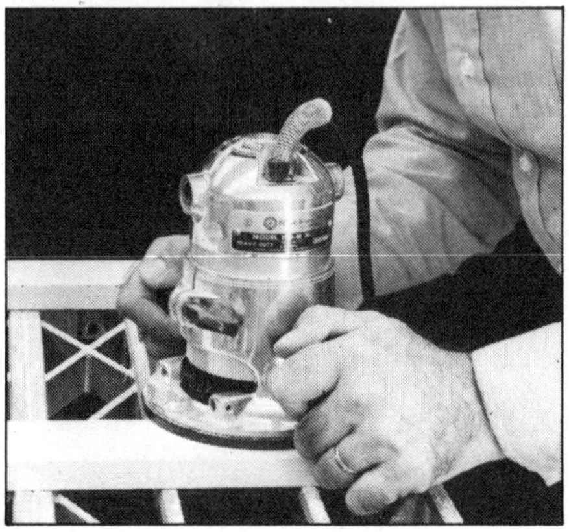

8. Doors are routed with small beading cutter. Back is rabbeted for ¼" panel.

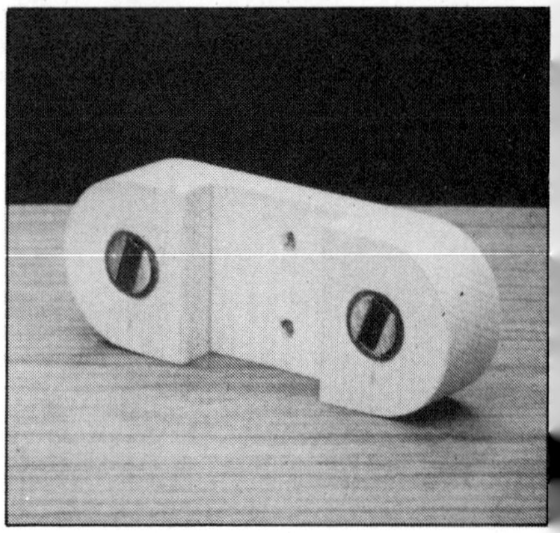

9. The magnets are mounted in notched block which screws to center divider.

in the usual manner. If you are painting, paint the cabinet first, then install the laminate.

The colorful decals (fruits, flowers, birds, etc.) add greatly to the appearance of the finished piece. The corner piece at the upper part of the door is not available in the shape shown, but it was made by simply cutting apart several of the ready made decals and rearranging them as shown.

BILL OF MATERIALS—DRY SINK
NOTE: Except where noted all lumber is common pine

Use	Size in inches	No. Req.
Base front	¾" x 5⅜" x 35½"	
Base rear	¾" x 4¾" x 34"	
Base sides	¾" x 5⅜" x 18"	2
Case bottom	¾" x 17¼" x 34"	
Case top	¾" x 17¼" x 34"	
Case sides	¾" x 17¼" x 26"	2
Frame upper	¾" x 1⅞" x 34"	
Frame center	¾" x 1⅜" x 34"	
Frame lower	¾" x 1⅞" x 34"	
Frame sides	¾" x 1⅛" x 27½"	2
Frame center	¾" x 1⅜" x 18⅜"	
Top front	¾" x 3¼" x 34"	
Top sides	¾" x 8¼" x 19½"	2
Top rear	¾" x 9½" x 34"	
Shelf	¾" x 5½" x 34"	
Door stiles	¾" x 2½" x 18⅞"	4
Door rail upper	¾" x 3½" x 10⅝"	2
Door rail lower	¾" x 2½" x 10⅝"	2
Door panel	¼" x 11⅛" x 15" plywood	2
Drawer front	¾" x 4½" x 32½"	
Drawer sub-front	½" x 3⅝" x 30½"	
Drawer sides	½" x 3⅝" x 15½"	2
Drawer rear	½" x 3" x 30½"	
Drawer bottom	¼" x 14⅝" x 31" plywood	
Button magnet support	¾" x 1⅜" x 3¾"	
Rear panel	¼" x 26¾" x 33¼" plywood	
Miscellaneous		
Nails 2" finishing		
Glue—white		
Button catches		2
Drawer slide hardware		1
Door pulls		2
Drawer pulls		2
Decals—Meyercord 1505-A, 1505-B		
Caster & brackets		

Classic China Cabinet *(p. 11)*

Wall Unit with
. . . .

Foldaway Bed (p. 18)

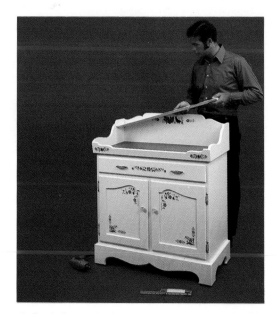

Colonial Dry Sink *(p. 24)*

Super Workbench (p. 28)

Cheese and Wine Cart *(p. 40)*

Butler's Tray Table *(p. 49)*

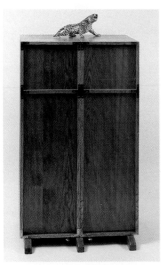

Hideaway . . . . Home Office *(p. 62)*

Gossip Bench *(p. 6*

Classic Rolltop Desk *(p. 82)*

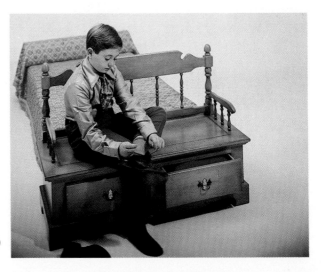

Child's Footlocker (p. 92)

6. *Assembled top's fastened to cabinet. Measure, cut plastic laminate to size.*

7. *Doors of dry sink are of dowelled construction. Top's cut before assembly.*

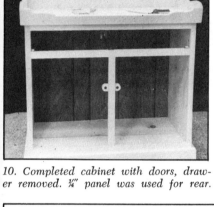

10. *Completed cabinet with doors, drawer removed. ¼" panel was used for rear.*

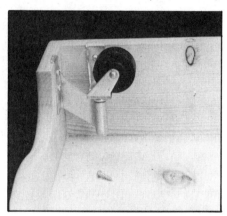

11. *Self-locating casters make the unit mobile, give added strength to corners.*

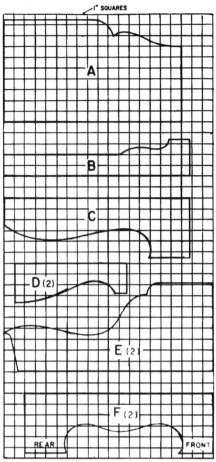

1" SQUARES

A

B

C

D (2)

E (2)

F (2)

REAR   FRONT

CONTOUR PATTERNS

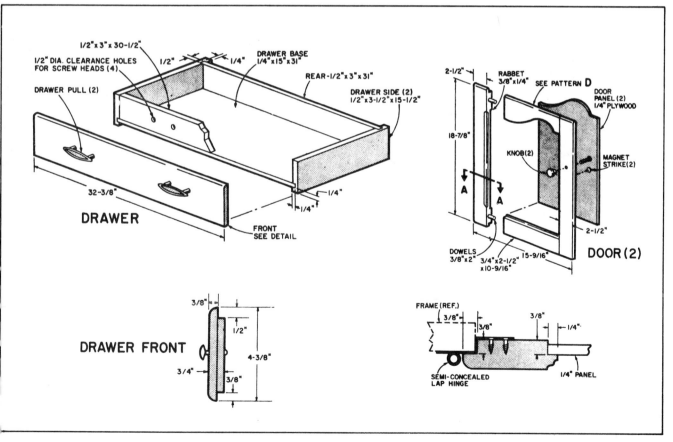

1/2" x 3" x 30-1/2"

1/2" DIA. CLEARANCE HOLES FOR SCREW HEADS (4)

DRAWER PULL (2)

1/2"   1/4"

DRAWER BASE 1/4" x 15" x 31"

REAR-1/2" x 3" x 31"

DRAWER SIDE (2) 1/2" x 3-1/2" x 15-1/2"

1/4"

1/4"

32-3/8"

DRAWER

FRONT SEE DETAIL

3/8"

1/2"

DRAWER FRONT

3/4"

4-3/8"

3/8"

2-1/2"

RABBET 3/8" x 1/4"

SEE PATTERN D

DOOR PANEL (2) 1/4" PLYWOOD

18-7/8"

KNOB (2)

MAGNET STRIKE (2)

A

A

2-1/2"

DOWELS 3/8" x 2"

3/4" x 2-1/2" x 10-9/16"

15-9/16"

DOOR (2)

FRAME (REF.)

3/8"

3/8"

3/8"

1/4"

SEMI-CONCEALED LAP HINGE

1/4" PANEL

SUPER WORKBENCH

Built for the professional and amateur alike this rugged workbench will give years of reliable service.

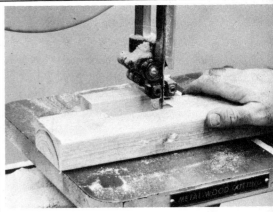

The notches on the leg piece are cut with a band saw. If none is available use a hand saw and chisel as an alternate.

After the hole is drilled in the stretcher piece transfer location of bolt to the leg by placing in the hole and tapping with hammer.

The completed workbench provides a sturdy work area for just about any kind of project you have in mind. Plenty of storage space too.

A sturdy, durable workbench is one of the most important items in any workshop, whether it be large or small, amateur or professional. This particular one features a novel hardwood top which is laminated to a plywood base. The combination provides the necessary stiffness and the hard surface will withstand abuse without splintering or denting. Hardwood strip flooring is ideally suited for this purpose because it is end-matched with tongue and groove edges which greatly simplify installation.

Other features of this fine workbench are a pegboard tool rack, roomy drawer, large storage compartment, and a work support for supporting long boards held in the vise. It also features a plug-in strip which

is fastened to the underside of the tool rack. This is not visible in the photos as it is placed toward the rear of the shelf as a safety precaution.

Also included are two frame-type pegboard panels which are mounted at the ends of the bench to utilize the otherwise wasted space.

The basic frame consists of 2 x 4 lumber fastened with lag screws which contribute to the sturdiness of this bench. Select straight 2 x 4's and try to choose those with a minimum of knots. Cut the various components to length then notch the legs to accept the stretchers. The method of notching depends on the tools available to you. If you have a band saw notching will be greatly simplified. Otherwise, you can use a hand saw

and chisel for this operation.

Carefully locate and layout the notches on the leg members. Note that only the lower rear notches are "U"-shaped. All others are "L"-shaped and thus edge cut. If the band saw is to be used, make the layouts on the proper face so the throat of the machine will not interfere. If the hand saw is employed be sure to make the cuts straight and square.

After notching the pieces set them aside and prepare the stretcher to take the lag screws. Locate the hole centers as indicated, then, using a one-inch diameter spade type bit bore the lag screw clearance to a depth of ⅜". This will allow room for the head and washer. The screw body hole is bored next. This i

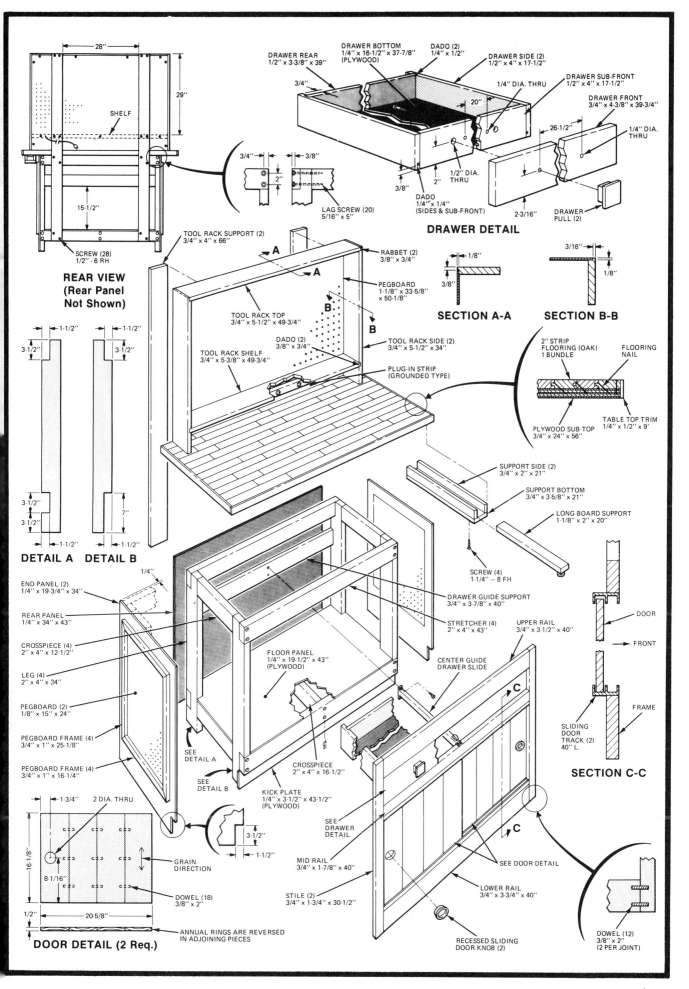

REAR VIEW (Rear Panel Not Shown)

28"

29"

SHELF

15-1/2"

SCREW (28)
1/2"- 6 RH

DETAIL A   DETAIL B

1-1/2"   1-1/2"

3-1/2"   3-1/2"

3-1/2"   7"

3-1/2"

1-1/2"   1-1/2"

3/4"   3/8"

2"

LAG SCREW (20)
5/16" x 5"

DRAWER DETAIL

DRAWER BOTTOM
1/4" x 16-1/2" x 37-7/8"
(PLYWOOD)

DRAWER REAR
1/2" x 3-3/8" x 39"

DADO (2)
1/4" x 1/2"

DRAWER SIDE (2)
1/2" x 4" x 17-1/2"

1/4" DIA. THRU

DRAWER SUB-FRONT
1/2" x 4" x 17-1/2"

DRAWER FRONT
3/4" x 4-3/8" x 39-3/4"

1/4" DIA. THRU

20"

26-1/2"

3/4"

1/2" DIA. THRU

3/8"

2"

2"

DADO
1/4" x 1/4"
(SIDES & SUB-FRONT)

2-3/16"

DRAWER PULL (2)

SECTION A-A

1/8"

3/8"

SECTION B-B

3/16"

1/8"

2" STRIP FLOORING (OAK)
1 BUNDLE

FLOORING NAIL

TABLE TOP TRIM
1/4" x 1/2" x 9"

PLYWOOD SUB-TOP
3/4" x 24" x 56"

TOOL RACK SUPPORT (2)
3/4" x 4" x 66"

A   A

RABBET (2)
3/8" x 3/4"

PEGBOARD
1-1/8" x 33-5/8" x 50-1/8"

B   B

TOOL RACK TOP
3/4" x 5-1/2" x 49-3/4"

DADO (2)
3/8" x 3/4"

TOOL RACK SIDE (2)
3/4" x 5-1/2" x 34"

TOOL RACK SHELF
3/4" x 5-3/8" x 49-3/4"

PLUG-IN STRIP
(GROUNDED TYPE)

SUPPORT SIDE (2)
3/4" x 2" x 21"

SUPPORT BOTTOM
3/4" x 3-5/8" x 21"

LONG BOARD SUPPORT
1-1/8" x 2" x 20"

SCREW (4)
1-1/4" – 8 FH

END PANEL (2)
1/4" x 19-3/4" x 34"

1/4"

REAR PANEL
1/4" x 34" x 43"

CROSSPIECE (4)
2" x 4" x 12-1/2"

LEG (4)
2" x 4" x 34"

PEGBOARD (2)
1/8" x 15" x 24"

PEGBOARD FRAME (4)
3/4" x 1" x 25-1/8"

PEGBOARD FRAME (4)
3/4" x 1" x 16-1/4"

FLOOR PANEL
1/4" x 19-1/2" x 43"
(PLYWOOD)

DRAWER GUIDE SUPPORT
3/4" x 3-7/8" x 40"

STRETCHER (4)
2" x 4" x 43"

CENTER GUIDE
DRAWER SLIDE

UPPER RAIL
3/4" x 3-1/2" x 40"

SEE DETAIL A

SEE DETAIL B

CROSSPIECE
2" x 4" x 16-1/2"

KICK PLATE
1/4" x 3-1/2" x 43-1/2"
(PLYWOOD)

SEE DRAWER DETAIL

MID RAIL
3/4" x 1-7/8" x 40"

STILE (2)
3/4" x 1-3/4" x 30-1/2"

LOWER RAIL
3/4" x 3-3/4" x 40"

RECESSED SLIDING
DOOR KNOB (2)

SEE DOOR DETAIL

C   C

DOOR

FRONT

FRAME

SLIDING DOOR TRACK (2)
40" L.

SECTION C-C

DOWEL (12)
3/8" x 2"
(2 PER JOINT)

DOOR DETAIL (2 Req.)

1-3/4"

2 DIA. THRU

16-1/8"

8-1/16"

1/2"

20-5/8"

3-1/2"

1-1/2"

GRAIN DIRECTION

DOWEL (18)
3/8" x 2"

ANNUAL RINGS ARE REVERSED
IN ADJOINING PIECES

WORKBENCH

5/16″ diameter and is bored through the center of each clearance hole.

Next, transfer the mounting holes to the cross members. Do this by aligning the pieces so the edges are flush, then insert the lag screws and tap gently with a hammer. When all the holes have been located, bore the 3/16″ root diameter for the lag screw, then assemble the frame. Be sure to place a washer under the head of each screw. Tighten securely, using a socket wrench. Be sure to work on a flat surface to ensure that the frame will assemble straight and square. Check for accuracy with a large square.

The front frame is made of pine lumber, but you may substitute hardwood if you like. Rip the parts to size then trim them to length. The materials list shows the stiles (the two vertical members of the front frame) as being 1¾″ wide. It's a good idea to make them 2 inches wide. This will permit final trimming to size, thus assuring that the width of the frame will align with the bench ends. Also, making the pieces oversize eliminates the need for cauls under the clamps. The dents left by the clamp jaws are simply trimmed off after assembly.

Two dowels per joint are used to assemble the frame. Locate the holes for the dowels carefully. Use dowel centers, a doweling jig or a combination of both. Bore the ⅜″ diameter holes 1-1/16″ deep. Spiral groove dowels are recommended. If you use smooth dowels, groove them with the splined jaws of a plier. This will permit air to escape as the dowel is driven into the hole. Failure to do this could result in the wood splitting.

Prepare the parts for assembly by applying a thin coat of glue to the three horizontal members of the frame. This is called sizing and its purpose is to prevent excessive absorption of glue, which would result in a dry or weakened joint. Allow the glue to set about 15 minutes, then recoat and join the parts. If the pieces were cut properly, the assembled frame should square up. However, be sure to check for squareness after applying the

After the holes are drilled, screw in the bolt with a ratchet. Remember to use washer under the bolt head to prevent wood from crushing. Drill hole deep enough for a good bite into the center brace.

Once the framework for the bench is bolted up, glue and clamp the front frame. Make sure to check the frame for squareness before the glue dries. Your workbench is already working for you.

After the frame is assembled, squared up and the glue has dried attach it to the bench frame. The front was cut oversize to ensure a perfect fit during sanding of the final assembly.

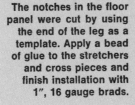

The notches in the floor panel were cut by using the end of the leg as a template. Apply a bead of glue to the stretchers and cross pieces and finish installation with 1″, 16 gauge brads.

The work area of the bench is topped with hardwood flooring. Rip the groove from the first strip. If possible the first strip should run the entire length of the bench. Fasten the flooring with 1½" spiral flooring nails.

The overhang of the strip flooring is trimmed with a panel saw. Leave about ⅟₁₆" for final trimming with a router. Strips should be staggered at least 8 inches. The last piece of flooring at the rear may have to be trimmed with a plane.

Use a good quality wood filler to fill in all the cracks and spaces between strips. Allow to dry and then sand. You may need to do this several times for a seamless finish.

The end and front edges of the top have been covered with a strip of trim ¼" thick by 1½" wide. To prevent cupping each sliding door is made up of 4 pieces with the annular rings reversed. These are glued up and installed.

clamps. If necessary, adjust and square up before the glue sets.

The end panels and bench floor are made from ¼" plywood. Cut these to size as indicated. The end pieces should line up with the front and rear edges of the 2 x 4 legs. Apply a bead of glue to the sides of the legs and crosspieces then install and assemble the ends, using 1"—16 gauge brads.

The front frame is installed now. Use glue and 2" finishing nails. Be sure to let the overhang at each end be equal. Allow the glue to set, then trim the overhang using a plane or router.

The top consists of a ¾" plywood base topped with hardwood flooring. Cut the plywood to size then fasten it to the plywood frame. If the top is to be fastened permanently, you can drive screws from above through the plywood into the 2 x 4's. If you prefer to make the top removable, fasten it from the underside by boring holes through the 2 x 4 frame then fasten with 3" lag screws.

The flooring is available in maple or oak and is sold at all lumber yards. It is sold by the bundle in random lengths. Size of the bundles varies so be sure to order enough to cover the 10 square feet of the workbench top.

The front or leading edge strip should be ripped to remove the groove as indicated. Do this on the table saw or use a plane. If possible, the first strip should extend the length of the top in one piece. Let the ends overhang and fasten the strip with 1½" spiral flooring nails. These are driven diagonally through the tongue of the strip. Before installing the first strip, bore six 3/32" diameter holes ¼" in from the leading edge. Counterbore these holes with a 5/32" diameter bit and make this hole ⅛" deep. Align the edge of the strip with the edge of the plywood and drive nails into each of the holes. Now proceed with the diagonal nailing. Drive the nails at a 45-degree angle. Drive the nails to a point where the nailheads are still slightly above the wood surface, then complete nailing with a nail set. This will prevent damage to the strip edges.

The strips for the second course

WORKBENCH

are installed with the groove fitted tightly against the tongue of the preceding course. Use a scrap of flooring to tap the strips tightly into place before nailing. When nailing near the strip ends, it may be necessary to drill pilot holes for the nails to prevent splitting. The end joints in each course must be staggered at least 8-inches apart. Each course must be installed so the ends overhang slightly. When the last row is installed, use the same procedure as used in the first course Bore holes near the rear edge and drive the nails straight down. If necessary, trim the rear strip.

The overhang is now trimmed with a saber saw or circular saw. Trim close to the plywood but leave about 1/16" overhang. This is then retrimmed using a router fitted with a panel trimming bit. Set the cutter so the guide of the bit rides against the end of the plywood edge. The result will be a cleanly trimmed edge with both the plywood and the hardwood perfectly flush. Be wary of voids in the plywood edge as this could cause the router bit to dip and cut an indent in the hardwood edge.

The end and front edges of the top are covered with a piece of trim ¼" thick by 1½" wide. Install the ends first, then follow with the front. Hold with brads.

The sliding doors are made of ½" pine. To prevent cupping, each door should be made of at least four pieces of wood, glued up to form the panel. Cut each door from a length of stock and reverse the annular rings as indicated on the drawing. This will insure that the doors will remain flat. Use dowels or if you have a shaper, you may want to use a glue joint instead. Make the doors slightly oversize in height, then trim to the necessary size. Note sliding door track varies among manufacturers so be sure to have the track installed before cutting the doors to height.

The drawer is made of ½" stock except for the front which is ¾" thick. Cut and assemble the pieces as indicated. The front and sub-front are installed temporarily with two screws installed in oversize holes bored through the sub front. This will allow adjustment of the front panel over the drawer opening.

Because of the width of the drawer, two drawer runners are used as indicated.

The frame for the pegboard is assembled from ¾" stock. Rabbet the rear edges of the sides and top member to take the pegboard. Install the pegboard with flat head screws.

The tool rack may be wall or table mounted. If wall-mounted, install it so it just clears the bench top. If mounted to the bench, let it rest on the bench and support it at the rear with two boards which span the frame.

The long work support is placed at the end of the table opposite the end where the vise is installed. The support is fitted with a knob on the underside and pulls out as required when working on long boards held by the vise. Installation details are shown on the drawing.

The small frames are made with mitered joints. The backs are rabbeted similar to the tool rack.

Add the rear panel to the bench to complete construction. Add the plug-in strip after the bench has been finished. The bench shown was finished with three coats of white shellac. The pegboard was given a couple of coats of semi-gloss latex paint.

Plenty of storage is provided by pegboard mounted to plywood end of workbench. Board holder slides out.

BILL OF MATERIALS FOR A STURDY WORKBENCH
(NOTE: 2 x 4's actually measure 1½" x 3½")

Description	Size	Quantity Needed
Leg	2" x 4" x 34"	4
Stretcher	2" x 4" x 43"	4
Crosspiece	2" x 4" x 12½"	4
Crosspiece	2" x 4" x 16½"	1
Floor panel	¼" x 19½" x 43"	1, plywood
End panel	¼" x 19¾" x 34"	2, plywood
Kick plate	¼" x 3½" x 43½"	1, plywood
Rear panel	¼" x 34" x 43"	1, plywood
Stile	¾" x 1¾" x 30½"	2, pine** (See Text)
Upper rail	¾" x 3½" x 40"	1, pine
Mid rail	¾" x 1⅞" x 40"	1, pine
Lower rail	¾" x 3¾" x 40"	1, pine
Drawer guide support	¾" x 3⅞" x 40"	1, pine
Sub-top	¾" x 24" x 56"	1, plywood
Top	2" strip flooring	1 bundle, oak
Door	½" x 16⅛" x 20⅝"	2, pine
Drawer front	¾" x 4⅜" x 39¾"	1, pine
Drawer sub-front	½" x 4" x 38⅝"	1, pine
Drawer side	½" x 4" x 17½"	2, pine
Drawer rear	½" x 3⅜" x 39"	1, pine
Drawer bottom	¼" x 16½" x 38⅞"	1, plywood
Tool rack side	¾" x 5½" x 34"	2, pine
Tool rack top	⅜" x 5½" x 49¾"	1, pine
Tool rack shelf	¾" x 5⅜" x 49¾"	1, pine
Pegboard	⅛" x 33⅝" x 50⅛"	1
Pegboard	⅛" x 15" x 24"	2
Pegboard frame	¾" x 1" x 16¼"	4, pine
Pegboard frame	¾" x 1" x 25⅛"	4, pine
Long board support	1⅛" x 2" x 20"	1, pine
Support side	¾" x 2" x 21"	2, pine
Support bottom	¾" x 3⅝" x 21"	1, pine
Table top trim	¼" x 1½" x 9 feet	pine
Tool rack support	¾" x 4" x 66"	2, pine
Center Slide Hardware		
Drawer Pull		
Sliding Door Track		
Recessed Sliding Door Knob		
Plug-In Strip (Grounded Type)		
Finishing Nails—2"		
Finishing Nails—1½"		
Lag Screws	⅝" x 5"	20 required
Screws	1¼" — 8 FH	16 required
Screws	½" — 6 RH	28 required

Compact BAR/CABINET Combo

This handy piece of furniture has everything. There is plenty of room for bottles, a compartment for recipes and utensils, a tray, and a glass rack.

THIS attractive bar-cabinet features a revolving door with racks for glasses and a detachable front panel which doubles as a serving tray. The use of prefinished panels for all exposed surfaces eliminates the need for finishing and gives the completed piece a swank professional appearance.

The well-proportioned bar has ample storage space for bottles, glassware, ice bucket and the like. The compartment to the left also has a small shelf near the top which is ideal for storing recipes, stirrers, tongs, etc. This shelf is placed high enough to clear the bottles stored below it.

To add further to the appearance, prefinished cove molding is used to edge the lid and base, thus solving the problem of what to do with exposed edges. When carefully cut and applied, the molding looks like it was cut from the panel with a shaper or router. Miters must be cut with a sharp blade; otherwise, the wood will tend to splinter resulting in an unsightly appearance.

Care must also be exercised when cutting the panels as the prefinished surface has a degree of brittleness which makes it prone to surface splitting. This is especially apparent when using dull tools.

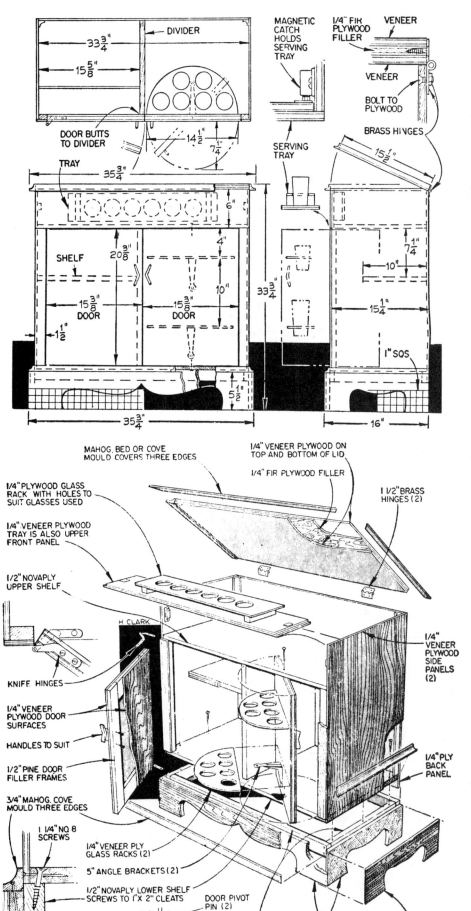

33 3/4"

15 5/8"

DIVIDER

MAGNETIC CATCH HOLDS SERVING TRAY

1/4" FIR PLYWOOD FILLER

VENEER

VENEER

BOLT TO PLYWOOD

DOOR BUTTS TO DIVIDER

14 1/2"

7 1/4"

SERVING TRAY

BRASS HINGES

TRAY

35 3/4"

15 1/2"

6"

4"

SHELF

20 3/8"

10"

33 3/4"

7 1/4"

10"

15 3/8" DOOR

15 3/8" DOOR

15 1/4"

1 1/2"

1" SQS

5 1/2"

35 3/4"

16"

MAHOG. BED OR COVE MOULD COVERS THREE EDGES

1/4" VENEER PLYWOOD ON TOP AND BOTTOM OF LID

1/4" FIR PLYWOOD FILLER

1 1/2" BRASS HINGES (2)

1/4" PLYWOOD GLASS RACK WITH HOLES TO SUIT GLASSES USED

1/4" VENEER PLYWOOD TRAY IS ALSO UPPER FRONT PANEL

1/2" NOVAPLY UPPER SHELF

H CLARK

1/4" VENEER PLYWOOD SIDE PANELS (2)

KNIFE HINGES

1/4" VENEER PLYWOOD DOOR SURFACES

HANDLES TO SUIT

1/2" PINE DOOR FILLER FRAMES

3/4" MAHOG. COVE MOULD THREE EDGES

1/4" PLY BACK PANEL

1 1/4" NO. 8 SCREWS

1/4" VENEER PLY GLASS RACKS (2)

5" ANGLE BRACKETS (2)

1/2" NOVAPLY LOWER SHELF SCREWS TO 1" X 2" CLEATS

DOOR PIVOT PIN (2)

WASHERS

1" X 2" CLEATS MOUNT CABINET (4)

1/2" NOVAPLY BASE FRAMES (3)

1/4" VENEER PLYWOOD FACING (3)

The brackets should be rivetted to the revolving door. Then the glass trays are rivetted to the brackets as shown here.

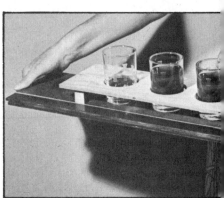

Use a hole saw attached to an electric drill to make cutouts for glasses on the serving tray and the revolving racks.

BAR/CABINET Combo

The best blade for a table or radial-arm saw when working with prefinished panels is a plywood blade. These are hollow ground and cut very smoothly.

Prefinished panels come in a wide variety of styles and woods. Some are solid panels without grooves while others have random grooves and still others have narrow bands or grooves with wide panels between. Prices vary depending upon location and quality. The wood selected and the grain pattern have a direct bearing on the price.

Use a non-staining white glue for assembling all sections and where necessary, use clamps. Clamping will not be practical when working with the cove molding. Here strips of masking tape are recommended to hold the piece while the glue dries.

Both doors are faced with the pre-finished material. A framing of ½-in. pine is sandwiched in between to build up the thickness and to prevent warping. The serving tray panel is held in place against the side panels by a friction fit bearing. The overhanging molding on the front edge of the lid also tends to hold the tray-panel securely. When the lid is raised the tray may be removed by pulling it forward slightly to overcome the slight side pressure. If desired, a pair of magnetic catches may be added at the ends.

A pair of knife hinges is used to support the swinging door. These are attached at the top and bottom into a recess cut in the door. The revolving door is affixed by means of a pivot that consists of a pair of 2-in. nails placed as shown. Two small washers at the bottom will allow the door to revolve freely.

The base is made by glueing the prefinished stock to a piece of ½-in. pine. Refer to the drawing as to edge treatment. When your bar-cabinet is completely assembled, break all sharp edges with fine sandpaper, then stain the inside if desired.

A headed 2-in. nail serves as a pivot for the revolving door. It was driven fully home after this photograph was taken.

The front panel of the bar, which nestles under the lid above the doors, can be detached and used as a serving tray.

White glue bonds prefinished molding to cabinet. Use masking tape rather than clamps to hold molding while glue dries.

BILL OF MATERIALS

No. Req.	Size in inches	Use
4 pcs. prefinished	¼ x 15⅜ x 20⅜	doors
4 pcs.	½ x 2½ x 20⅜	door frame
4 pcs.	½ x 2 x 11⅜	door frame
2 pcs. prefinished	¼ x 1½ x 20⅜	end strips
pine	¾ x 1¼ x 20⅜	end strips, rear
1 pc.	½ x 15 x 33¾	upper shelf
1 pc.	½ x 15 x 33¾	lower shelf
1 pc. pine	¾ x 10 x 16	small shelf
1 pc. pine	¾ x 14 x 20½	divider
2 pcs. prefinished	¼ x 15¼ x 29⅜	sides
1 pc. pine	¼ x 33 x 34¼	rear
	1 x 1 x 6 ft.	cleats
1 pc. prefinished	½ x 5½ x 35¼	front base, inner
1 pc. prefinished	¼ x 5½ x 35¾	front base, outer
1 pc.	½ x 5½ x 15½	side base, inner
2 pcs. prefinished	¼ x 5½ x 15½	side base, outer
12 ft. prefinished	cove molding	
2 pcs. prefinished	¼ x 15½ x 34¼	lid
1 pc. fir plywood	¼ x 15½ x 34¼	lid, inner
2 pcs. prefinished	7¼ x 14½ x ¼	glass rack
1 pc. prefinished	¼ x 6 x 34¼	outer serving tray
1 pc. prefinished	¼ x 6 x 33¾	inner serving tray
1 pc. fir plywood	¼ x 4½ x 24	serving tray glass rack
White glue		
Screws		
Door pulls		
1 pair knife hinges		
2-in. nails (2) pivot		
2 washers		
2 shelf brackets (Stanley)	5	shelf bracket
1 prefinished Fruit-wood panel	4 x 8 ft.	
1 pair 1" hinges	1 in.	lid

Early American Dowry Chest

Made from pine, this handsome replica of bygone days provides ample storage for today's homemakers. It's easy to build, too

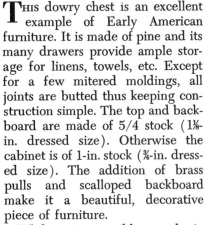

THIS dowry chest is an excellent example of Early American furniture. It is made of pine and its many drawers provide ample storage for linens, towels, etc. Except for a few mitered moldings, all joints are butted thus keeping construction simple. The top and backboard are made of 5/4 stock (1⅛-in. dressed size). Otherwise the cabinet is of 1-in. stock (¾-in. dressed size). The addition of brass pulls and scalloped backboard make it a beautiful, decorative piece of furniture.

While it is possible to obtain wide boards at most lumberyards, you will save considerably on costs by gluing up your own. You can also economize by using common lumber instead of clear. Just be sure to choose boards with good sound knots. Loose knots will not do and should be avoided.

Basic tools are used for this piece: table saw, router, drill, band saw or saber saw (for the backboard). Another tool you should have is a doweling jig. Although not essential, it makes easy work of gluing up the boards and butt joints for the front frame.

Top. Choose good flat boards for the top. Use 6-in. stock and arrange them so the knots are not too close to the ends of edges. Cut the

boards slightly longer than needed. After gluing, they can be trimmed to the final length.

Place the boards on a pair of saw horses and mark the locations of the dowels. Identify each board so you will know how each piece goes together later on during assembly. If you have a doweling jig, align it with the marks and drill the ⅜-in. diameter holes 1-1/16-in. deep. You can do this with the portable drill or on the drill press. The doweling jig shown in photo automatically centers the drill on the board. Apply a little glue to the dowels and drive them in with a hammer. Use spiral dowels—smooth dowels may split the boards as there is no way for the air to escape from the holes when they are driven in.

Prepare your clamps by opening them to the proper size, then apply glue to all surfaces to be joined. Be sure to include the protruding dowels. Bring the parts together and clamp securely. Do not wipe the glue droplets that ooze from the joints. When the glue has hardened, remove the excess droplets with a chisel. This is especially important if you plan to stain the piece. Wiping the excess will spread the glue on the wood surface and tend to size the wood. This will result in uneven and spot-

ty staining later on.

Cabinet Sides. While the glue is setting for the top, you can prepare the sides. The procedure is the same as for the top except that the lumber used is ¾-in. thick. After the glue has set, trim the sides to the proper length and width. If you have a jointer, use it to plane the front and rear edges. At this time you can also cut the rabbet at the rear edges. Make the rabbet ¼-in. deep.

Front Frame. Choose clear lumber for the front frame, especially for the narrower pieces. Cut these to the sizes shown then drill the dowel holes following the procedure used for the sides and top.

The assembly sequence of the front frame is important. Note that the upper grid is glued up as a unit. This is the part that contains the six drawer openings. After the glue has set, remove the clamps and install the lower rail and center stile. When the assembly is completed, mark the dowel locations for the end stiles. Again use the dowel jig to align the holes.

With the front frame completed, sand the surface so that all joints are smooth and flush. Then assemble the front frame to the side panels. Note that dowels are used here also. Since the front frame is only

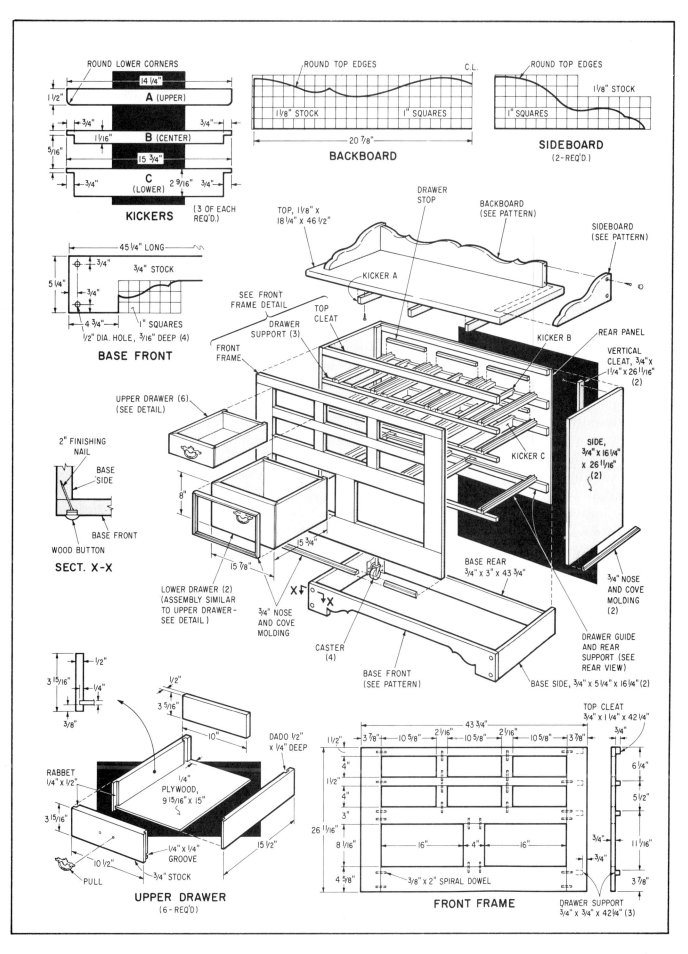

ROUND LOWER CORNERS

14 1/4"

A (UPPER)

1 1/2"

3/4"   3/4"

1 1/16"   B (CENTER)

5/16"

15 3/4"

3/4"   C (LOWER)   2 9/16"   3/4"

KICKERS   (3 OF EACH REQ'D.)

ROUND TOP EDGES   C.L.

1 1/8" STOCK   1" SQUARES

20 7/8"

BACKBOARD

ROUND TOP EDGES

1 1/8" STOCK

1" SQUARES

SIDEBOARD   (2-REQ'D.)

45 1/4" LONG

3/4"

3/4" STOCK

5 1/4"

3/4"

4 3/4"   1" SQUARES

1/2" DIA. HOLE, 3/16" DEEP (4)

BASE FRONT

DRAWER STOP

TOP, 1 1/8" x 18 1/4" x 46 1/2"

BACKBOARD (SEE PATTERN)

SIDEBOARD (SEE PATTERN)

KICKER A

SEE FRONT FRAME DETAIL

DRAWER SUPPORT (3)

TOP CLEAT

FRONT FRAME

KICKER B

REAR PANEL

VERTICAL CLEAT, 3/4" x 1 1/4" x 26 11/16" (2)

UPPER DRAWER (6) (SEE DETAIL)

KICKER C

SIDE, 3/4" x 16 1/4" x 26 11/16" (2)

2" FINISHING NAIL

BASE SIDE

BASE FRONT

WOOD BUTTON

SECT. X-X

8"

15 3/4"

15 7/8"

LOWER DRAWER (2) (ASSEMBLY SIMILAR TO UPPER DRAWER - SEE DETAIL)

3/4" NOSE AND COVE MOLDING

X

X

CASTER (4)

BASE REAR 3/4" x 3" x 43 3/4"

3/4" NOSE AND COVE MOLDING (2)

DRAWER GUIDE AND REAR SUPPORT (SEE REAR VIEW)

BASE FRONT (SEE PATTERN)

BASE SIDE, 3/4" x 5 1/4" x 16 1/4" (2)

1/2"

3 15/16"

1/4"

3/8"

1/2"

3 5/16"

10"

DADO 1/2" x 1/4" DEEP

RABBET 1/4" x 1/2"

1/4" PLYWOOD, 9 15/16" x 15"

3 15/16"

1/4" x 1/4" GROOVE

PULL

10 1/2"

3/4" STOCK

15 1/2"

UPPER DRAWER   (6-REQ'D)

TOP CLEAT 3/4" x 1 1/4" x 42 1/4"

43 3/4"

1 1/2"   3 7/8"   10 5/8"   2 1/16"   10 5/8"   2 1/16"   10 5/8"   3 7/8"   3/4"

4"

1 1/2"

4"

3"

26 11/16"

8 1/16"   16"   4"   16"

4 5/8"

3/8" x 2" SPIRAL DOWEL

6 1/4"

5 1/2"

11/16"

3/4"

3/4"

3 7/8"

FRONT FRAME

DRAWER SUPPORT 3/4" x 3/4" x 42 1/4" (3)

Dowry Chest

¾-in. thick, the dowels can only penetrate about ½-in. Use care when drilling these holes. As an alternative, you can use nails to join the front to the sides. If you do, use 2-in. finishing nails and be sure to sink the heads. Use protective cleats under the clamps when assembling the front frame to the sides. Be sure the sides are square to the front frame. Check with a large square. If necessary, use

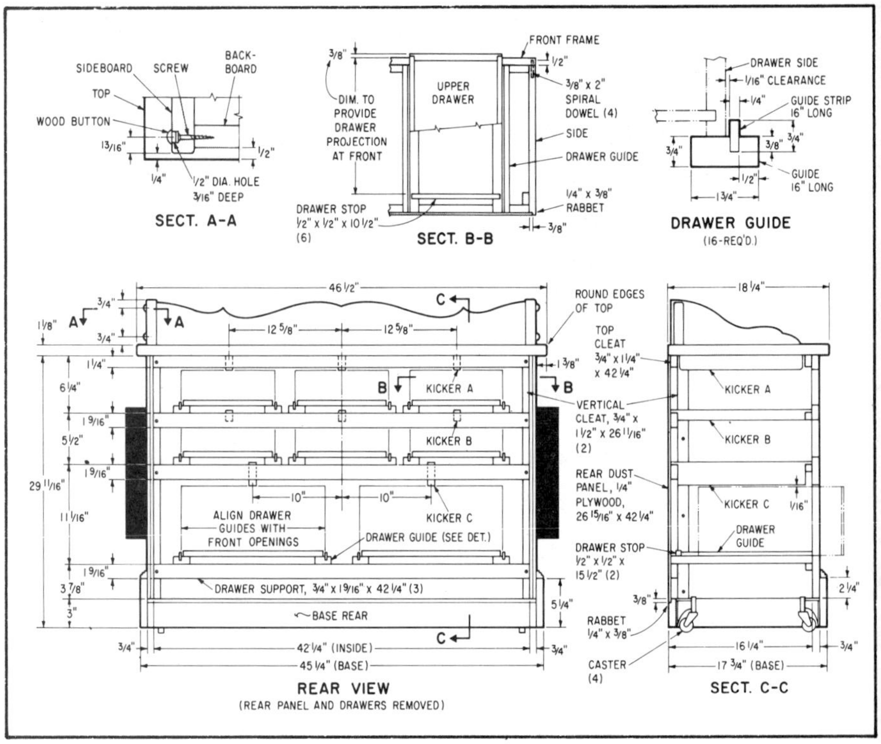

SIDEBOARD
SCREW
BACK-BOARD
TOP
WOOD BUTTON
13/16"
1/2"
1/4"
1/2" DIA. HOLE 3/16" DEEP
SECT. A-A
3/8"
DIM. TO PROVIDE DRAWER PROJECTION AT FRONT
UPPER DRAWER
FRONT FRAME
1/2"
3/8" x 2" SPIRAL DOWEL (4)
SIDE
DRAWER GUIDE
1/4" x 3/8" RABBET
DRAWER STOP 1/2" x 1/2" x 10 1/2" (6)
SECT. B-B
3/8"
DRAWER SIDE
1/16" CLEARANCE
1/4"
GUIDE STRIP 16" LONG
3/4"
3/8"
1/2"
GUIDE 16" LONG
1 3/4"
DRAWER GUIDE
(16-REQ'D.)
46 1/2"
12 5/8"
12 5/8"
ROUND EDGES OF TOP
TOP CLEAT 3/4" x 1 1/4" x 42 1/4"
1 3/8"
KICKER A
KICKER B
KICKER C
VERTICAL CLEAT, 3/4" x 1 1/2" x 26 11/16" (2)
REAR DUST PANEL, 1/4" PLYWOOD, 26 15/16" x 42 1/4"
DRAWER STOP 1/2" x 1/2" x 15 1/2" (2)
29 11/16"
6 1/4"
1 9/16"
5 1/2"
11 1/16"
3 7/8"
3"
10"
ALIGN DRAWER GUIDES WITH FRONT OPENINGS
DRAWER GUIDE (SEE DET.)
DRAWER SUPPORT, 3/4" x 1 9/16" x 42 1/4" (3)
BASE REAR
5 1/4"
42 1/4" (INSIDE)
45 1/4" (BASE)
REAR VIEW
(REAR PANEL AND DRAWERS REMOVED)
RABBET 1/4" x 3/8"
CASTER (4)
18 1/4"
DRAWER GUIDE
2 1/4"
16 1/4"
17 3/4" (BASE)
SECT. C-C

BILL OF MATERIALS— EARLY AMERICAN DOWRY CHEST

Note: Except where indicated all lumber used is common pine.

Use	Size & Description	No. Req.
top	1⅛x18¼x46½"	1
backboard	1⅛x4¾x41¾"	1
sideboard	1⅛x4¾x14¼"	2
side	¾x16¼x26 11/16"	2
base side	¾x5¼x16¼"	2
base front	¾x5¼x45¼"	1
front stile	¾x3⅞x26 11/16	2
stile	¾x2 1/16x4"	4
stile center	¾x4x8 1/16"	1
rail, upper	¾x1½x36"	2
rail, center	¾x3x36"	1
rail, lower	¾x4⅝x36"	1
top cleat, front	¾x1¼x42¼	2
drawer support front	¾x¾x42¼"	3
vertical cleat	¾x1½x26 11/16"	2
drawer support rear	¾x1 9/16x42¼"	3
rear base	¾x3x43¾"	1
kicker, upper	¾x1½x14¼"	3
kicker, center	¾x1 1/16x15¾"	3
kicker, lower	¾x2 9/16x15¾"	3
drawer guide	¾x1¾ x 16"	16
drawer guide strip	¼x¾x16" plywood	16
drawer stop	½x½x10½"	6
drawer stop	½x½x15½"	2
drawer upper front	¾x3 15/16x10½"	6
drawer upper rear	½x3 5/16x10"	6
drawer upper, side	½x3 15/16x15½"	12
drawer upper, bottom	¼x9 15/16x15" plywood	6
drawer lower, front	¾x8x15⅞"	2
drawer lower, rear	½x7⅜x15⅜"	2
drawer lower, side	½"x8"x15½	4
drawer lower, bottom	¼x15x15" 5/16	2
nose & cove molding	⅝x¾"	15 feet
dust cover	¼x26 15/16x42¼ plywood	1
screws	1¼" x 8 FH	36
screws	2½x10 FH	13
nails	2" finishing	
brads	1" finishing	
wood buttons		8
pulls		8
casters w/bracket		4

braces to hold the assembly square while the glue sets.

Base. The base pieces are cut to the sizes indicated. Trace the scallop design on the front piece then round off all outer edges with a router or sandpaper. Drill the button holes at each end of the front piece. These will conceal the nail heads. Note that the holes are drilled ¾-in. from the edge. This is done for the sake of appearance. The nails into the side pieces will have to be driven at an angle as shown in the drawing.

After the base is completed, fasten it to the cabinet with glue and 1¼-in. screws.

Drawer Supports. The drawers ride on corner guides. To keep the drawers from tipping when extended, a kicker is used above each drawer. The kicker is a strip of wood placed so the top rear of the drawer rides against it.

Cut all the necessary strips and install them as indicated in the drawing. Drill screw clearance holes and install with screws. The two vertical strips at the rear must be set back to allow for the horizontal crosspieces. Although the crosspieces are different widths, they must be installed with the top edges aligned.

Cut the sixteen corner guides from flat stock. Make the lengths uniform, then cut the groove for the thin plywood strip. This is best done on the table saw with a blade of proper thickness. Apply a little glue to the plywood strips then insert them into the grooves. Clamping is not necessary. Do not install yet.

Drawers. Drawers are rabbeted with flush sides and these are rather simple to make. The two larger drawers are similar to the smaller ones except that they have mouldings added to the face. Note that the drawer fronts are ¾-in thick. The sides are ½-in. and the bottoms are made of ¼-in. plywood.

Cut all pieces to size according to the bill of materials. If you find that the wide side and rear members of the larger drawers are bowed, you can relieve them by sawing narrow grooves as shown. This will not affect the operation of the drawers. Cut the rabbets and dadoes using either the table saw with a dado blade or the router. If you lack a dado blade or router, you can make several passes with a regular blade. This method is not easy but it does work.

After all parts are cut, drill the clearance holes for the pulls, sand each piece, and then assemble with glue and finishing nails. To keep

If possible, use a doweling jig when you're drilling holes for the spiral dowels.

As illustrated here, the wide boards can be made up by gluing six-inch stock.

Front frame is also assembled with dowels Glue and clamp upper section first.

Assembling front, side panels. Use a stick under clamps to prevent marring.

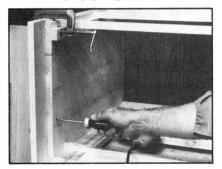

Base is installed with screws driven from inside. Use clamps to hold the base.

"Worn" corners are made with a sander. Rock sander back, forth for round look.

Drawers are made of ½-inch pine except for fronts. Drive nails through sides.

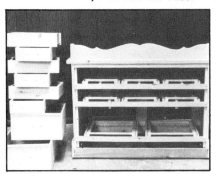

Rear view of the cabinet with drawers. Note stops at rear of each guide set.

Here is a view from the rear showing the drawer guides and the kicker also.

the assembly square, the bottoms should be ready to insert. Place a little glue in the grooves and slide the bottom into place. The two large drawers are fitted with ¾-in. nose and cove molding. Miter the corners and install as shown, using glue and brads. The edges of the six small drawers are rounded.

The drawer guides are now installed. Do each drawer individually. Just in case there is some discrepancy between drawers, number each drawer and the corresponding opening. Dab a little glue at the points where the bottoms of the guides contact the crosspieces. Insert a drawer and position the guides so that the drawer front is flush with the front frame. This will indicate that the

guides are perpendicular to the front. Allow a little play between the drawer sides and the guide. Repeat this procedure for the remaining drawers. Be careful not to move the guides while the glue is setting. After the glue has set, you can drive a couple of finishing nails into the joint. Actually, the glue should suffice.

The kickers are cut and installed next. Note that there are three different sizes. The uppermost ones are fastened to the underside of the cabinet top. Add the drawer stops. Position them so the drawers project ⅜-in. from the front.

Completing the Chest Top. The cabinet top is trimmed to size and all corners are rounded. The top front corners are "worn" by using

a file or plane. File until the corners slant downward. Finish with sandpaper.

Cut the backboard and side pieces according to the plan. Round the top edges then assemble with screws and glue. Screw heads are concealed with wood buttons.

Attach the backboard to the top with screws from the underside. Next attach the top to the cabinet with screws through the front and rear cleats.

Mount the concealed casters at each corner, then install the rear dust panel.

Finish the piece as desired. If you plan to use stain, apply a thin coat of penetrating sealer and allow it to dry before applying the stain.

Cheese and Wine Cart

Construction is simplified with ready-made legs and spokes

HOME CRAFTSMEN are often discouraged from making a rolling cart on wheels because they don't have a lathe for the spokes. This elegant cart was designed and built without a lathe. The turnings are ready-made and available at most lumberyards and home improvement centers. Even the wheel hubs and rims are made with conventional tools—a router and saber saw.

The cart is made of ¾″, 1⅛″ and 1⅜″ pine stock, nominal sizes 1″, 1¼″ and 1½″. It measures 18″ x 29″ x 29″ and has a roomy drawer for storing odds and ends. Most rolling carts have a movable hand grip which must be dropped out of the way to permit the drawer to open. We used a fixed hand grip and simply made the drawer open from the front. It looks better and is more practical.

The top of the cart is made of 1⅜″ pine. Four boards, each 5-inches wide, are glued up to obtain the necessary width. Note

that the materials list shows the lengths to be 3-inches longer than the finished size. The excess will be trimmed away after gluing. Dowel pins are necessary to assure a good permanent glue line. To prevent warping, invert the first and third boards so the annular rings will alternate. Use four dowels in each section. These should be located carefully. If you have a doweling jig, the dowel holes will be automatically centered. If you do not have a jig, drill the holes in the first board, then use dowel centers to transfer the location of the holes to the mating board. Repeat for the four boards, then apply glue and clamp. After glue sets, trim ends to size.

If the surface joints are uneven, use a belt sander to even the surface. Belt sanders cut fast, especially on pine, so use care when sanding. Start with a medium grit belt followed by fine.

The upper rails are made of 1⅛″ stock. After ripping the

pieces to width, run a groove along the lower edge using the router fitted with a "V"-shaped cutter. Tack a wood strip to the rail to guide the cutter. You will need two side rails and one for the rear. The front is left open for the drawer.

The lower side rails are made in a similar manner except that they are narrower. The front and rear rails are a bit more tricky to make. The upper edge is contoured. In addition, the upper edge is contour grooved. This requires a shaped wood template which is used to guide the router. Trace the contour of the end panel onto a piece of scrap about two inches longer than the panel. The template strip is a narrow piece of wood nailed to the base piece. It is contour-cut parallel to the shape of the panel. Use a marking gauge to draw the shape of the template. To set the gauge, measure the radius of the router base and then add ½ inch. Trace the shape onto the guide

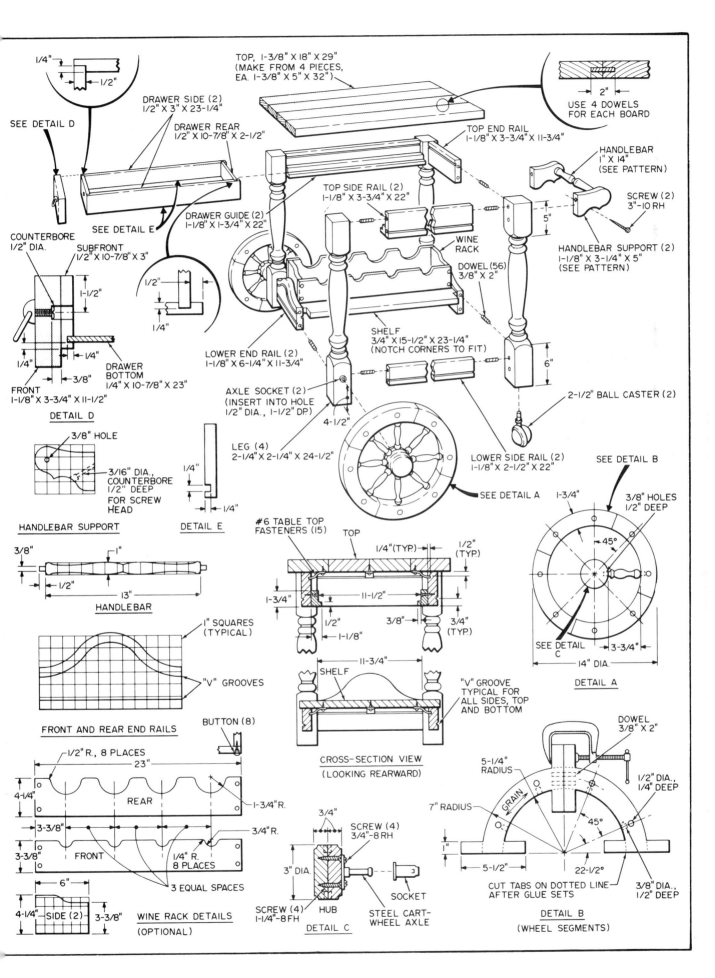

1/4"
1/2"

TOP, 1-3/8" X 18" X 29"
(MAKE FROM 4 PIECES,
EA. 1-3/8" X 5" X 32")

2"
USE 4 DOWELS
FOR EACH BOARD

SEE DETAIL D

DRAWER SIDE (2)
1/2" X 3" X 23-1/4"

DRAWER REAR
1/2" X 10-7/8" X 2-1/2"

TOP END RAIL
1-1/8" X 3-3/4" X 11-3/4"

HANDLEBAR
1" X 14"
(SEE PATTERN)

SCREW (2)
3"-10 RH

SEE DETAIL E

DRAWER GUIDE (2)
1-1/8" X 1-3/4" X 22"

TOP SIDE RAIL (2)
1-1/8" X 3-3/4" X 22"

5"

WINE
RACK

HANDLEBAR SUPPORT (2)
1-1/8" X 3-1/4" X 5"
(SEE PATTERN)

COUNTERBORE
1/2" DIA.

SUBFRONT
1/2" X 10-7/8" X 3"

1/2"

1/4"

DOWEL (56)
3/8" X 2"

SHELF
3/4" X 15-1/2" X 23-1/4"
(NOTCH CORNERS TO FIT)

1-1/2"

1/4"

3/8"

DRAWER
BOTTOM
1/4" X 10-7/8" X 23"

FRONT
1-1/8" X 3-3/4" X 11-1/2"

DETAIL D

LOWER END RAIL (2)
1-1/8" X 6-1/4" X 11-3/4"

AXLE SOCKET (2)
(INSERT INTO HOLE
1/2" DIA., 1-1/2" DP.)

4-1/2"

LEG (4)
2-1/4" X 2-1/4" X 24-1/2"

2-1/2" BALL CASTER (2)

LOWER SIDE RAIL (2)
1-1/8" X 2-1/2" X 22"

SEE DETAIL B

SEE DETAIL A

3/8" HOLE

3/16" DIA.,
COUNTERBORE
1/2" DEEP
FOR SCREW
HEAD

1/4"

1/4"

1-3/4"

3/8" HOLES
1/2" DEEP

45°

HANDLEBAR SUPPORT

DETAIL E

3/8"

1"

1/2"

13"

HANDLEBAR

#6 TABLE TOP
FASTENERS (15)

TOP

1/4"(TYP.)

1/2"
(TYP.)

1-3/4"

11-1/2"

1/2"

3/8"

3/4"
(TYP.)

1-1/8"

SEE DETAIL
C

3-3/4"

14" DIA.

DETAIL A

1" SQUARES
(TYPICAL)

"V" GROOVES

11-3/4"

SHELF

"V" GROOVE
TYPICAL FOR
ALL SIDES, TOP
AND BOTTOM

CROSS-SECTION VIEW
(LOOKING REARWARD)

DOWEL
3/8" X 2"

5-1/4"
RADIUS

1/2" DIA.,
1/4" DEEP

FRONT AND REAR END RAILS

BUTTON (8)

1/2" R., 8 PLACES

23"

7" RADIUS

GRAIN

45°

4-1/4"

REAR

1-3/4"R.

3-3/8"

3/4"R.

FRONT

1/4" R.
8 PLACES

3/4"

1"

5-1/2"

22-1/2°

3/8" DIA.,
1/2" DEEP

3-3/8"

3 EQUAL SPACES

3" DIA.

SCREW (4)
3/4"-8 RH

CUT TABS ON DOTTED LINE
AFTER GLUE SETS

6"

SOCKET

DETAIL B
(WHEEL SEGMENTS)

4-1/4"

SIDE (2)

3-3/8"

WINE RACK DETAILS
(OPTIONAL)

SCREW (4)
1-1/4"-8 FH

HUB

STEEL CART-
WHEEL AXLE

DETAIL C

Treasury of Woodworking Projects / 41

Cheese Cart

strip and cut with a saber saw. Fasten it to the base with a couple of nails, then place the panel into the shaped base. Hold it securely with a stop on the table or with a clamp.

Cut the ⅜″ deep groove in the rail pieces. These are for the top fasteners. Locate the groove ½-inch from the top edge. The width of the saw kerf is not important. Cut the lower shelf to size, but do not notch the corners yet.

The legs are standard 3″ x 32″ turnings available at lumber yards everywhere. Since the finished length required is 24½ inches, you will have to trim the lengths to size. The square block at the top should measure 5-inches and the lower one 6-inches. (See drawing.) Note: If you have a lathe, simply make a template on kraft paper, then turn in the usual manner.

Use the doweling jig to locate and drill the ⅜″ diameter holes at the ends of the rail pieces. The holes should be one-inch deep. The holes for the caster and wheel sockets are also drilled into the legs at this time.

Use dowel centers to transfer the dowel holes from the rail ends to the legs. Drill the holes carefully to insure that they are straight.

The legs are fastened to the side (long) rails with dowels as shown. Use care when applying glue to the rail ends. Use it sparingly. Clamp the sections and when the glue has set, remove the clamps and fasten these sections to the end (short) rails. To keep the unit square while clamping, nail a temporary cleat across the upper front, which lacks a rail because of the drawer.

The top and lower shelf are now installed. Use table top brackets to fasten them. The lower shelf must be notched at the corners before installation. Place the shelf in position and, with a pencil, mark exactly where the cuts are to be made. Cut and fit into place, then fasten with the brackets. The next step is to cut and install the drawer runners, and then make the drawer as shown.

The wheels are made by cutting eight curved pieces with tabs as indicated. The tabs are used as an aid to gluing and are removed when the glue has set. Drill the dowel holes in each section. Also drill the spoke holes by supporting the segments in a scrap of wood cut to the same contour as the segment. Drill the ⅜″ dia. holes ½″ deep. After the holes are drilled, glue up pairs of segments to make half rims. Insert the dowels, glue, and then clamp as shown. When the glue has set, glue up the half sections to complete the rims. Use a saber saw or table jig saw to cut away the tabs. You will now have a rim with 8 spoke holes on the inside diameter. Make a curved sanding block and smoothen the rim until all saw marks are removed. Drill the eight ½″ dia. button holes around the face of each rim and drill four holes on the back side.

The spokes are cut from 11-inch spindles. Each spindle will yield two spokes. Cut the spindles in half and then with a sharp knife shape the ends to form the ⅜″ tenon. Fit these into the rim without glue.

Now make the hub: Screw two 4″ square pieces of ¾″ pine together and be sure to cross the grain of each at right angles to each other. Do not glue at this time. Lay out a 13¾″ circle on the lay-up and cut with a saber saw. Sand the disc until perfectly smooth, then shape the outer edge with a router. Next, drill eight ⅜″ dia. equally spaced holes around the circumference of the disc. The holes must be centered on the parting line.

Remove the screws from the hub to disassemble it. Place the spokes into the sockets formed by drilling, then apply glue to the inner hub surface. Add the second half of the hub and rescrew. Add buttons to complete the wheel.

A special wheel shaft with socket is available. (See materials list). It is fastened to the wheel with three round head screws. The socket part is simply forced into the holes previously drilled into the legs. The ball casters are likewise inserted into the holes made at the bottom of the rear legs. Add the ornaments to complete the piece. The wine rack is optional. Finish as desired. We used Sapolin stain and three coats of clear gloss lacquer.

BILL OF MATERIALS

NOTE: Except for the legs, all lumber used is pine.

Quantity	Size and Description	Purpose
1	1⅜″ x 18″ x 29″ (Make from 4 pieces, ea. 1⅜″ x 5″ x 32″)	Top
2	1⅛″ x 3¾″ x 22″	Side rail (top)
1	1⅛″ x 3¾″ x 11¾″	End rail (top)
2	1⅛″ x 3¼″ x 5″	Handlebar support
1	1″ x 14″	Handlebar
4	2¼″ x 2¼″ x 24½″	Leg
1	¾″ x 15½″ x 23¼″	Shelf
2	1⅛″ x 2½″ x 22″	Side rail, (lower)
2	1⅛″ x 6¼″ x 11¾″	End rail, (lower)
1	1⅛″ x 3¾″ x 11½″	Drawer front
2	½″ x 3″ x 23¼″	Drawer side
1	½″ x 10⅞″ x 3″	Drawer subfront
1	½″ x 10⅞″ x 2½″	Drawer rear
2	1⅛″ x 1¾″ x 22″	Drawer guide
8	1⅛″ x 5″ x 12½″	Wheel segment
4	¾″ x 2¾″ dia.	Wheel hub
16	¾″ x 4¾″	Spoke
32	½″ x ⅝″	Buttons
1	3⅜″ x 23″	Wine rack front
1	4¼″ x 23″	Wine rack rear
2	4¼″ x 6″	Wine rack side
3		Ornament
2	Ball casters, 2½″	
15	Table top fasteners #6	
2	Wheel axle assembly	
56	Dowels, ⅜″ x 2″	

Top panel is made by dowelling and gluing several boards together. When the glue dries, trim excess at ends of the panel.

The decorative bead on end panels is made with a router. Make a wooden template (see diagram) for the router base to follow.

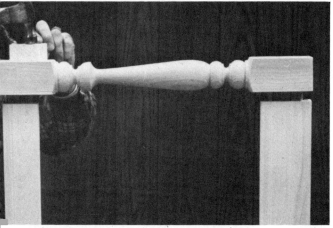

Using ready-made legs saves a lot of work. Cut legs to size and join to apron with glue and dowels. Use block to protect legs.

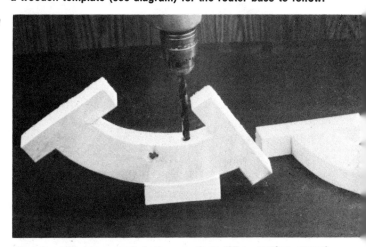

Rims for wheels are made in four sections. When cutting curved rims leave end "tabs" for later assembly. Predrill for spokes.

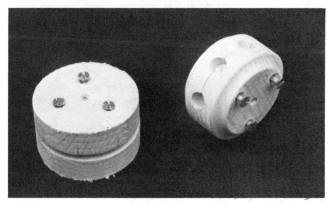

Cut hubs from ¾" stock, then saw in half. Reassemble with wood screws and drill for spokes. Hubs are cross-grain for strength.

Separate hub halves, insert spokes, glue and rejoin hubs with screws. Spokes are made from ready-made spindles cut in half.

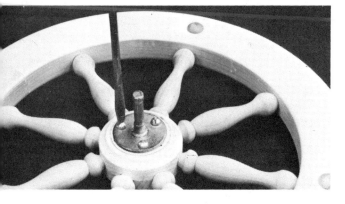

The wheel shaft is attached to the hub with three screws. The metal stem will snap into the socket which is placed in leg.

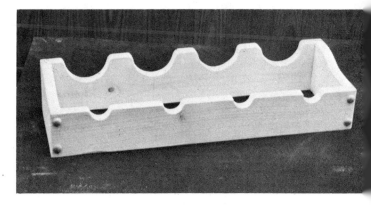

The wine rack is made to be removable. Bottle rests are cut so that bottles lie with necks down. Add wood buttons for looks.

DIVIDER UNIT WITH DESK

This contemporary, modular style project is quite easy to build and just as easy to dismantle and reassemble if you ever wish to move it

THE OPEN, INFORMAL DESIGN of the combination desk and storage unit makes it attractive but unobtrusive. You can install it at the end of a room or in a corner, or use it as a divider without overwhelming the rest of the decor.

The unit is not difficult to build and requires few power tools. A power drill, of course would make the work go faster, but accurate holes can be drilled by hand.

One power tool is a must. This is a saw, either a table saw or a portable circular saw, to cut out the parts accurately and to cut the dadoes in the magazine rack (unit A). The latter task could also be done with a router.

If you have no power tools, or don't want to do all the work yourself, have a carpenter build the modules. Then, you can assemble the unit yourself.

Layout the parts on plywood, as shown in the plans, and cut them out. True the edges with coarse sandpaper and, if necessary, fill any cracks with filler.

Next, cut the 2 x 2s and 1 x 4s to the dimensions shown in the drawing of the framing. If you wish, you can use the dimensions shown or you can extend the uprights to ceiling height.

At the same time, cut the 1 x 4s for the drawer sides and backs and for the table edges. Sand all

surfaces smooth and round the edges slightly.

Once the parts are ready, assemble the modules, following the step-by-step instructions in the plans. Do this in your workshop. When they are finished and painted, carry them to the place where you intend to erect the unit. Do the same thing with the framing.

When all the parts and assemblies are on site, erect the unit with screws as shown in the plans. Don't use glue at this stage. You may wish to move the unit some day. If it is merely screwed together, it can be broken down into easily handled parts and reassembled at its new location.

Stain or paint all framing members and allow to dry thoroughly, then move framing into room for assembly.

Predrill and screw together all 2 x 2 and 1 x 4 framing members, attaching members marked 1-4 last.

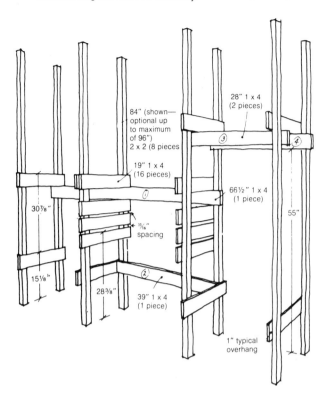

84" (shown—optional up to maximum of 96") 2 x 2 (8 pieces)

28" 1 x 4 (2 pieces)

19" 1 x 4 (16 pieces)

66½" 1 x 4 (1 piece)

30⅞"

1¹¹⁄₁₆" spacing

15⅛"

28⅜"

39" 1 x 4 (1 piece)

55"

1" typical overhang

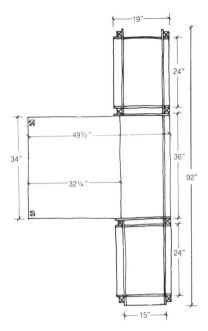

19"

24"

49½"

34"

36"

32¼"

92"

24"

15"

Set up desk as shown. To fold desk down, unlatch screen door hooks on legs, fold legs under and latch with screen door hook. Remove desk assembly from support framing and place assembly into channels directly above the previous channels. Desk top will fold down compactly without touching floor.

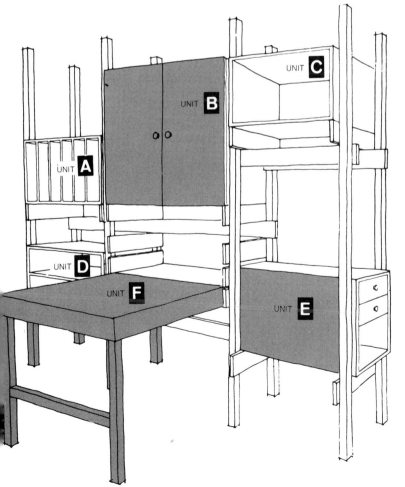

UNIT **C**

UNIT **B**

UNIT **A**

UNIT **D**

UNIT **F**

UNIT **E**

When thoroughly dry, install hinges on doors, and doors on cabinet; apply door pulls and magnetic catches.

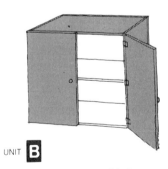

UNIT **B**

Glue and nail basic cabinet parts together, including the shelf. Countersink nail holes before glue sets, and wipe away excess glue. Fill nail holes, allow to dry, and sand smooth.

Diagrams continue on following page→

DIVIDER UNIT WITH DESK

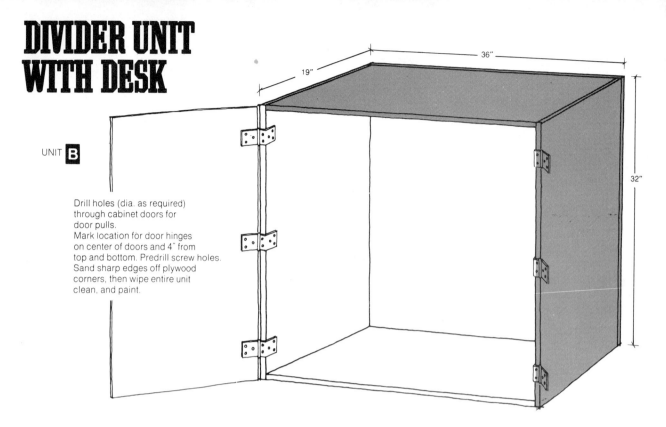

UNIT **B**

Drill holes (dia. as required)
through cabinet doors for
door pulls.
Mark location for door hinges
on center of doors and 4" from
top and bottom. Predrill screw holes.
Sand sharp edges off plywood
corners, then wipe entire unit
clean, and paint.

UNIT **A**

On top and bottom, rout or saw and chisel five
¼" x ¼" channels for dividers, spacing them
as shown. (Note: six additional channels are
shown as optional so dividers can be moved
closer together or farther apart, or to
accommodate up to six additional dividers.

**Each one of the six units
is built separately, then
joined together in final
assembly. The five shelf
and cabinet units offer a
good deal of storage space**

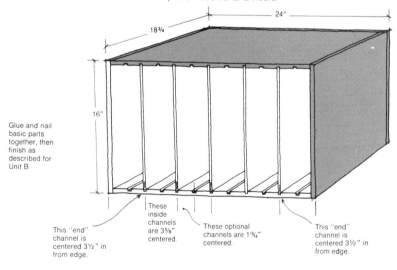

Glue and nail
basic parts
together, then
finish as
described for
Unit B.

This "end"
channel is
centered 3½" in
from edge.

These
inside
channels
are 3⅝"
centered.

These optional
channels are 1¹³⁄₁₆"
centered.

This "end"
channel is
centered 3½" in
from edge.

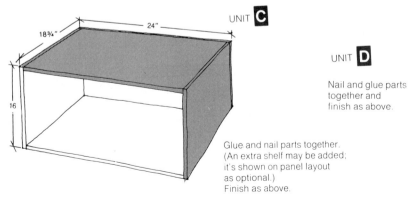

UNIT **C**

Glue and nail parts together.
(An extra shelf may be added;
it's shown on panel layout
as optional.)
Finish as above.

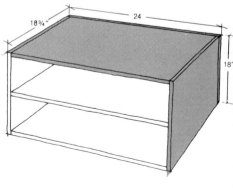

UNIT **D**

Nail and glue parts
together and
finish as above.

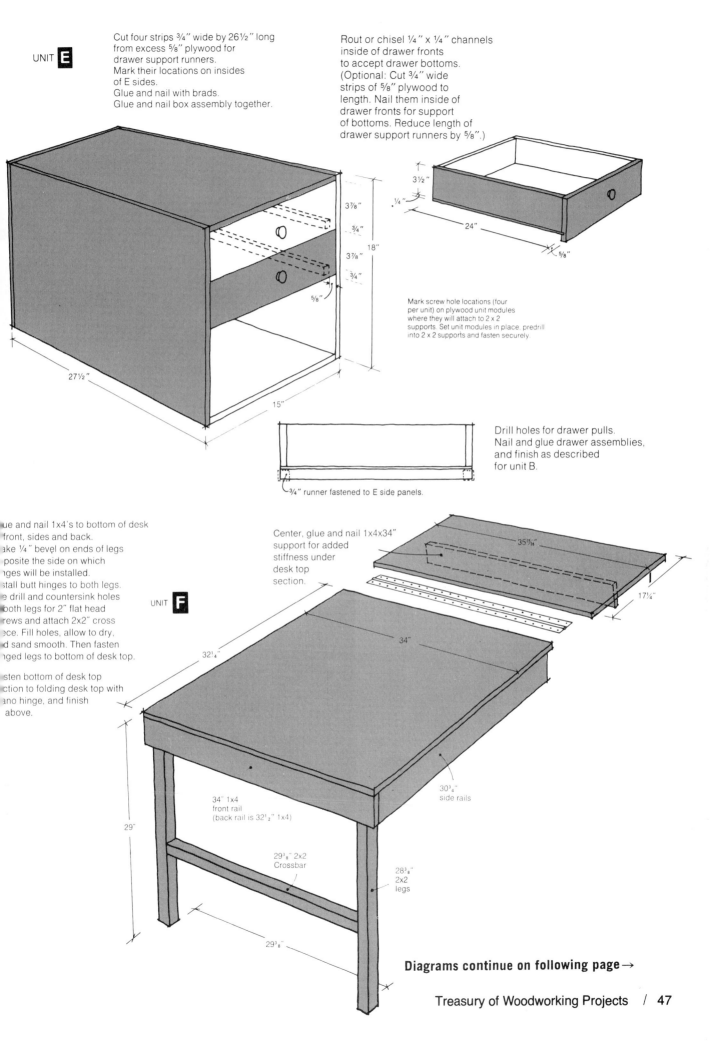

UNIT E

Cut four strips ¾" wide by 26½" long from excess ⅝" plywood for drawer support runners.
Mark their locations on insides of E sides.
Glue and nail with brads.
Glue and nail box assembly together.

Rout or chisel ¼" x ¼" channels inside of drawer fronts to accept drawer bottoms. (Optional: Cut ¾" wide strips of ⅝" plywood to length. Nail them inside of drawer fronts for support of bottoms. Reduce length of drawer support runners by ⅝".)

3⅞"
¾"
3⅞"
¾"
18"
⅝"

27½"
15"

3½"
¼"
24"
⅝"

Mark screw hole locations (four per unit) on plywood unit modules where they will attach to 2 x 2 supports. Set unit modules in place, predrill into 2 x 2 supports and fasten securely.

Drill holes for drawer pulls. Nail and glue drawer assemblies, and finish as described for unit B.

¾" runner fastened to E side panels.

...ue and nail 1x4's to bottom of desk ...front, sides and back.
...ake ¼" bevel on ends of legs ...posite the side on which ...ges will be installed.
...stall butt hinges to both legs.
...e drill and countersink holes ...both legs for 2" flat head ...rews and attach 2x2" cross ...ece. Fill holes, allow to dry, ...d sand smooth. Then fasten ...nged legs to bottom of desk top.

...sten bottom of desk top ...ction to folding desk top with ...ano hinge, and finish ...above.

UNIT F

Center, glue and nail 1x4x34" support for added stiffness under desk top section.

35¹⁵⁄₁₆"
17¼"
34"
30¾" side rails
32¼"
29"

34" 1x4 front rail (back rail is 32½" 1x4)

29⅜" 2x2 Crossbar

28⅜" 2x2 legs

29⅜"

Diagrams continue on following page →

DIVIDER UNIT WITH DESK

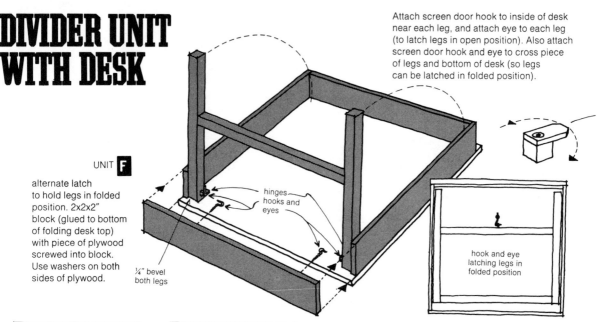

Attach screen door hook to inside of desk near each leg, and attach eye to each leg (to latch legs in open position). Also attach screen door hook and eye to cross piece of legs and bottom of desk (so legs can be latched in folded position).

UNIT **F**

alternate latch to hold legs in folded position. 2x2x2" block (glued to bottom of folding desk top) with piece of plywood screwed into block. Use washers on both sides of plywood.

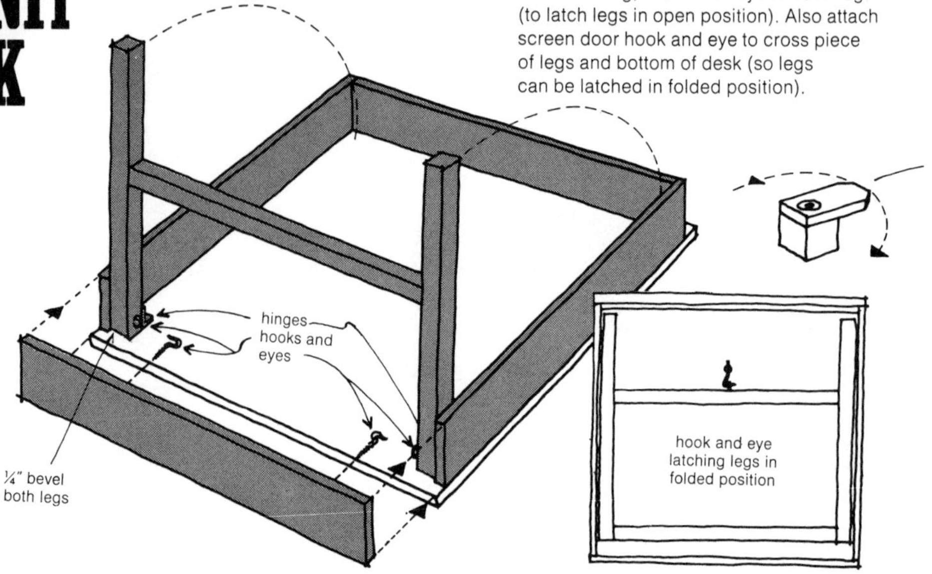

hinges
hooks and
eyes
¼" bevel
both legs
hook and eye
latching legs in
folded position

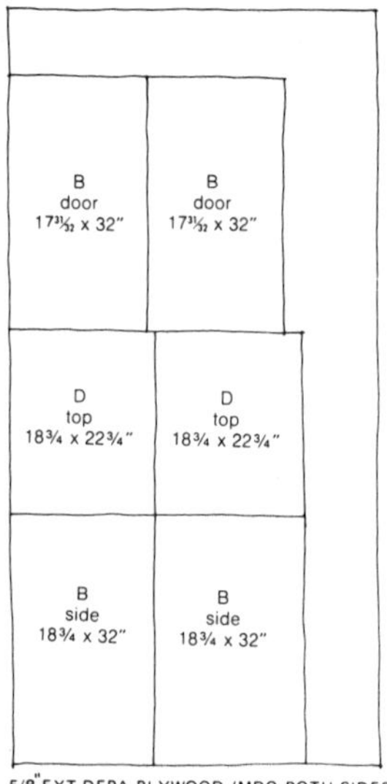

B door 17³¹⁄₃₂ x 32"
B door 17³¹⁄₃₂ x 32"
D top 18¾ x 22¾"
D top 18¾ x 22¾"
B side 18¾ x 32"
B side 18¾ x 32"

5/8" EXT·DFPA PLYWOOD (MDO BOTH SIDES)

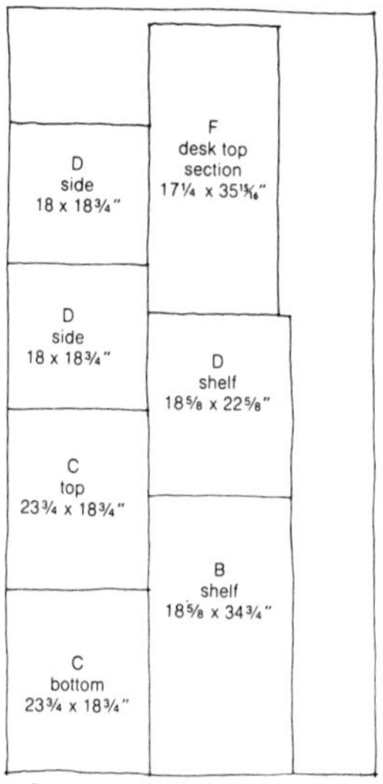

D side 18 x 18¾"
F desk top section 17¼ x 35¹⁵⁄₁₆"
D side 18 x 18¾"
D shelf 18⅝ x 22⅝"
C top 23¾ x 18¾"
B shelf 18⅝ x 34¾"
C bottom 23¾ x 18¾"

5/8" EXT·DFPA PLYWOOD (MDO BOTH SIDES)

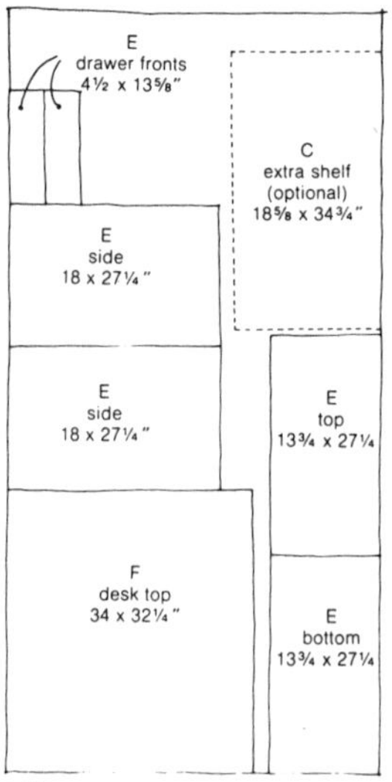

E drawer fronts 4½ x 13⅝"
C extra shelf (optional) 18⅝ x 34¾"
E side 18 x 27¼"
E side 18 x 27¼"
E top 13¾ x 27¼
F desk top 34 x 32¼"
E bottom 13¾ x 27¼

5/8" EXT DFPA PLYWOOD (MDO BOTH SIDES)

Most of the unit is made from plywood. Drawings at left give suggestions for making various cuts

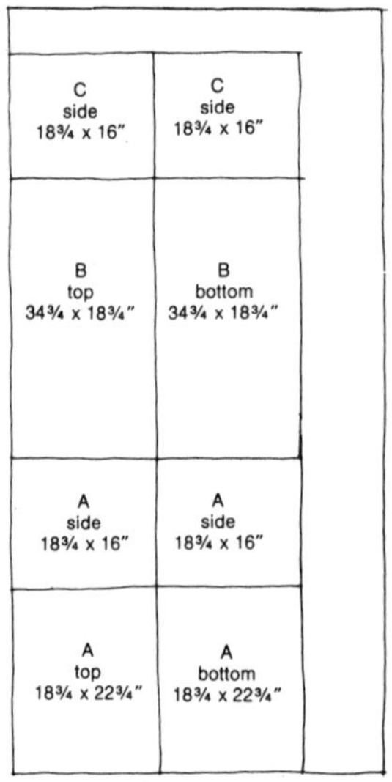

C side 18¾ x 16"
C side 18¾ x 16"
B top 34¾ x 18¾"
B bottom 34¾ x 18¾"
A side 18¾ x 16"
A side 18¾ x 16"
A top 18¾ x 22¾"
A bottom 18¾ x 22¾"

5/8" EXT·DFPA PLYWOOD (MDO BOTH SIDES)

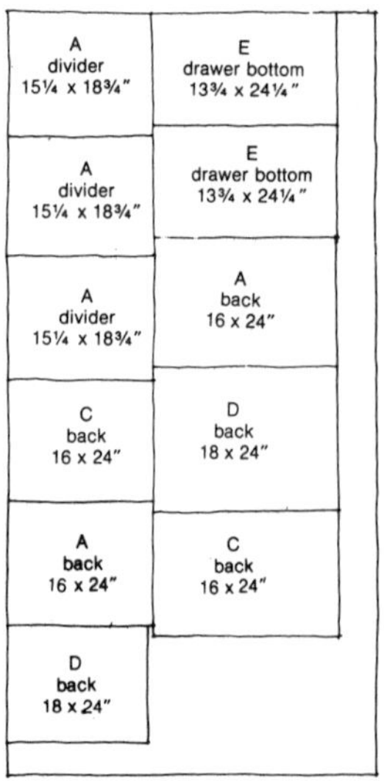

A divider 15¼ x 18¾"
E drawer bottom 13¾ x 24¼"
A divider 15¼ x 18¾"
E drawer bottom 13¾ x 24¼"
A divider 15¼ x 18¾"
A back 16 x 24"
C back 16 x 24"
D back 18 x 24"
A back 16 x 24"
C back 16 x 24"
D back 18 x 24"

1/4" B·B INT·DFPA PLYWOOD

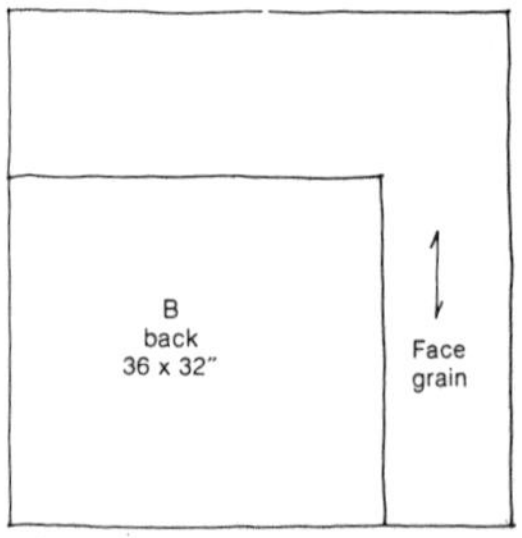

B back 36 x 32"
Face grain

1/4" B·B INT·DFPA PLYWOOD

BILL OF MATERIALS

Quantity	Size and Description		Purpose
4	⅝"	4'x8' EXT-DFPA plywood (medium density overlay both sides)	cabinets, shelves, etc.
1½	¼"	4'x8' B-B INT-DFPA plywood	dividers, backs and drawer bottoms
1	2"	2"x72' select grade lumber	frame and desk legs
1	1"	4"x60' select grade lumber	frame and desk drawers
as needed	1¼"	#8 oval head screws and finish washers	
as needed	2"	#8 flat head screws	

NOTE: Also need cabinet door hinges, door pulls, magnetic door catches, brads, piano hinge, butt hinges, hooks and eyes (small), 6d finishing nails, and finishing materials.

Here's a neat woodworking project that you'll be proud of—a butler's tray table. As the name implies, it serves two purposes—a sturdy table and a handsome serving tray. Special butler tray hinges have no projections and are spring loaded so they will hold in any position. A clever self-cen-

Butler's Tray Table

With this clever design you can build a dual-purpose piece of furniture which is a spring-hinged tray that self-centers as a table top

tering arrangement on the underside of the tray holds it in place on the base so it cannot accidentally slide off. The unit shown was made of lumber-core birch, but other woods may be substituted. For a colonial look, pine may be used.

Start with the base. Cut the squares for the legs to size, then clip the diagonal on the table saw. Be sure to place the fence so the waste will fall away from the blade, otherwise a kickback may result.

The legs are now ready to be grooved. This can be done either on the shaper, if you have one, or with the router. If the router is used, it would be best to mount it inverted on a table, as shown. This converts it to a mini-shaper and makes it much easier to use. Insert a "V" cutter in the router collet and set the proper depth of cut. Cut should be ⅛-inch deep. A makeshift fence consisting of a small piece of wood and a couple of clamps will do. Set the fence so the cut is ⅜-inch in from the edge of the work. Run the work through, then change cutters and round off the three corners shown. If your cutter has a pilot, you will not require the fence.

Rails for the table are cut to size and drilled to take two ⅜-

When ripping the diagonal for the legs. it is best to set the fence on the proper side to give you the maximum safety.

The router is being used to groove the legs. The inverted position shown makes it easier working small pieces.

Accuracy makes the drill press ideal for holes. If you use a portable drill, be sure it's straight and square.

Place base on top, center carefully Mark off the inside edges of the rail, then slowly cut along the guides.

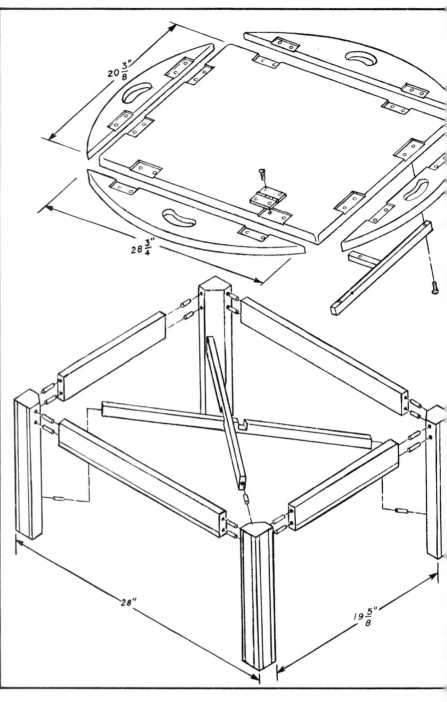

inch dowels. Dowel transfer points are used to locate the holes. Prop up the work as shown for proper alignment. Center punch the prick marks left by the points, then proceed to drill the holes for the dowels. The depth of the holes should be 1 1/16-inch. Insert dowels with glue and assemble the base.

The top board is prepared next. If your table saw fence will not extend far enough, try this. Clamp a strip of wood to the underside of the work, then use the edge of the table as a guide. Place the

assembled base on the table top and carefully center it. Next mark off the jig which consists of four cleats, two long and two short. They are cut so they will be a trifle smaller than the inner dimension of the rails. Align and then install.

The curved sides are made next. These can be cut either on the band saw or with a saber saw. After cutting, sand the edges smooth then shape the edge still using the router as a shaper.

The hinges are mortised next.

Some butler hinges have half-round ends while others are square. Regardless of the hinge used, a mortising jig made of 1/4-inch plywood can be used advantageously. Simply note the distance from the outside of the cutter to the outside of the router base plate. Trace the outline of your hinge onto a piece of 1/4-inch plywood, then enlarge the outline by adding the dimension obtained from the edge of the cutter to the edge of the base plate. This will give you an out-

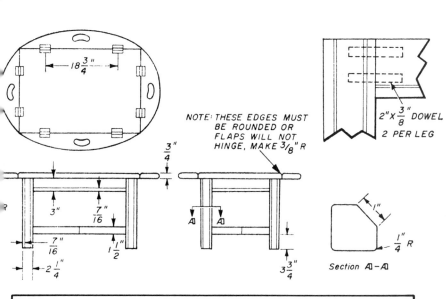

The aligning jig on the underside of the top is made with rounded corners to make the tray "fall" into its place.

NOTE: THESE EDGES MUST BE ROUNDED OR FLAPS WILL NOT HINGE, MAKE 3/8" R

2" x 3/8" DOWEL 2 PER LEG

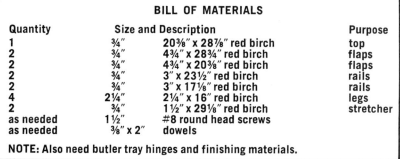

Section A–A

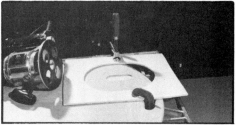

Shown here is the easy way to mortise hings. The plywood jig will give perfect results every time. Note center lines.

BILL OF MATERIALS

Quantity	Size and Description		Purpose
1	¾"	20⅜" x 28⅞" red birch	top
2	¾"	4¾" x 28¾" red birch	flaps
2	¾"	4¾" x 20⅜" red birch	flaps
2	¾"	3" x 23½" red birch	rails
2	¾"	3" x 17⅛" red birch	rails
4	2¼"	2¼" x 16" red birch	legs
2	¾"	1½" x 29⅛" red birch	stretcher
as needed	1½"	#8 round head screws	
as needed	⅜" x 2"	dowels	

NOTE: Also need butler tray hinges and finishing materials.

One hinge is already mounted and the other is ready to be. Remember other types of wood, as pine, may be used.

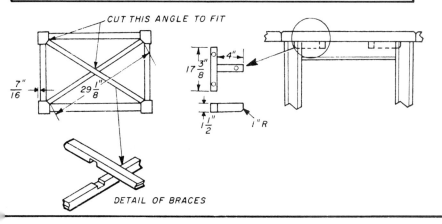

CUT THIS ANGLE TO FIT

DETAIL OF BRACES

One advantage of lumber-core plywood is that edges can be sanded easily. Here the table base is ready for finishing.

line of your hinge measuring something like 8 x 14-inches. Cut this out, saving the outside part. This is now a guide for the router and if you will make a trial cut on scrap wood, you should find that the hinge will fit perfectly into the mortise.

The butler hinge is unique in that the leaves are not the same thickness. This means that the mortise will have to be made to the deepest part of the hinge. Shims are made to be placed under the thinner part, as shown. Some

butler hinges have the same thickness leaves, so it is recommended that you not mortise for the hinge until you have it in hand. The dimension for the mortise was purposely left out of the drawing.

When mortising, place both the sides and table top in position and mortise them together.

Stretchers are added to complete the construction. Stretchers are glued in place and held with screws driven diagonally.

To finish the table, remove the hinges and sand all parts thor-

oughly. Then finish to your liking. Antique red (with the base coat thinned so the rich grain pattern of the red birch would show through) was used on this tray table. Many finishes are possible, and if antiquing is not your cup of tea, try a wood-tone stain topped off with a French polish.

STORAGE WALL WITH FOLDAWAY DINING TABLE

CRAMPED FOR SPACE? This wall unit can work well in any room and serves a dual purpose. It provides storage space and also can be transformed into an instant dining area of some elegance when needed. Its secret is a space-saving hideaway dining table which is housed in the lower center section, hidden behind two swing-away doors. The table seats four adults comfortably. The secret of successful folding is a gateleg foot and a pair of special hinges. The heavy-duty hinges not only support the two halves of the table, but, when folded, they leave a space to clear the gateleg foot which is mounted at one end. The gateleg foot is cleverly designed so that it locks in both the folded and open positions.

The cabinet has been made with adjustable shelves in the lower sections. These are optional and need not be used, especially if you would like to install large speakers in the cabinets.

The piece is made in six sections which makes it easily transportable.

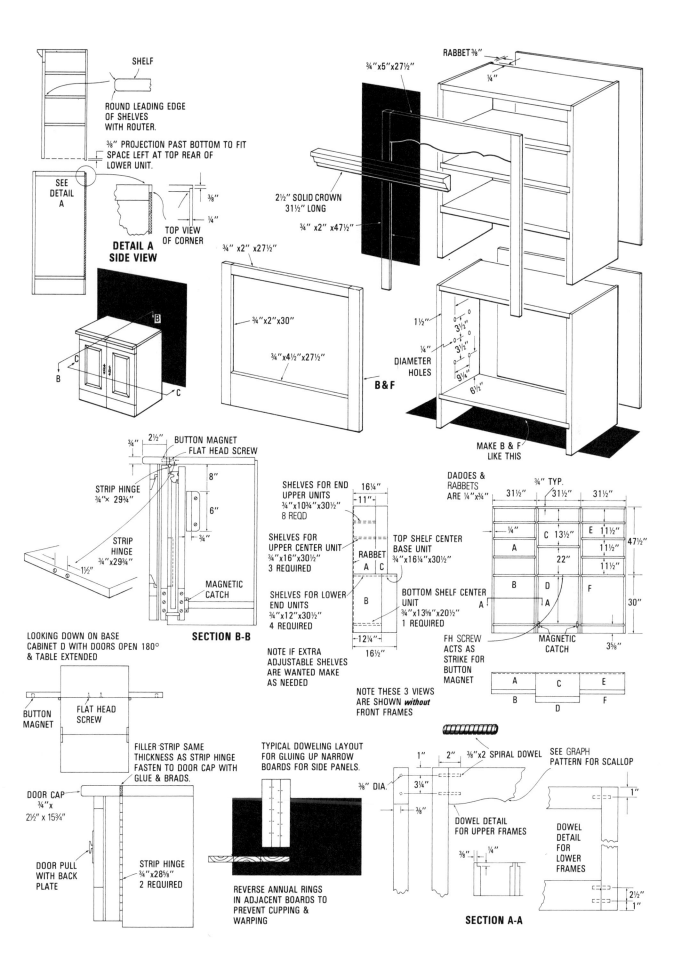

SHOP-BUILT SQUARE made from 1 x 4 pine is clamped in place to guide router when making dado cuts.

TEST FIT shelves in dados before applying glue to dado and shelf ends, squaring, and clamping assembly.

CARPENTER'S SQUARE checks frame after applying glue and long clamps. Slotted boards guide and support clamps.

BEVEL EDGES on door panel making angle cuts on table saw, then separate scrap with shallow vertical cut.

PROTECTIVE WOOD STRIPS keep clamp jaws from marring door assembly that fits over folded table while glue dries.

The overall width is 91½ in. and the height is 77½ in. Lumber used was one-in. pine.

The bill of materials calls for 260 spiral dowels. This is not an error. The pine boards must be edge-glued to obtain the width required. If you use wide boards, they should be ripped and glued. The widest individual pieces should be about 4-in. The annular rings must alternate up and down in adjacent boards as shown in the drawing, otherwise the boards will cup badly as the wood ages. If you have a shaper equipped with a glue joint cutter, you can eliminate the dowels and use the glue joint instead.

Cut the parts to size as indicated in the materials list then, if necessary, rip the boards, reverse, them and then lay out and drill the dowel holes. A doweling jig is recommended as it will assure accurate alignment of the dowels and a good flat joint. Use a good grade of glue and clamp the parts securely.

When all the wide boards have been glued, sand them with a belt sander or use a jack plane. Follow with a finishing sander. When done, the boards must be flat and smooth. The cross members or shelves (as they are called in the materials list) will be held by dadoes cut into the uprights (sides). Be sure the ends are free of any burrs which could cause problems when you must fit them into the dadoes. Note that the shelves are cut ¼ in. narrower than the uprights. This is to allow clearance for the rear panel.

The dadoes and rabbets are cut into the uprights using a router. A Tee square made of ¾-in. stock simplifies cutting the dadoes. Make the square about 28 in. long. This enables it to straddle two panels side-by-side, as shown in the photo. Lay out the position of each dado on the boards, then clamp the square as shown and cut the dado ¾ in. wide and ¼ in. deep. A ¼ x ⅜-in. rabbet is also cut along the rear edge of the uprights to take the rear panel.

Each section is now ready to be assembled. Check the fit of the shelves into the dadoes and make any necessary adjustments. You may want to round the edges of the

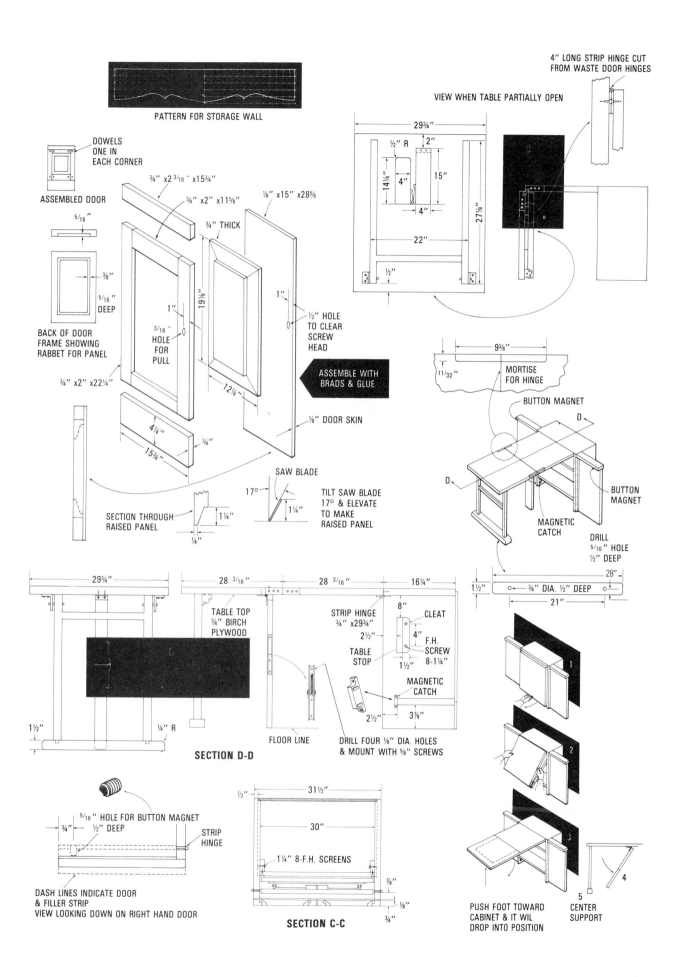

PATTERN FOR STORAGE WALL

DOWELS ONE IN EACH CORNER

ASSEMBLED DOOR

5/16"

3/8"

5/16" DEEP

BACK OF DOOR FRAME SHOWING RABBET FOR PANEL

3/4" x2" x22 1/4"

3/4" x2 3/16" x15 3/4"

3/4" x2" x11 5/8"

1/8" x15" x28 5/8"

3/4" THICK

19 1/8"

1"

3/16" HOLE FOR PULL

1"

1/2" HOLE TO CLEAR SCREW HEAD

ASSEMBLE WITH BRADS & GLUE

1/8" DOOR SKIN

12 1/4"

4 1/4"

3/4"

15 3/4"

SECTION THROUGH RAISED PANEL

1 1/4"

1/4"

SAW BLADE

17°

1 1/4"

TILT SAW BLADE 17° & ELEVATE TO MAKE RAISED PANEL

4" LONG STRIP HINGE CUT FROM WASTE DOOR HINGES

VIEW WHEN TABLE PARTIALLY OPEN

29 3/4"

1/2" R

2"

14 1/4"

4"

15"

4"

22"

27 1/8"

1/2"

9 3/8"

11/32"

MORTISE FOR HINGE

BUTTON MAGNET

D

D

BUTTON MAGNET

MAGNETIC CATCH

DRILL 5/16" HOLE 1/2" DEEP

1 1/2"

3/4" DIA. 1/2" DEEP

28"

21"

29 3/4"

28 3/16"

28 3/16"

16 1/4"

TABLE TOP 3/4" BIRCH PLYWOOD

STRIP HINGE 3/4" x29 3/4"

2 1/2"

TABLE STOP

8"

CLEAT

4"

F.H. SCREW 8-1 1/4"

1 1/2"

MAGNETIC CATCH

2 1/2"

3 7/8"

1 1/2"

1/4" R

FLOOR LINE

SECTION D-D

DRILL FOUR 1/8" DIA. HOLES & MOUNT WITH 5/8" SCREWS

1

2

3

5/16" HOLE FOR BUTTON MAGNET

3/4"

1/2" DEEP

STRIP HINGE

DASH LINES INDICATE DOOR & FILLER STRIP VIEW LOOKING DOWN ON RIGHT HAND DOOR

1/2"

31 1/2"

30"

1 1/4" 8-F.H. SCREENS

7/8"

1/8"

3/4"

SECTION C-C

4

PUSH FOOT TOWARD CABINET & IT WIL DROP INTO POSITION

5 CENTER SUPPORT

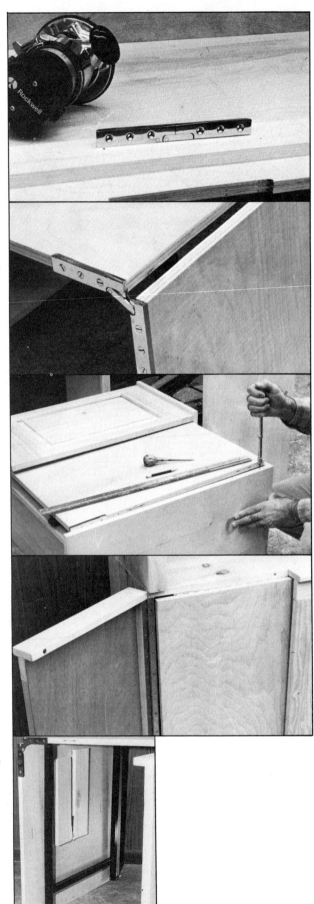

GUIDE BOARD clamped to table top controls router when cutting the mortise for special table-folding hinge.

HINGE CLOSEUP shows action that allows the table top sections to move away from each other so they can fold over.

PREDRILL screw holes to prevent splitting frame when mounting the strip hinges for the table cover doors.

CLEARANCE under front frame for top section allows table cover doors to close flush with the edge of the bottom shelf.

CENTER SUPPORT hinges to under side of table top and swings around 180° in the middle to lie flat when folded.

shelves before assembly. Use a router fitted with a 1/8-in. rounding bit. Do only the eight exposed shelves of the upper cabinets.

Apply glue to the dadoes and shelf ends then mate the parts and clamp as shown. Use a large square to make sure that the case is square and remains so after clamping.

Make the front frames next. Dowel the joints as shown in the diagram. The lower frames are closed top and bottom but the upper frames are open at the bottom. The top rails of the upper frames are scalloped before assembly. Use a saber saw or jig saw to cut the scallops. After these have been assembled and the glue has set, remove the clamps and then round the edges with the 1/4-in. rounding bit. When rounding the outer edges near the top, stop the router short of the end. The cut should stop at the point where the solid crown will be. Draw a stop line by laying the crown in position, then scribe a light pencil line as a guide for the router. The lower frames are rounded on all edges, inside and out.

The frames are now attached to the cabinets. Apply glue to all joints and fasten with 2-in. finishing nails. Countersink the nail heads then fill the holes with a suitable filler. Add the solid crown molding to the top, fastening it with glue and nails driven in angularly along the top edge as shown.

If you decide to build the storage wall without the table, make a center frame and install it so it matches the end cabinets.

The table mechanism is especially designed for this application. Make the table top in two sections using birch plywood or other suitable finish. Place the two sections on the workbench with the ends butted as shown, then clamp a guide to the top for the router. This will be used to cut the mortise for the hinge. Set the guide, so that the depth of the cut will be exactly $1\frac{1}{32}$ in. deep and $9\frac{3}{8}$ in. long. The gateleg foot is installed at the far end of the table. The opposite end of the table is fastened to the base cabinet with a strip or piano hinge.

Note: The table hardware is imported from Spain and it is designed for a table height of less than our standard of 30 in. with a table top thickness of 1½ in. which is quite heavy. To compensate for the higher table and thinner top we used a foot base piece which is placed under the legs after the table is opened. The base piece is stored in the cabinet when not in use.

The center support is hinged to the underside of the table and drops down automatically when the table is raised. Because of its length, it is hinged at its side using a modified spring-loaded drop leaf support. Rework the support by removing the rivets at each end. Do this by grinding the rivet head or by filing it until it drops out. Discard the rivets and end flaps. Now drill four ⅛-in. diameter holes along the backbone as indicated in the drawing. Mount the support to the two wood pieces using round head screws. The spring will block one of the screw holes, but you can get a narrow screwdriver in from the edge to drive the

screw. In use, the center support hinges along its top as well as its side. Operate it as follows: When the table is open, the folded support will dangle from the underside. Swing it toward the front of the table slightly then open at the joint to extend the support fully. Now swing it to a vertical position where it will stiffen and support the table top.

The two doors are made with raised panels. Glue up boards for the panels then trim to size (12¼ x 19⅛ in.). Raise the panels on the table saw by elevating the blade 1¼ in. (vertical measurement) and tilting the arbor 17°. Adjust the fence so there will be a ¼-in. flat at the outer edge. Hold the work securely and run it through the blade slowly. When all four sides are cut, the waste should still be hanging on as shown in the photo. Lower the blade and set the arbor to 0°. Then set the fence and raise the blade as necessary to remove the waste. This operation will also

square off the angular cut left by the edge of the tilted saw blade.

Make up the frame for the doors and rabbet the rear edges to take the raised panel. You can run the rabbets off the ends of the stiles as they will be concealed when the ⅛-in. plywood is fastened to the rear of the frame. The plywood is made long enough to cover the apron and base pieces which are assembled to make up the door. Assemble the door as shown and be sure to add the filler strip at the rear edge of the door filler cap. When the door is fastened to the cabinet you will notice a gap at the top equal to the thickness of the strip hinges used. Cut the strip accordingly, and install with brads and glue.

Install the button magnets at the rear of the caps and then install two flat head screws into the edge of the cabinet. These keep the doors closed. At the lower part of the cabinet and just before the lower shelf, two magnetic catches are installed. These hold the hinged table top secure and flat when the table is not in use.

The table stop and cleats must be installed firmly. The stop acts as a support for the table as it is being extended and also when it is being retracted. It acts as a fulcrum.

The rear panels are cut from wall paneling. Note that the upper panels are made to project ⅜ in. below the side members. This is done so it will extend ⅜ in. below the top shelf of the lower cabinets, thus covering a raw edge.

When in place, the upper cabinets are secured to the lower units at the rear with steel mending plates. These are available at hardware shops. Use the straight type.

Sand all exposed surfaces then stain and finish as desired. Before you apply stain, test the product on scrap lumber. If you find the stain too dark or mottled, you may want to seal the wood lightly before staining. Do this with shellac thinned about 1-to-5 with alcohol (5 parts alcohol to one part shellac). Apply with a brush, allow to dry, then sand lightly with 220 paper. Now apply stain. You will notice the stain covers evenly without hot spots.

MATERIALS LIST

Note: All lumber is ¾-in. pine except for rear panels.

No. Req'd	Size and Description	Use	No. Req'd	Size and Description	Use
4	12¼"x30"	Side (end cabinet)	2	4¼"x15¾"	Door base
4	12¼"x30½"	Shelf (end cabinet)	2	¾"x28³⁄₁₆"x29¾" plywood	Table top
2	16½"x30"	Side (center cabinet)	1	4"x14¼"	Center support
1	16¼"x30½"	Shelf, top (center cabinet)	1	4"x15"	Center support
1	13⅝"x30½"	Shelf, lower (center cabinet)	1	1½"x1½"x28"	Foot base
3	¼"x25¾"x47⅞" plywood	Rear panel	2	DP	Pull/backplate
4	2"x30"	Stile, lower	2	MC	Magnetic Catch
2	2"x27½"	Rail, upper	2	BM	Button Magnet
2	4½"x27½"	Rail, lower	1	¾"x29¾"	Table strip hinge
1	6"x30"	Table stop	2	¾"x28⅝"	Door strip hinge
2	1½"x6"	Cleat	1	¾"x4"	Center support hinge
2	⅞"x28⅝"	Door filler	1 set	FTH	Foot & hinges
2	⅛"x15"x28⅝" plywood	Door back	2	½" No. 8 FH	Screw
2	2½"x15¾"	Door cap	8	1¼" No. 8 FH	Screw
2	2³⁄₁₆"x15¾"	Door apron	4	⅝" No. 6 RH	Screw
2	³⁄₁₆"x15¾"	Door cap filler	1	DLS	Drop leaf hinge for support
2	12¼"x19⅛"	Raised panel	48	¾"—18	Brad
4	2"x11⅝"	Door rail	70	2"	Nail, finishing
4	2"x22¼"	Door stile	260	⅜"x2"	Dowels spiral

Colonial Hutch

Professional tricks make this handsome hutch easy-to-build at an inexpensive cost. It's a most desirable furniture piece, too

Hᴇʀᴇ is a fair-sized hutch dimensioned so that it can be constructed by using a single panel of 4 x 8-ft. lumber core plywood for the main assembly. Pleasantly proportioned, the basic colonial design has been cleverly reworked to permit the piece to blend with a wide range of decor, enabling you to use it in the dining area, living room, or den.

The upper section features two good-sized shelves and a wide single drawer. This drawer front is made to appear as a double, simply for purpose of design, by cutting a partial saw kerf down the center and adding two drawer pulls. The delightful deceit is again repeated on the lower section. A horizontal saw kerf across both door panels and a pair of pulls relieves the otherwise "heavy" look of the lower cabinet, while ample storage space is provided behind the doors. If an actual set of drawers are your preference you can, of course, easily make the substitution.

Two professional tricks are utilized in the construction. The cabinet door trim appears to be carved right out of the panel but it is actually created by adding on ready-made straight and curved molding available as a stock item at most lumber supply dealers. Additionally, molded accent edges are shaped separately, cut into strips and also added on.

The project illustrated was made of birch lumber core plywood, with solid birch for trim and base. Many fine hardwoods are available in lumber core form so the choice is yours.

Console Cabinet and Mirror   *(p. 102)*

Tile-Top Table with Built-in Planter   *(p. 107)*

Modern Storage Cabinet   *(p. 118)*

Trestle Desk   *(p. 123)*

Drop-Leaf Secretary   *(p. 130)*

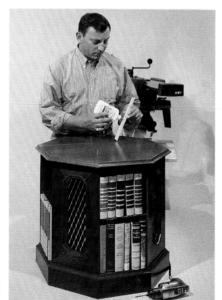

Decorative Bookshelf Table (p. 140)

End Table Cellarette **(p. 143)**

Foldaway Bed . . . .

Storage Unit **(p. 14**

Mobile Server **(p. 152)**

Library Wall Cabinet **(p. 157)**

Drop-Leaf Table **(p. 19**

Drop-Leaf Movable Server (p. 190)

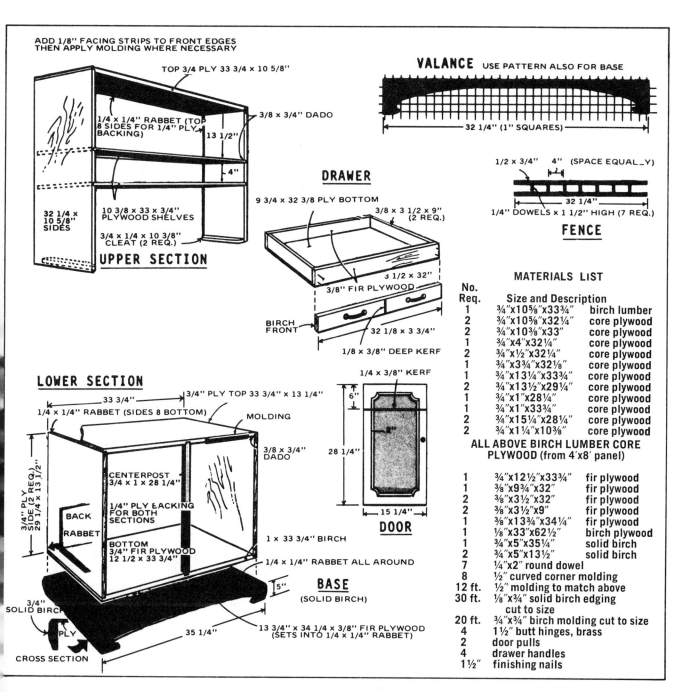

ADD 1/8" FACING STRIPS TO FRONT EDGES
THEN APPLY MOLDING WHERE NECESSARY

TOP 3/4 PLY 33 3/4 x 10 5/8"

1/4 x 1/4" RABBET (TOP
8 SIDES FOR 1/4" PLY
BACKING)

3/8 x 3/4" DADO

13 1/2"

4"

32 1/4 x
10 5/8"
SIDES

10 3/8 x 33 3/4"
PLYWOOD SHELVES

3/4 x 1/4 x 10 3/8"
CLEAT (2 REQ.)

UPPER SECTION

VALANCE USE PATTERN ALSO FOR BASE

32 1/4" (1" SQUARES)

1/2 x 3/4"   4"   (SPACE EQUALLY)

32 1/4"

1/4" DOWELS x 1 1/2" HIGH (7 REQ.)

FENCE

DRAWER

9 3/4 x 32 3/8 PLY BOTTOM

3/8 x 3 1/2 x 9"
(2 REQ.)

3 1/2 x 32"

3/8" FIR PLYWOOD

BIRCH
FRONT

32 1/8 x 3 3/4"

1/8 x 3/8" DEEP KERF

MATERIALS LIST

No. Req.	Size and Description	
1	¾"x10⅝"x33¾"	birch lumber
2	¾"x10⅝"x32¼"	core plywood
2	¾"x10⅜"x33"	core plywood
1	¾"x4"x32¼"	core plywood
2	¾"x½"x32¼"	core plywood
1	¾"x3¾"x32⅛"	core plywood
1	¾"x13¼"x33¾"	core plywood
2	¾"x13½"x29¼"	core plywood
1	¾"x1"x28¼"	core plywood
1	¾"x1"x33¾"	core plywood
2	¾"x15¼"x28¼"	core plywood
2	¾"x1¼"x10⅜"	core plywood

ALL ABOVE BIRCH LUMBER CORE PLYWOOD (from 4'x8' panel)

1	¾"x12½"x33¾"	fir plywood
1	⅜"x9¾"x32"	fir plywood
2	⅜"x3½"x32"	fir plywood
2	⅜"x3½"x9"	fir plywood
1	⅜"x13¾"x34¼"	fir plywood
1	⅛"x33"x62½"	birch plywood
1	¾"x5"x35¼"	solid birch
2	¾"x5"x13½"	solid birch
7	¼"x2" round dowel	
8	½" curved corner molding	
12 ft.	½" molding to match above	
30 ft.	⅛"x¾" solid birch edging cut to size	
20 ft.	¾"x¾" birch molding cut to size	
4	1½" butt hinges, brass	
2	door pulls	
4	drawer handles	
1½"	finishing nails	

LOWER SECTION

33 3/4"

3/4" PLY TOP 33 3/4" x 13 1/4"

1/4 x 1/4" RABBET (SIDES & BOTTOM)

MOLDING

3/8 x 3/4"
DADO

CENTERPOST
3/4 x 1 x 28 1/4"

1/4" PLY BACKING
FOR BOTH
SECTIONS

BOTTOM
3/4 FIR PLYWOOD
12 1/2 x 33 3/4"

3/4" PLY
SIDE (2 REQ.)
29 1/4 x 13 1/2"

BACK
RABBET

1 x 33 3/4" BIRCH

1/4 x 1/4" RABBET ALL AROUND

3/4"
SOLID BIRCH

PLY

CROSS SECTION

BASE
(SOLID BIRCH)

5"

35 1/4"

13 3/4" x 34 1/4 x 3/8" FIR PLYWOOD
(SETS INTO 1/4 x 1/4" RABBET)

1/4 x 3/8" KERF

6"

2"

28 1/4"

15 1/4"

DOOR

1. An accurate layout of the pieces will minimize errors and prevent any waste. Panel of lumber core plywood is sold in 4 x 8-ft. size which is ample for the main assembly.

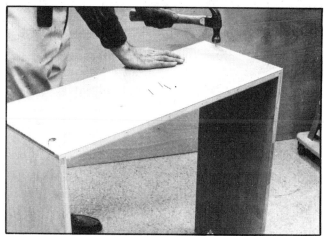

2. Finishing nails are used to hold the glued sections together until the clamps can be applied. Note the novel use of the parallel clamps to hold sections steady for nailing.

Colonial Hutch

Construction begins with layout. The first step is one which should be carried out with care because one wrong cut could prove quite costly. The reason is that lumber core is quite generally sold only as an entire 4 x 8-ft. panel so you can't go back to buy an additional small piece should the need arise. Thus, it is advisable to carefully measure and mark off the various pieces *right on the panel*. Use a hard-leaded pencil and mark lightly. Be sure to make allowance for the thickness of the saw kerf at all cuts.

The radial arm saw is, by far, the most useful power tool for such construction but a table or portable circular saw can also be used. If yours is a small shop and the handling of a full 4 x 8-ft. panel presents a problem, allow for several rough cuts in your layout (there'll be sufficient waste for this

purpose). Use a saber or even a hand saw to cut the panel into four bite-size pieces which will handle easily.

Use a planer or plywood blade on your saw to obtain clean, smooth cuts which will not require finish sanding. Cut all the main pieces and follow up by marking them for dado and rabbet cuts. Use of a dado cutter simplifies the operation but a regular saw blade can also do the job if necessary. In the latter case, make twin cuts ¾-in. apart, then a series of passes to clean out in-between.

The upper and lower side pieces are dadoed ¾-in. wide and ⅜-in. deep to receive the horizontal members and drawer shelves. A ¼-in. rabbet cut is made at the inside back of the top, bottom and side pieces. The drawer shelves and top of the lower cabinet are not rabbetted since they were cut ¼-in. narrower at the onset. This is to allow the back panel to set in flush. *Note:* The bottom member of the cabinet is ¾-in. fir plywood; the

front edge faced with 1 in. length of birch.

Although some craftsmen like the effect of the exposed raw edge of lumber core, the trick used by the pro's to conceal the edge is to simply add on a thin strip of solid stock about ⅛-in. thick. After all panels are cut to size, rip up a supply of such strips and glue onto all front edges of the panels. Sand flush to sides.

Assembly and gluing are the next steps. Use of white glue is recommended because of its good holding, quick setting, and non-staining characteristics. Use 1½-in. finishing nails for holding the parts while clamps are affixed to the work. In a number of places the nails will eventually be concealed by the molding trim; elsewhere they should be set and the holes filled with plastic wood or similar material. If you don't have large clamps to handle the job you'll have to resort to the use of flathead wood screws to provide gluing pressure. Here again, holes will

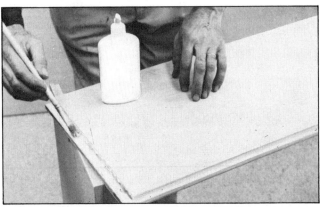

3. Use a brush to spread white glue over both surfaces of joints. Glue has good holding and is also quick setting.

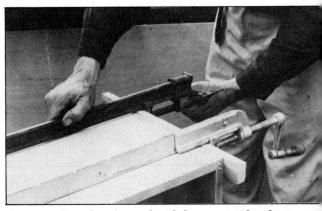

4. Large bar clamps are big help to provide gluing pressure. If not available, you can use flathead wood screws

7. Glue and small finishing nails are needed to apply the molding trim. Set nails, fill holes with plastic wood.

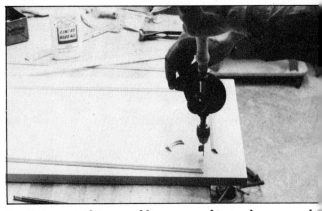

8. Before applying molding on cabinet doors, pre-drill holes for ⅝" brads which are left protruding slightly

require filling after the screws have been countersunk.

The base of the unit is made of ¾-in. solid stock, birch or maple being equally suitable. If a less expensive wood is preferred, bass or poplar can be used. This applies to the trim as well. Cut the parts for the base noting that the dimensions allow for the cabinet to set *into* the base. Thus the inside dimensions of the base wall are equal to the outside dimensions of the cabinet. Cut a ⅜-in. dado ¼-in. deep and ¼-in. from the top of the three pieces (two sides and front) before gluing. Since the ⅜-in. set-in panel will add much strength, ordinary butt joints will suffice between front and sides. The curved cross-section of the base is accomplished by hand planing to shape. If a planer jointer is available, so much the better.

Fancy treatment of the cabinet doors is next. This is a rather simple operation. The curved molding is positioned at each corner, 2-in. from each edge and the outline is marked lightly in pencil. A couple of ⅜-in. brads are nailed about two thirds into the panel. The heads are then clipped off with a diagonal cutter or pliers to form a point of sorts. The molding is again put into place and pressed lightly to get an impression of the nail positions for drilling. Drill same-size holes, apply a few small beads of glue and finally press the corner firmly into place. The protruding nail points will usually suffice to hold the molding in place while the glue sets. If not, apply clamp pressure.

Inasmuch as the ends of the corner molding are pre-cut to a 45° angle you will need only to cut matching 45° angles on the straight lengths and apply, following the same procedures as for the corners.

Butt hinges are set into mortised recesses in the door so they will lay almost flush with the edge. This will eliminate the need to mortise on the cabinet side. Position the doors so they will set back ⅛-in. from the cabinet front and measure and mark for hinge screw holes. Before finally attaching doors make the partial saw cut ⅜-in. deep across both doors, 6-in. from the top to simulate the set of drawers.

The upper drawer is a simple box construction made with ⅜-in. plywood to which the front panel is attached. Accent molding is made by cutting the pattern on shaper or saw with shaper cutters. Rip down the lengths required using 45° miters for corner joints, then nail and glue into place. Set all nails and fill the holes.

Addition of the decorative fence and valance on the upper shelf completes construction. Screw the three sections together for rigidity, glue in the back panel (⅛-in. birch plywood) and smooth-sand the entire job. Stain to suit and surface with several coats of satin brushing lacquer for a fine, lasting finish.

5. *A spoke shave is used to smooth over curved sections that have been cut to plan contour with band or jig saw.*

6. *After the base is assembled a plane is used to contour the cross section after which it is sanded thoroughly.*

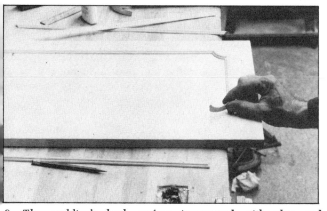

9. *The molding's back surface is covered with glue and molding is then pressed down on protruding brad points.*

10. *View of completed base. Plan dimensions allow for the cabinet to set into the base. Molding trim's added later.*

HIDEAWAY HOME OFFICE

Efficiency plus describes this oak and oak plywood dandy which hides away in just 20 by 30 by 50 inches

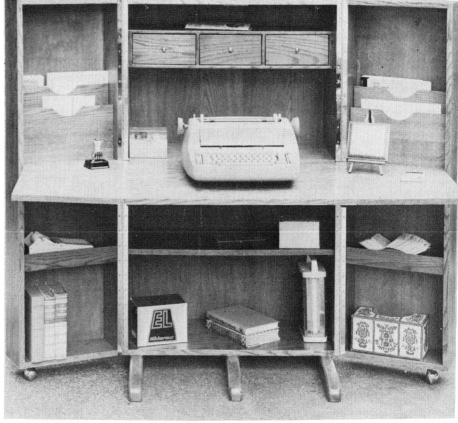

THIS HIDEAWAY HOME OFFICE is an unobtrusive piece of furniture when closed, but open the two doors and—presto!—you have a large size writing desk, filing space and ample storage. Everything is within easy reach so you can handle the complexities of bills, taxes, credit accounts, and other chores common to all householders.

The size of the cabinet when closed is 20″ × 30″ × 50-½″. When open, it measures 30″ × 60″ × 50-½″. The desk surface is 21″ × 56″. A unique method is used to support the flaps of the desk: a pin located on the door shelf engages a matching hole in the desk flap. This rigidly supports the flap and locks the door in the open position. Flip-top hinges enable the flaps to fold onto the main desk section: all can then fold up compactly Two retractable supports add to the sturdiness of this piece.

Lumber used for this project was ¼″, ½″ and ¾″ plywood. Some solid lumber is also utilized. The most difficult part of this project is the mitering of the panels to form the cabinet and doors. All other construction is rather basic and easy to do.

Mitering. Oak plywood was used in construction but other species may be substituted. Rip the panels to size as shown in the materials list, then proceed to miter the ends. The mitered joint may be made in several ways, either on the table saw using saw and router, or with the shaper. Choose the method best suited to your equipment and skill. We used the offset miter, which consists of a miter with a rabbet, but two other methods are shown in the detail: the lock miter and the spline joint. The lock miter should be done with a shaper or router using a matched set of cutters. The spline can be done on the table saw.

To make the offset miter, cut a ⅜″ × ¾″ rabbet across the ends of the top and bottom panels and the four top and bottom door panels (two tops, two bottoms), using a dado head. We used a Rockwell wobble head which makes a very accurate cut.

When the tops and bottoms are rabbeted, reset the blade or fence, then proceed to make a ⅜″ × ⅜″ rabbet at the ends of the six vertical members (two cabinet sides and four door sides). Now remove the dado

blade and replace it with the regular saw blade, set to an angle of 45-degrees. For this operation, an auxiliary wood fence must be fastened to the metal saw fence (most fences are provided with holes for this purpose); simply screw it to the fence as shown in the detail. Before mounting the wood fence, cut an arc out of the piece to clear the saw blade. With the blade set at 45-degrees, adjust the fence to make the angle cuts—and be sure to make them accurately. See detail.

The advantage of this joint is that it provides plenty of gluing surface and it helps keep the corners square.

After all miters have been made, cut the stopped dado for the desk piece and the ¼″ × ¼″ groove at the rear of the cabinet members and at the front of the door members. The groove is placed ⅝″ from the edges. The ¼″ plywood panels are placed in the grooves and the ends, top and bottom are assembled dry to check the fit: miters should close flush with no space at the joints. If okay, install the desk piece and other members, apply glue to the miters and clamp securely. Note: do not glue in the ¼″ panel. This should be made to float

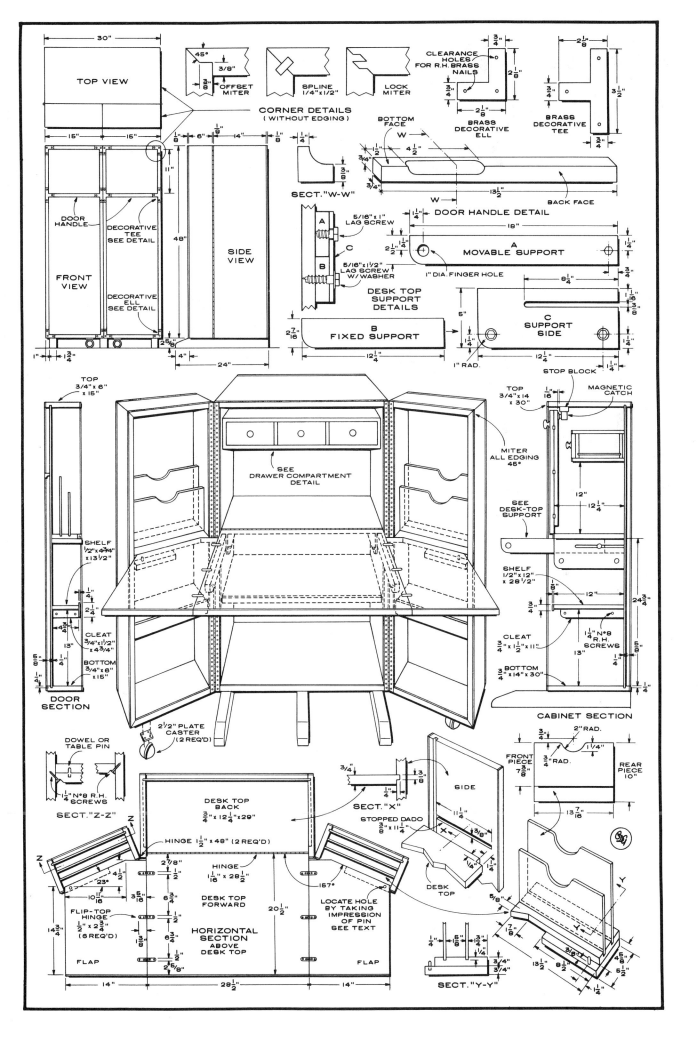

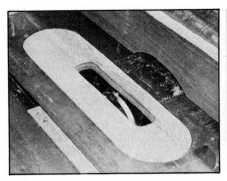

Wide-slot plywood insert replaces regular insert in table saw. Wobble head is used to rabbet panels. Alternative cutting methods are shown in detail drawing.

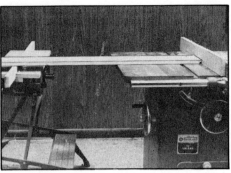

Support is needed for long sides when you are rabbeting them on table saw. Workmate is used here. Wax on the saw table allows the work to slide easily.

Auxiliary wood fence and the regular saw blade are used to rabbet vertical members (cabinet and door sides). Note arc cut in fence so that it clears saw blade.

Saw blade at 45 degrees is used to make the angle cuts; broken lines indicate the miters here. This joint offers good gluing surface, and keeps corners square.

After ¼" slot has been cut for rear panel, the panel is installed and cabinet is clamped up on short ends until glue sets. Rear panel floats free in slots.

Closeup of mitered corner; miters should close flush with no space at the joint. In this photo, a wood scrap protects the work from clamp damage while glue sets.

in the frame or cabinet. The same procedure is followed in making the doors. Remember when applying clamps to protect the work by using cauls (strips of wood) under the clamps. With the ¼" panels in place, the glued-up assembly should be square, but be sure to check for squareness with a large square before the glue sets. Adjust as necessary.

All exposed plywood edges must be concealed. This can be done with veneer tape or with a solid band. The solid band will stand up better and is therefore recommended. The strips are ripped from solid stock, making each strip ⅛" × ¾". Let the ends slightly extend the piece to be edged, then measure the pieces carefully and miter the ends. Fit each piece individually, apply glue to the plywood edge and to the back of the band, then fasten with brads. You can use ordinary brads but "Beauty Brads," especially made for applying molding and edging, are recommended. These very thin brads are made of hardened steel, have no heads, and do not require setting as

an ordinary brad does. In use, they are driven into the work leaving about ¼" exposed, then are snapped across the grain with a hammer blow to the side. The brad will snap slightly below the surface, thus eliminating the need for setting. Also, the hole left is so small that the finishing materials will usually fill it.

Desk Top. The desk top and flaps are cut as indicated, then the three are placed on a flat surface and the hinge locations are laid out. The hinges used are the flip-top type which permits the flaps to flop 180-degrees. The hinges are ½" wide and 2-¾" long and must be mortised so the tops are flush with the desk top. Use a router fitted with a ½" straight cutter. To assure accuracy and uniformity, you should use a jig (the one shown is made of ⅜" plywood). Make the width of the opening equal to the diameter of the router base and the length of the cutout 2¼" longer than the diameter of the router base. Note that the hinge is deeper at the center, thus you will have to mortise this part deeper for clearance.

The flaps and desk top must be aligned at the front edge when cutting the mortise. The rear edges of the flaps must match the shelf when the doors are swung open 157 degrees. Because of possible discrepancies, you may have to re-work the rear flap edges to obtain a good fit. You can check this after the side doors are hung.

The piano hinges for the doors measure 1-½" × 48" and the desk hinge measures 1-1/16" × 28-½". Install the end and center screws on all hinges and check the fit. If okay, install the rest of the screws. The plate casters are used under the doors to help take some stress off the door hinges. The casters are installed after the cabinet is mounted onto the base pieces. The base piece height should be the same as the caster height measured from the bottom of the wheel to the top of the plate.

To support the desk flaps, a projection on the door shelves is provided. A locating pin on the shelf prevents the door from swinging away from the flap which would leave

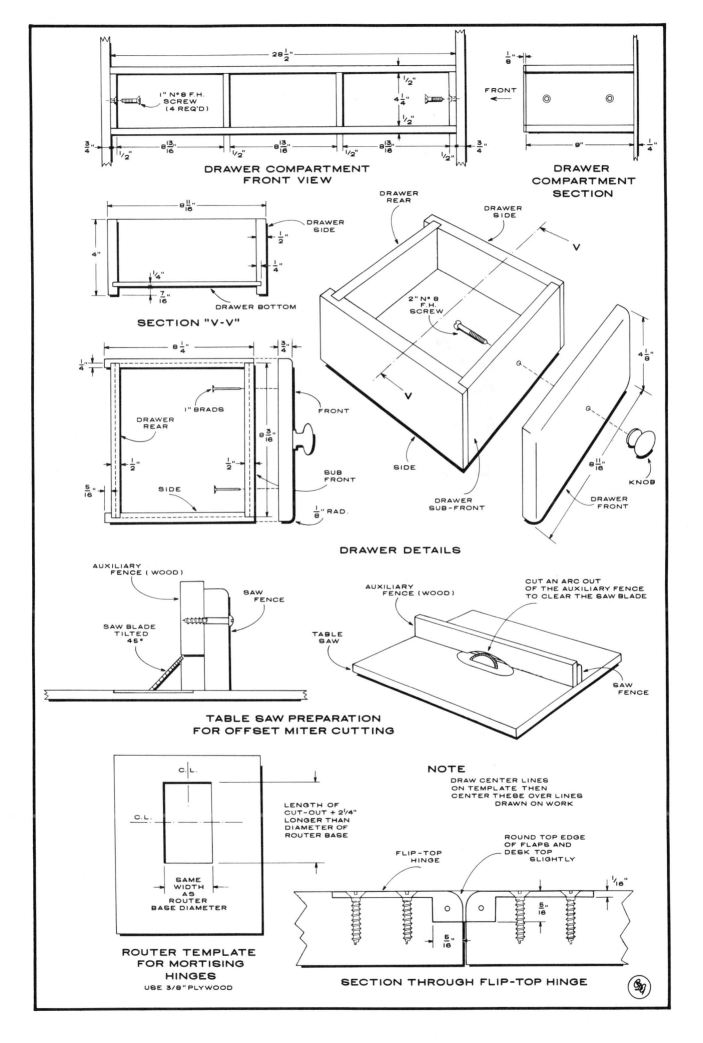

DRAWER COMPARTMENT
FRONT VIEW

DRAWER COMPARTMENT
SECTION

SECTION "V-V"

DRAWER DETAILS

TABLE SAW PREPARATION
FOR OFFSET MITER CUTTING

ROUTER TEMPLATE
FOR MORTISING
HINGES
USE 3/8" PLYWOOD

SECTION THROUGH FLIP-TOP HINGE

NOTE
DRAW CENTER LINES
ON TEMPLATE THEN
CENTER THESE OVER LINES
DRAWN ON WORK

Stopped dado, which will accept the desk top, is cut with a router. Side glides, for accuracy with the router, will be removed later. Study drawings carefully.

With router guides removed, fit of rabbeted desk top to stopped dado is tested by designer in this photograph. For professional job, fit should be precise.

Though veneer tape can be used to correct exposed plywood edges, solid strips are recommended. Here they are ripped from solid stock. Each strip is ⅛″ by ¾.″

Ends of the strips are mitered and each piece is carefully fitted. Apply glue to the plywood edge and strip and fasten with brads. See text regarding edging brads.

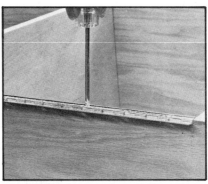

Make pilot holes for hinges slightly under screw size with portable drill; then attach hinge temporarily with end screws for check before proceeding with balance.

Cutting squares for the handles (refer to drawings). Note push stick in photo.

Base pieces are cut from thick stock and then rounded with the router. Round ends where base meets the cabinet, as indicated by pencil in this photograph.

With base pieces attached, casters can be installed with adequate clearance from center base piece. If necessary, you can use shims under caster plates.

Jig made from ⅜″ plywood is used to mortise desk top for hinges. Flap and desk top must be butted for this operation. Use ½″ straight cutter in router.

the flap unsupported and place a great strain on the flip-top hinges. Therefore, it is important that whenever the desk top flaps are extended, they must rest on the shelf support provided.

The pins are installed on the shelves as shown. To locate the holes on the underside of the flaps, lower the flaps into place and let the pin point mark the location. A piece of carbon paper placed carbon-side up on the pin will leave a distinct mark.

The rails near the top of the door fronts serve to break up the monotony of the plain doors and also serve as door pulls. Finger clearance is provided in each piece toward the center. Installed after the staining and finishing operations are completed, they are held firmly by the decorative Tees. No other support is necessary. The finger clearance can be made with a router or shaper. If the proper cutter is not available, you can use a chisel to cut the clearance.

ance.

Drawers. The drawer compartment and drawers are first cut as indicated. The compartment is made of ½″ plywood with butt joints and oak edging ripped to ½″ widths is used to conceal the plywood edge. When assembling the drawers, insert the bottom panel then glue and brad the sides to the sub-front and rear. The drawer fronts are fastened to the sub-fronts with glue and brads. Install the door shelves and large

In its retracted position, desk support clears flap support permitting the door to close. In use, the finger hole is employed to pull out the support for solidity.

shelf with screws driven through the cleats.

This completes construction. Stain and finish as desired. We used Golden Oak paste wood filler followed by sanding sealer, then clear lacquer. The paste filler stains and fills the open pores of the oak in one operation. In use, the filler is thinned with benzine to the consistency of heavy cream, then is brushed on with the grain. When it starts to set (about 10 minutes) it is rubbed off across the grain using burlap or excelsior. This will work the filler into the pores leaving a smooth surface. Do not do too large an area at one time, for once the filler has set it will be difficult to remove. Allow the work to dry overnight before applying the sealer coat. Before the sealer is applied, very lightly sand the filled wood then dust with a tac cloth.

When finishing is completed, add the decorative corners and Tees, magnetic catches and brass pulls. The desk supports are also fastened using 1-½" Lag screws.

Partially completed drawer. When assembling, insert bottom panel, then glue and brad sides to the sub-front and rear. Fronts are fastened in the same way.

Drawer compartment is constructed of ½" plywood with butt joints, as indicated in drawing. Oak edging, ½" wide, mitered at ends, is applied to plywood.

BILL OF MATERIALS

Except as noted, lumber used is ¾" oak plywood. Oak, when specified after the measurement, signifies solid oak.

Description	Size (in inches)	Quantity
Side	¾ × 14 × 48	2
Top	¾ × 14 × 30	1
Bottom	¾ × 14 × 30	1
Rear	¼ × 29 × 47, oak plywood	1
Desk top rear	¾ × 12-¼ × 29	1
Shelf	½ × 12 × 28-½, oak plywood	1
Shelf edge	⅛ × ¾ × 28-½, oak	1
Shelf cleat	¾ × 1-½ × 11, oak	2
Stop	¼ × ¾ × 3-½, oak	1
Base	1-¾ × 2-⅝ × 24	3
Desk top forward	¾ × 20-½ × 28-¼	1
Flap	¾ × 14 × 19-¼	2
Support, movable	¾ × 2-½ × 18, oak	2
Support, fixed	¾ × 2-7⁄16 × 12-¼, oak	2
Support, side	¼ × 5 × 12-¼, plywood	2
Drawer box top	½ × 9 × 28-½, oak plywood	1
Drawer box bottom	½ × 9 × 28-½, oak plywood	1
Drawer box side	½ × 4-¼ × 9, oak plywood	4
Drawer rear	½ × 4 × 8-3⁄16, oak plywood	3
Drawer sub-front	½ × 4 × 8-3⁄16, oak plywood	3
Drawer front	¾ × 4-⅛ × 8-11⁄16, oak plywood	3
Drawer side	½ × 4 × 8-¼, oak plywood	6
Drawer bottom	¼ × 7-7⁄16 × 8-3⁄16, oak plywood	3
Door side	¾ × 6 × 48	4
Door top	¾ × 6 × 15	2
Door bottom	¾ × 6 × 15	2
Door front	¼ × 14 × 47	2
Door handle	¾ × ¾ × 13-½	2
Door shelf	¾ × 5-¼ × 13-½	2
Separator front	¼ × 7-⅜ × 13-7⁄16, oak plywood	2
Separator rear	¼ × 10 × 13-7⁄16, oak plywood	2
Flap support	¾ × 5-½ × 8-½	2
Pin	5⁄16 × 1, dowel	2
Shelf lower	½ × 4-¾ × 13-½	2
Shelf edge	¼ × 2-¼ × 13-½ oak plywood	2
Shelf cleat	¾ × 1-½ × 4-¾	4
Plywood edging	⅛ × ¾ oak	65 feet
Hinge door	1-½ × 48	2
Hinge desk	1-1⁄16 × 28-½	1
Hinge, flip-top	½ × 2-¾ FTT	6
Corner	AC	8
Tee	AT	4
Knob	Knobs	5
Magnetic catch	PM	2
Caster, plate	2-½"	2
Screw	1-½" × 8 RH	20
Screw	1" × 8 FH	8
Lag screw	5⁄16 × 1	2
Lag screw	5⁄16 × 1-½	4
Beauty Brads	BBDS	1 pk.
Brads	1"	12

Gossip Bench: Versatility Plus

Attractive addition to any room in your home is made of pine and a little plywood, easily built in a weekend

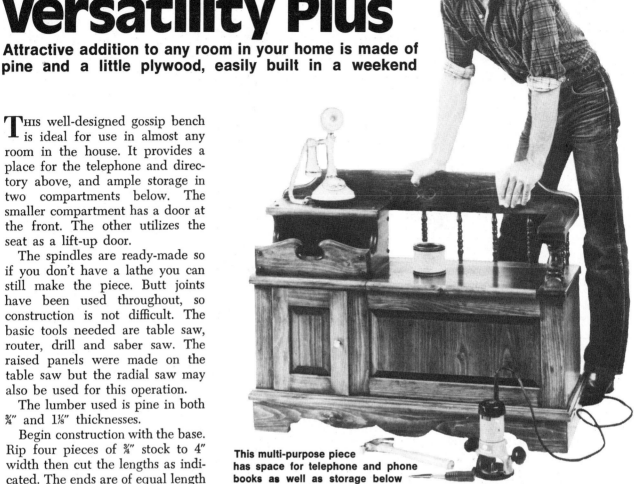

This well-designed gossip bench is ideal for use in almost any room in the house. It provides a place for the telephone and directory above, and ample storage in two compartments below. The smaller compartment has a door at the front. The other utilizes the seat as a lift-up door.

The spindles are ready-made so if you don't have a lathe you can still make the piece. Butt joints have been used throughout, so construction is not difficult. The basic tools needed are table saw, router, drill and saber saw. The raised panels were made on the table saw but the radial saw may also be used for this operation.

The lumber used is pine in both ¾" and 1⅛" thicknesses.

Begin construction with the base. Rip four pieces of ¾" stock to 4" width then cut the lengths as indicated. The ends are of equal length

This multi-purpose piece has space for telephone and phone books as well as storage below

The base cleats for the Gossip Bench are tacked in place with nails and then permanently screwed in place, as shown above. Next, the bottom frame ends are all sanded smooth and flush with a belt sander.

After the bottom frame is completely assembled, a router fitted a rabbeting bit is used to make a rabbet along the top rear edge the bottom frame to accept the plywood panels to be inset a bit la

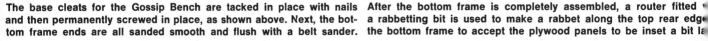

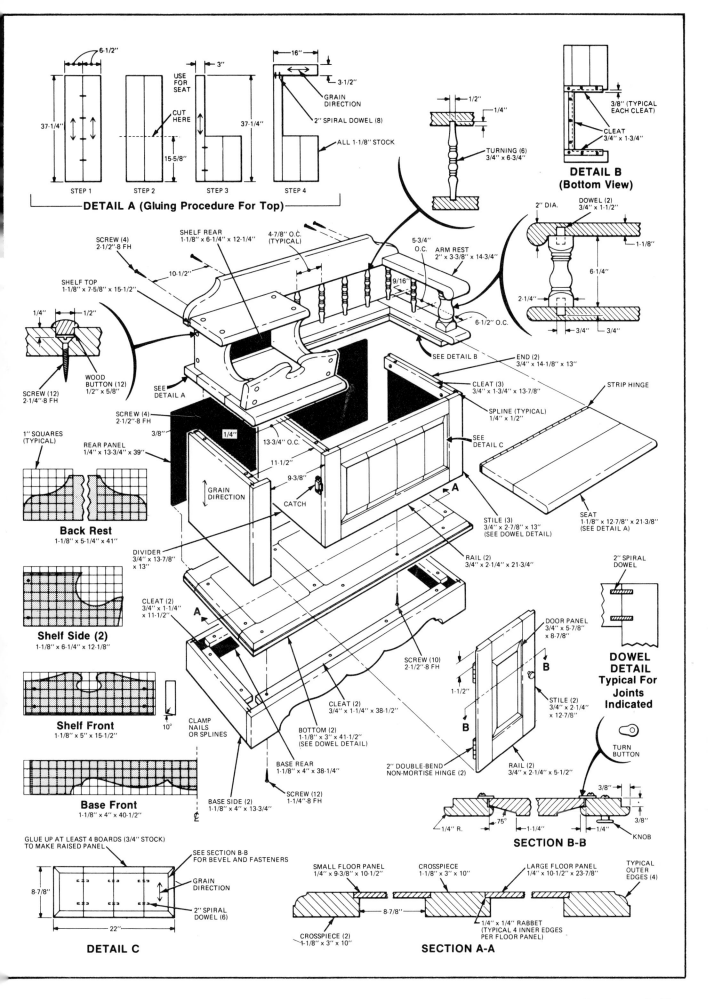

DETAIL A (Gluing Procedure For Top)

6-1/2"

37-1/4"

15-5/8"

STEP 1 STEP 2 STEP 3 STEP 4

USE FOR SEAT

CUT HERE

3"

16"

37-1/4"

3-1/2"

GRAIN DIRECTION

2" SPIRAL DOWEL (8)

ALL 1-1/8" STOCK

1/2"

1/4"

TURNING (6)
3/4" x 6-3/4"

**DETAIL B
(Bottom View)**

3/8" (TYPICAL EACH CLEAT)

CLEAT
3/4" x 1-3/4"

2" DIA.

DOWEL (2)
3/4" x 1-1/2"

1-1/8"

6-1/4"

2-1/4"

3/4" 3/4"

SCREW (4)
2-1/2"-8 FH

SHELF REAR
1-1/8" x 6-1/4" x 12-1/4"

4-7/8" O.C.
(TYPICAL)

5-3/4"
O.C.

ARM REST
2" x 3-3/8" x 14-3/4"

10-1/2"

SHELF TOP
1-1/8" x 7-5/8" x 15-1/2"

9/16"

SEE DETAIL B

6-1/2" O.C.

END (2)
3/4" x 14-1/8" x 13"

CLEAT (3)
3/4" x 1-3/4" x 13-7/8"

SPLINE (TYPICAL)
1/4" x 1/2"

SEE DETAIL C

STRIP HINGE

1/4" 1/2"

SCREW (12)
2-1/4"-8 FH

WOOD BUTTON (12)
1/2" x 5/8"

SEE DETAIL A

SCREW (4)
2-1/2"-8 FH

3/8"

1/4"

13-3/4" O.C.

11-1/2"

9-3/8"

CATCH

A

STILE (3)
3/4" x 2-7/8" x 13"
(SEE DOWEL DETAIL)

SEAT
1-1/8" x 12-7/8" x 21-3/8"
(SEE DETAIL A)

1" SQUARES
(TYPICAL)

REAR PANEL
1/4" x 13-3/4" x 39"

GRAIN DIRECTION

Back Rest
1-1/8" x 5-1/4" x 41"

DIVIDER
3/4" x 13-7/8"
x 13"

RAIL (2)
3/4" x 2-1/4" x 21-3/4"

2" SPIRAL
DOWEL

Shelf Side (2)
1-1/8" x 6-1/4" x 12-1/8"

A

CLEAT (2)
3/4" x 1-1/4"
x 11-1/2"

DOOR PANEL
3/4" x 5-7/8"
x 8-7/8"

B

**DOWEL
DETAIL
Typical For
Joints
Indicated**

Shelf Front
1-1/8" x 5" x 15-1/2"

10°

CLAMP
NAILS
OR SPLINES

SCREW (10)
2-1/2"-8 FH

1-1/2"

B

STILE (2)
3/4" x 2-1/4"
x 12-7/8"

TURN
BUTTON

CLEAT (2)
3/4" x 1-1/4" x 38-1/2"

BOTTOM (2)
1-1/8" x 3" x 41-1/2"
(SEE DOWEL DETAIL)

3/8"

3/8"

KNOB

Base Front
1-1/8" x 4" x 40-1/2"

BASE REAR
1-1/8" x 4" x 38-1/4"

BASE SIDE (2)
1-1/8" x 4" x 13-3/4"

SCREW (12)
1-1/4"-8 FH

2" DOUBLE-BEND
NON-MORTISE HINGE (2)

RAIL (2)
3/4" x 2-1/4" x 5-1/2"

1/4" R. 75° 1-1/4" 1/4"

SECTION B-B

GLUE UP AT LEAST 4 BOARDS (3/4" STOCK)
TO MAKE RAISED PANEL

SEE SECTION B-B
FOR BEVEL AND FASTENERS

GRAIN
DIRECTION

8-7/8"

2" SPIRAL
DOWEL (6)

22"

DETAIL C

SMALL FLOOR PANEL
1/4" x 9-3/8" x 10-1/2"

CROSSPIECE
1-1/8" x 3" x 10"

LARGE FLOOR PANEL
1/4" x 10-1/2" x 23-7/8"

TYPICAL
OUTER
EDGES (4)

8-7/8"

CROSSPIECE (2)
1-1/8" x 3" x 10"

1/4" x 1/4" RABBET
(TYPICAL 4 INNER EDGES
PER FLOOR PANEL)

SECTION A-A

Gossip Bench

but the front and rear sections are not. After the lengths are cut, check the ends for squareness then proceed to cut the splines. The kerf of the spline will depend on the spline used. You can use steel splines or ¹⁄₁₆", ⅛" or ¾" wood splines. The wood spline should be made of plywood. After the splines are made, cut the contour in the front piece then proceed to assemble the base. Apply a thin coat of glue to the end grain of the rear piece and the front ends of the side pieces. Allow the glue to dry (about 15 minutes) then recoat with glue and assemble. Follow this procedure for all end grain gluing. The splines should be fitted carefully. Check the assembly for squareness then clamp securely and set aside while the glue sets.

Prepare the four base cleats and bore the screw clearance holes. Be sure the vertical and horizontal holes are offset so the screws will clear.

Install the cleats to the upper inside edge of the base with glue and flat head screws.

The bottom frame is made next. Use flat lumber, and after cutting the five pieces to size, lay them on a flat surface to mark the location of the dowels. Use two dowels per joint. To prevent errors in assembly, mark each joint with matching numbers or letters, such as A-A, B-B, etc. Use ⅜" x 2" dowels and bore each hole about 1¹⁄₁₆" deep. Glue and clamp in the usual manner.

Use a router fitted with a rabbeting bit and make a rabbet along the top rear edge of the bottom frame to take the rear panel. Use it also to cut the clearance in the bottom frame for the ¼" panels. The router is also used to shape the end and front edges of the frame. Use a suitably shaped cutter and if necessary, you can use two or more cutters in several passes to achieve the desired shape.

The left and right end pieces and the divider are made by gluing two or three narrow boards (preferably three). This will prevent cupping. Be sure to reverse

Turned upside-down we see the bottom of the bench. Note how base is fastened to bottom frame: wood screws through cleats.

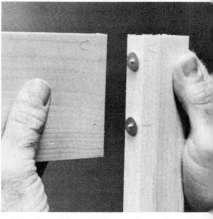

Dowel centers are used to transfer location of the holes from stile to rail. T will ensure an aligned fit between piec

Top cleats being installed. The horizontal member shown forms the great support. Strengthen top member joints with dowels.

Large clamps are used to keep the j tight while the glue sets. All glued ar must be clamped for a good, solid bo

LIST OF MATERIALS

Except where noted, all lumber used is pine.

Description	Size	Number of Pieces Required
Base front	¾"x4"x40½"	1
Base end	¾"x4"x14⅛"	2
Base rear	¾"x4"x39"	1
Base cleat	¾"x1¼"x11½"	2
Base cleat	¾"x1¼"x38½"	2
Bottom front/ rear	1⅛"x3"x41½"	2
Bottom cross-piece	1⅛"x3"x10"	3
End	¾"x14⅛"x13"	2
Divider	¾"x13⅞"x13"	1
Stile	¾"x2⅞"x13"	3
Rail	¾"x2⅞"x21¾"	2
Cleat	¾"x1¾"x13⅞"	3
Rear panel	¼"x9⅜"x10½" Plywood	1
Floor panel	¼"x10½"x23⅞" Plywood	1
Floor panel	¼"x13¾"x39" Plywood	1
Seat cleat, rear	¾"x1¾"x20⅞"	1
Seat cleat, side	¾"x1¾"x13⅞"	2
Top front	1⅛"x13"x37¼"	1
Top rear	1⅛"x3"x37¼"	1
Top end piece	1⅛"x3½"x16"	1
Back rest	1⅛"x5¼"x41"	1
Shelf rear	1⅛"x6¼"x12¼"	1
Shelf top	1⅛"x7¾"x15½"	1
Shelf end	1⅛"x6¼"x12¼"	2
Shelf front	1⅛"x5"x15½"	1
Arm rest	1⅛"x3⅜"x14¾"	1
Arm rest end	1⅛"x3⅜"x2"	1
Door stile	¾"x2¼"x12⅞"	2
Door rail	¾"x2¼"x5½"	2
Door panel	¾"x5⅞"x8⅞"	1
Seat panel	¾"x8⅞"x22"	1
Spline	¼"x½"x6 feet	
Spindle	¾"x6¾"	6
Post	2¼"x2¼"6¼"	1
Post dowel	¾"x1½"	2
Button	½"x⅝"	12
Dowel	⅜"x2"	52
Screws	1¼ – 8 FH	
Screws	2½ – 8 FH	
Turn button retainer		12
Non-mortise double bend hinge		2
Strip hinge	1"x21⅜"	1
Knob		1
Magnetic catch		1

nt frame is assembled to the end panel the above photo. Here you may use nes or finishing nails; countersink them.

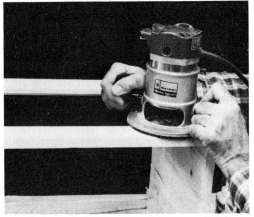

The opening in the front frame is rounded with an appropriate rounding bit or two or more cutters to achieve the desired shape.

The top cleats are completely pre-assembled and shaped before mounting onto frame. Rounding tool breaks sharp corners.

e the end piece is being attached to top frame with nails. Always use a :k to protect wood from hammer blows.

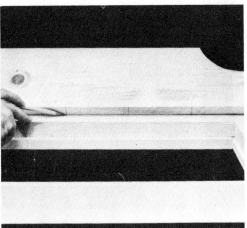

After aligning the two pieces, hole locations from the backrest are transferred to the rear of the top frame with pencil marks.

The curved end of the bench's armrest is easily cut on a band saw. If you don't have one, the alternative is to use a coping saw.

the annual rings in adjacent pieces. Use dowels or, if you have a shaper, you may want to use a glue joint instead. Of course you will require a glue joint cutter for this operation. Regardless of the joint used, be sure the glue line is straight and clean. The width of the boards should be made oversize so they can be trimmed after gluing. The divider is trimmed ¼" narrower than the end pieces. This will allow clearance for the rear panel and align it with rabbets cut in the end pieces.

Trim the three pieces to length and width required, then cut ¼" x ⅜" rabbets along the rear edge of the end pieces.

The front frame is made with doweled joints. Follow the same procedure used when making the bottom frame. After the glue has set, trim the height to match that of the end pieces then use the router to round off the face of the

opening. Rabbet the back edge to take the raised panel.

Sand the face of the front frame, then prepare to assemble it to the divider and end pieces. Use a spline or, if you do not want to go to the trouble, you can assemble with nails. In any event, use glue to assure a good tight joint. The front member for the left end panel is assembled similarly.

The front frame with side members can now be assembled to the bottom frame. Place the frame with sides onto the bottom piece. Align the rear of the divider and right side with the rear edge of the bottom piece. The right side should be set-in ⅞" from the edge of the bottom frame. Let the frame rest in this position then locate the left side piece with its front member. The left side should be set-in ⅞", as was the right end. The front edge of this piece should be in a straight line with the front frame.

If required, make the necessary adjustments, then gauge a light pencil line around the frame and side members. Draw the line inside and out. Now remove the frame pieces and bore screw clearance holes through the bottom frame. Center the holes between the lines and space them two over the side pieces and three along the front. After the holes are bored, place the vertical members on a flat surface upside down. Then lay the bottom frame (also upside down) onto the verticals. Align the pieces using the pencil marks as a guide. Mark the centers for the screw holes, bore pilot holes, then assemble with glue and screws. Use the glue sparingly to avoid it from squeezing out along the outer edges of the base. The assembly can now be fastened to the base by means of the cleats.

The top is made of 1⅛" stock. The procedure is a bit unusual be-

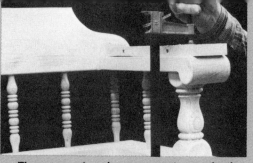

Pre-lathed spindles from your lumber shop are inserted into the ½" diameter holes to form the backrest. Spindles are glued in.

The arm rest and corner post are glued and tightly clamped. Note the use of waste stock under jaw prevents marring of wood.

The raised effect of the door panel is ccomplished with a table saw. A sharp bl and care is required for this operati

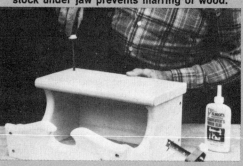

The door is hung with double-bend non-mortise hinges designed for cabinet doors. Note the retainer buttons on the door.

The telephone shelf is assembled separately with screws and glue and fastened to the bench top with screws from beneath.

Thorough sanding is very importa Curved parts are done by hand, a po sander is used on flat areas. Apply sta

Gossip Bench

cause of the hinged seat and grain direction in the right end piece. The sketch will clarify this.

First, two boards each 7½" wide and 38" long are doweled and glued, Fig. A. After the glue has set, trim both ends to 37¼" long. Then make one cut 15⅝" from the left end, to form the seat, fig. B. Allowing for the kerf cuts, the seat should measure 21⅜". If there is a discrepancy, trim it to this size.

Set the seat aside, and dowel and glue the remaining piece to the rear strip, Fig. C. Trim the "L"-shaped piece to size then cut a rabbet for the rear panel. Place the rabbet along the bottom rear edge. Add the right end piece, securing it with two dowels as indicated, Fig. D. The seat should now be trimmed in length so it has about ⅛" clearance at each end.

Cut and install the seat cleats along the ends and rear of the seat opening. Allow the cleats to project into the seat area ⅜" all around. The fastening cleats to hold the frame and side members to the top are now cut and installed. Secure the members with flat head screws.

The back rest is cut to size and shaped at the ends with a saber saw. The spindle spacing is care-

fully laid out along the bottom edge of the backrest. The marks are then transferred to the rear edge of the top frame. Bore the blind holes to take the spindle tenons. The hole diameter and depth will depend on the spindles used.

The arm rest is given thickness at the end by gluing a piece of stock as indicated. After gluing, it is rounded with a coping saw or band saw if one is available. A saber saw won't work because of the width of the piece.

The corner post should be on hand before you bore its mounting holes. When installed, the corner post and spindles should be exposed equally.

Cut the parts for the telephone holder from 1⅛" stock. Counterbore the ½" diameter button holes ¼" deep then bore the screw clearance holes clear through. Bevel the bottom edge of the front panel to an angle of 10 degrees. Do this on the table saw and be sure to do it before you shape the top edge.

When assembled, the telephone shelf is fastened to the bench top with screws driven from the underside of the top and through the lower edge of the backrest.

The door frame is doweled and glued, then the rabbets for the door frame and raised panel are cut with the router. The door frame

rabbets are cut only along the sides. The top and bottom edges of the door are not rabbetted.

The raised panels are made on the table saw by tilting the blade 15 degrees. Let the blade project 1⅜" and make a trial cut on scrap lumber before raising the panels. The panels should be made from glued-up stock to prevent them from cupping.

The panels are made with ⅛" clearance at the ends to allow for expansion. They are held without glue, using turn button retainers. These will hold the panels securely but permit movement due to weather conditions. (The panels will be shorter in cool dry weather and longer in hot humid weather.)

The door is fastened with double-bend non-mortise hinges. These are especially designed for cabinet doors and do not require mortising. The door catch is a novel magnetic type. It is fully adjustable and simply snaps into two predrilled holes in the divider.

Cut the strip hinge to size and install it with the top edge flush with the seat top. Install all other hardware at this time, then remove and sand the work thoroughly.

Finish the piece as desired. We used walnut stain and three top coats of lacquer. This was followed by a final application of rubbing compound.

Break-front China Cabinet

It measures 77½ in. x 33½ in. and is made in two separate sections for easy construction

PLEASE your wife by building this elegant piece of furniture to display her fine china. Made of birch lumber core, it has the appearance of a very expensive piece but it can be built for relatively little cost. Featured are a curved molded pediment, raised panels, glass shelves, and ample storage space in the base. The glass shelves are easily removed for washing and they allow light to penetrate and thus brighten up the chinaware.

The cabinet is made in two separate sections thus making it easier to build. The lower part is made first. Cut the sections to size, then rabbet the rear edges to accommodate the back panel and assemble using glue and finishing nails.

Nails are used only where they will be hidden by mouldings; otherwise dowels are used as in the doors. The one exception is the use of brads to attach the mouldings.

The rabbeting can be done by one of several methods. The shaper, jointer or router are fine. Another tool often used for rabbeting is the table saw. If the saw is used, make the vertical cut first. Since lumber core birch is used, it is not necessary to hide the edges. Simply sand them smooth.

Add the base pieces next. These are cut so the front piece overlaps the sides. Use dowels to join the pieces. You'll need clamps for this operation. Dowels should be the grooved type. If you use plain

dowels, crimp the edges with a pair of pliers to form grooves. This will make for a tighter joint.

The upper section of the china cabinet differs from the lower in at least two respects. The top features a graceful curved pediment, and the base piece (of the top) is notched at the sides. Cut the sections to size, and then cut the curved pediment. While we used a band saw, it can be done with a saber saw. Use poplar or other hardwood for this piece. The bottom piece is best notched on the table saw using the miter gauge to support the work.

Before assembling, sand the pediment to remove all saw marks then join the sections. A nail can be

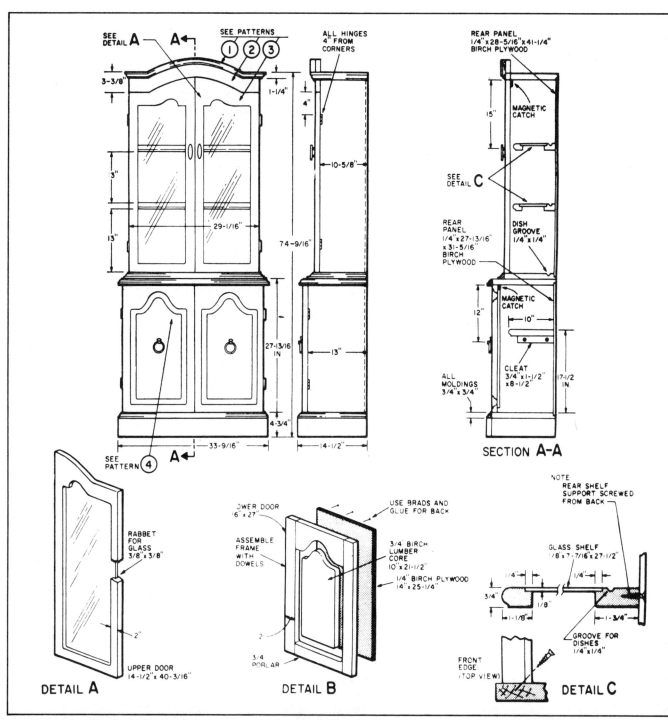

SEE DETAIL A

A

SEE PATTERNS
①②③

ALL HINGES
4" FROM
CORNERS

REAR PANEL
1/4"x 28-5/16"x 41-1/4"
BIRCH PLYWOOD

3-3/8"

1-1/4"

4"

15"

MAGNETIC
CATCH

13"

10-5/8"

SEE
DETAIL C

13"

29-1/16"

74-9/16"

REAR
PANEL
1/4"x 27-13/16"
x 31-5/16"
BIRCH
PLYWOOD

DISH
GROOVE
1/4"x 1/4"

MAGNETIC
CATCH

12"

10"

27-13/16
IN.

13"

CLEAT
3/4"x 1-1/2"
x 8-1/2"

17-1/2
IN.

4-3/4"

ALL
MOLDINGS
3/4"x 3/4"

33-9/16"

14-1/2"

SECTION A-A

SEE
PATTERN ④

A

RABBET
FOR
GLASS
3/8"x 3/8"

2"

UPPER DOOR
14-1/2"x 40-3/16"

DETAIL A

LOWER DOOR
16"x 27"

ASSEMBLE
FRAME
WITH
DOWELS

USE BRADS AND
GLUE FOR BACK

3/4 BIRCH
LUMBER
CORE
10"x 21-1/2"

1/4" BIRCH PLYWOOD
14"x 25-1/4"

2

3/4
POPLAR

DETAIL B

NOTE
REAR SHELF
SUPPORT SCREWED
FROM BACK

GLASS SHELF
1/8"x 7-7/16"x 27-1/2"

1/4"

1/4"

3/4"

1/8"

1-1/8"

1-3/4"

GROOVE FOR
DISHES
1/4"x 1/4"

FRONT
EDGE
(TOP VIEW)

DETAIL C

Curved pediment adds to the appearance of cabinet. Sand edges before assembly.

The router is used to cut the rabbets to accept the back panels. Use a square bit.

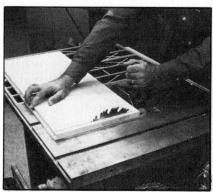

Notches for the bottom pieces are made on table saw. Stop and cut as shown here.

China Cabinet

BILL OF MATERIALS—CHINA CABINET

Lower Section

Quan.	Size and Description	Use
2	¾"x13¾"x32 1/16" birch	top and base
2	¾"x13⅛"x31⅞" birch	sides
1	¼"x27 13/16"x31 5/16" birch plywood	rear
2	¾"x1½"x8½" poplar	shelf cleats
1	¾"x10¼"x30 9/16" birch	shelf
2	¾"x4"x13¾" poplar	base sides
1	¾"x4"x33 9/16" poplar	base front
4	¾"x2"x27" poplar	door sides
4	¾"x2"x12" poplar	door top and bottom
2	¾"x10"x21½" birch	raised panel
2	¼"x14"x25¼" birch plywood	door back

Upper Section

Quan.	Size and Description	Use
1	¾"x10 11/16"x27 9/16" birch	top
1	¾"x11⅜"x29 1/16" birch	base
2	¾"x10⅝"x42" birch	sides
1	¼"x28 5/16"x41¼" birch plywood	rear
2	¾"x1¾"x27 9/16" poplar	rear shelf supports
2	¾"x1⅛"x27 9/16" poplar	front shelf supports
1	¾"x6"x29 1/16" poplar	pediment
1	¾"x1¼"x25" poplar	top molding
1	¾"x3¾"x31" poplar	curved molding
2	¾"x2"x37¾" poplar	outer door sides
2	¾"x2"x40 3/16" poplar	inner door sides
2	¾"x4¾"x10½" poplar	door top
2	¾"x2"x10½" poplar	door bottom
	¾"x182" poplar	molding for entire unit

Misc.—screws, glue, hinges, pulls, nails, brads, glass, dowels.

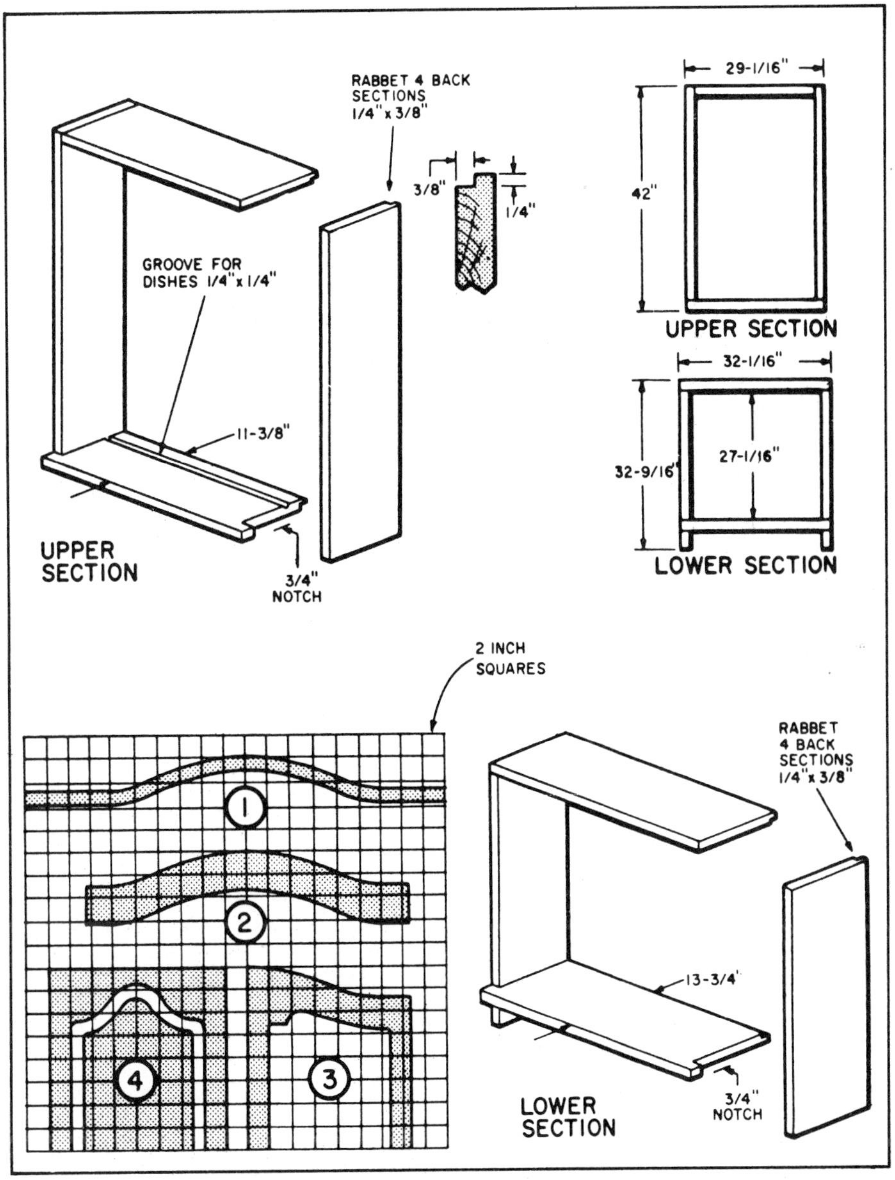

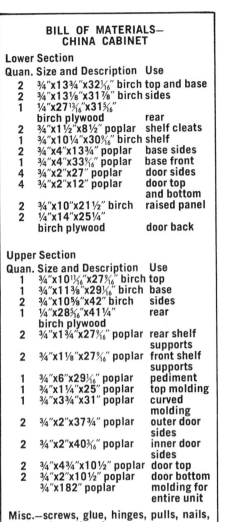

placed at the upper part of the pediment as the molding will conceal it. There is nothing wrong in using nails even where the heads will show, but it makes for a finer, better finished piece of furniture if they are hidden. Use clamps to hold the pieces while the glue sets. We have found that Weldwood white glue is fine for this type of work as it sets fast, is non-staining, and has a very strong glue line.

The curved pediment molding looks tricky but it is quite easy to make. Draw the outline of the molding onto a piece of poplar about 4-in. wide (see the accompanying drawing). Then, using router or shaper, cut the desired profile. The advantage of using the shaper is that a larger profile is possible than with the router. If the shaper is used, insert the starting pin to prevent kickback.

After the piece is shaped, cut the top line on the band saw, miter the corners, and mount it as shown in the photograph. Using the same profile cutter, make the rest of the moulding for the base and midsection.

The lower doors are made from poplar and consist of three sections: frame, raised panel, and backpiece. Cut the framing to size and assemble it with dowels. (A dowel drilling jig is handy as it assures alignment of the pieces.) The curved part of the upper rail is not cut until after the frame is glued. Should it be cut before gluing, clamping pressure may split the narrow part. When the glue has set, cut the curve and then rout the edges to suit using a beading or ogee bit.

After routing the inside edge, cut the rear panel to size and mount it with glue and brads. Next, cut the panel inserts to size and use the router (with the same bit) to shape the edges. Center the panel in the door frame and again assemble with brads and glue. As an aid to centering the panel, cut three scraps of wood, one inch wide, and use them as temporary spacers at the sides and bottom. This will automatically center the panel.

The upper doors are made in a similar manner, but they are left open to accept the glass. After cutting the decorative bead on the inner edge, cut the rabbet on the underside for the glass. If desired, a brass grille may also be used with the glass. The depth of the rabbet will be determined by the thickness of the glass and grille.

The lower shelf is supported by means of the two cleats shown in the photo. The wood strips to sup-port the glass shelves are held with screws, as indicated. The glass shelves should be of double strength glass. This is a little thicker than window glass and is available at glazier shops. The door glass can be single strength. Brass butt hinges are used for the doors. Cut full mortises in the side panels and mount the hinges carefully.

Sand the entire cabinet, then stain the desired shade. To complete the job, apply a suitable finish.

With suitable cutter head, cut molded edge on the shaper. Cut top curve after shaping.

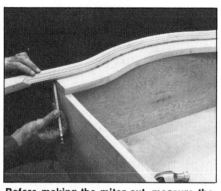

Before making the miter cut, measure the shaped piece carefully for the best fit.

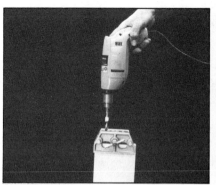

Dowling jig simplifies drilling holes in the door members. Tape on drill shows depth.

Spiral-grooved dowels are recommended —they hold better. Buy at lumber yards.

Door frame before assembly: Test parts for an accurate fit before you begin gluing.

The raised panels for front of doors are made by shaping the outline with a router.

Use one-inch wide strips of scrap wood to center the raised molded panel in the door.

The shaped molding is mitered, attached to edges. You can make molding yourself.

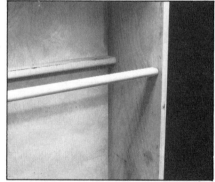

The shelf supports for glass shelves are rabbeted (¼" wide x ⅛" deep) for glass.

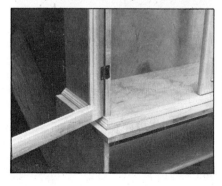

Hinges are fully mortised in the sides of cabinet. Brass butts will work well.

Corner detail showing construction of the door and the top piece.

TRESTLE TABLE and BENCHES

Another fine project styled in the Early American tradition, this sturdy furniture set will provide years of good service

THESE EARLY AMERICAN trestle table and bench sets are almost as popular today as they were in the Colonial days. These furniture pieces are rugged rather than fragile, and beautiful in their simplicity. If you shop around in the furniture stores, you will find that these pieces are available in both 1⅛-in. stock and in 2-in. stock. The heavier 2-in. stock is the better, although more expensive choice. Prices in the better furniture stores were five times higher for a set similar to the one constructed here. Ours costs more to build, due to the New York area's sky-high lumber prices. With shrewd shopping it can cost you considerably less elsewhere.

When buying your lumber, choose boards that are fairly flat and be sure to avoid any that have sap streaks. If possible try to avoid boards that are not edge dressed. Another thing to watch for are the knots. These should not be missing, loose or chipped. With a little patience you can purchase wood that will be easier to work with and most important, will help you to turn out a choice piece of furniture.

If the board edges are not dressed, (sides are rough and uneven), the first step must be to even them up. The best way to do this is to draw a line with a straight edge then trim freehand with a saber saw or on the band saw. Trim one edge only then rip both edges of the stock on the table saw. This will assure that they are square and parallel. The boards for the tops of the table and benches should be left a few inches oversize in length. This will be trimmed off later after the boards are glued up.

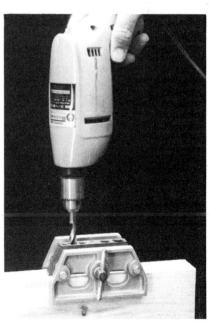

Dowels are used to join together the top sections. Using a jig like the one above is a good way to locate and align them.

The glue used on the top boards should be a water resistant type. When applying clamps, insert scrap wood between clamp and work which will prevent marring of the table top edges.

After the glue sets, plane the surface joints of the table top so that the top will be smooth and free of steps and bumps. The length may now be trimmed with a portable saw.

Draw the outline of the support ends on a 2-in. board. Be sure to include the top and bottom lines. Cut out scroll design with band saw and end trim with radial or portable saw.

Above are the two trestle ends. These have slots cut to hold the fake pegs. The dowels hold these ends to the table ends and simulate the old fashioned mortise and tenon with peg.

Dowels are used when glueing the top. This will make for a stronger joint and will greatly simplify the alignment of the boards when clamping. There are several methods of locating the dowels. A jig as shown is very good. Simply clamp it in place and drill through the dowel sized bushing. These are small metal plugs with pointed centers. They are easy to use and inexpensive.

Arrange boards so the grain and knot patterns are to your liking, then mark them accordingly. Drill the necessary holes then dab a little glue on one end of the fluted dowels and drive them home with a hammer. The glue used should be of the water resistant type, especially for the table top. The benches and table bases may be assembled with white glue. Before applying the glue have your gluing area set up so that you will not waste time later. Have clamps open to proper size and have clamp pres-

sure strips ready. The reason for this "ready-for-action" is that it will take considerable time to apply glue to all the edges of the boards and it is necessary to clamp the boards before the glue begins to set. Apply the glue with a small paint brush.

To prevent bowing of the top, the clamps should be alternated between top and bottom. After glue sets, plane the surface joints so the top will be smooth and free of steps or bumps. The length may now be trimmed with a portable saw. Use a strip of wood as a guide to assure a straight square cut.

The bench tops and ends are made of one-piece wide boards, however the table ends must be glued-up because of the width. Follow the same procedure used when making the top. If you can make the width with two boards, fine. If not, use as many boards as needed to make the width. Again make the length a little longer than the fin-

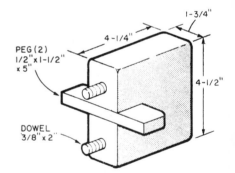

PEG (2)
1/2"x1-1/2"
x 5"

1-3/4"

4-1/4"

4-1/2"

DOWEL
3/8"x2"

TABLE TRESTLE END (2)

NOTE:
BE SURE DOWELS DO NOT INTERFERE WITH SCREWS HOLDING TRESTLES.

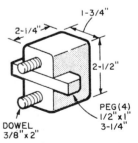

1-3/4"

2-1/4"

2-1/2"

PEG (4)
1/2"x1"
3-1/4"

DOWEL
3/8"x2"

BENCH TRESTLE END (4)

As shown above, a special router cutting bit used to round off the edges of the trestle supports for both the table and the benches.

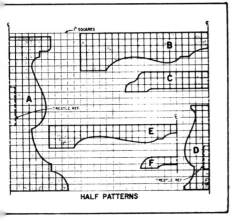

HALF PATTERNS

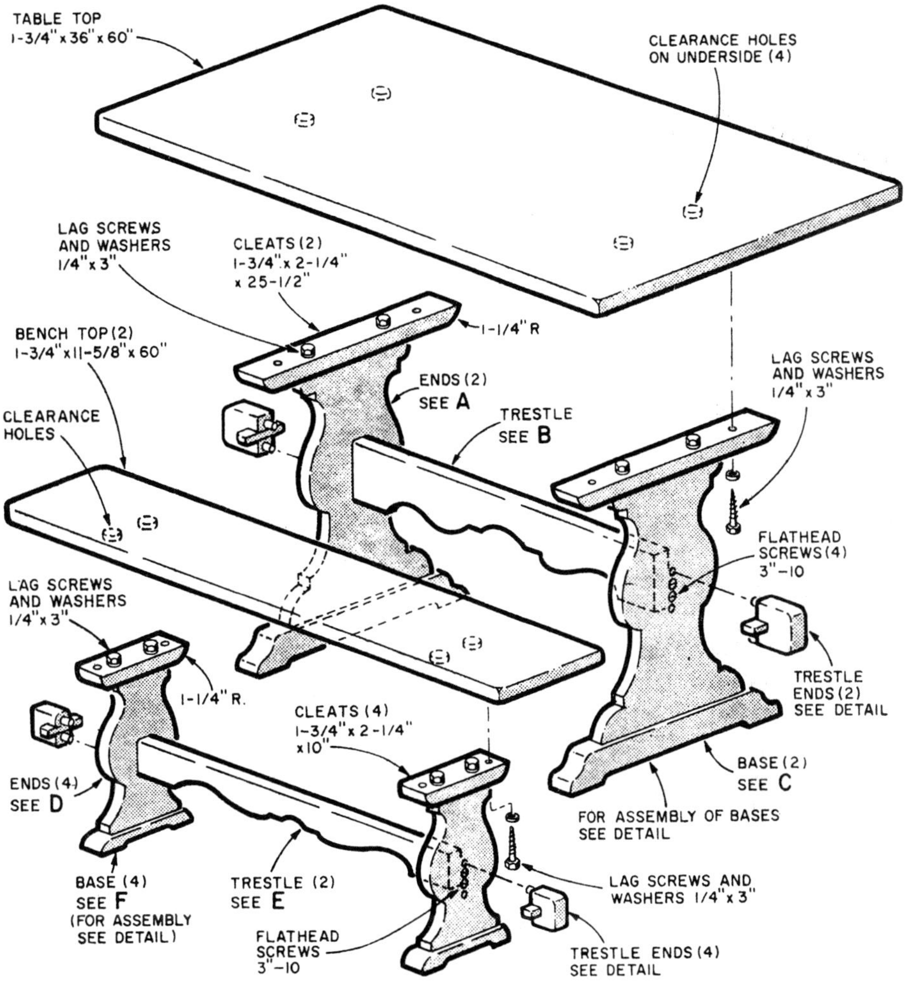

ished size to allow for trimming. Two inches in the overall should suffice.

After the glue has set, plane the joint. Then draw the outline of the design onto the board. Be sure to include the top and bottom lines. If you have a radial-arm saw trim the top and bottom lines, then cut the scroll design using a bandsaw or saber saw. After cutting, sand smooth, then round off all corners with a router.

The base and upper supports of the end panels are cut from 2-in. stock. After cutting and before assembling to the ends, sand smooth and round edges as done with the end sections. Assemble with glue and lag screws. Washers must be used under the lag screw heads.

The trestles are cut next. Note that these are "fakes" with ends added on. In olden days before glue and screws were so plentiful, cabinet makers had to use the mortise and tenon with peg to hold

their work together but thanks to progress, a difficult task becomes a very simple one.

Make up the ends as indicated, notching the "slot" for the peg. Add peg using glue and nails. Two dowels hold the end to the table. Use glue when assembling. The benches are assembled in a similar manner.

To give the table a worn colonial look, the corner edges are well rounded with a plane or spokeshave. If you desire you can add a few gouges along the ends and sides.

The type of finish is a matter of preference, but generally a dark walnut stain is most suitable for this type of furniture. There are numerous stains and finishes available. Choose one to your liking and be sure to test the color on a piece of scrap wood before applying to your work. Prepare the surface by giving a thorough sanding until all work is smooth.

BILL OF MATERIALS

Use	Description	No. Req.
Table Top	1¾"x36"x60" pine	1
Trestle	1¾"x5¾"x40" pine	1
Trestle ends	1¾"x4¼"x4½" pine	2
End	1¾"x18"x23½" pine	2
Base	2¼"x3⅛"x26¼" pine	2
Cleats	1¾"x2¼"x25½" pine	2
Pegs	½"x1½"x5" pine	2
Bench top	1¾"x11⅝"x60" pine	2
Trestle	1¾"x3½"x40" pine	2
Trestle ends	1¾"x2¼"x2½" pine	4
End	1¾"x7¾"x12⅞" pine	4
Base	1¾"x2¼"x11½" pine	4
Cleats	1¾"x2¼"x10" pine	4
Pegs	½"x1"x3¼" pine	4
Fluted dowels	⅜"x2"	24
Flat head screws	3"—10	12
Lag screws	¼"x3"	36
Washers		
Glue		

NOTE: All lumber indicated as 2" will measure approximately 1¾". Table and Bench Tops and Ends are listed above as one piece. These are glued up from appropriate number of pieces. Four inch or six inch pieces may be used.

Colonial Canopy Bed

This handsome pine bed is quite easy to build and will add a warmth to your bedroom that will never go out of style. It's a faithful reproduction of our Early American tradition of fine furniture

FASHIONS that are going out of style now will be back in years to come. This applies to clothes, hair styles—and furniture.

The pine canopy bed shown here is a case in point. Its dignified 18th Century quality is bound to please those who prefer traditional furniture to modern. And like so many other home workshop projects, it can be built for a fraction of what its commercial counterpart would cost.

The four corner posts are the biggest job, so start working on them first. Since it is impossible to turn these 63⅜-inch-long posts on the ordinary lathe, you will have to make them in two sections and then join the sections.

Rip the 1¾-inch pieces of pine to two-inch widths and 36-inch lengths for the upper and lower pieces. The bottom sections will be 32 inches long after they are turned, and the top sections 32⅔ inches. In addition you will have to make ⅞ x 2½-inch dowels which will join all of the top and bottom sections.

Mark and cut both the mortises and the holes for the dowels before going ahead and turning the post sections on the lathe. The holes in the bottom sections are 1½-inch deep, and in top sections one inch.

Before assembling the sections mortise the lower halves of the posts to take the headboard and footboard crosspieces, and the top of the two head posts for the headboard.

Next, turn the two sections of the footboard rail, also ripped from 1¾-inch stock. The rail has 1⅛-inch tenons at each end which fit into holes drilled in the posts, and where these two sections are joined each has a two-inch hole to accept half of the four-inch dowel. Glue turned rail and 8 x 37½-inch footboard into their respective holes and mortises.

Three boards glued together make the headboard. To be sure of strong joints where the three boards join, use ¼-inch plywood splines set in the grooves, which are cut with a router. Use a table saw to cut the tenons for the headboard.

When working on the bed rails an important concern is the strength of the metal brackets, since most commercial furniture has a more elaborate system for holding the bed rails in place. However, by using ¼ x 1¼-inch carriage bolts and drilling through both the bed rails and the brackets (after first determining their correct position), the problem can be solved.

The next step is to position the bed rails against the completed footboard and headboard and make a light outline of the brackets on the posts. This will mark the position of the steel pins that support the bed rails in each post. Cut the grooves in the posts for the brackets before assembling the headboard and footboard. Then drill holes in all four of the posts for the pins, drive the pins below the surface and plug the four holes with dowels.

Now begin working on the canopy frame. By laying out a full-size view on a piece of plywood, you will find it easier to do the actual construction. For each side piece use five separate cuts of wood, each three inches wide, splined together. Three of the crosspieces are 7/16 x 1¼-inch, but the two end ones are larger (1¼ x 1¼-inch) for added strength. The corners can be strengthened by gluing in corner blocks.

After completing the canopy turn to the last items, the finials. The large one is mounted in a ⅝-inch hole drilled into the block glued to the back center of the headboard (see drawing). The other four are smaller and fit over pins protruding from the posts.

Thoroughly sand all the pieces and spray an alcohol-base stain on the entire bed to give it that Early American look. Then apply a semi-gloss, alcohol-resistant-type lacquer. After the first coat has dried, lightly steel-wool the entire bed, and give it a final coat of clear lacquer.

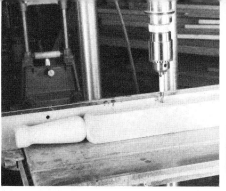

Corner posts represent biggest job, and are made in halves. Drill holes in lower halves for rail bracket pins.

Above is footboard of bed before top sections of corner posts are added. Rail is made in two sections.

After cutting bracket grooves in posts and joining halves, next cut post mortices for the headboard tenons.

Bed rails are secured to corner posts with brackets seated in grooves. Note that carriage bolts are used.

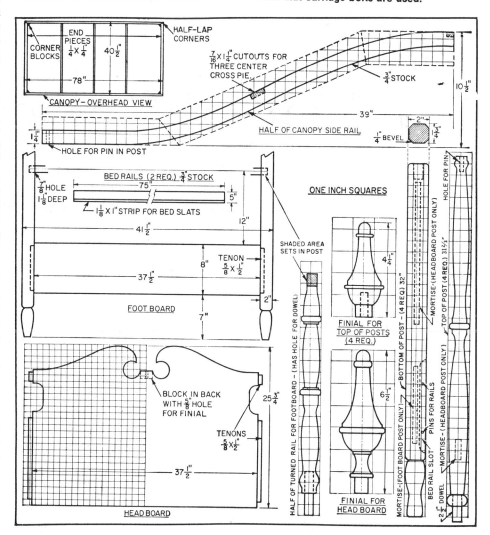

CLASSIC ROLLTOP DESK

**This classic oak rolltop desk, which is worth thousands, can be
built for around $200. What's more, it has storage space galore.**

THIS ELEGANT rolltop desk is designed along the lines of those
which were popular in the 19th century. Constructed of solid and veneer
oak, this functional masterpiece will
make a fine addition to any home.
The all-wood tambour operates with
ease in a graceful curve and when
retracted it disappears behind the
pigeonhole shelves. Two manuscript
boards are also included. These are
located at the top of each pedestal.

The desk has seven drawers. Two
of these are made to hold letter-size
folders. Additionally, the drawers
have aluminum rails to support hanging files. Center guides allow the
drawers to operate without binding.
Dust panels between each drawer
are included.

Happily, the value is tremendous. Materials will cost you
around $200; store bought the unit
would cost thousands.

Simple Construction. To simplify
construction, the top is made as a
separate unit which is fastened to the
pedestal base with lag screws. All
frame members are doweled for added
strength.

Begin construction by cutting all
parts to size as shown in the materials
list. The one-inch oak stock is $^{13}/_{16}$"
thick and all measurements are based
on this thickness. If you decide to
use pine for construction, be sure to
allow for the difference in thickness
of the pine, which is $^{3}/_{4}$".

Work on the base section first. Rip
the stiles and rails for the end frame

section to size, then trim them to
length. Locate the $^{3}/_{8}$" dowel holes
as indicated then drill to a depth of
1-$^{1}/_{16}$". The use of a dowel jig is recommended for this operation as accuracy is most imporant. After the
holes are drilled in one member, use
dowel centers to transfer the hole
locations to the mating parts.

When setting up the pieces for the
frames, note that the stiles at the rear
are wider than those at the front. To
avoid errors, identify each joint
matching numbers or letters, such
as A-A, B-B, etc.

After the frame members have
been drilled for the dowels, groove
them to take the $^{1}/_{4}$" plywood panels.
Note that the grooves are not centered; they are closer to the outside.

The ¼″ × ¼″ groove runs through from end to end on the short rail pieces, but they do not run through on the stiles. Instead, they stop ¼″ before the dowel holes. The grooves can be made with a router, shaper or table saw fitted with a dado blade.

After the pieces are grooved, assemble the frames temporarily. Do this by with loose fitting dowels, which can be made this way by sanding the dowels down slightly.

With the frames temporarily assembled, bead the edges using a router; or use a shaper if available. Bead (or round) only the exposed edges adjacent to the grooves. See detail drawing. When making the bead or round, be sure the pilot of the router cutter is riding on a solid surface. If necessary, place a filler strip into the groove while the cut is being made.

Disassemble the members, then proceed to drill the holes for the front frame assembly. These holes are made in the edge of the forward stiles. These holes will take dowels from the front frame. Likewise, the dowel holes for the rear apron and center frame are also made at this time. The holes should be drilled before the frame is assembled as it

is easier to handle the separate pieces rather than the assembled frame.

After the necessary holes have been drilled, cut the rabbets into the rear stiles for the rear panel. Note carefully into which pieces the rabbet is to be made.

The rear crosspieces, upper and lower, are drilled for dowels. Drill two holes in each and make them 1-½″ deep. This will allow the dowel to protrude ½″, which will later be inserted into the rear stiles. After the holes are made, use dowel centers to transfer the dowel hole centers to the stiles. Be sure that the rear edge

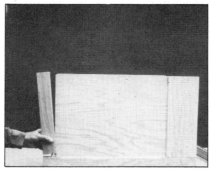

Glue is applied to all mating surfaces and parts are assembled. Do not glue the panel in place—it should float free.

of the crosspiece is flush with the rabbeted edge of the stile.

The pedestals, when completely assembled, will be fastened to the top with flat head screws.

Cut the four end panels from ¼″ oak plywood. Each piece is 5-½″ × 21-7⁄16″, but check this out carefully with the actual opening, as these pieces will be inserted into the grooves of the stiles and rails. The best way to check the size is to dry-assemble one end frame (without glue), then use two thin sticks telescoping them into the grooves. Tape the sticks so they won't move apart, then disassemble the frame and measure the overall length of the sticks. Do this for the length and width measurements. Cut the plywood panels accordingly. The size of the panels should be very close to the size called out in the bill of materials. However, because of possible discrepancies, it is best to check the size as outlined above.

Assembling the frame pieces must be done with care.

First, size the end grain surfaces of each of the rail pieces with glue. Simply thin some glue and brush well into the surface. You can apply glue directly from a squeeze bottle,

Cauls are used under jaws of clamps to protect the work. Be sure to wipe away any excess glue which squeezes out.

This is a view of the end frame after the dadoes have been cut. You can use various tools; a dado head will do the trick.

When you assemble the pedestal sections bar clamps are indispensable. The proper pressure must be applied.

Front frame stiles being notched on a table saw equipped with dado blade. You can dado four pieces in a single pass.

Dowel hole in desk must be accurately drilled. Here a disassembled dowel jig section is clamped to guide for drilling.

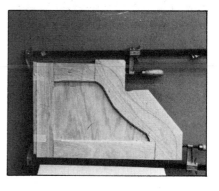

Rolltop frame being squared. Waste pieces are used so that pressure is applied evenly to all frame members.

ROLLTOP DESK

then brush out with a brush dipped in water.

Allow the side to dry then apply full-strength glue to one end of each dowel and insert into the holes drilled previously into each of the rail pieces. Be sure to use spiral or grooved dowels: These will allow air to escape thus preventing the wood from splitting. Assemble the pieces with the panel in place, then clamp securely. Be sure to use sticks under the clamp jaws to prevent damaging the stile edges.

The dadoes for the drawer dust frames are cut next. These can be made in several ways. You can use a router, table saw or radial arm saw. If the router is used, care must be taken to assure that all dadoes are parallel to each other and that they are in perfect alignment with each other. Clamp a wood guide to the work, positioning it so the dado will be in the proper location. When using the table saw, the fence is used to guide the work over the dado blade. If you use the radial arm saw, clamp stops to the fence for each set of dadoes to be cut. The width of the dado is ¾" and the depth is 3/16".

The frame pieces are made next. These are cut from ¾" pine. Make 16 long pieces and 16 short ones. The width should be exactly 2". After the pieces are cut, groove them to take the dust panels. Make the groove ¼" wide and ¼" deep. Center it along one edge of the long piece and on one edge and two ends of the short pieces. Use the router, table saw or shaper, to cut the grooves.

Make up 32 splines, each ¼" × ¼" 1-5/8", using plywood scraps. Next, cut the plywood panels and assemble one frame dry without glue to check the fit. If fit is okay, proceed to assemble the eight frames with glue. Clamp securely and be sure the frames are perfectly square before glue sets. A simple gluing jig can be made to clamp the assembly and assure squareness. One tapered piece is nailed to the baseboard. The free taper is wedged into place using a hammer. Make sure the baseboard is flat, otherwise the frames will set with a twist.

When the frames are glued, they can be assembled and glued to the pedestal sides. This assembly consists of the two pedestal sides, four

Template guide has been inserted into router base. Cutter projects distance of the groove depth, template thickness.

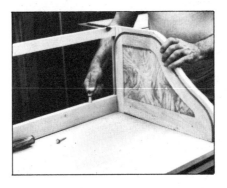

Here, crosspieces with end frames attached are being fastened to the top of the desk with lag screws for strength.

After tambour is in place, the corner guides are nailed to backboard to assure that all of the slats are correctly aligned.

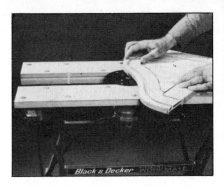

After the groove has been cut, the corners of the frame are rounded or beaded. Router makes an excellent tool for job.

In this view desk is partially completed. Tambour, drawers and other components can be fitted into the partially built unit.

View of the completed tambour. Tape used is removed so the tambour is lifted from the supporting backboard.

frames and two aprons. Prepare the necessary clamps and clamp sticks or cauls, which will protect the work surfaces. If you are working alone, you may want to tape the sticks into place so you can work the clamps unhindered.

Insert the dowels into the upper and lower aprons, then apply glue to all mating surfaces. If you are good at this, you can glue the entire pedestal at one time. Otherwise, apply glue to the dadoes on one side and coat only one edge of the frame pieces. If you decide on this method, install only one set of dowels to the aprons. It may help to install loose fitting dowels to the dry end of the

aprons. This will help in aligning the pieces. To make loose-fitting dowels, sand the surface of the dowels until the dowels fit the hole loosely, as was done previously. Clamp the assembly firmly and make sure that all pieces are in alignment. When the glue has set, remove the clamps, separate the dry side of the pedestal, apply glue as above, replace the loose dowels with regular dowels, then reclamp. Repeat this procedure for the second pedestal.

The pieces for the front frames are cut and notched as indicated. They are then assembled with glue to form the frame assembly. Transfer the holes made previously in the ped-

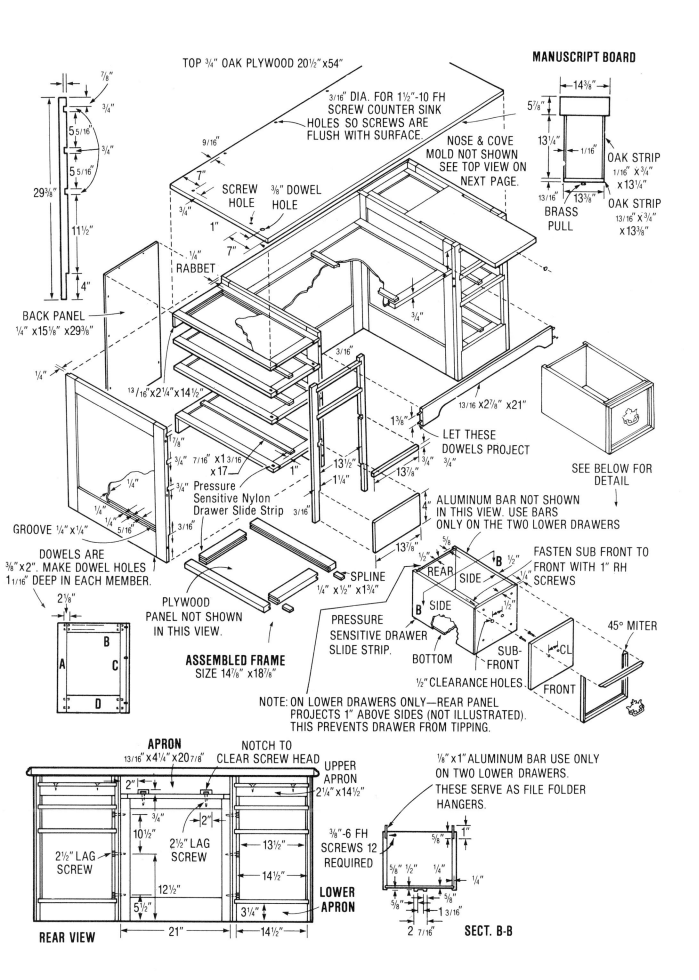

TOP ¾" OAK PLYWOOD 20½" x54"

MANUSCRIPT BOARD

3/16" DIA. FOR 1½"-10 FH SCREW COUNTER SINK HOLES SO SCREWS ARE FLUSH WITH SURFACE.

NOSE & COVE MOLD NOT SHOWN SEE TOP VIEW ON NEXT PAGE.

14⅜"
5⅞"
13¼"
1/16"

OAK STRIP 1/16" X ¾" x 13¼"

13/16" 13⅜"

BRASS PULL

OAK STRIP 13/16" X ¾" x 13⅜"

7/8"
¾"
5 5/16"
¾"
5 5/16"
29⅜"
11½"
4"

9/16"
7"
¾"

SCREW HOLE
⅜" DOWEL HOLE
1"
7"

¼"
RABBET

¾"

3/16"

BACK PANEL ¼" x15⅛" x29⅜"

¼"

13/16"x2¼"x14½"

LET THESE DOWELS PROJECT

13/16 x2⅞" x21"

1⅜"
¾" ¾"

1 7/8"
¾" 7/16" x1 3/16" x 17
¾"
1"
13½"
13⅞"

1¼"

SEE BELOW FOR DETAIL

ALUMINUM BAR NOT SHOWN IN THIS VIEW. USE BARS ONLY ON THE TWO LOWER DRAWERS

¼"
¼"
1/4" 5/16"
3/16"

Pressure Sensitive Nylon Drawer Slide Strip

4"

13⅞"

GROOVE ¼" x ¼"

DOWELS ARE ⅜" x 2". MAKE DOWEL HOLES 1 1/16" DEEP IN EACH MEMBER.

2⅛"

B
A   C
D

SPLINE ¼" X ½" X1¾"

PLYWOOD PANEL NOT SHOWN IN THIS VIEW.

ASSEMBLED FRAME SIZE 14⅞" x18⅞"

PRESSURE SENSITIVE DRAWER SLIDE STRIP.

5/8
½"   B ½"
REAR   ¼"
SIDE   ¼"
½"
SIDE
BOTTOM
B
SUB-FRONT
½" CLEARANCE HOLES.
FRONT

FASTEN SUB FRONT TO FRONT WITH 1" RH SCREWS

CL
45° MITER

NOTE: ON LOWER DRAWERS ONLY—REAR PANEL PROJECTS 1" ABOVE SIDES (NOT ILLUSTRATED). THIS PREVENTS DRAWER FROM TIPPING.

⅛" x1"ALUMINUM BAR USE ONLY ON TWO LOWER DRAWERS. THESE SERVE AS FILE FOLDER HANGERS.

APRON 13/16"x4¼"x20⅞"

NOTCH TO CLEAR SCREW HEAD

UPPER APRON 2¼" x14½"

2"
¾"
2"
10½"

2½" LAG SCREW

13½"

14½"

12½"
5½"

2½" LAG SCREW

3¼"

LOWER APRON

⅜"-6 FH SCREWS 12 REQUIRED

1"
5/8"
5/8" ½"   ¼"   ¼"
5/8"   5/8"
1 3/16"
2 7/16"

SECT. B-B

REAR VIEW

21"   14½"

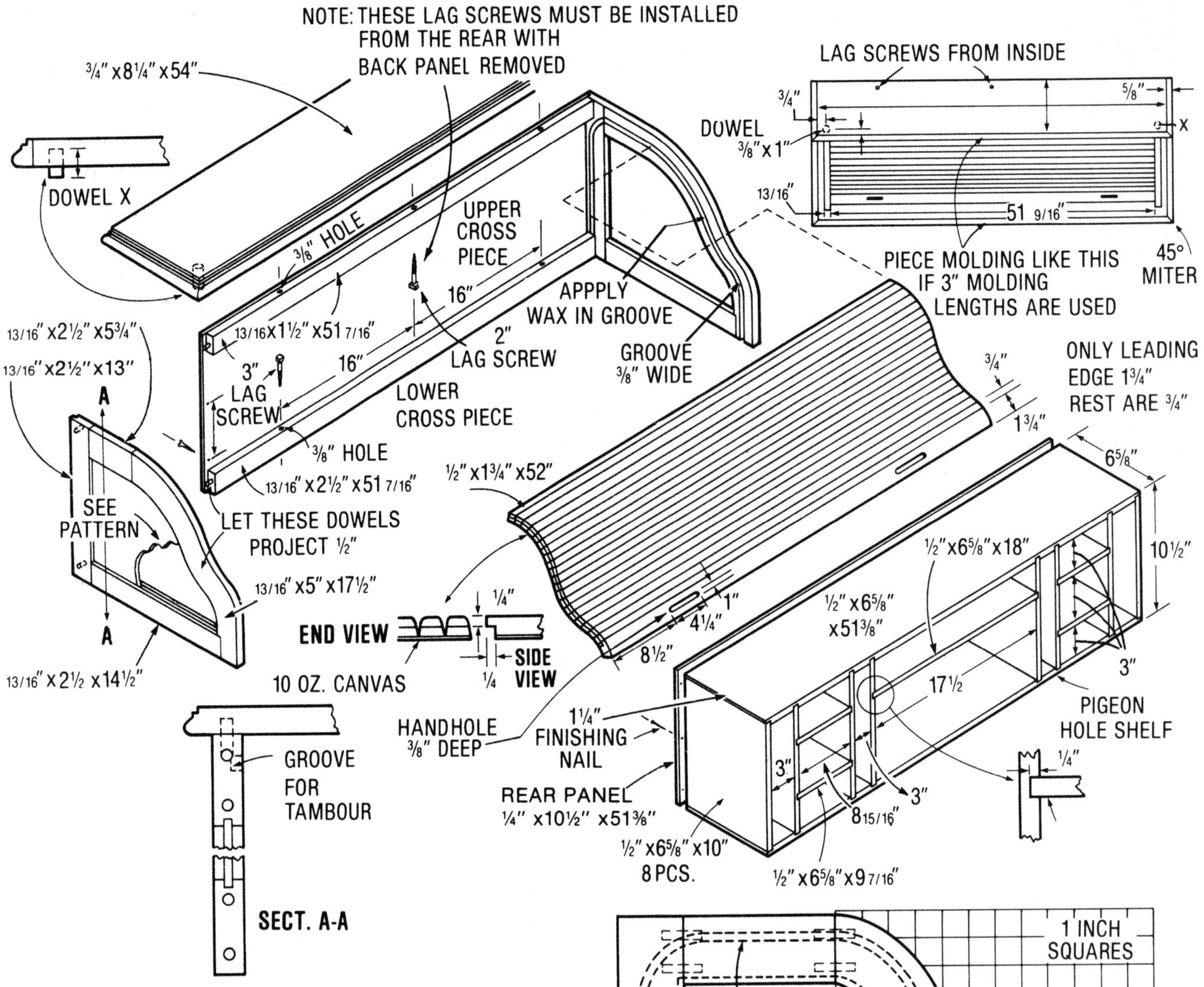
NOTE: THESE LAG SCREWS MUST BE INSTALLED FROM THE REAR WITH BACK PANEL REMOVED
3/4" x8 1/4" x54"
DOWEL X
3/8" HOLE
UPPER CROSS PIECE
16"
2"
LAG SCREW
13/16x1 1/2" x51 7/16"
3"
LAG SCREW
16"
LOWER CROSS PIECE
3/8" HOLE
13/16" x2 1/2" x51 7/16"
APPPLY WAX IN GROOVE
GROOVE 3/8" WIDE
13/16" x2 1/2" x5 3/4"
13/16" x2 1/2" x13"
A
SEE PATTERN
LET THESE DOWELS PROJECT 1/2"
13/16" x5" x17 1/2"
A
13/16" x2 1/2 x14 1/2"
LAG SCREWS FROM INSIDE
3/4"
DOWEL 3/8" x1"
5/8"
X
13/16"
51 9/16"
45° MITER
PIECE MOLDING LIKE THIS IF 3" MOLDING LENGTHS ARE USED
1/2" x1 3/4" x52"
3/4"
1 3/4"
ONLY LEADING EDGE 1 3/4" REST ARE 3/4"
6 5/8"
10 1/2"
1/2" x6 5/8" x18"
1/2" x6 5/8" x51 3/8"
1"
4 1/4"
8 1/2"
3"
PIGEON HOLE SHELF
17 1/2
1/4"
END VIEW
SIDE VIEW
1/4
10 OZ. CANVAS
HANDHOLE 3/8" DEEP
1 1/4" FINISHING NAIL
REAR PANEL 1/4" x10 1/2" x51 3/8"
3"
3"
8 15/16"
1/2" x6 5/8" x10" 8 PCS.
1/2" x6 5/8" x9 7/16"
GROOVE FOR TAMBOUR
SECT. A-A

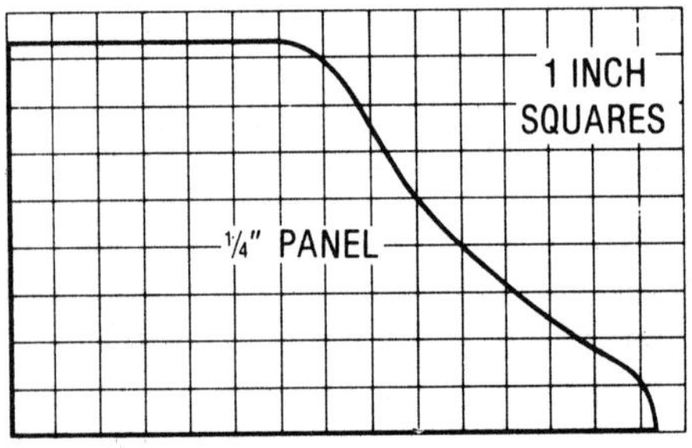
1 INCH SQUARES
1/4" PANEL

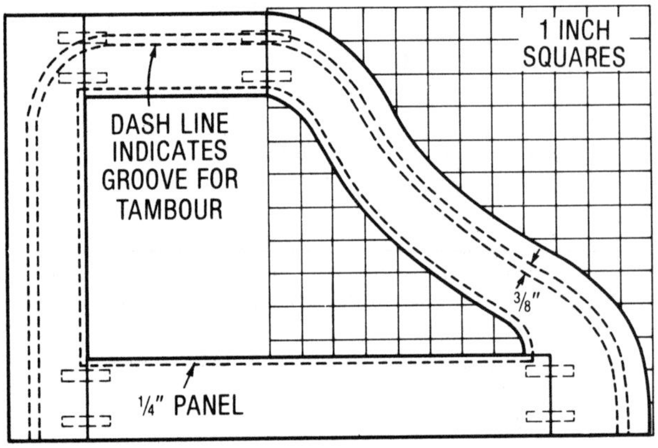
1 INCH SQUARES
DASH LINE INDICATES GROOVE FOR TAMBOUR
3/8"
1/4" PANEL

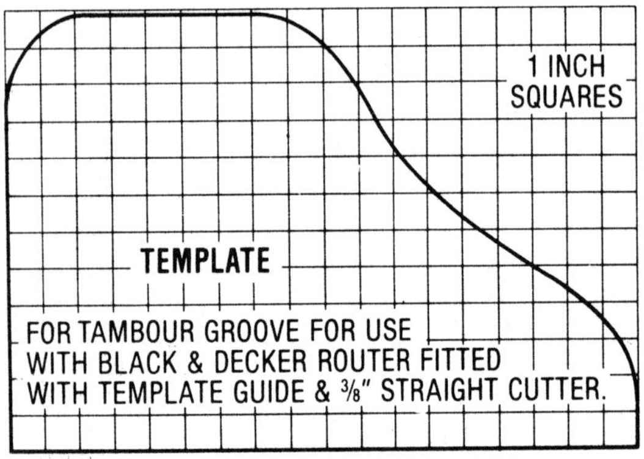
1 INCH SQUARES
TEMPLATE
FOR TAMBOUR GROOVE FOR USE WITH BLACK & DECKER ROUTER FITTED WITH TEMPLATE GUIDE & 3/8" STRAIGHT CUTTER.

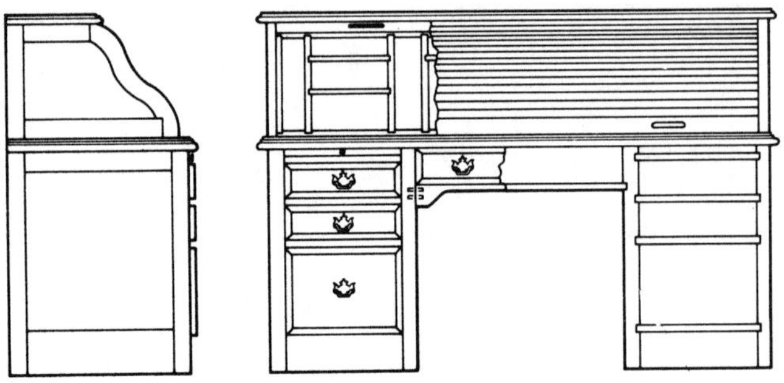

Pigeonhole compartments are assembled in sections. The top and the bottom boards of each will be added later.

Squeeze bottle makes a convenient way to apply adhesive; apply a wiggly bead. Here it is being used to secure the stile.

For good looks, miter nose and cove moldings. Here, they're being secured to drawer front. Use glue and brads for job.

Drawer members being clamped. Squareness is crucial in making drawers. Check for it before the adhesive sets. Take care.

After the stile is positioned squarely, use nails to secure it. Nails used in front of the stile should be driven in at angle.

Detail of the completed drawer. This is lower drawer for file folders. Folders can be hung in place with aluminum runners.

estals to the rear side of the front frames. Drill these holes ½" deep then apply glue and clamp the frames to the pedestals.

The pedestals are now joined to the rear center panel with lag screws. Be sure both pedestals are on a perfectly flat surface for this operation.

The drawers' sides, rear and sub-front are made of ½" poplar. The front panels are made of ¾" plywood. Drill the holes for the pulls, then assemble the drawers with glue and brads. Lay out the fronts so the grain patterns match pleasingly.

The panel effect in the drawer fronts is achieved by the use of nose and cove moldings. Miter the mold-

ings carefully and install with glue and brads.

The drawer slides are cut to size and grooved, then installed to the center bottom of each drawer. Accuracy is important here. The center guides are cut 1/16" narrower than the width of the groove in the slides. Install them to the top center of each dust frame. Be sure to set them back as indicated so they won't interfere with the drawer sub-fronts. Install with brads. Do not use glue at this time as it may be necessary to make some adjustments. Check the drawer fit. If okay, remove the guide, apply glue then reassemble in the same position.

Cut the manuscript boards as shown, using ¾" plywood. Face the sides and front with oak then lay into place.

Join Moldings. The top panel is cut from ¾" oak plywood. Use either lumber core or plywood core. Edge the ends and front with nose and cove molding Miter the corners as shown. Since most hardwood nose and cove moldings are available in 3-foot lengths, it will be necessary to join the molding along the front edge of the top. Use either a square butt joint or miter the butt as desired.

Fasten the top to the pedestals with flathead screws. Countersink the heads so they are flush with the surface. The screw heads will be concealed by the roll-top unit.

The roll-top consists of the end frames fastened to two crosspieces. A ¼" panel closes off the rear. The top panel is fastened with dowels.

Make the end frames as shown, then cut a groove for the tambour. This groove is ⅜" wide and 5/16" deep. It is placed ⅝" from the curved section of the end frame. The groove is cut with a router fitted with a template guide. The guide screws into the router base and allows the tool to follow a template, resulting in a perfectly cut groove. The template is made of hard-board, particleboard or other rigid material. It is cut with allowance made for the guide wall thickness and tool clearance. This allowance will differ from one manufacturer to another. You must determine the allowance for your particular tool. The template shown was made to work with a Black & Decker router. Fasten the template to the work with screws then proceed to cut the grooves.

After the grooves are cut, the corners of the end frames are rounded. Assemble the frames to the rear crosspieces, and set them aside.

Prepare the tambour by cutting the slats from ½" stock. You will have to use several boards for this. Cut the boards to length then, before ripping into narrow strips, rabbet the ends to fit into the groove of the end panels. Make the rabbet ¼" wide and ¼" deep. Now rip the boards into strips ¾" wide, except for the leading strip which should be 1-¾" wide.

After the strips are cut, bevel them to permit the tambour to ride the groove without binding. Do this on the table saw, with the blade set at an angle of 10-degrees.

ROLLTOP DESK

Cut 10-ounce duck (canvas) about 18" × 52". Tape it to a flat square board. Stretch the canvas smoothly and tape the ends down securely. The material is cut slightly oversize to allow for taping; the excess will be cut away later.

Apply contact cement to the cloth and back of each slat. Apply liberally, following manufacturer's instructions. Do not use flammable type contact cement indoors, as it can be dangerous. For indoor application, a nonflammable latex type cement is recommended.

Allow the cement to set about 45 minutes, then start to fasten the strips to the canvas. A side guide consisting of a piece of 1 × 2 lumber, is recommended to assure that the strips are installed straight and square. When all pieces are in place, trim the excess canvas with a knife or razor blade.

Move the assembled top frame forward so the grooves are off the desk top. This will allow you to install the tambour into the grooves. Roll the tambour up as far as it will go, then check it for fit. It will most likely be stiff which can be corrected later by rubbing the grooves with paraffin or candle wax. Don't use the wax before applying the finish, as this will cause problems with staining and topcoats.

The top unit is fastened to the desk top with lagscrews at the rear lower crosspiece. The forward ends are doweled as shown, thus allowing the upper unit to be removable. You will find it much easier to apply the stain, filler and topcoats with the parts disassembled. Make and install the pigeonholes next, as indicated.

For a good finish apply a paste wood filler to the oak. We use Golden Oak Filler. This fills and stains in one operation. After the filler, several coats of sanding sealer is applied, followed by three coats of lacquer. After the lacquer has dried for about a week, it should be rubbed with rubbing compound. The results will be well worth the effort.

BILL OF MATERIALS

Note: All measurements are given in inches.

Purpose	Size and Description		Quantity
Roll Top Unit			
Top	3/4 x 8 1/4 x 54	plywood	1
Crosspiece upper	13/16 x 1 1/2 x 51 7/16	poplar	1
Crosspiece lower	13/16 x 2 1/2 x 51 7/16	poplar	1
Rear panel	1/4 x 13 x 52 7/16	plywood	1
End frame rear	13/16 x 2 1/2 x 13	oak	2
End frame top	13/16 xx 2 1/2 x 5 3/4	oak	2
End frame front	13/16 x 5 x 17 1/2	oak	2
End frame bottom	13/16 x 2 1/2 x 14 1/2	oak	2
End panel	1/4 x 8 1/2 x 14	plywood	2
Tambour slat	1/2 x 3/4 x 52	oak	21
Tambour lead slat	1/2 x 1 3/4 x 52	oak	1
Pigeonhole Unit			
Top	1/2 x 6 5/8 x 51 3/8	oak	1
Bottom	1/2 x 6 5/8 x 51 3/8	oak	1
Shelf	1/2 x 6 5/8 x 18	oak	1
Shelf	1/2 x 6 5/8 x 9 7/16	oak	4
Panel	1/2 x 6 5/8 x 10	oak	8
Rear	1/4 x 10 1/2 x 51 3/8	plywood	1
Desk Unit			
Top	3/4 x 20 1/2 x 54	oak plywood	1
End frame stile rear	13/16 x 2 1/2 x 29 3/8	oak	4
End frame stile front	13/16 x 1 11/16 x 29 3/8	oak	4
End frame rail upper	13/16 x 2 1/2 x 15	oak	4
End frame rail lower	13/16 x 6 x 15	oak	4
End frame panel, rear	1/4 x 15 1/8 x 29 3/8	plywood	2
End frame apron, upper	13/16 x 2 1/4 x 14 1/2	oak	2
End frame apron, lower	13/16 x 3 1/4 x 14 1/2	oak	2
End frame panel	1/4 x 15 3/8 x 21 3/8	plywood	4
Dust frame side	3/4 x 2 x 18 7/8	pine	16
Dust frame front	3/4 x 2 x 10 7/8	pine	8
Dust frame rear	3/4 x 2 x 10 7/8	pine	8
Dust frame panel	1/4 x 11 1/4 x 15 3/8	plywood	8
Spline	1/4 x 1/2 x 1 3/4	plywood	36
Front frame stile	13/16 x 1 1/4 x 29 3/8	oak	4
Front frame rail	3/4 x 13/16 x 13 7/8	oak	6
Front frame rail, lower	13/16 x 4 x 13 7/8	oak	2
Manuscript board	3/4 x 14 3/8 x 19 1/8	plywood	2
Manuscript trim	1/16 x 3/4 x 13 1/4	oak	4
Manuscript front edge	3/4 x 13/16 x 13 3/8	oak	2
Desk Unit Center			
Rear apron	13/16 x 4 1/4 x 20 7/8	oak	1
Rear frame, upper rail	13/16 x 2 1/2 x 16	oak	1
Rear frame, lower rail	13/16 x 6 x 16	oak	1
Rear frame stile	13/16 x 2 1/2 x 24 1/4	oak	2
Rear frame panel	1/4 x 16 3/8 x 24 5/8	plywood	1
Dust frame side	3/4 x 2 x 18 7/8	pine	2
Dust frame front	3/4 x 2 x 17 5/8	pine	1
Dust frame rear	3/4 x 2 x 17 5/8	pine	1
Dust frame panel	1/4 x 15 7/16 x 17 7/8	plywood	1
Front apron	13/16 x 2 7/8 x 21	oak	1
Drawers			
Upper Drawer			
Side	1/2 x 5 x 18	poplar	8
Rear	1/2 x 4 1/8 x 12 1/2	poplar	4
Sub-front	1/2 x 5 x 12 1/2	poplar	4
Front	3/4 x 5 3/16 x 13 7/16	plywood	4
Bottom	1/4 x 12 1/2 x 17	plywood	4
Lower Drawer			
Side	1/2 x 10 3/8 x 18	poplar	4
Rear	1/2 x 10 1/2 x 12 1/2	poplar	2
Sub-front	1/2 x 10 3/8 x 12 1/2	poplar	2
Front	3/4 x 11 3/8 x 13 7/16	plywood	2
Bottom	1/4 x 12 1/2 x 17	plywood	2
Center Drawer			
Side	1/2 x 4 x 17 1/2	poplar	2
Rear	1/2 x 3 1/8 x 20	poplar	1
Sub-front	1/2 x 4 x 20	poplar	1
Front	3/4 x 4 1/8 x 20 15/16	oak plywood	1
Bottom	1/4 x 16 1/2 x 20	plywood	1
Drawer Slide	1/2 x 2 7/16 x 16 3/4		7
Drawer Guide	7/16 x 1 3/16 x 17		7
Other Materials			
Nose & Cove molding	5/8 x 3/4	oak	45 ft.
Lag Screws	5/16 x 3		3
Lag Screws	5/16 x 2 1/2		8
Lag Screws	5/16 x 2		3
Screws	3/8 – 6 FH		12
Screws	1" – 8 RH		28
Screws	1 1/2" – 10 FH		16
Nail, finishing	1 1/4"		1 box
Aluminum bar	1/8 x 1 x 16 1/4		2
Chippendale pull	3" centers		8
Brass knob			2
Drawer Slide Strip, nylon			28
Dowels	3/8 x 2		70
Canvas	10 oz., 18" x 52"		1
Nylon Slide Strip			28

Sawhorse-Tool Box

A two-in-one project for craftsmen that combines a lot of use into a little space—this deluxe sawhorse includes a carry-about tool box, handy storage space and an extra sawhorse

THIS is not just a sawhorse, but a workshop which will save you many steps around the house because it can be easily moved from one job to another. Hand tools can be stored in the space beneath the top, while bins located between the legs hold small portable electric tools, such as a drill, sander and saw. A shelf holds a carry-all tool box for additional storage.

The tool box also serves as a base into which a rack may be inserted to make a support the same height as the sawhorse. When used in conjunction with the sawhorse, this rack is useful for supporting full sheets of plywood or long lengths of lumber when sawing them to smaller pieces, or for dressing down doors.

Building the sawhorse. To insure the proper fitting of the parts for the sawhorse, pay particular attention to the compound angles to which these parts are cut. Unlike making right angle ripping or crosscuts on a circular saw, the compound angles used here require settings of either 4° or 15°, or a combination of both.

While the circular saw simplifies the cutting of these compound angles, satisfactory results can be obtained with a crosscut handsaw. The blade of a T-bevel, set to the proper degree with the aid of a protractor, is used as a visual guide for determining the required slant to which the saw is held. The handle of the T-bevel is positioned on the work at a 90° angle from the cutting line. The 4° and 15° bevels on the edges can also be made with a hand plane. Retail lumberyards will rip stock to the widths designated in the Materials List. Unless

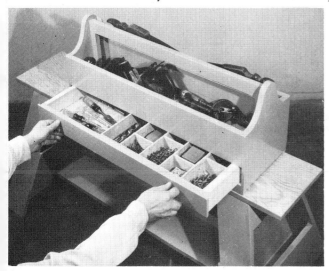

The drawer is partitioned to hold the small workshop necessities such as screwdrivers, chisels, bits and assorted nails and screws. To protect the cutting edges of the chisels, install some special brackets or clips in the larger compartment.

Convenient bins at each end can hold an assortment of portable electric tools such as a drill, sander and saw. Hand tools can be stored in space below top—their weight prevents the sawhorse from creeping when planing boards held in vise.

Sawhorse-Tool Box

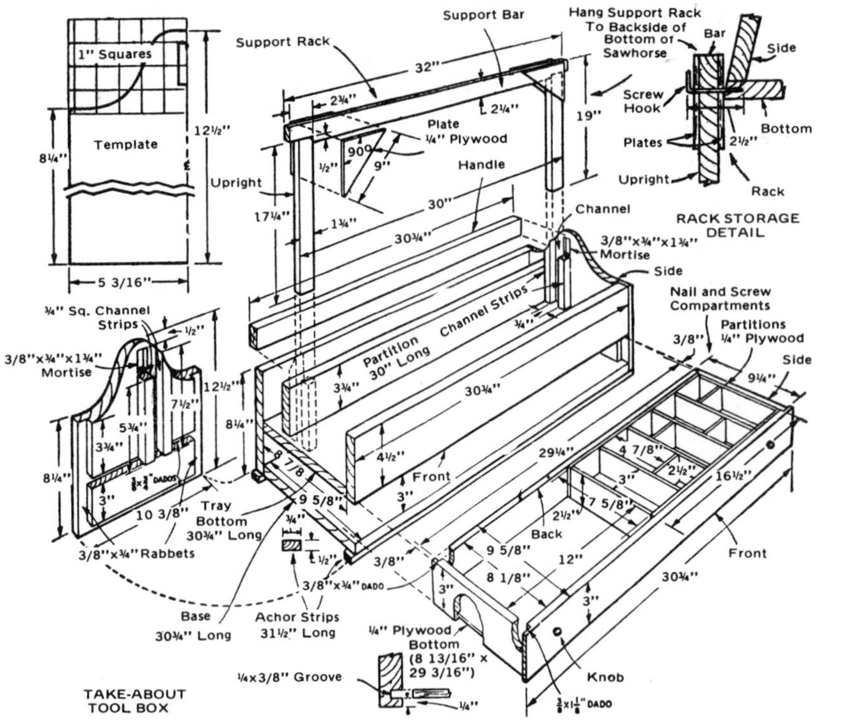
1" Squares
Template
8¼"
12½"
Upright
5 3/16"
Support Rack
Support Bar
32"
2¾"
2¼"
Plate
¼" Plywood
90°
9"
½"
Handle
30"
17¼"
1¾"
30¾"
19"
Hang Support Rack
To Backside of
Bottom of
Sawhorse
Screw
Hook
Bar
Side
Plates
Bottom
2½"
Upright
Rack
RACK STORAGE
DETAIL
Channel
3/8"x¾"x1¾"
Mortise
Side
Nail and Screw
Compartments
Partitions
¼" Plywood
Side
¾" Sq. Channel
Strips
½"
3/8"x¾"x1¾"
Mortise
12½"
7½"
8¼"
5¾"
3¾"
8¼"
3"
10 3/8"
Tray
Bottom
30¾" Long
3/8"x¾" Rabbets
Partition
30" Long
Channel Strips
¾"
3¾"
30¾"
4½"
Front
3"
8 7/8
9 5/8"
¾"
½"
3/8"
3/8"x¾" DADO
Base
30¾" Long
Achor Strips
31½" Long
3/8"
9¼"
29¼"
4 7/8"
2½"
16½"
3"
7 5/8"
2½"
Back
9 5/8"
12"
8 1/8"
3"
3"
30¾"
Front
¼" Plywood
Bottom
(8 13/16" x
29 3/16")
¼x3/8" Groove
¼"
Knob
TAKE-ABOUT
TOOL BOX

MATERIALS LIST—Tool Box

No. Req.	Size and Description	Use
2	¾" 10⅜"x12½" pine	box sides
1	¾" 8⅞"x30¾" pine	box tray bottom
1	¾" 1¾"x30¾" hardwood	box handle
1	¾" 9⅝"x30¾" pine	box base
1	¾" 4½"x30¾" pine	box front
1	¾" 8¼"x30¾" pine	box back
2	¾" ¾"x5¾" pine	box channel strips
2	¾" ¾"x7½" pine	box channel strips
1	¾" 3¾"x30" pine	box partition
2	¾" ½"x31½" pine	anchor strips
1	¾" 3"x30¾" pine	drawer front
2	¾" 3"x9¼" pine	drawer sides
1	¼" 8 13/16"x29 3/16" plywood	drawer bottom
1	¾" 3"x29¼" pine	drawer back
6	¼" 2½"x7⅝" plywood	nail compartment ends and partitions
2	¼" 2½"x16½" plywood	nail compartment front and back
4	¼" 2½"x3" plywood	nail compartment partitions
2	¾" 1¾"x17¼" pine	support rack uprights
1	¾" 2¼"x32" hardwood	rack support bar
4	¼" 4½"x9" plywood	support rack plates

NOTE: Also required are knobs, screw hooks and finishing materials.

otherwise specified, all ¾-inch stock members for the sawhorse and tool box are joined with coated 8*d* common wire nails, and an adhesive applied to the joints.

Cut all of the pieces for the sawhorse from the dimensions given in the drawing and start assembling them by nailing the compartment sides and ends together to form a frame. Add the compartment bottom which is beveled 15° on all four edges. The four legs are sawed alike in size and shape up to the point when the rail notches are made. Make duplicate notches on the legs. When notching the legs, the cutting angles of the first set of legs are the reverse of those used on the second set. Attach the legs to the compartment sides, cutting off or clinching over any nails which protrude on the inside. Add the rails next, then install the shelf.

Fasten the bin bottom fillers to the rails with 6*d* nails and nail the bin backing to the legs with 4*d* nails. Before installing the hooks, eyes and chain to the top, give the wood (except for the working surface of the top) an enamel undercoating. When dry, smooth with steel wool and apply two coats of an interior enamel. Give the unpainted portion of the top two coat of boiled linseed oil.

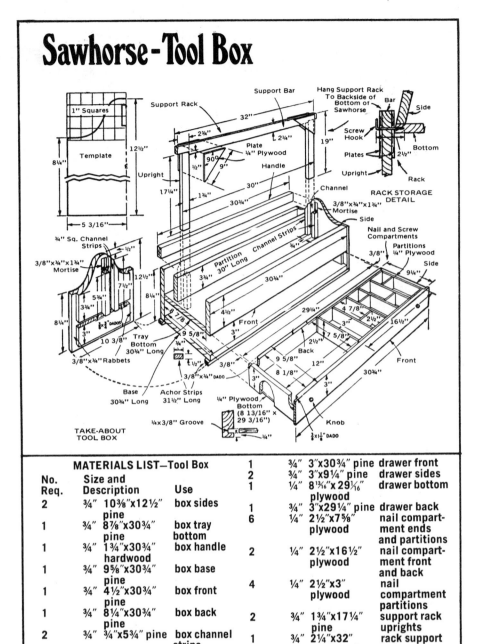

Take-about tool box and racks Scribe the cutting lines for the contoured portions of the side or end with the aid of a cardboard half template, as shown in the drawing After cutting the dadoes, rabbet and handle mortises, join the side to the tray bottom and handle Next add the base, front and back

When installing the channe strips, check their spacing so tha the ¾-inch stock, used for the up rights of the supporting rack, slide freely in the channels thus formed Shape the upper ends of the longe channel strips to conform to th contoured portion of the sides. Th partition, which forms a compar ment for handsaws, rests again the channel strips and is anchore with 8*d* finishing nails driven i through the sides. Anchor strip nailed to the bottom prevent th tool box from sliding off the shel

Cut the end dadoes on the draw er front and sides and then mak the ¼ x ⅜-inch grooves in thes

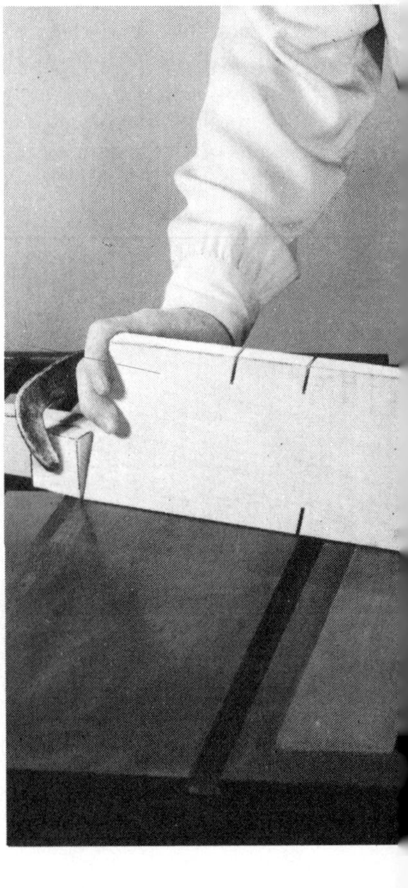

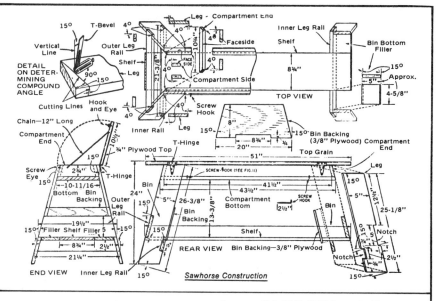

DETAIL ON DETERMINING COMPOUND ANGLE

Vertical Line
T-Bevel
Cutting Lines
Hook and Eye
Chain—12" Long
Compartment End
Screw Eye
T-Hinge
Bottom Bin Backing
Outer Leg Rail
Filler Shelf Filler
END VIEW
Inner Leg Rail

Leg - Compartment End
Inner Leg Rail
Shelf
Bin Bottom Filler
Faceside
Outer Leg Rail
Shelf
Leg
FACE SIDE
Compartment Side
Inner Rail
Screw Hook
TOP VIEW
Bin Backing (3/8" Plywood) Compartment End
Top Grain
Screw Hook
Compartment Bottom
Bin Backing
Bin
Leg
Notch
Shelf
3/4" Plywood Top
REAR VIEW
Bin Backing—3/8" Plywood
Notch

Sawhorse Construction

	MATERIALS LIST—Sawhorse					
No. Req.	Size and Description	Use	1	3/4"	8¾"x51¼" pine	shelf
2	3/4" 3"x41½" pine	compartment sides	4	3/4"	4¾"x5⅛" pine	bottom bin fillers
2	3/4" 3"x10¼" pine	compartment ends	2	3/8"	8"x20" plywood	bin backing
1	3/4" 10¹¹⁄₁₆"x43½" pine	compartment bottom	1	3/4"	10½"x51" plywood	top
4	3/4" 5⅛"x26½" pine	legs	1		24" link or safety chain	
2	3/4" 2¾"x21¼" pine	inner leg stretchers	as needed	#7	¾" round head screws	
2	3/4" 5¼"x19½" pine	outer leg stretchers				

NOTE: Also required are T-hinges, hooks and eyes, glue, coated wire nails, finishing nails, lath nails, enamel, enamel undercoater and boiled linseed oil.

members (including the back) for the bottom. Join the sides to the front, slide the bottom in the grooves and add the back. Cross-nail with 6d finishing nails. Assemble the parts for the nail and screw compartments with ¾-inch brads and glue before installing in the drawer. Anchor the unit in place with brads and add the knobs to complete the drawer.

The support rack is made of a hardwood bar (preferably oak) and two uprights. Drive 10d finishing nails through the bar and into the uprights. Coat the plywood plates with glue and attach them to the rack with lath nails. When not in use, the rack can be hung on the sawhorse.

Recess the heads of the finishing nails and paint the box, except the sides, back, bottom and inside of the drawer, with an enamel undercoater. When dry, fill the nail holes with wood putty and smooth the surface with steel wool. Apply two coats of interior enamel of the same shade as you used on the sawhorse. As with the sawhorse, coat the unpainted surfaces with boiled linseed oil.

When assembling the tool box, left, mount the tray and the handle to one of the sides, then add the other side. Below, making the lateral cuts in the legs for the rail notches. Note the stop block clamped to the 2-inch high fence which in turn, is fastened to the miter gauge extension.

Child's Footlocker

A lumber-plywood combination and the use of ordinary hand tools simplifies the building of this handy furniture piece

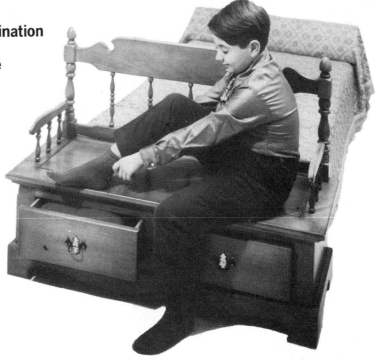

Y ou don't need a lathe or other specialized tools to make this attractive child's footlocker. The spindles are assembled from stock items and, except for a few scroll cuts made with a saber saw, every bit of the construction can be done with ordinary hand tools.

The combination of solid lumber and plywood used in construction eliminates the problems that often confront the home craftsman. Wide flat boards are hard to come by in solid lumber except perhaps for knotty pine which is not suitable in this case. Our solution was to use plywood which is available in many types of wood and in several thicknesses. Birch was selected for the child's footlocker illustrated as it has a lovely grain and is smooth, close grained, and easy to finish.

The problem with using plywood, however, is the edge grain which is unsightly and difficult to finish. We decided to use solid lumber to edge the plywood thus eliminating the second problem. A good wood to use for edge work is poplar. It, too, has an excellent grain pattern, is close grained and is easy to work.

Assembly is accomplished with

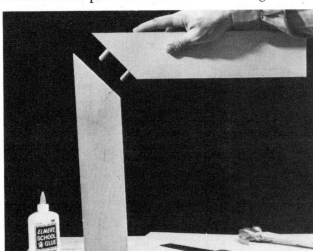

The frame of the footlocker seat is cut from ¾-in. poplar. First miter the corners, then assemble with the aid of both dowels and glue, as pictured in this photograph.

As shown here, nails and dowels are used to attach th poplar frame to the birch plywood seat. If they are readi ly available, clamps will prove to be very helpful, also

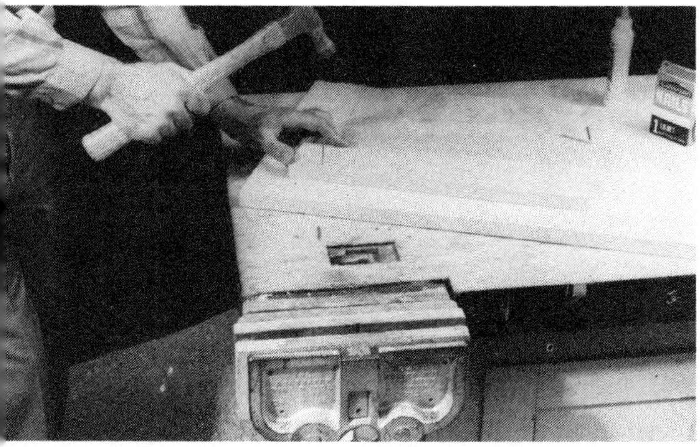

The cleats are attached to the underside of the footlocker seat with the aid of both nails and glue. Note the dimensions for same as listed in the adjacent Bill of Materials.

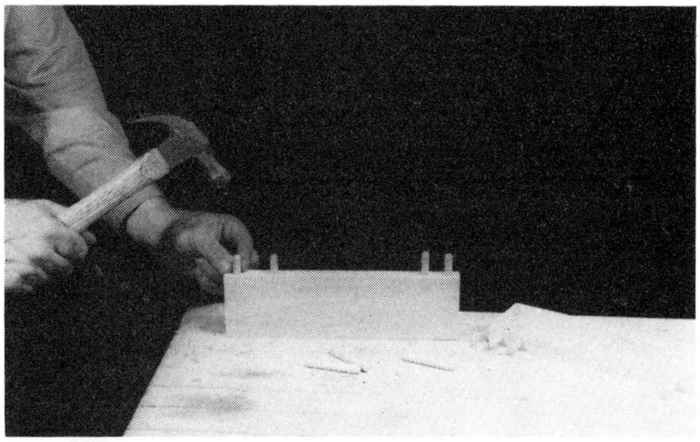

The poplar front framing is doweled as pictured here. Before beginning the assembly, lay all the pieces on a flat table and sand the joints until they are flat and smooth.

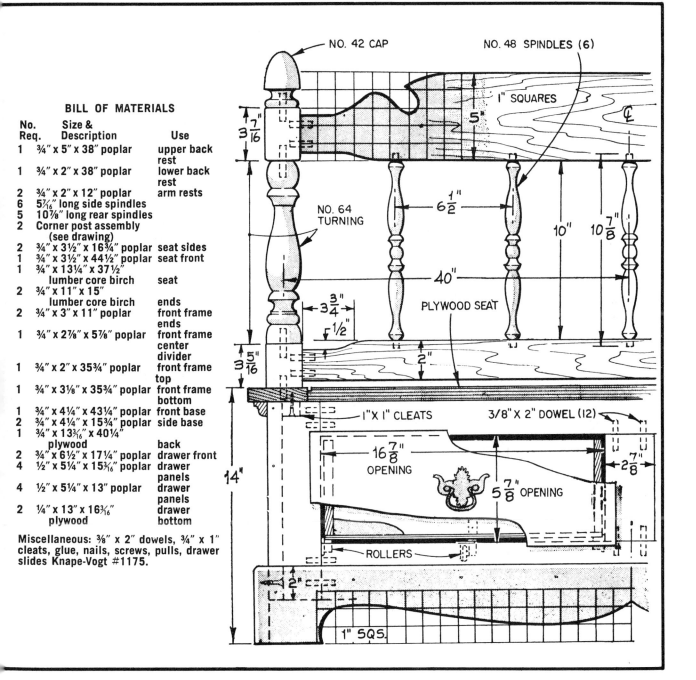

BILL OF MATERIALS

No. Req.	Size & Description	Use
1	¾" x 5" x 38" poplar	upper back rest
1	¾" x 2" x 38" poplar	lower back rest
2	¾" x 2" x 12" poplar	arm rests
6	5 7/16" long side spindles	
5	10⅞" long rear spindles	
2	Corner post assembly (see drawing)	
2	¾" x 3½" x 16¾" poplar	seat sides
1	¾" x 3½" x 44½" poplar	seat front
1	¾" x 13¼" x 37½" lumber core birch	seat
2	¾" x 11" x 15" lumber core birch	ends
2	¾" x 3" x 11" poplar	front frame ends
1	¾" x 2⅞" x 5⅞" poplar	front frame center divider
1	¾" x 2" x 35¾" poplar	front frame top
1	¾" x 3⅛" x 35¾" poplar	front frame bottom
1	¾" x 4¼" x 43¼" poplar	front base
2	¾" x 4¼" x 15¾" poplar	side base
1	¾" x 13 3/16" x 40¼" plywood	back
2	¾" x 6½" x 17¼" poplar	drawer front
4	½" x 5¼" x 15 3/16" poplar	drawer panels
4	½" x 5¼" x 13" poplar	drawer panels
2	¼" x 13" x 16 3/16" plywood	drawer bottom

Miscellaneous: ⅜" x 2" dowels, ¾" x 1" cleats, glue, nails, screws, pulls, drawer slides Knape-Vogt #1175.

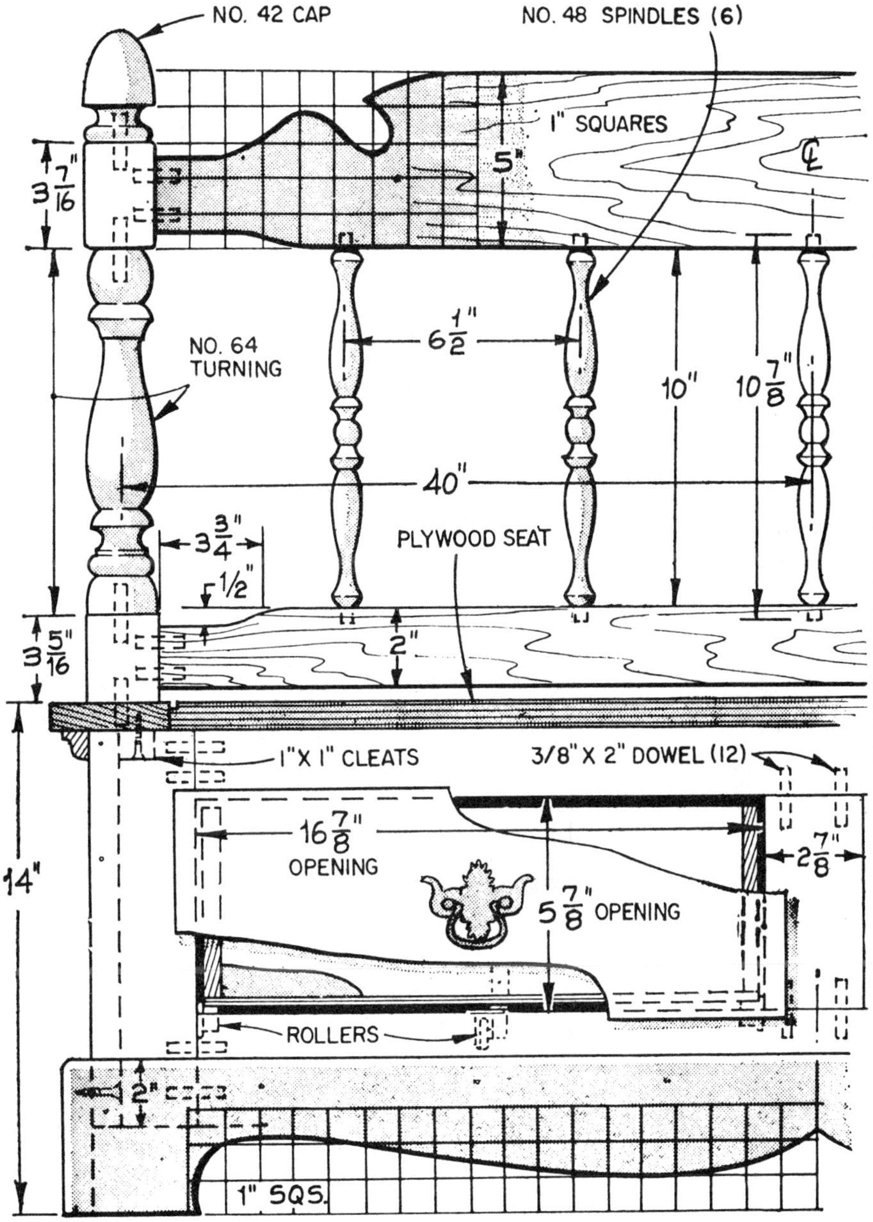
NO. 42 CAP
NO. 48 SPINDLES (6)
1" SQUARES
5"
3 7/16
NO. 64 TURNING
6 1/2"
10"
10 7/8"
40"
3 3/4"
1/2"
PLYWOOD SEAT
3 5/16
2"
14"
1"X 1" CLEATS
3/8"X 2" DOWEL (12)
16 7/8" OPENING
2 7/8"
5 7/8" OPENING
ROLLERS
2"
1" SQS.

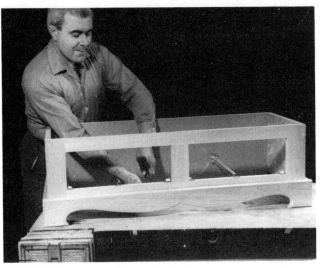

The base section is fastened to the main section with the aid of screws. Note the single track drawer slide hardware. Knape-Vogt #1175 was selected for use in this project.

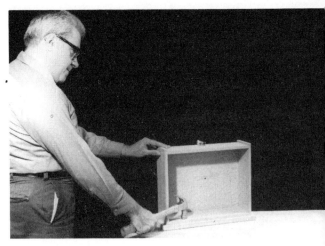

Drawer construction is greatly simplified by the use of false fronts which also eliminate need for shaping, undercutting. Drawer's completed first, then false front added.

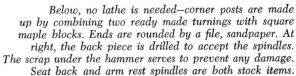

Below, no lathe is needed—corner posts are made up by combining two ready made turnings with square maple blocks. Ends are rounded by a file, sandpaper. At right, the back piece is drilled to accept the spindles. The scrap under the hammer serves to prevent any damage. Seat back and arm rest spindles are both stock items.

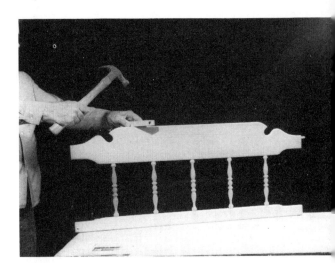

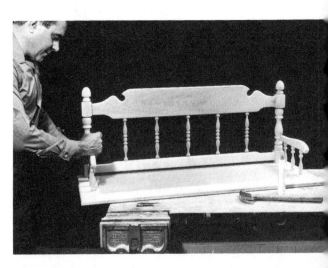

For the two poplar arm rests, the 5-7/16-in. long side spindles are cut in half. You will have to whittle their cut ends so as to fit the holes drilled into the seat, as shown here. For further information, refer to the drawing.

Child's Footlocker

screws, dowels, nails and glue. Cut all sections to size, check for proper fit, then assemble as shown in the photographs. The edging for the seat section is mitered and assembled with dowel pins. If you cut the miters by hand be sure they are straight and square. Plywood is also used for the end panels. Cut the pieces so the grain runs vertically.

The front framing is cut from poplar and dowelled as shown. Before assembling, lay pieces on a flat table and sand until the joints are flat and smooth. Assemble to the side panels with glue and a couple of nails. Place the nails at the ends where they will be hidden by the base and upper mouldings. For added strength, use corner glue blocks on the inside corners.

The turned corner posts are made up by combining two ready made turnings and square maple blocks as shown. The squares are cut from a length of maple base block. The ends are rounded by using a file and following up with sandpaper. Assemble with dowels and white glue. Ordinary dowels may be used, but grooved dowel pins are best as they will retain the glue better.

The spindles for the seat back and arm rests are also stock items. For the arm rests, the spindles are cut in half. The cut end of the spindles will have to be whittled so they will fit the holes drilled into the seat. Refer to the drawing.

The drawers are made of ½-in. lumber with ¼-in. plywood bottoms. Three-quarter-inch false fronts are added to the drawers. This greatly simplifies construction and eliminates the need for shaping and undercutting. Single track drawer hardware is recommended. The type used here was Knape-Vogt #1175.

The base is cut to shape then assembled by means of screws from the inside. Likewise, the seat is assembled to the side, rear and front by means of cleats and roundhead screws.

After assembly, sand smooth then stain and finish as desired.

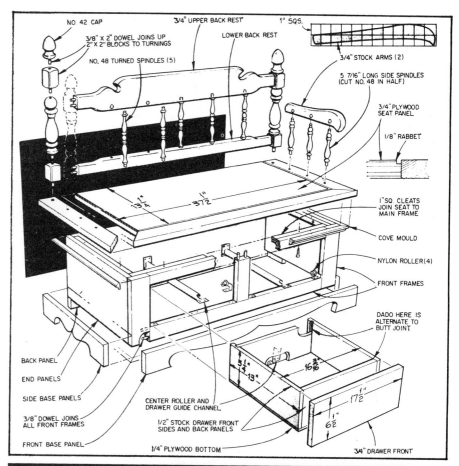

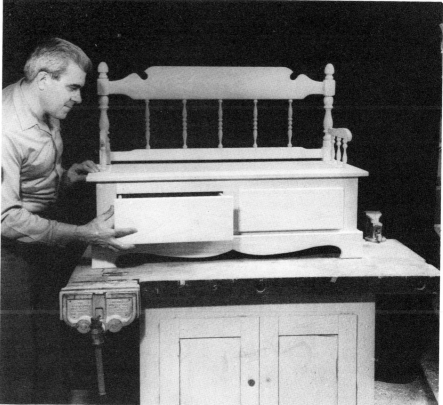

The drawers are made of ½-in. lumber with ¼-in. plywood bottoms and must be made with the proper allowance for the drawer hardware that is to be used. Therefore, you should obtain the necessary hardware before you actually make the drawers.

Captain's Trundle Bed

This fine furniture piece can be built from common lumber and is functional and decorative—lower drawer rolls out for use as bedding or storage space

THIS CAPTAIN'S TRUNDLE BED has a lower drawer that rolls out to be used as an extra bed or as a bin for clothes, bedding, toys, or whatever. It is designed so that both upper and lower sections take a 39-in. x 75-in. mattress (standard twin size). The drawer is mounted on casters and rolls out easily from either side. Prefinished paneling, in the head and footboards as well as the roll-out bin, simplifies construction and adds to the appearance of this fine furniture. Finish of the solid lumber can be made to match or contrast with the paneling.

Common lumber is used for construction. By carefully choosing and cutting, you can eliminate most knots. The knots are not objectionable however, and some folks prefer them, so take your pick.

Rip the legs from a length of 8/4 (2-in.) x 12-in. pine. The actual size of the board is 1-13/16-in. x 11¼-in. Cut four pieces, each 2-1/16-in. wide. After cutting, use a plane or jointer if you have one and smoothen the rough edges left by the saw blade.

Next rip the two side pieces from 5/4 x 10 stock (actual size 1-3/16-in. x 9¼-in.), and trim the ends to make them 7⅜-in. long. Cut the cross members from the same mamaterial. Make two pieces each 6-in. x 39-in. and from the remaining strip, make two pieces each 3-in. x 39-in.

Make a pattern for the scroll at the top of the cross pieces. Draw the necessary squares and plot the shape onto the pattern, using wrapping paper or thin cardboard. Cut the curved portion of the pattern,

then trace onto the cross pieces. Cut the shape with a saber saw fitted with a 10-tooth contour blade —this should leave a fairly smooth cut.

The side rails are made next. The offset step can be cut in several ways. You can rip most of the long section, then use a sabre saw to finish at the offset. You can also use a band saw, or (although slower), you can cut the entire length with a sabre saw. In either case, you will have to smooth out the edge. The best way to do this is to use the router and template. The template is made only for the offset. A straight edge is then used for the long straight part. The router is fitted with a flush cutter at least 1¼-in. long. Make the template from a piece of ⅛-in. hardboard. See detailed drawing.

Tack the template in place so that the cutter just bites into the rough saw cut edge of the board. Nail the template to the inner surface of the side so the holes won't show.

Of course you can finish the edge by using a plane on the straight part and sandpapering the offset. Round the two upper edges and outer edge of the lower part of the sides. The cross members are rounded on all four edges.

Cut a groove for the end panels in each of the cross pieces. Note that the groove is centered. Use either a dado blade or make several passes with a regular blade on your table saw. The upper pieces are cut on the lower edge. The top edge is cut in the lower pieces.

Before making the cut in the work-piece, check the width of the cut on a scrap piece. The panel should fit snugly. Make the groove 11/32-in. deep.

Reset the fence for the posts, placing the grooves in the center. Note that blind grooves are made. Place masking tape on the saw table and draw starting and stopping lines as shown. Make test cuts on scrap lumber first. Hold the work slightly above the revolving blade with the end of the piece aligned with the pencil mark. Carefully lower the work into the blade and advance until the rear end of the post reaches the mark on the second piece of tape. Grooves (dadoes) should start and stop 3″ before ends of posts. See detail.

Locate the screw holes in each of the posts. Note that the spacing is different at the tops and bottoms. Drill the ½-in. counterbore hole fisrt. Make it ⅜-in. deep. then follow with the screw clearance hole. After the holes have been drilled, round off the edges of the posts and form the slight curve at the top. Do this on a lathe if possible, otherwise use a block of wood wrapped with rough sandpaper and do it by hand. Drill a dowel hole at the top to receive the dowel for the acorn ornament. The ornaments are available at home improvement centers and lumber yards. Some of these have a rather large threaded dowel. To simplify matters, insert the threaded dowel, cut it off at the base, then redrill a ⅜-in. hole to take a regular dowel.

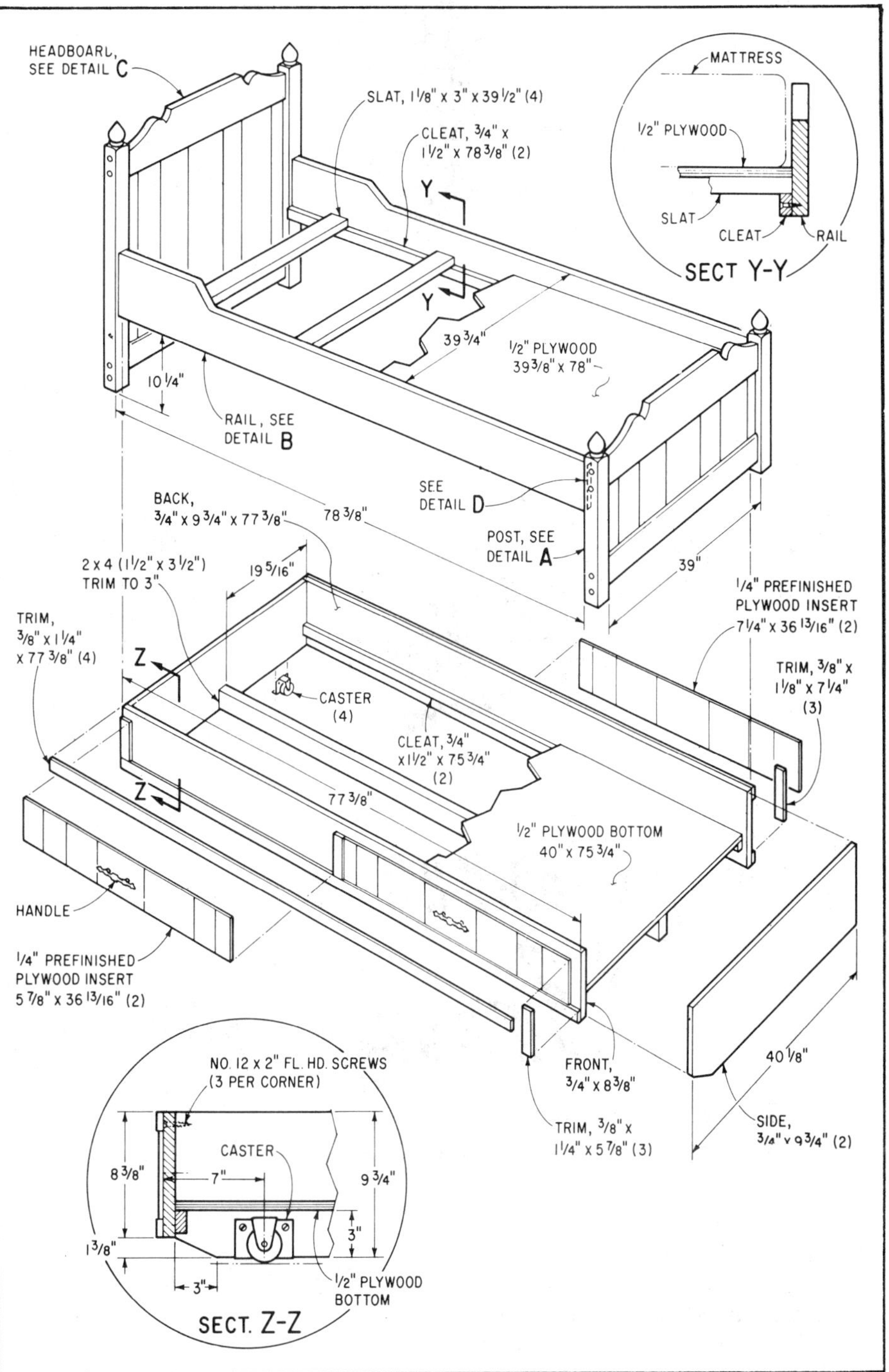

BILL OF MATERIALS

Use	No. Reg.	Size
Post, rear	2	1 13/16″x2″x33¾″
Post, front	2	1 13/16″x2″x17½″
Header rail	2	1 3/16″x6″x39″
Bottom rail	2	1 3/16″x6″x39″
Side	2	1 3/16″x9″x78⅜″
Front panel	1	¼″x9 3/16″x39 11/16″
Rear panel	2	¼″x25½″x39 11/16″
Cleats	1	¾″x1½″x78⅜″
Slats	6	1 13/16″x3″x39⅝″
Bed hooks		4 sets with ¾x8 FH screws
Acorns	4	
Buttons	16	(to conceal screws.)
Plywood	1	½″x39⅜″x78″
Glides	4	
Screws	16	3½″—14 RH

NOTE: If you are making the Trundle, you will also need the following:

Front & rear	2	¾″x8⅜″x77⅜″
Sides	2	¾″x9¾″x40⅛″
Plywood	1	½″x40″x75¾″
Cleat	2	¾″x1½″x75¾″
Center support	1	1½″x3″x75¾″
Trim		⅜″x1¼″x34′
Panel insert	4	¼″x5⅞″x36 13/16″
casters	4	
screws	12	2″—12 FH

Trundle Bed

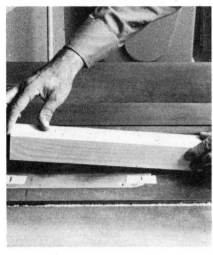

Cut the slots for the paneling on a table saw. Notice the tape marks which indicate the start and stop points of blind slots.

The pilot holes for the screws in the bed posts are drilled as pictured above. The countersunk holes should be drilled first.

Use a sabre saw to cut the shaped edges of both the head and the foot boards. For the best results, use a smooth cutting blade.

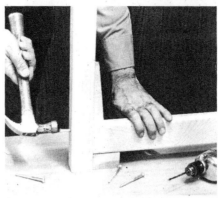

Place a piece of scrap paneling in corners to align posts and cross members. Put scrap wood under crosspiece to position it.

Assemble the head and foot board sections with glue and screws. Countersunk screw heads will be concealed by wood buttons.

Having cut side pieces with a sabre saw, you can clean edges using a router and template, or else plane and sandpaper.

The ends of the side pieces are dadoes to receive the bed hooks. Use a side cutter about ⅜-in or ½-in. deep and use a guide.

Here we see the side piece ends, one with hooks, the other without. The larger holes are drilled clearance for rear projections.

To locate the mating parts of the hook hardware, match posts to side which are on trundle with ½-in. spacer in between.

The casters shown here are a special type made for the trundle beds. They can be installed quite easily with just three screws.

Round off the edges of the posts with a small rounding cutter in your router. A ¼-in. radius cutter is recommended.

Before assembling the parts, sand all pieces carefully. Install a scrap piece of ¼-in. paneling into the corners to align the posts and cross members. Place a piece of 1½-in. wood under the crosspiece to position it on the post. Then mark and drill pilot holes for the screws into the ends of the cross members. Assemble the parts with glue.

The ends of the side pieces are dadoes to receive the bed hooks. Use a side cutter about ⅜-in. or ½-in. deep. Nail a guide strip on the inner surface of the rail. Place it so the depth of cut will match the thickness of the hardware. For the hooks shown, the depth is ⅛-in. Make the cut just a trifle deeper. At the rear end of the side rail, the dado is blind. At the front, only the top need be blind. The bottom can run off the edge. See detailed drawing. You will have to file the back of the hook to match the curve of the blind dado, or you can chisel out the corner so the hardware will fit.

You will have to make two passes with the router to obtain the correct width for the hook. Drill out clearances for the protrusions at the rear of the male hooks, then attach with FH screws.

Note that the female plate is not symmetrical. The slots are closer to one end than the other. Orient them properly then mate with the male. Stand the bed up with props and with trundle in place, lay a ½-in. spacer on the trundle, then rest the rail on it. Carefully mark the posts, indicating the location of the plate vertically. Now place the post assembly on the work table and draw the exact position for the plate. Route with an end cutter, then clean out the corners with a chisel. Also, chisel out the clearance for the male sections. Install the plate with FH screws.

To make the trundle, rip four pieces of pine. Make two of them 8⅜-in. wide by 77⅜-in. long and two pieces 9¾-in. by 40⅛-in. Bevel one corner of each of the 40⅛-in. pieces as shown. Assemble these with nails and glue, using two nails in

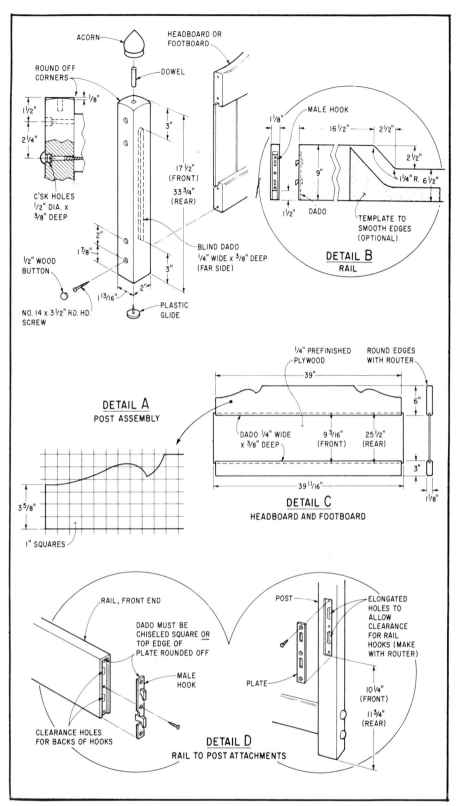

each side. After the piece has been assembled and squared, add a few screws as shown.

Add two long cleats with their top edge 6⅜-in. from the top of the frame. Apply glue and nail from the inside, using 1½-in. nails, slanting them slightly. Add a piece of 1½x 3-in. stock to the center. Be sure its top edge is level with the

two cleats.

Add trim to the front and rear as shown then cut the inserts to size and install with glue. Drill holes for the pulls centering the pulls in each panel.

Finish the piece as desired. Place masking tape on the paneling to simplify finishing then remove.—

Layout sections on the plywood and cut apart with saber saw. To make cutouts for bookshelves drill entry hole in one corner.

Judicious use of cleats permits assembling sections without screws or nails on any exposed surfaces—a professional technique.

Compact Writing Desk

It has a considerable amount of storage space for its size, with book shelves, drawer, and a storage well under the lid

THIS graceful desk features a storage well, a drawer and two bookshelves which run completely through the unit. A modern version of the famous Davenport styling, it is generously proportioned and equally suitable for child or grown-up. The lid slopes slightly toward the front, making it far more comfortable than the usual flat-topped desk. A lid support bracket holds the top open so that both hands are free while tidying up, etc. If the desk is to be used by a girl, a mirror may be mounted on the underside of the lid, so the desk can also double as a vanity.

Plywood construction eliminates the need for glueing boards to make up wide panels, and it also does away with bothersome framing. Construction is clean and simple. Judicious use of cleats permits assembling sections without screws or nails on any exposed surfaces. This is the way professional furniture is made.

You can build this desk using hand tools alone, but the work will go much quicker and easier if you have a saber saw, portable drill and sander. Through judicious

Curves are cut free hand with a saber saw. One piece construction of the sides saves time spent on separate cuts and assembly.

planning of your cuts, one 4' x 8' panel of ¾" plywood should be sufficient. You'll need a piano hinge and a 10" lid support.

Lay out the sections on the plywood with the grain running the length of the pieces. Inasmuch as the sides are not symmetrical, be sure to lay them out one face up and the other face down.

When all sections are laid out, cut them apart with the sabre saw. This should be a rough cut close to the line, just to separate the large board into easy-to-handle sections. Curves are cut freehand, but straight lines should be made with the guide wherever possible. Use a new blade and feed the saw slowly to prevent chipping or splintering. To make the cutouts for the bookshelves, drill entry holes for the blade near one corner, then proceed to drop out the center. When you near the end of the cut, support the waste to prevent it from falling prematurely, since this could damage the work.

Cut all cleats to size and drill pilot holes for the screws as indicated. A screw pilot bit will make the necessary clearance hole including the countersink for the screw head. Spring clamps are fine for holding the cleats.

Fasten the cleats with glue and screws, then follow by assembling the sections, adding the front panel last. The drawer compartment and lid are added to complete the main construction. The drawer is made by dadoing the ends as indicated. Make two parallel cuts ½" apart and halfway through the stock, then clean out in between with a chisel. Assemble as shown using a small triangular glue block at the bottom front.

Sand all surfaces thoroughly, first with medium grade paper, followed by fine and extra fine.

Finish as desired. A good treatment consists of two coats of clear brushing lacquer followed with paste wax.

The finished desk will beautify any unused space in your home whether it be the bedroom, living room or entry hall, and its usefulness will more than equal its decorative value.

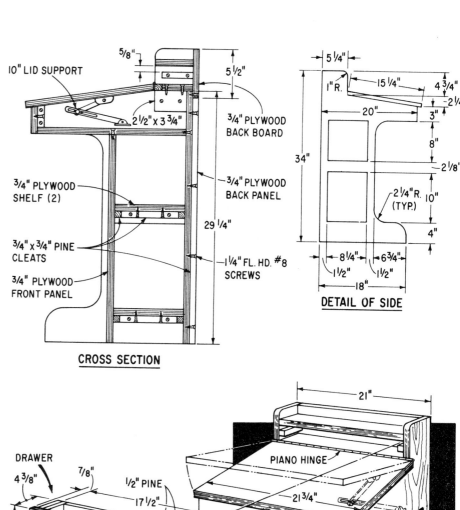

CROSS SECTION

DETAIL OF SIDE

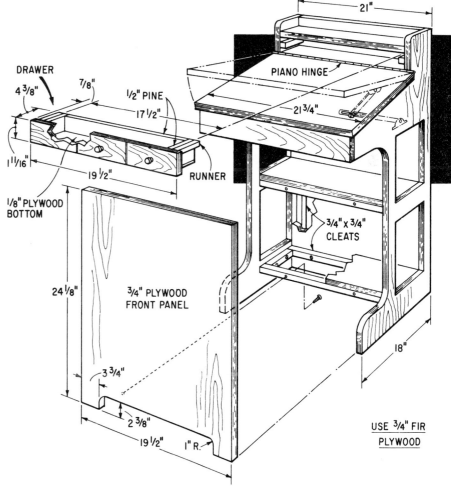

USE ¾" FIR PLYWOOD

Console
Cabinet
and
Mirror

This handsome set sells for at least $400 in the better furniture stores. Build both pieces from pine for under $100.

This beautiful set was made with just one machine, a Sears 10-in. table saw. All routing or shaping was eliminated by the use of standard stock moldings. Another outstanding feature is that by using common pine for the construction, the cost was kept to a minimum. Both pieces were built for under $100. This included $15 for a good plate glass mirror. If you were to buy this combination in one of the better furniture stores, it would cost you at least $400.

The construction is not difficult. If you haven't had much experience cutting angles on the table saw, you most certainly will after this project. Both blade tilting and miter gauge angle cutting are used extensively. The only tricky cutting involves the crown moulding at the base of the cabinet and top of the mirror. The crown moulding must be cut at the angle in which it will be used. This means that it must rest against the miter gauge at this angle. In addition, the miter gauge must be set at an angle either 22½° or 45°. The 45° cut is made for the mirror, but the console requires 22½° cuts. See photo 8 which shows how the crown is

held for cutting. If you don't already possess one, you should fit your miter gauge with an auxiliary back stop. This will facilitate the cutting of mouldings and it also makes for more accuracy, as it prevents any "give" in the work piece.

Before starting work, check the calibration on the miter gauge and the blade tilt. If it is off, make the necessary adjustments. To check

for accuracy, make two sets of 45° cuts on scrap wood. Make one set using the miter gauge and the other with the blade tilt. When joined, each set should make a perfect 90° corner which you can easily check with a try-square.

Cut the lumber to size and where possible, cut between knots. If the knots must be included, try to locate them where they will be

1. *Use table saw for top, bottom board diagonal cuts; check miter gauge for accuracy. Before beginning work, check calibration on miter gauge, blade tilt. To check, make 2 45° cuts on scrap wood—one set using miter gauge, the other with blade tilt. When joined, each set should make 90° corner that you can easily check with a try-square.*

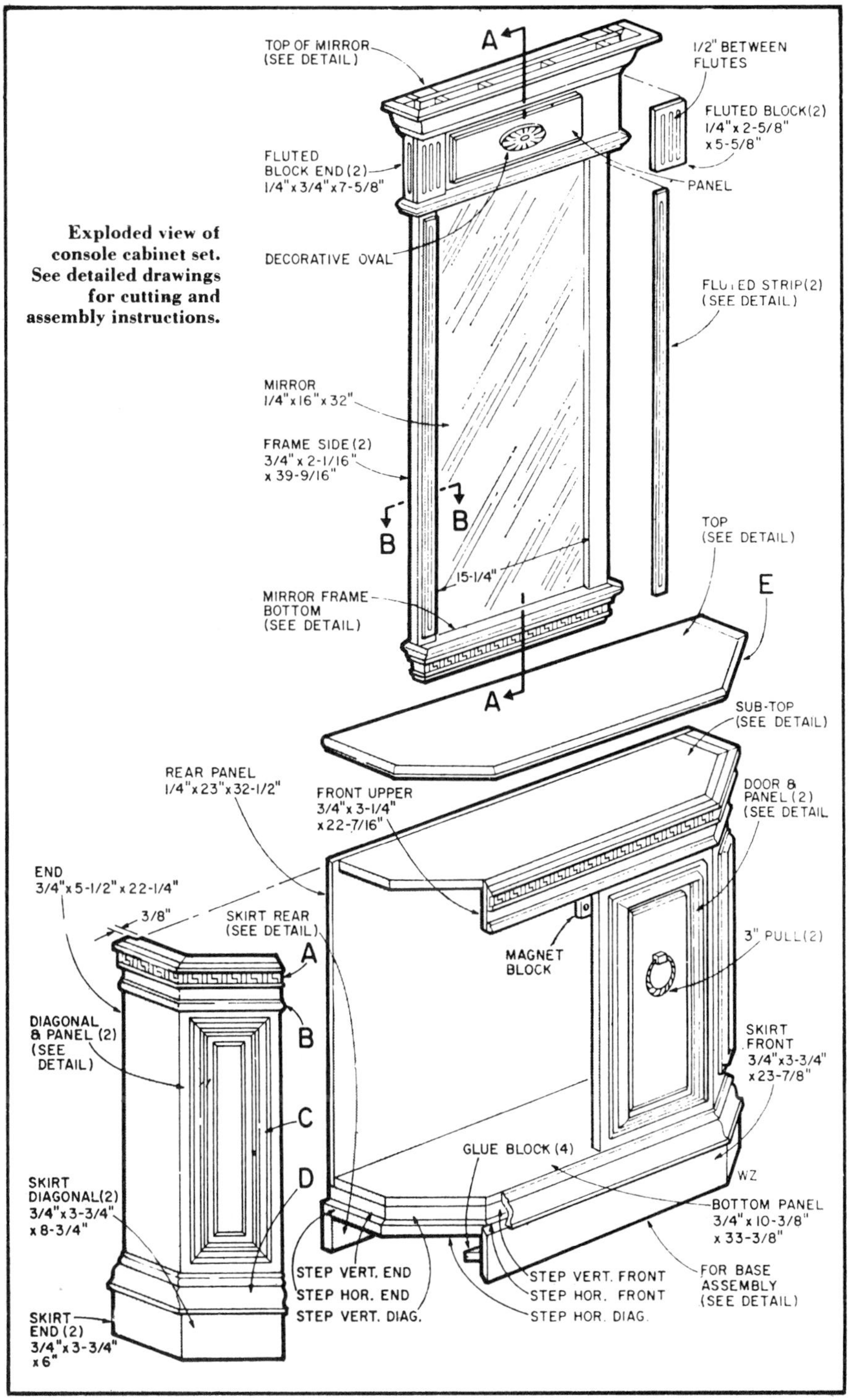
TOP OF MIRROR (SEE DETAIL)
A
1/2" BETWEEN FLUTES
FLUTED BLOCK(2) 1/4"x 2-5/8" x 5-5/8"
FLUTED BLOCK END (2) 1/4"x 3/4"x 7-5/8"
PANEL
DECORATIVE OVAL
FLUTED STRIP(2) (SEE DETAIL)
MIRROR 1/4"x 16"x 32"
FRAME SIDE (2) 3/4"x 2-1/16" x 39-9/16"
B
B
TOP (SEE DETAIL)
15-1/4"
E
MIRROR FRAME BOTTOM (SEE DETAIL)
A
SUB-TOP (SEE DETAIL)
REAR PANEL 1/4"x 23"x 32-1/2"
FRONT UPPER 3/4"x 3-1/4" x 22-7/16"
DOOR & PANEL (2) (SEE DETAIL
END 3/4"x 5-1/2"x 22-1/4"
3/8"
SKIRT REAR (SEE DETAIL)
A
MAGNET BLOCK
3" PULL(2)
DIAGONAL & PANEL (2) (SEE DETAIL)
B
SKIRT FRONT 3/4"x 3-3/4" x 23-7/8"
C
GLUE BLOCK (4)
SKIRT DIAGONAL(2) 3/4"x 3-3/4" x 8-3/4"
D
WZ
BOTTOM PANEL 3/4"x 10-3/8" x 33-3/8"
STEP VERT. END
STEP HOR. END
STEP VERT. DIAG.
STEP VERT. FRONT
STEP HOR. FRONT
STEP HOR. DIAG.
FOR BASE ASSEMBLY (SEE DETAIL)
SKIRT END (2) 3/4"x 3-3/4" x 6"

Exploded view of console cabinet set. See detailed drawings for cutting and assembly instructions.

BILL OF MATERIALS—CONSOLE CABINET & MIRROR

All lumber is pine except for rear panel which is plywood.

Use	No. Req.	Size
Top	1	¾" x 11⅝" x 35⅛"
Sub-top	1	¾" x 9¾" x 31⅞"
Front upper	1	¾" x 3¼" x 22-7/16"
End	1	¾" x 5½" x 22¼"
Diagonal	2	¾" x 7¾" x 22¼"
Door	2	¾" x 11-3/32" x 18⅞"
Diagonal panel	2	½" x 2½" x 13¾"
Door panel	2	½" x 6" x 13¾"
Magnet block	1	¾" x 3¼" x 3½"
Rear panel	1	¼" x 23" x 32½"
Bottom panel	1	¾" x 10⅜" x 33⅜"
Skirt end	2	¾" x ¾" x 6"
Skirt diagonal	2	¾" x 3¾" x 8¾"
Skirt front	1	¾" x 3¾" x 23⅞"
Skirt rear	1	¾" x 5" x 34½"
Step horizontal end	2	¾" x 1¼" x 5⅝"
Step horizontal diagonal	2	¾" x 1¼" x 8¼"
Step horizontal front	1	¾" x 1¼" x 23¼"
Step vertical end	2	¾ x 1¼" x 5⅛"
Step vertical diagonal	2	¾" x 1¼" x 7½"
Step vertical front	1	¾" x 1¼" x 22½"
Nose & cove moulding		⅜" x 48"
Nose & cove moulding		¾" x 60"
Greek key		1¾" x 60"
Base moulding		¾" x 20 ft.
Crown moulding		2½" x 60"

Miscellaneous items—2 pr. 1½" butts, 2 pulls, 2 magnet catches, screws, nails, glue.

Mirror

Use	No. Req.	Size
Frame upper	1	¾" x 8⅜" x 15¼"
Frame side	2	¾" x 2$\frac{1}{16}$" x 39$\frac{9}{16}$"
Filler strip	1	¼" x 2" x 20"
Frame bottom	1	¾" x ⅞" x 19¾"
Panel	1	½" x 4¾" x 14"
Fluted block	2	¼" x 2⅝" x 5⅝"
Fluted block end	2	¼" x ¾" x 7⅝"
Fluted strip	2	⅜" x 1⅛" x 30"
Crown moulding		2½" x 36"
Nose & cove moulding		¾" x 60"
Greek key		1¾" x 24"
Decorative oval		2½" x 5"

covered with panels or mouldings later. The lumber used for the sub-top and bottom was badly warped, but rather than waste it, we cut a few longitudinal grooves on the hidden side. When assembled, the sections flattened out perfectly.

The lumber used was 1-in. x 12-in. (actual size ¾-in. x 11¼-in.) The depth of the top measures 11⅝-in. so we had to glue up a strip to make this piece. The other choice would have been to buy a wider board.

The sub-top is not an essential piece but it greatly simplifies assembly. The same results are possible using nailing cleats but the assembly would be more difficult. When nailing the sub-top to the top, set the back edge in ⅜-in. thus forming a rabbet for the rear panel. The end panels are rabbeted on one edge and mitered on the other. Note that the miters are 22½° because the shape of the cabinet is actually half of an octagon.

The raised panel effect is achieved by the use of beveled boards framed with base moulding. Note that the mouldings are used in reverse, low side out and the high edge toward the center.

Assemble all parts with white glue and nails. When gluing mitered mouldings be sure to apply

Console Cabinet and Mirror

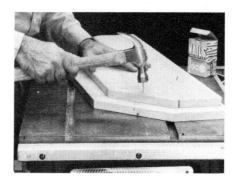

the glue to the miters and wipe off excess before glue sets.

When assembling the end and diagonal panels together drive a couple of nails along the edges to close the joint while the glue sets.

Before cutting and adding the step for the set-out at the base, check the altitude of the 2½-in. crown moulding. The altitude of the moulding is the vertical measurement taken when the moulding is resting on a horizontal surface. See drawing. The mouldings will vary in size between manufacturers, so check this carefully. The step must be cut so that when the moldings rest on it, the top of the molding will be flush with the top edge of the bottom panel.

Doors are cut with about ¹⁄₁₆-in. clearance all around. Gain for the hinges is cut fully on the doors. This eliminates the need for cutting into the door frame. Before assembling the doors, drill the holes for the pull screw. Note the clearance for the screw head.

The addition of the mouldings completes the base. Use ¾-in. nose and cove at the top and note that it is set down ¹⁄₁₆-in. to form a step. The Greek key is added next, followed by the miniature nose and cove just above the door line. The crown moulding takes care of the bottom.

The mirror frame is not as difficult to build as it may seem. Mouldings again play an important part in construction. Like the console, all lumber is pine.

The fluted pieces are made on the table saw using a moulding head. We used the groove part of a tongue and groove set. The tip of the cutters was ground round to form the half-round groove, but it could be left square to achieve the same effect. To determine where to start and stop the cut, it is best to make trial cuts on scrap wood.

2. Sub-top is nailed with a set-back at rear, allowing for thickness of the rear panel. While not an essential piece, it greatly simplifies assembly.

4. Base moulding's used to frame panels. Temporary gauge block facilitates assembly. Mouldings are reversed—low side out, high edge toward the center.

3. Rabbets are cut on saw using the rip fence as shown. Make the vertical cut first. You'll have experience cutting angles on saw with this project.

5. Here beveled panels are given coat of glue, then centered in frame. The raised panel effect is achieved by use of boards framed with base moulding.

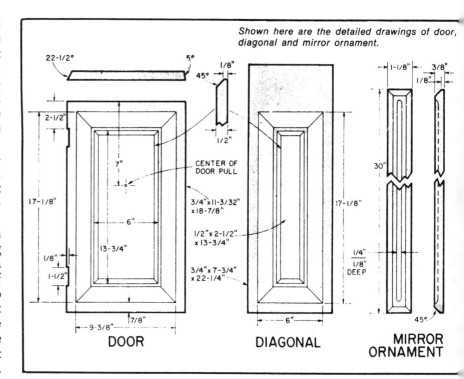

Shown here are the detailed drawings of door, diagonal and mirror ornament.

DOOR   **DIAGONAL**   **MIRROR ORNAMENT**

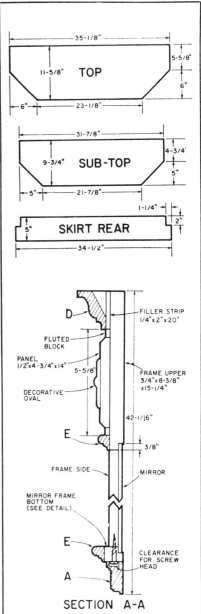

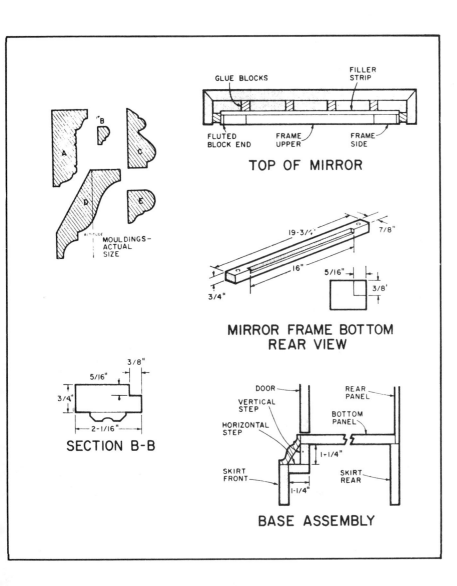

SECTION A-A

There are two ways to make the cut; in each case the fence is used to guide the work. You can elevate the blade to the proper height (3/16-in.), then carefully lower the work onto it; or you can place the work in position, hold it firmly, then raise the blade to its 3/16-in.

6. Toe nail panels when assembling for greater strength, using nails generously. When assembling the end and diagonal panels together drive a couple of nails along edges to close joint while glue sets.

Console
Cabinet
and
Mirror

protrusion and feed the work until you reach a predetermined stop marked onto the table. The built-up columns at the top are made by adding blocks as indicated in the drawings. The decorative oval in the top panel of the mirror is available at most lumber yards that carry carvings. Most carved wood mouldings are bowed slightly. To remedy this, simply moisten the back with water and flatten. Apply with glue and a couple of brads.

When the construction is completed, fill all nail holes then sand thoroughly. Dust and finish as desired. We used antique green, highlighting the high spots and letting the corners go dark. Antiquing kits are readily available in a variety of colors with easy-to-follow instructions.

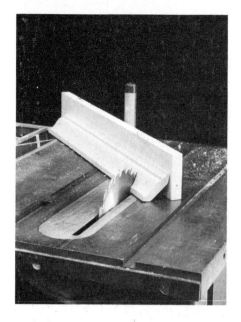

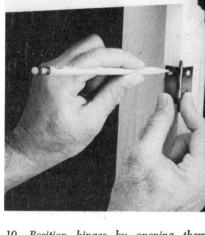

10 Position hinges by opening them all the way. Fit into corner; locate screw holes. 11. Bottom piece of the mirror frame's held with screws and glue, below. Other joints are nailed.

8. When cutting the crown moulding, support it in the angle in which it'll be used. 9. Below, Greek-key moulding adds the finishing touch to the cabinet. Check the miters before gluing.

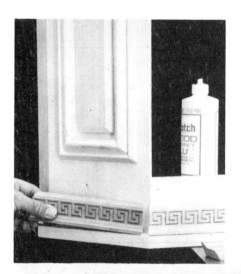

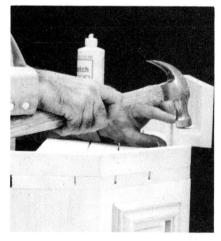

7. The bottom step is added as shown. Lumber used was badly warped, so the kerf cuts were made to straighten the board. When assembled, the sections flattened out perfectly.

12. Pictured here is the mirror panel which is cut from ½" pine lumber. The carved applique will be centered in the panel. The decorative oval in the top panel of the mirror is available at most lumber yards that carry carvings.

TILE-TOP TABLE with built-in PLANTER

Construction is simplified—so even a novice can do it easily

If you're searching for a coffee table that is beautiful, distinctive and unique, you won't be able to resist this one. This table features a lovely ceramic tiled top (your own selection) and a planter insert which can hold real live plants for the green thumbed or artificial plants for the non-gardener. The planter is made with acrylic plastic and is easily removable so you can plant, replant, or transplant plants away from the table without fear of messing it up with soil or water.

The table is made of butternut wood which has a lovely grain pattern. This wood must be handled carefully however, as it tends to split easily. The ceramic tiles are 8-inches square and ⅜-in. thick. Ceramic tiles for a table top make a lot of sense. They are durable, not affected by alcohol or heat, easily cleaned, require no upkeep, and pattern choices and colors are almost limitless. We used ⅛-in. Plexiglas for the plants, which is readily available at most glass shops.

Simplified construction methods

have been devised so even the novice can make this table without much difficulty. A router is used to form the flutes on the lower part of the apron. It is also utilized for the cove cut at the upper part of the legs and for the add-on strip at the bottom edge of the apron.

The legs are constructed first. Glue-up two pieces of one-inch stock. Note that one-inch refers to the nominal size of the lumber. The dressed size is the actual size of the stock and it is ¾-in. for softwoods and ¹³⁄₁₆-in. for hard woods. Although the difference between the two is not very great, is can cause problems. If you use hardwood, follow the measurements shown; otherwise make the slight adjustment needed for softwoods.

After the glue has set, the leg squares must be cut to size. Next layout the shape of the leg on one face of each piece. Mark the center line for the ½-in. concave cut on each piece, then square over the line around each piece using a try square. Clamp two legs as shown, and drill a ½-in. diameter hole through each pair. After each hole

is drilled, rotate each leg 90-degrees, clamp, and repeat the drilling operation. When done, each leg will have a clean semicircular cut as shown. The angular cuts just below the curved section are made with a saber saw or band saw.

The narrow kerf cuts near the bottom of each leg must be made while the legs are still square. Square a pencil line around the leg 1½-in. from the bottom end. Use a hack saw to make the kerf cuts. Make them ⅜-in. deep and be sure they are in perfect alignment around the leg.

The tapers are cut with the saber saw or band saw. An alternative is to use the table saw for taper ripping with a tapering jig. This method works very well, but because of the small size of the legs, the hands are rather close to the blade and this could be dangerous. The drawing shows how the jig is made and used. A push stick is recommended for this operation.

The legs are fluted using a core box cutter and a jig which is clamped to the router base. The router is used upside down and in

A leg is set up for cutting flutes with the router. Note jig clamped to base of router to position and limit the cut.

The legs are then clamped together in pairs to bore the half rounds. This is best done, as here, on a drill press.

To smooth out the half round sandpaper is wrapped round a dowel which is fixed in the drill as a sanding drum.

This is the approved method of sanding small pieces with a belt sanding. If tool is lightweight, clamp it to table.

Here the tapers are being cut on band saw. Note that the pencil lines for the second side will have to be redrawn.

Pieces of scrap wood should be used to raise it to the proper height when the dowel holes are being transferred.

this manner it works like a shaper. The jig is cut in the shape of an "L." A scrap piece of ⅜-in. or ½-in. plywood works fine. The long side of the "L" serves as a fence against which the work is pushed. The short part of the "L" acts as a stop, limiting the length of the flute. We made one wide flute, but you may prefer to substitute a narrower cutter and make two or even three flutes. You will have to move the jig for each cut however. Regardless of the number of flutes you make, test the cut on scrap wood the same width as the legs before cutting the actual pieces.

After the legs are cut and shaped, they must be sanded. The curved part is best done with a piece of sandpaper wrapped around a ½-in. dowel. Use it by hand or mount the dowel in a drill for a faster and smoother operation. The tapered part can be done on a belt sander. If you use a portable belt sander, mount it upside down and move the work back and forth until flat and smooth.

The aprons are ripped to size then cut to the proper length. Note that we have made a series of 9/16-in. deep kerf cuts on the back side of the long pieces. This was done because the wood was badly bowed. If your lumber is flat, disregard this operation.

The double flute near the lower edge of the apron is made with the router. This can be done in the conventional manner by clamping a guide strip on the work, or by clamping one to the router base. If you have a router guide, set it for the proper depth and cut the flutes first, one on all the pieces, then reset to cut the second flute.

The strip at the bottom of the apron is ripped to size then rounded at the outer edge. After shaping, sand it smooth and likewise sand the face of the apron, then add the strip to the lower edge of the apron. Use glue and brads.

Drill and counterbore the apron mounting holes. The depth of the counterbore must be fairly accurate or you may find the mounting screws penetrating the top frame. If you use the drill press, set the depth gauge. If a portable drill is

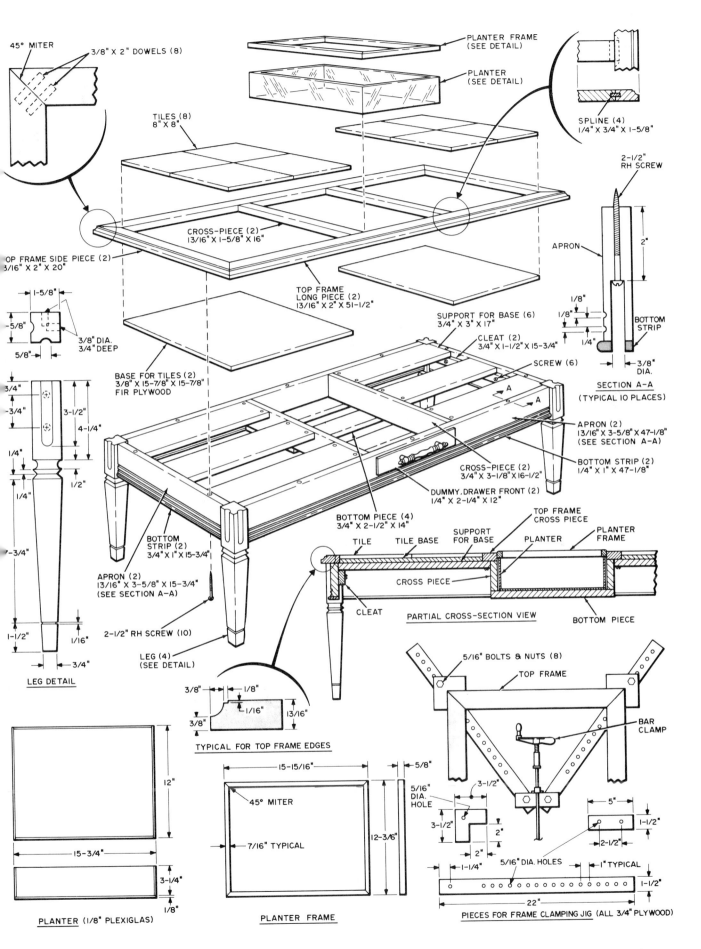

45° MITER

3/8" X 2" DOWELS (8)

PLANTER FRAME
(SEE DETAIL)

PLANTER
(SEE DETAIL)

SPLINE (4)
1/4" X 3/4" X 1-5/8"

TILES (8)
8" X 8"

TOP FRAME SIDE PIECE (2)
3/16" X 2" X 20"

CROSS-PIECE (2)
13/16" X 1-5/8" X 16"

2-1/2"
RH SCREW

APRON

BOTTOM
STRIP

SECTION A-A
(TYPICAL 10 PLACES)

1-5/8"

5/8"

5/8"

3/8" DIA.
3/4" DEEP

TOP FRAME
LONG PIECE (2)
13/16" X 2" X 51-1/2"

SUPPORT FOR BASE (6)
3/4" X 3" X 17"

CLEAT (2)
3/4" X 1-1/2" X 15-3/4"

SCREW (6)

3/8"
DIA.

BASE FOR TILES (2)
3/8" X 15-7/8" X 15-7/8"
FIR PLYWOOD

3/4"

3-1/2"

4-1/4"

1/4"

1/2"

APRON (2)
13/16" X 3-5/8" X 47-1/8"
(SEE SECTION A-A)

BOTTOM STRIP (2)
1/4" X 1" X 47-1/8"

CROSS-PIECE (2)
3/4" X 3-1/8" X 16-1/2"

DUMMY DRAWER FRONT (2)
1/4" X 2-1/4" X 12"

BOTTOM PIECE (4)
3/4" X 2-1/2" X 14"

TOP FRAME
CROSS PIECE

PLANTER
FRAME

TILE   TILE BASE   SUPPORT   PLANTER
                     FOR BASE

CROSS PIECE

BOTTOM PIECE

CLEAT

PARTIAL CROSS-SECTION VIEW

BOTTOM STRIP (2)
3/4" X 1" X 15-3/4"

APRON (2)
13/16" X 3-5/8" X 15-3/4"
(SEE SECTION A-A)

2-1/2" RH SCREW (10)

LEG (4)
(SEE DETAIL)

7-3/4"

1-1/2"

1/16"

3/4"

LEG DETAIL

3/8"   1/8"

1/16"

3/8"

13/16"

TYPICAL FOR TOP FRAME EDGES

5/16" BOLTS & NUTS (8)

TOP FRAME

BAR
CLAMP

5/16"
DIA.
HOLE

3-1/2"

3-1/2"

2"

2"

5"

1-1/2"

2-1/2"

1-1/4"

5/16" DIA. HOLES   1" TYPICAL

22"

1-1/2"

PIECES FOR FRAME CLAMPING JIG (ALL 3/4" PLYWOOD)

12"

15-3/4"

3-1/4"

1/8"

PLANTER (1/8" PLEXIGLAS)

15-15/16"

5/8"

45° MITER

7/16" TYPICAL

12-3/16"

PLANTER FRAME

The apron pieces which make up the sides of the coffee table planter must be sanded before the basic unit is finally put together. The final sanding, shown here, should be done with an oscillating belt-type sander loaded with fine grit paper.

A special procedure must be used in assembling the top frame. Parts must be installed in pairs, one long and one short per section. Then the sections are drawn together in this jig, made from scrap wood and assembled with drawn bars shown.

The apron is fastened to the top with screws. Note that the holes are counterbored. The pieces of pine which are used as supports for the tiles are cut and screwed to the crosspieces in position. The other end will be held with a cleat.

used, wrap a piece of tape on the drill bit to indicate the proper depth.

Drill the dowel holes at each end of the apron. Make these holes 1¼-in. deep then drill the mating holes in each of the legs ¾-in. deep. (Note: If you are to use a doweling jig to drill the holes into the apron ends, do this before adding the strip at the bottom as it will interfere with the jig.)

The legs are glued to the long aprons first. After the glue has set, the two assemblies are glued to the short aprons. To attempt to glue and clamp the four aprons and four legs at one time would be tricky. You will need long bar clamps when gluing the legs to the long aprons. As a substitute, you can use a wedge-type clamp utilizing your workbench top or other flat surface for this purpose. Screw or clamp a stop at one end of the table. At the other end fasten a wedge-shaped piece the same way with clamp or screws. Position the wedge so another wedge can fit between it and the workpiece. Carefully strike the loose wedge with a hammer so it tightens up the assembly. Leave it until the glue sets.

The top frame is made with mitered corners. Cut the stock to the proper width and make each slightly oversize. Mark the lengths accurately then miter. Be sure the corners are perfect 45-degree cuts. The grooves for the crosspieces are made with the router. Keep the router setting the same and cut the grooves in the ends of the two crosspieces. Best way to groove the crosspieces is to make the groove in a wide board which has been cut to exact length. After grooving, rip into the narrow strips required. Cut plywood splines and insert them into the ends of the crosspieces. Use glue.

Drill the dowel holes into the mitered frame ends.

A special procedure must be used in assembling the top frame. If three sides of the frame were doweled and assembled, it would be impossible to install the last section. The parts must be installed in pairs, one short and one long per section. Bear in mind that the assembly cannot be delayed too long as the glue will start to set and of course hits can ruin the job.

Take four dowels and sand them so they fit the holes easily without force. Set them aside. Prepare a miter frame clamp. This is easily made with scrap wood. Drill a series of holes, spaced one-inch apart, then assemble with corners and draw bars as shown. Use 5/16-in. bolts in assembling the parts. The jig is self-adjusting and can be used for all miter frame gluing.

Apply dowels and glue to two diagonal corners and to one end only of the cross pieces. Insert the loose-fitting dowels into the other diagonal corners. Do not use glue here. Install the jig and draw the parts together by tightening the clamp. Align the crosspieces making sure they are in proper position. When the glue sets, separate the two sections, replace the dowels with proper fitting ones, apply glue to the miters and dry end of the splines and repeat the clamping operation. Note that if you prefer to glue and clamp the entire frame at one time, a slow-setting glue should be used.

The supports for the tiles and planter are made of pine. Cut the pieces to size and fasten with screws. If you use 7/16-in. thick tiles, the tile base should be 3/8-in. plywood. When this is placed onto the base supports, the tiles will fit into the recess with the top surface flush with the frame. We did not use a grout between the tiles. If you use grout, select one that matches the tiles.

The planter is made of 1/8-in. Plexiglas. Cut the pieces to size then assemble using thickened solvent cement. Simply apply a bead to the joint edge and gently join the pieces. Clamp or hold firmly until set. The resulting high-strength joint will not be affected by moisture. A wood frame is made to loosely fit into the opening and rest on the planter.

The table should be given a good sanding, followed by stain and suitable top coat. If the wood used has open grain, paste wood filler should be used to fill the pores. The filler can be mixed with the stain. Follow the manufacturer's directions for the proper procedure.

The tiles used are Bizantino Orange #67 and are made by United Ceramic Tile Co. Your local tile dealer should be able to get these for you. If you have difficulty, write the company directly at 923 Motor Parkway, Hauppauge, New York, 11787.

To use the planter for living plants, place a layer of gravel at the bottom. Over this place a layer of charcoal, followed by potting soil.

The planter support is being installed here. It will be held in place with screws driven diagonally through ends.

This view shows how the tiles rest on the tile base. And this, in its turn rests on the tile-bases supports.

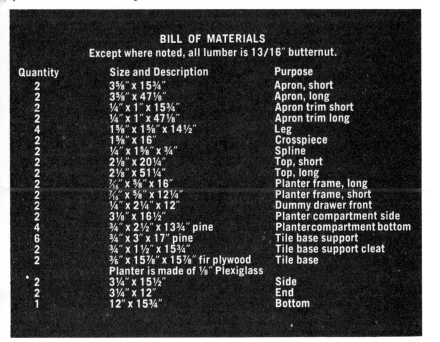

BILL OF MATERIALS
Except where noted, all lumber is 13/16" butternut.

Quantity	Size and Description	Purpose
2	3⅝" x 15¾"	Apron, short
2	3⅝" x 47⅛"	Apron, long
2	¼" x 1" x 15¾"	Apron trim short
2	¼" x 1" x 47⅛"	Apron trim long
4	1⅝" x 1⅝" x 14½"	Leg
2	1⅝" x 16"	Crosspiece
2	¼" x 1⅝" x ¾"	Spline
2	2⅛" x 20¼"	Top, short
2	2⅛" x 51¼"	Top, long
2	7/16" x ⅝" x 16"	Planter frame, long
2	7/16" x ⅝" x 12¼"	Planter frame, short
2	¼" x 2¼" x 12"	Dummy drawer front
2	3⅛" x 16½"	Planter compartment side
4	¾" x 2½" x 13¾" pine	Planter compartment bottom
6	¾" x 3" x 17" pine	Tile base support
2	¾" x 1½" x 15¾"	Tile base support cleat
2	⅜" x 15⅞" x 15⅞" fir plywood	Tile base
	Planter is made of ⅛" Plexiglass	
2	3¼" x 15½"	Side
2	3¼" x 12"	End
1	12" x 15¾"	Bottom

After planter has been made, assembled and the cement has set an extra bead should be placed along inside corners.

ANTIQUE DESK

With this design you can produce a good looking, high quality piece of furniture at a really low cost, because all you use is second hand lumber

Y OU COULD PAY hundreds of dollars for a ready-made secretary-desk like that above—or you can build it in your home workshop for about a tenth of the price.

The economy trick is largely in the gold-antiqued finish that conceals surface flaws so completely you can use board grade or even second-hand lumber in the construction. All finishing materials, even the cloth pads for blending and texturing, are supplied in a nationally-available kit.

To begin, round up as much scrap board and used lumber as you can to fill out the items specified in the Materials List. Edge-trim and sand any old lumber going into the job. You need not get it smooth, just free of rough fibers. Squeegee a spackling compound over any pits; the antiquing process will hide this filler completely.

Cut the sides, tops, and bottoms of the upper and lower units, making certain the ends are square. The backs may be plywood or tongue and groove (T&G), though it's a good idea to use plywood for the back of the lower unit to insure rigidity, as the weight of the upper unit rests on it.

Use an original corner of the plywood panel for one of the cabinet corners and you'll square it immediately. Fasten all lumber-to-lumber joints with 8d finishing nails; sink the heads and spackle them flush. If 1¼-inch plywood is used for the back, install it with 1-inch brads. Try a gap-filler glue such as casein or aliphatic resin to reinforce the joints.

To prepare doors rim the lower doors with 1 x 2 stock on all sides except where the hinges will go. There, install 1 x 3 to allow the

door to overlap the cabinet side.

Upper doors are made from stock screen frame. Recess an inside edge of the stock ¼ x ¾-inch and cut the horizontal and vertical frame pieces. Lay out the mitered framing and attach with corrugated fasteners.

Instead of screening, cut ¾-inch welded wire mesh on the diagonal to fit the rabbetted area of each top door. A few shots from your staple gun will anchor the mesh, then run casein or aliphatic glue along the channels to lock it firmly all around. The diagonal position is not only decorative but it also braces the doors.

There's a simple trick to shaping the rounded upper portion of the doors. Merely cut a circle from scrap plywood and then use the cut off sections in the doors. Fasten the plywood fillets in place at upper corners against the wire mesh using 6d finishing nails through their tapered ends and glue along the edges. Conceal the seams with a spackling compound. Use corner plates to stiff the doors at their lower corners, corrugated fasteners at the upper ones.

Desk lid supports slide out automatically through front guide holes when the lid is opened; return when it is closed. Two long screen door springs connected to these slides by a chain provide the loco

Working with used lumber is a cheap way to obtain sturdy material with an authentic look for an antiqued project. Squaring edges will take care of any notches of uneveness.

Since the finishing process will hide any flaws in the wood, a light sanding, followed by squeegeeing some spackling into hole and deep cuts, will do for the roughest surfaces.

Make both sections at the same time to make sure they will match in width. Favor plywood for the back of the lower unit; tongue and groove boards work well for upper half.

For stiffness, strengthen the lower corners of upper doors with corner plates. Corrugated fasteners, reinforced by curved sections, will hold the miters at upper corners.

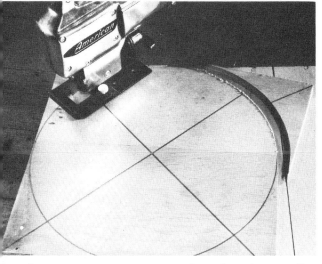

Here is an easy way to get curved sections for rounding the door tops. Cut a circle from a square equal to the diameter needed. Two cut corners combine to make a top.

Use spackling compound to fill in every crack and seam that remains after gluing and nailing each curved section in place. The final finish will hide any touch-up.

ANTIQUE DESK

Rim the lower doors with 1 x 2 stock on all sides except where the hinges will be placed. There, install 1 x 3 stock which allows the door to overlap the cabinet side.

The first step in the finishing process is the application of base paint with brush in the conventional manner. If second coat is necessary, let the first coat dry overnight

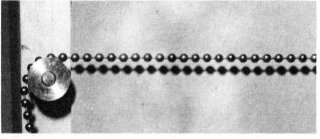

A bead chain operates the writing lid supports. It runs over standard bead chain sprockets located at the rear of slots in writing top; it connects the lid slide, and spring.

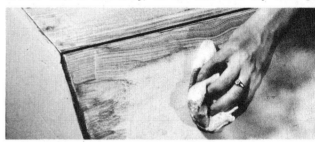

Having applied base paint, next step is to brush on the gold antique, and then wipe it off central panel areas. A gold luster remains; it's more prominent around the rims

motion, doing away with any carefully fitted metal levers.

After installing the channel bottom in the lower section and cutting and fitting the writing top, insert the support slides and check them for proper fit. Attach a long shank screw eye on the top of each slide about 4 inches from the inside end and on one side so that it will ride along the recessed side of the writing top. Install a standard ⅛-inch diameter bead chain sprocket on each recessed edge of the writing top about 1-inch in from the end.

Now, attach ⅛-inch bead chain to the inside of the lid 4 inches from the hinge, using a small staple or screw eye. Feed the chain through the long-shank screw eye on the slide, pass it over the chain sprocket and down in back to the screen door spring. Clinch the screw eye over the chain to lock it. With lid closed, attach chain to spring with moderate tension.

As you open the desk lid, the screw eye will slide forward in its slot and the chain should slide the support until it is fully extended. Close the lid and the slide should retract out of sight. If any adjustment is needed, increase or decrease the spring tension. Once this is set correctly, cut off excess chain and hook up the other slide in the same manner.

Shelves in both upper and lower units may be placed to suit your individual needs. If reinforced with glue and held by 6d finishing nails driven through the sides, no cleats are needed for normal loading.

Applying a finish to a cabinet built with wood would appear to present a tedious and expensive finishing problem. The secretary-desk, however, was transformed into a fine piece of furniture with materials obtained in an antiquing kit.

If you wish to do the job as it was done in the photos, choose white as a base color. Stir the base

paint and apply, after making sure the surface is clean and dry. Some of the used lumber may already have paint on it. You can go over this if you first sand off the gloss.

One coat of paint is usually enough. If the wood is badly blemished, add a second coat; let it dry before you start antiquing.

Antique gold is brushed on after the base paint has dried overnight, it's not a gilt and not intended to cover like one. The base color will be partially visible through it. While the brushed-on gold is still wet, gently wipe the central area of the panel so the outer rim area will have a heavier coat. A subtle gold luster will still remain over the whole area.

Work only one panel at a time. Use the cloth pads from the kit to create any effect you want, using a patting or swirling motion and a light touch to blend out the gold and eliminate any brush marks. Stir the gold frequently while you

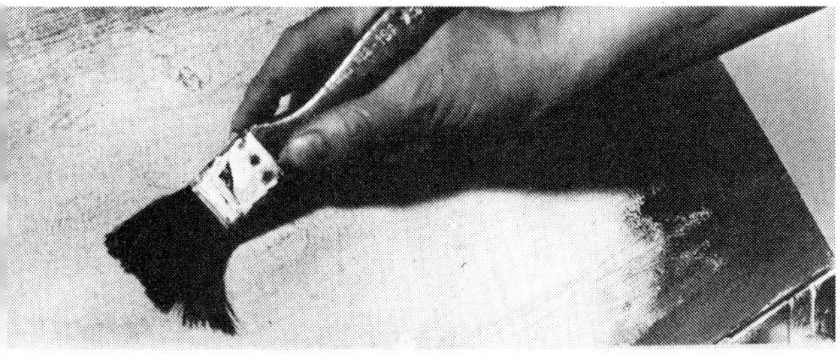

Finally, when the gold application has completely dried, cover the piece with a coat of vinyl liquid laminate to make it scrubbable. For more luster, apply second coat.

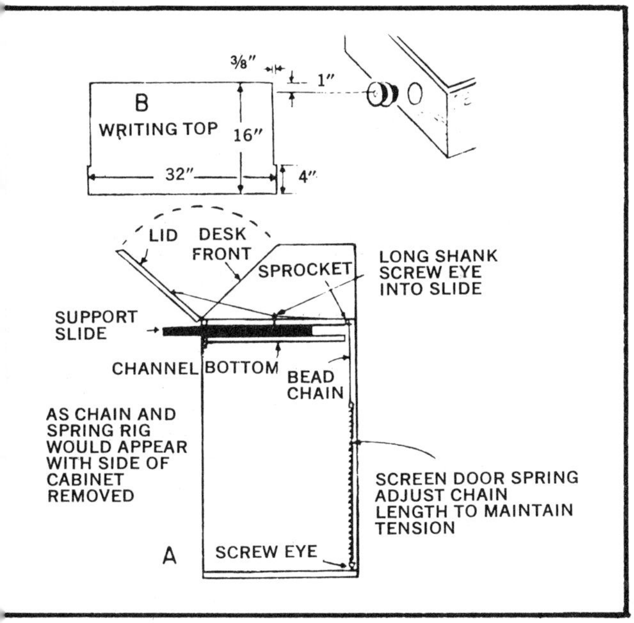

3/8″
1″
B
WRITING TOP
16″
32″
4″
LID
DESK FRONT
SPROCKET
LONG SHANK SCREW EYE INTO SLIDE
SUPPORT SLIDE
CHANNEL
BOTTOM
BEAD CHAIN
AS CHAIN AND SPRING RIG WOULD APPEAR WITH SIDE OF CABINET REMOVED
SCREEN DOOR SPRING ADJUST CHAIN LENGTH TO MAINTAIN TENSION
A
SCREW EYE

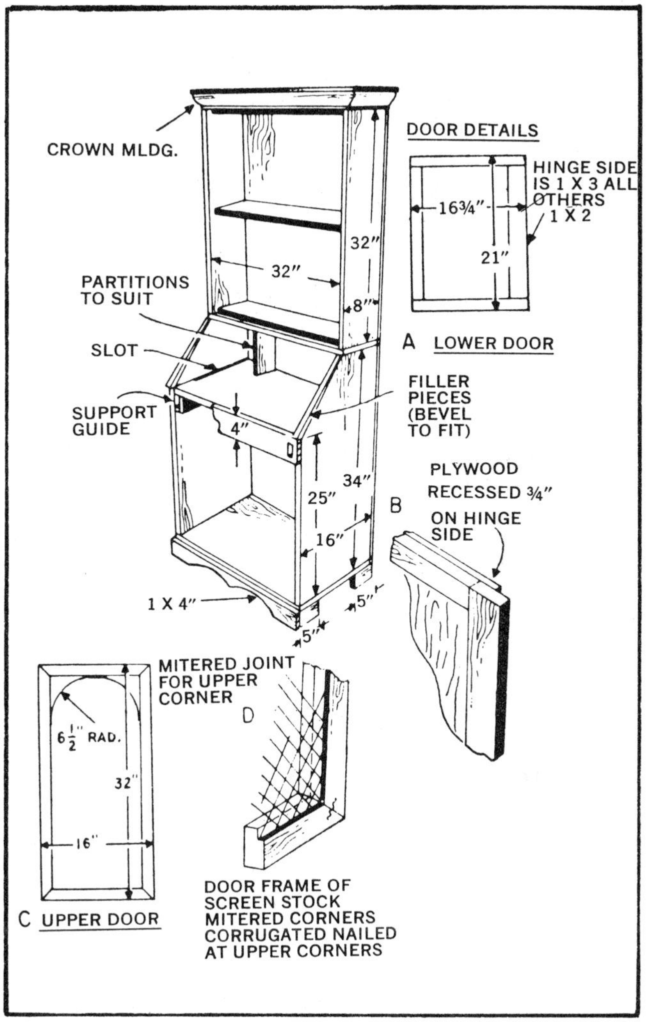

CROWN MLDG.
DOOR DETAILS
HINGE SIDE IS 1 X 3 ALL OTHERS 1 X 2
16¾″
21″
32″
32″
PARTITIONS TO SUIT
8″
SLOT
A LOWER DOOR
SUPPORT GUIDE
4″
FILLER PIECES (BEVEL TO FIT)
PLYWOOD RECESSED ¾″ ON HINGE SIDE
34″
25″
B
16″
1 X 4″
5″
5″
MITERED JOINT FOR UPPER CORNER
D
6½″ RAD.
32″
16″
C UPPER DOOR
DOOR FRAME OF SCREEN STOCK MITERED CORNERS CORRUGATED NAILED AT UPPER CORNERS

work to keep the gold metallic particles dispersed through it.

If you prefer a wavy or stippled pattern, use the pads to create it. There is no set style for antiquing. The finest examples represent the preference of the craftsman who produced them. So you use your own ideas. Take plenty of time to work as the gold dries slowly, and you can add more after the first coat dries. Let it deposit in the crevices of moldings for emphasis.

Don't aim for a straight-lined mass-production look. The beauty of an authentic antiqued finish is in its individuality.

The vinyl liquid laminate goes on after the gold has dried overnight. This is the crystal clear coating that makes your antiquing job completely scrubbable. And wet glasses won't leave rings on it. One coat is enough but if you want a higher luster you can add another coat after the first one has dried overnight.

BILL OF MATERIALS

Quantity	Size and Description		Purpose
4	1″	8″x32″ used or scrap wood	top unit and rear writing surface
4	1″	8″x34″ used or scrap wood	bottom unit sides
5	1″	8″x33½″ used or scrap wood	top and bottom of lower unit, and desk lid
4	1″	8″x21″ used or scrap wood	door panels, lower unit
2	1″	4″x33½″ used or scrap wood	base front and cross member above lower doors
1	1″	4″x24″ used or scrap wood	base side
2	1″	4″x16″ used or scrap wood	lid support channels
2	1″	4″x17½″ used or scrap wood	lower door rim
4	1″	2″x16¾″ used or scrap wood	lower door rim
2	1″	2″x17½″ used or scrap wood	lower door rim
2	1″	2″x32″ used or scrap wood	vertical frame, upper doors
4	1″	2″x16″ used or scrap wood	horizontal frame, upper doors
2	1″	2″x16″ used or scrap wood	lid support slides
1	¼″	33½″x35½″ plywood	bottom unit back
1	¼″	33½″x32″ plywood	upper unit back
1	½″	13¼″x14¼″ plywood	upper door top corners
1	5″x5′ crown molding		top unit
2 yds.	36″ welded mesh		upper door grilles
2	screen door springs		lid support slide returns
2	⅝″ bead chain sprockets		lid support slide extensions
1	⅛″x60″ bead chain		lid support slide extensions

NOTE: Also need 6d and 8d finishing nails, 1″ brads, screw eyes, casein or aliphatic resin glue, spackling compound, hardware and antiquing kit.

Two Shaving Bars

Here you can choose between two contemporary-style projects that you can build quickly and easily. They will help you keep your shaving gear together and the bathroom nea

IF YOU FIND your shaving gear cramped for space in the medicine cabinet, build a wall-hung shaving bar. Here are two excellent models styled by a noted industrial designer. Each of these is easily constructed of cabinet wood, aluminum, glass and mosaic tile.

One model features a mirror that slides up for access to the interior of the cabinet, and a lower drop-front that doubles as a closure and shelf. This cabinet is made of ½-inch solid walnut, except for the hardboard back and plywood mirror panel. Remember that the side pieces must be mirror images of each other, not exact duplicates. These are grooved at the rear to take the back panel, and at the front for sliding mirror unit. Note that a supporting plywood panel, not the mirror itself, slides in the grooves. The mirror is simply cemented to the panel. The panel is rabbeted at the top and bottom for long aluminum angle "irons" that serve as handles, and along the sides to fit into approximately 9/16-inch wide grooves on the sides.

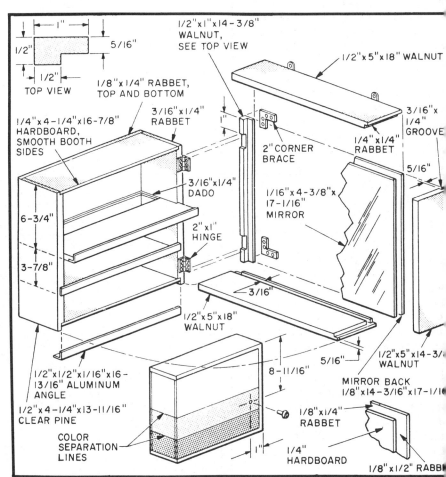

TOP VIEW

1/2"x1"x14-3/8" WALNUT, SEE TOP VIEW

1/2"x5"x18" WALNUT

1/8"x1/4" RABBET, TOP AND BOTTOM

3/16"x1/4" RABBET

3/16"x 1/4" GROOVE

1/4"x4-1/4"x16-7/8" HARDBOARD, SMOOTH BOOTH SIDES

2" CORNER BRACE

1/4"x1/4" RABBET

5/16"

3/16"x1/4" DADO

1/16"x4-3/8"x 17-1/16" MIRROR

6-3/4"

2"x1" HINGE

3-7/8"

3/16"

1/2"x5"x18" WALNUT

1/2"x1/2"x1/16"x16-13/16" ALUMINUM ANGLE

1/2"x4-1/4"x13-11/16" CLEAR PINE

COLOR SEPARATION LINES

8-11/16"

5/16"

1/2"x5"x14-3/ WALNUT

MIRROR BACK 1/8"x14-3/16"x17-1/1

1/8"x1/4" RABBET

1/4" HARDBOARD

1/8"x1/2" RABB

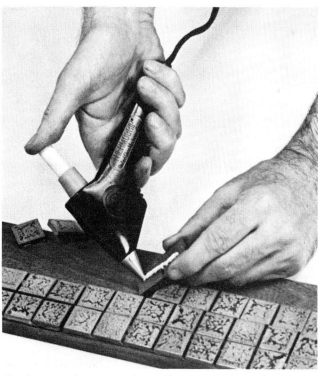

A desk-lid type arm supports the panel when it is in the open position and a magnetic catch keeps it closed. The mirror slides up and down, providing more storage space.

The hot glue is used to bond the ceramic tile to the drop-front. Also be sure to heat the aluminum strips, which are used in both bars, before applying to achieve a better bond.

The mirror is held in the raised position by magnetic catches. Mount these catches onto the mirror backing and fit the mirror unit into place *before* you glue the sides of the cabinet into position.

The hot glue is used to bond the ceramic tile to the drop-front. An aluminum angle across the top provides a handle for this door. Heat the aluminum (and those on the mirror panel) before applying the stick glue. A desk-lid type arm supports the panel in the open position; a magnetic catch keeps it closed.

The other model has a front that swings out. Study the diagrams carefully, and note that the front *rests* over the main part of the cabinet which is made of pine and a hardboard back panel. Retaining edges on the shelves consist of angle-aluminum cemented onto the rabbeted shelf edges.

The swinging front is a three-sided affair with a mirror on the inside. It is made of ½-inch solid walnut and a hardboard back. Metal corner braces are used on the right-hand hinge post for added strength.

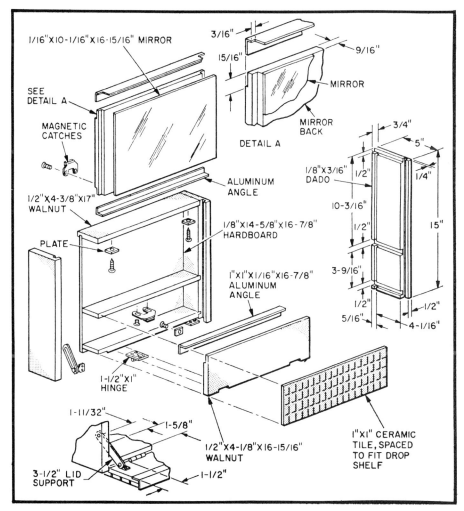

MODERN STORAGE CABINET

Simple elegance describes this wood and glass unit, sure to be a bright spot in any home and built with a few ordinary tools and inexpensive plywood

THIS MODERN CHINA cabinet/storage unit, elegantly sleek and stylishly simple in appearance, will blend in well with other contemporary furniture pieces. The simplicity of its design and lack of ornamentation makes it fairly easy to build. It features a storage compartment at the bottom and smoked glass doors at the top. The center section is left open. It is made entirely of plywood except for the edging which is cut from solid stock.

The pivot hinges for the glass doors are quite novel. They do not require holes to be drilled into the glass. Instead, they are furnished with nylon studs which securely hold the glass. Another feature of these new hinges is the built-in bullet catch stop.

The two basic tools needed for this project are the table saw and router. Dado joints are used throughout and this is where the router comes in handy.

The lumber used was ¾-inch red birch plywood and solid stock. You will need two 4′ × 8″ panels and one ¼″ panel for the back. Most lumber yards will rip the plywood free or for a nominal charge. If your lumber dealer will do it, have the boards ripped to 16-inch widths. This will make it easier to carry. You can then recut the boards to the final width in your shop. Lumber yard dealers can rough-cut the stock to size but most will not or cannot maintain the accuracy required in cabinetmaking, such as for this project. Also, they use coarse blades leaving less than smooth edges.

Start construction with the two side members. Trim them to the

You may choose to use smoked glass on your unit. Clear glass was used in our model to show off the display area. But smoked glass can give it the jazzy contemporary look of expensive pieces.

proper length then rip them to the necessary width. Place them on the work table back-side up and proceed to lay out the double line for the dado. The lines are to be exactly ¾″ apart. No need to run the lines across the board. Marking them along one edge will suffice.

One of the most effective ways for cutting dadoes requires the use of a router guide. This is a homemade gadget and consists of a "T" square made of ¾-inch stock. Make the guide as shown and bear in mind that it must be perfectly "square." If it is off, the dadoes will likewise be off.

Fit your router with a ¾″ straight cutter, preferably carbide tipped. Set the depth of cut to ³⁄₁₆″ then clamp the guide to a piece of scrap wood, and take two cuts, one on either side of the straight-edge. These will serve as locators when cutting the dadoes.

Sides. To cut the dadoes, slide the guide along the work until the pencil marks previously drawn at the edge of the board line up with the dado groove in the guide. Clamp the guide at the far end then proceed to cut the dado. When done, slide the guide to the next set of marks and repeat the procedure. To prevent damage to the work, be sure to use a wood pad under the clamp where it contacts the work.

When the dado operation is completed, run a ¼″ × ⅜″ rabbet along the rear inner edges to accept the rear panel. If the router left fuzz at the edges of the rabbet or dadoes, clean with a piece of 220 sandpaper.

Shelves. The shelves are made next. Cut the seven pieces to length (31⅜″), but not to width. The solid

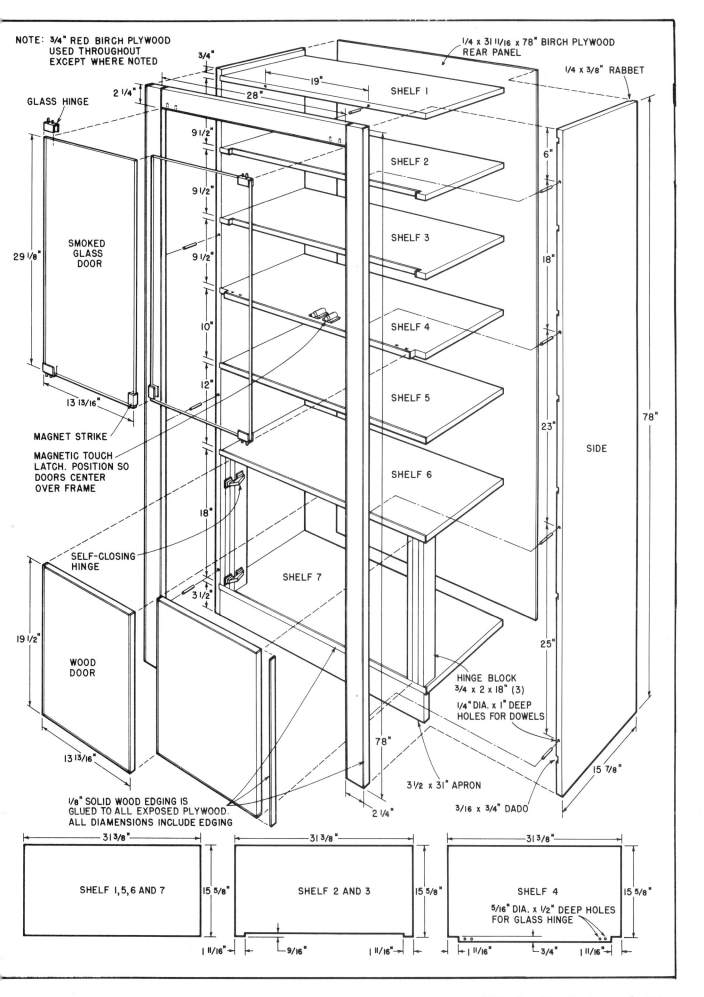

NOTE: 3/4" RED BIRCH PLYWOOD USED THROUGHOUT EXCEPT WHERE NOTED

GLASS HINGE

SMOKED GLASS DOOR

29 1/8"

13 13/16"

MAGNET STRIKE

MAGNETIC TOUCH LATCH. POSITION SO DOORS CENTER OVER FRAME

SELF-CLOSING HINGE

18"

19 1/2"

WOOD DOOR

13 13/16"

1/8" SOLID WOOD EDGING IS GLUED TO ALL EXPOSED PLYWOOD. ALL DIAMENSIONS INCLUDE EDGING

3/4"

2 1/4"

28"

19"

SHELF 1

9 1/2"

SHELF 2

9 1/2"

SHELF 3

9 1/2"

10"

SHELF 4

12"

SHELF 5

SHELF 6

SHELF 7

3 1/2"

78"

2 1/4"

1/4 x 31 11/16 x 78" BIRCH PLYWOOD REAR PANEL

1/4 x 3/8" RABBET

6"

18"

23"

SIDE

25"

78"

HINGE BLOCK 3/4 x 2 x 18" (3)

1/4" DIA. x 1" DEEP HOLES FOR DOWELS

3 1/2 x 31" APRON

3/16 x 3/4" DADO

15 7/8"

31 3/8"

SHELF 1,5,6 AND 7

15 5/8"

1 11/16"   9/16"   1 11/16"

31 3/8"

SHELF 2 AND 3

15 5/8"

31 3/8"

SHELF 4

5/16" DIA. x 1/2" DEEP HOLES FOR GLASS HINGE

15 5/8"

1 11/16"   3/4"   1 11/16"

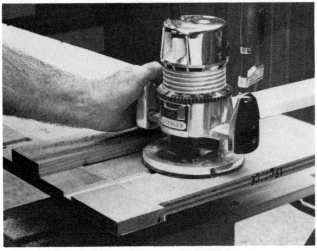

The use of a homemade dado guide eases the cutting of dadoes for the cabinet sides. Use a guide for straight cuts.

The dadoes cut in the sides of the cabinet will hold the shelves, so be certain they are equal for level shelves.

The edging is prepared by ripping ⅞"-wide strips of hardwood to match the plywood. Trim the overhang.

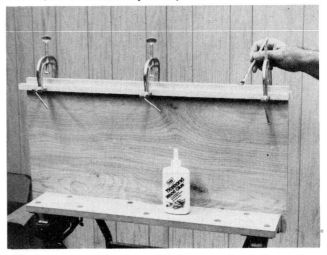

Edging clamps are in place and glue is applied to fasten the edging. When clamping, center the strip over the ¾" shelf.

MODERN STORAGE CABINET

wood strip must be added to the front edge of the shelves. You can cut these strips and add them with glue and brads. A better method is to glue a thicker piece to the edge, then trim it later. The advantage here is that the thicker piece assures better contact under clamping pressure and easier handling.

Prepare the edging by ripping ⅞"-wide strips of hardwood to match the red birch plywood. The ⅞"-width will leave a slight overhang which will be trimmed off later.

Edging clamps are ideal for this operation, but are not essential. Regular clamps can be used in the conventional manner. When clamping, be sure to center the ⅞" strip over the ¾" shelf. Apply glue to both surfaces then clamp and watch out for the strip creeping.

When all the edges have been glued, set the saw table fence so that ⅛" of the trim will be left on the edge. Next, reset the saw fence to 15⅝", then recut the shelves trimming off the excess at the rear edge of the shelves.

You will note that four of the shelves are identical rectangles, and the other three are not. Shelves #2 and #3 are notched along the front edge to allow clearance for the swinging glass doors. Shelf #4 is deeper than the others and is notched at the front corners. The added depth is necessary to support the sockets for the glass hinge.

When all shelves are cut, add the solid edging to the fronts. Note that the dimensions shown are for the shelves with the edging included.

The assembly and gluing of the shelves to the sides must be done with great care. A pair of saw horses is recommended. Straddle them with a pair of 2 × 3's about 7 feet long.

These will support the cabinet and also serve as cauls under the clamps. The rear panel should be cut to size at this time.

To assure a good strong joint, glue size the ends of the shelves. Do this by thinning some glue with water and brush on the ends of all the shelves. Allow to dry about 15 minutes. The glue we used was an aliphatic resin type which is strong and fast-drying. This fast-drying feature may pose a problem unless you work fast and with an assistant. If you are too slow in this operation, the first-glued joints may start to set before you get to the last joint. If you think this will be a problem, it is suggested that you use a glue with a longer standing time. Most hide glues will serve this purpose.

Apply undiluted glue to the dado grooves and to the shelf ends, then install the shelves into the grooves. Add glue to the other ends of the

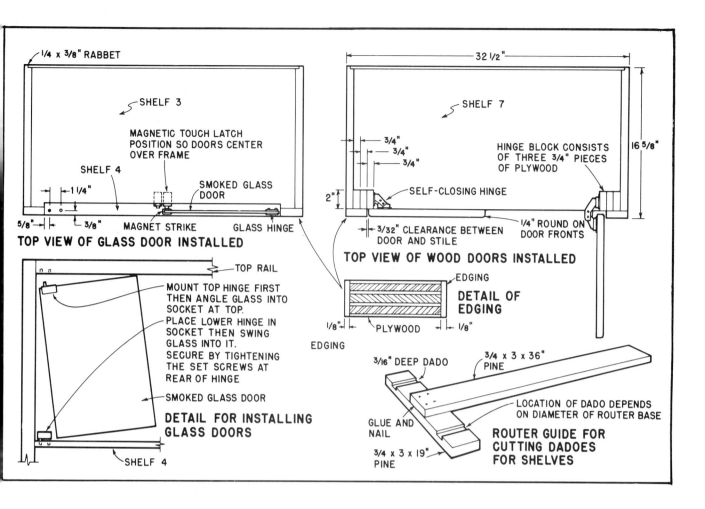

TOP VIEW OF GLASS DOOR INSTALLED

1/4 x 3/8" RABBET

SHELF 3

MAGNETIC TOUCH LATCH POSITION SO DOORS CENTER OVER FRAME

SHELF 4

SMOKED GLASS DOOR

1 1/4"

5/8" 3/8" MAGNET STRIKE GLASS HINGE

32 1/2"

SHELF 7

3/4"
3/4"
3/4"

HINGE BLOCK CONSISTS OF THREE 3/4" PIECES OF PLYWOOD

16 5/8"

2"

SELF-CLOSING HINGE

1/4" ROUND ON DOOR FRONTS

3/32" CLEARANCE BETWEEN DOOR AND STILE

TOP VIEW OF WOOD DOORS INSTALLED

TOP RAIL

MOUNT TOP HINGE FIRST THEN ANGLE GLASS INTO SOCKET AT TOP.

PLACE LOWER HINGE IN SOCKET THEN SWING GLASS INTO IT. SECURE BY TIGHTENING THE SET SCREWS AT REAR OF HINGE

SMOKED GLASS DOOR

DETAIL FOR INSTALLING GLASS DOORS

SHELF 4

EDGING

DETAIL OF EDGING

1/8" PLYWOOD 1/8"

EDGING

3/16" DEEP DADO

3/4 x 3 x 36" PINE

GLUE AND NAIL

3/4 x 3 x 19" PINE

LOCATION OF DADO DEPENDS ON DIAMETER OF ROUTER BASE

ROUTER GUIDE FOR CUTTING DADOES FOR SHELVES

Take great care when assembling and glueing shelves to the sides. Use a pair of sawhorses and 2 x 3s for support.

To check for assembly squareness, temporarily insert the rear panel. After panel is removed check with square.

---

shelves and to the grooves of the other side member. Assemble carefully then apply the clamps as shown.

To assure that the assembly is square, insert the rear panel temporarily. If the top or bottom shelf is parallel to the end of the rear panel, the assembly will be square. After the panel is removed, you can check for squareness with a builder's square.

The front frame consists of two side stiles and a top rail. Rip these to size then edge and recut so they will be 2-1/4" wide. The frame members are fastened to the cabinet sides with 1/4" dowels. Locate and drill the holes in the front edges of the side and top shelf. Use dowel centers to transfer the hole locations to the

frame members. The holes in the cabinet are drilled one-inch deep and those in the frames 1/2" deep. Fasten the frame members to the cabinet with glue and clamp securely.

The apron and hinge blocks are added next. The blocks are necessary if you use the hinges shown. These are self-closing, adjustable and surface mounted. They open flush with

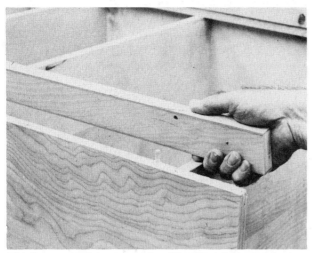

The frame members are fastened to the cabinet sides with ¼" dowels. Fasten them with glue and clamp securely till dry.

Special hinges are used in this project. They are self-closing, adjustable, surface mounted and open flush with inside.

Detail shows the strike for the glass doors before it has been fully inserted. These strikes keep the doors closed.

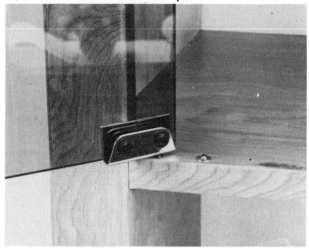

The glass is held in place by tightening the nylon screws at the rear edge. Lower hinge is placed into socket first.

MODERN STORAGE CABINET

the inside, but they are designed to be used from zero to full overlay.

Cut the doors to size then edge with the side edging running the full length of the door. See drawing. To allow for clearance, the outer corners of the door must be rounded.

The glass doors are purchased cut to size. Ask for smoked glass. These are ¼" plate glass and are quite expensive, so be sure the size is correct. To make sure the size shown will fit your cabinet, you may want to make a pair of dummy doors out of ¼" plywood. Install them and check them out carefully. The doors should clear the side stiles as well as the #2 and #3 shelves.

Install the glass doors by fastening the top hinge to the glass. Hold in place by tightening the nylon screws at the rear edge. Now place the lower hinge into the lower socket then swing the glass into place.

Bill of Materials

All lumber is ¾" red birch plywood except as noted.

Side	¾ × 15-⅞ × 78	2
Rear	¼ × 31-11/16 × 78	1
Shelf	¾ × 15-⅝ × 31-⅜	6
Shelf	¾ × 16-⅜ × 31-⅜	1
Hinge block	¾ × 2 × 19	6
Apron	¾ × 3-½ × 31	1
Frame top	¾ × 2-¼ × 28	1
Frame side	¾ × 2-¼ × 78	2
Dowel	¼ × 1-7/16	10
Door, wood	¾ × 13-13/16 × 19-½	2
Door, glass, smoked	13-13/16 × 29-⅛	2
Edging	⅛ × ¾, solid birch	40 ft.
Glass hinge (GDH)		2 pr.
Hinge, self-closing (IH)		2 pr.
Touch Latch (TL)		2
Strike (MAS)		2

Trestle Desk

This fine piece recaptures the simplicity and handsome styling of the Early American tradition in furniture design

THIS FINE DESK can be easily built with ordinary tools. It features three full depth drawers which provide ample storage for stationery, books, etc. The dividers at the rear are useful for keeping bills, letters and important papers in order. The large writing area allows you to write easily without feeling cramped.

Lumber. The material used for the main part of the desk is 5/4″ pine (which is 1⅛″ dressed). However, ½″ pine and plywood are also utilized. In addition, 1¾″ stock is used for the pedestal base. The ½″ pine is used to keep costs down. The desk top and shelf are both made of ½″ material with the edges built up to give the appearance of heavier lumber. The side pieces are 11-inches wide and while it is available in one piece, 5/4″ x 12″, the cost is much higher than narrower boards, and so we decided to glue up to make the necessary width. Also, wider boards have a tendency to warp and cup. Glueing up narrower pieces eliminates this problem. The plywood is used for the bottom of the desk compartment.

Construction starts with the side pieces. Assuming that you will use two or more pieces to make the necessary width, rip enough stock for both side pieces. Allow a little extra stock for trimming after glueing. The glued joint should be doweled. In order to place the dowels properly, make a kraft paper pattern of the side section using the squares provided. Layout the pattern carefully, then cut with a scissor or razor blade. Use the pattern as a guide to determine where to place the glue line. Bear in mind that the dowels will penetrate each section by one inch. The pieces to be glued must be square and true. After ripping, the edges should be trued up with a jointer or jack plane. Take light cuts; only remove enough stock to clean the glue line edges.

The dowels used are ⅜″ x 2″.

Trestle Desk

The dowel holes must be accurately located and aligned. Perhaps the best way to drill these holes is with a doweling jig which will assure perfect alignment of the mating pieces automatically. Drill the holes about 1⅛″ deep. Insert the dowels after coating them lightly with glue. Apply glue to the mating surfaces then bring them together and clamp. After the glue has set, remove the clamps and trace the outline of the side. Be sure to mark the button hole centers. The two rear buttons conceal screw heads, the front two are dummies and used only for appearance. Cut the outline with a saber saw then sand smooth to remove all kerf marks. Next, drill the button holes—½″ diameter and ¼″ deep. At the rear location drill the 3/16″ screw clearance holes. Round off edges with a router. Do not round off the inside bottoms.

Rear Panel is also made up of glued stock. Again, use dowels and follow procedure outlined above. In this case, however, the location of the dowels is not critical. After gluing the board, rip it to size then cut the rabbet along the lower edge. Do this on the table saw, making two passes, one with the board held vertically, the second with the board held horizontally. Set the depth and width of the cut for ½″. Cut the ½″ grooves for the desk top and shelf also. Make a series of cuts on the table saw or use the router. Use the router to round off the top and outside bottom corners.

The shelf is made with ½″ wood. The edge is thickened with a strip of 1⅛″ stock. Rabbet the top edge of the strip to accept the ½″ board. Shape the leading edge of the strip with a router. Use a rounding cutter for the lower edge and a beaded cutter for the top edge. Glue the strip to the board carefully. The joint should be tight so it will look like one piece. Repeat the procedure for the desk top. Because of the width, glue up several pieces of ½″ boards to obtain the required size.

Pedestals are cut next. These are straight-sided and do not require special treatment. Likewise, the trestle is straight. Cut these to the proper lengths, then rip to width. Round off the corners. Make up the two pedestal support blocks. These are cut to size, then drilled to accommodate the flat head mounting screws. Countersink the holes for the screw heads. Also drill and counterbore the screw holes for the trestle.

Base pieces are cut from 1¾″ stock. Make a layout on kraft paper, then cut and trace onto the lumber. The lumber should be 3½″ wide so that only the shaped ends of the pieces need be cut with the saber saw. Sand the pieces after cutting and be sure to remove all saw marks.

Layout the two lag screw mounting holes. Counterbore the holes to accept the washers.

Prior to assembling the sections, sand all surfaces smooth. Start with a medium grit paper such as 80 then work with finer grits ending with 220.

The desk compartment top and bottom are glued to two spacers cut from ½″ wood. These are butted and held in position with a few brads. Clamp securely. When the glue sets, add the rear panel and shelf. The sides are installed and fastened to the rear piece with flat head screws. The spacers are also screwed to the side pieces. This will bring all members of the desk compartment together. The leading edge of the shelf is fastened to the sides with 10d finishing nails, one at each end. Sink the heads and fill.

Install the pedestal support blocks at the top of each pedestal. Use glue and nails. Invert the pedestal and mount the base pieces. Drill pilot holes to correspond to the lag screw holes drilled earlier in the base pieces. Use glue and join all pieces. Be sure to use washers under the lag screw heads. Mount the cross piece after both pedestals have been completed. Stand the pedestals on a flat surface while installing the cross piece. Join with flat head screws

Dowel holes must be accurately loca and aligned. It's best to use a dowe for aligning and centering the holes.

Drive dowels so only one inch shows If you're using smooth dowels, taper e and cut grooves along dowel length.

It will be necessary to cut dadoes in both the shelf and desk top sections v a router. Use a piece of wood as guide

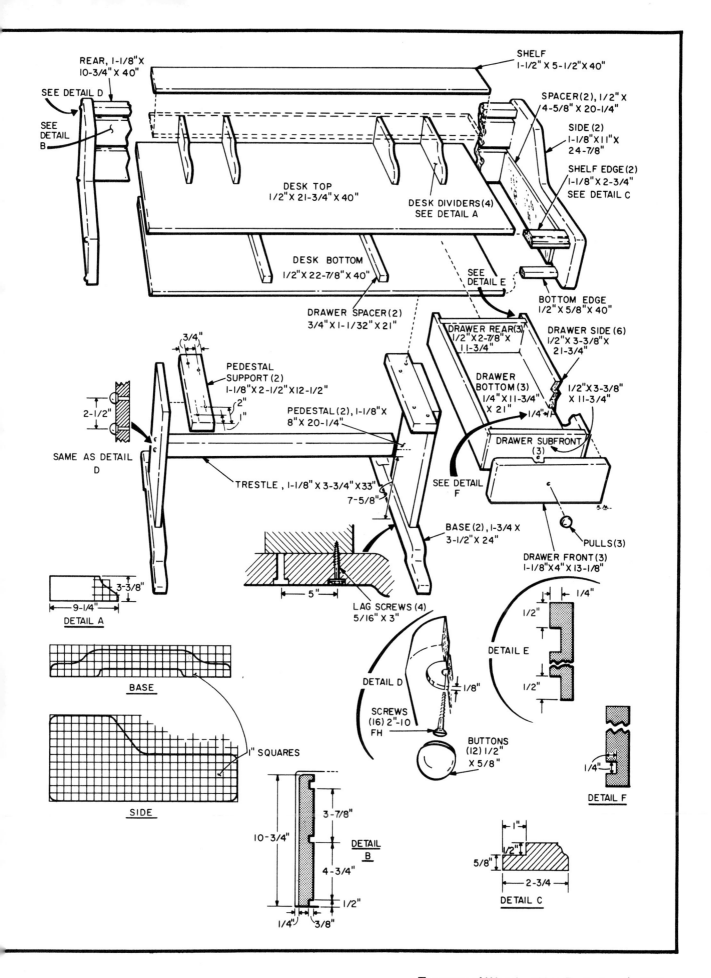

REAR, 1-1/8" X 10-3/4" X 40"

SEE DETAIL D

SEE DETAIL B

SHELF 1-1/2" X 5-1/2" X 40"

SPACER(2), 1/2" X 4-5/8" X 20-1/4"

SIDE (2) 1-1/8" X 11" X 24-7/8"

SHELF EDGE (2) 1-1/8" X 2-3/4" SEE DETAIL C

DESK TOP 1/2" X 21-3/4" X 40"

DESK DIVIDERS(4) SEE DETAIL A

DESK BOTTOM 1/2" X 22-7/8" X 40"

SEE DETAIL E

BOTTOM EDGE 1/2" X 5/8" X 40"

DRAWER SPACER(2) 3/4" X 1-1/32" X 21"

DRAWER REAR(3) 1/2" X 2-7/8" X 11-3/4"

DRAWER SIDE (6) 1/2" X 3-3/8" X 21-3/4"

DRAWER BOTTOM(3) 1/4" X 11-3/4" X 21

1/2" X 3-3/8" X 11-3/4"

1/4"

DRAWER SUBFRONT (3)

3/4"

PEDESTAL SUPPORT (2) 1-1/8" X 2-1/2" X 12-1/2"

2"

1"

2-1/2"

SAME AS DETAIL D

PEDESTAL(2), 1-1/8" X 8" X 20-1/4"

TRESTLE, 1-1/8" X 3-3/4" X 33"

7-5/8"

SEE DETAIL F

BASE(2), 1-3/4 X 3-1/2" X 24"

PULLS(3)

DRAWER FRONT(3) 1-1/8" X 4" X 13-1/8"

5"

LAG SCREWS (4) 5/16" X 3"

1/4"

1/2"

DETAIL E

1/2"

3-3/8"

9-1/4"

DETAIL A

BASE

SIDE

1" SQUARES

DETAIL D

SCREWS (16) 2"-10 FH

1/8"

BUTTONS (12) 1/2" X 5/8"

1/4"

DETAIL F

3-7/8"

10-3/4"

DETAIL B

4-3/4"

1/2"

1/4"

3/8"

1"

1/2"

5/8"

2-3/4"

DETAIL C

Trestle Desk

and glue. The pedestal assembly is now fastened to the underside of the desk compartment. Use 1¾"-10 flat head screws. Note—the screws will penetrate the ½" plywood bottom. Since the drawer bottoms are raised slightly, the points will clear the drawers. If smaller screws are used, they won't have the necessary holding power.

Drawers are made with 1⅛" fronts and ½" sides, rear and subfront. Joints are rabbeted at the front and dadoed at the rear. A groove at the lower edge holds the ¼" plywood bottoms. Cut the parts to size and dado as shown. The subfront must be drilled for the screw clearance before assembly. The drawer fronts are cut to size and the edges rounded with the router.

Assemble the drawers with glue and brads. Place the brads through the sub-front angling them slightly. The heads will be hidden when the fronts are installed. Note that the fronts are raised 1/16" above the drawer bottoms. Add the drawer spacers between the drawers.

Finally, cut the compartment dividers and install below the shelf. They are not held with nails or glue. Simply cut them so they slide in with a snug fit. Finish the desk with stain and gloss top coat.

BILL OF MATERIALS FOR TRESTLE DESK

NOTE: Except where noted, all lumber is pine.

Use	No. Req.	
sides	2	1⅛"x11"x24⅞"
rear	1	1⅛"x10¾"x40"
shelf	1	½"x5½"x10"
shelf edge	2	1⅛"x2"¾x40"
desk top	1	½"x21¾"x40"
desk bottom	1	½"x22⅞"x40" plywood
bottom edge	1	½"x⅝"x40"
pedestal support	2	1⅛"x2½"x12½"
pedestal	2	1⅛"x8"x20¼"
trestle	1	1⅛"x3¾"x33"
base	2	1¾"x3½"x24"
spacer	2	"½x4⅝"x20¼"
drawer spacer	2	¾"x1⅓₂"x21"
drawer side	6	½"x3⅜"x21¾"
drawer rear	3	½"x2"⅞x11¾"
drawer subfront	3	½"x3⅜"x11¾"
drawer front	3	1⅛"x4"x13⅛"
drawer bottom	3	¼"x11¾"x21"
desk dividers	4	½"x9⅜"
buttons	12	"½x⅝"
pulls	3	
screws	16	2"-10 FH
lag screws	4	5/16"x3"

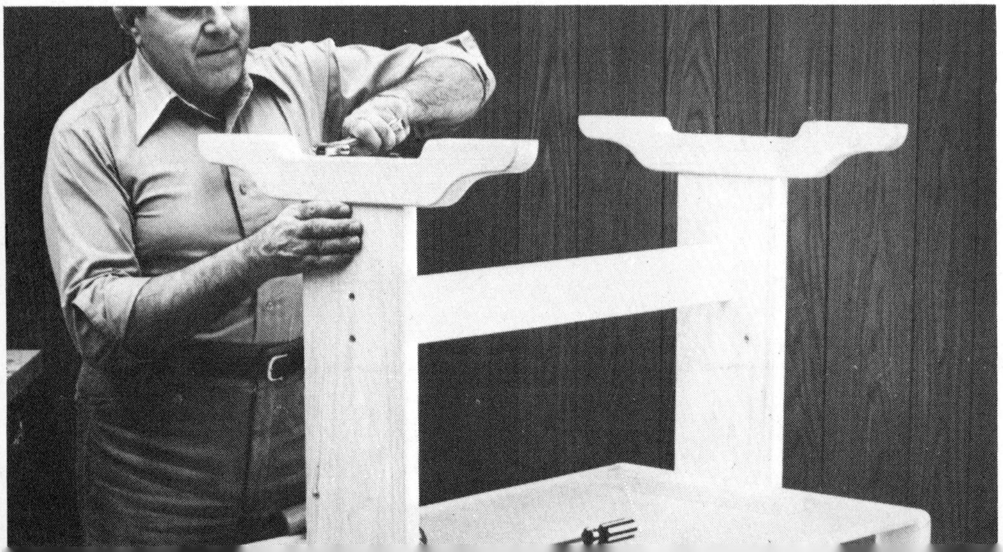

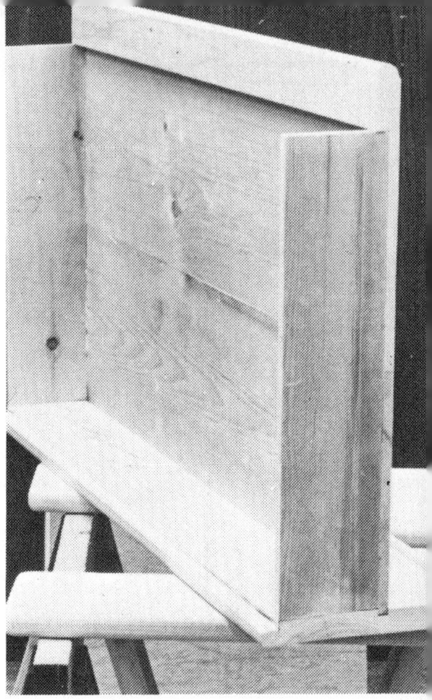

This view shows the spacer and des assembled. Note at the top of the pict the thickened edge of the desk top.

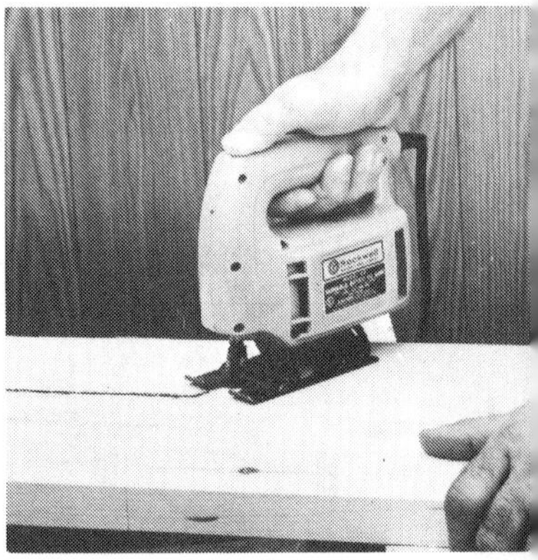

Use a saber saw to cut out the diag edges of the side pieces for the des Then round off and sand edges smo

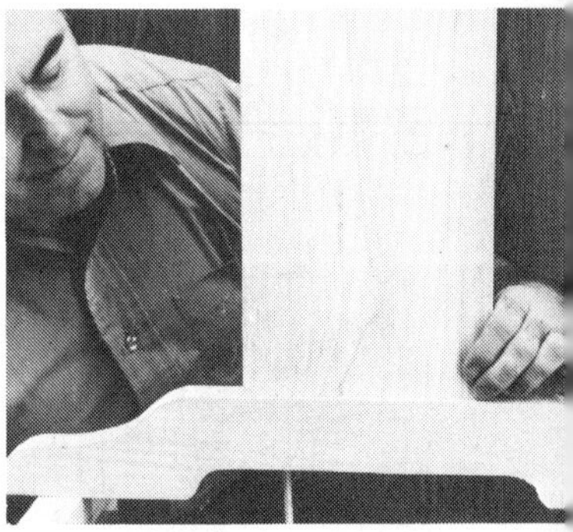

To locate pilot holes for the lag scre arrange pieces as shown and adju until you find alignment with pencil.

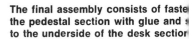

The final assembly consists of faste the pedestal section with glue and to the underside of the desk sectior

BOOK AND MAGAZINE TABLE

Here's a modern-style piece that you can build quickly and cheaply

THIS GRACEFUL TABLE conveniently holds your favorite books and magazines. The interesting surfboard shape not only goes well with contemporary furniture, but a slight tilt to the end panel creates a handy book display area. Sturdy, unusual wrought iron legs add character to the low lines of this design, which is easily assembled when you study the drawings and take it a step at a time.

Begin by having a metal workshop fabricate the wrought iron legs according to the plan. To take care of minor variations in angles and dimensions, you probably will save yourself extra work by having the legs bent before beveling and drilling the bottom shelf and cutting the support partition for the top shelf to proper height. Paint the legs with flat black enamel or in a color to contrast with the shelves.

Using a large steel square, lay out the parts on a panel of ¾-inch thick interior-type plywood, as shown on the cutting diagram. Remember to allow for saw kerfs while laying out the parts. Next saw out all parts to size, drill holes to receive legs and then dado bottom shelf to receive the support partition. Make an angular cut on the wide end of the bottom shelf to fit the rabbet on end panel, then rabbet the end of the top shelf to receive the support partition. With glue and 6d finish nails, fasten end panel and the partition to bottom shelf. Then support the top shelf on a block while attaching to this partition. Some adjustment for length of legs can be obtained by drilling blind holes on the underside of the top shelf; plates can be threaded up or down a few turns to bring top shelf level. Use screws to fasten leg frames and plates as shown.

Finish by smoothing edges and joints with coarse sandpaper on a block and filling nail holes and plywood edge grain with wood paste filler. Next smooth up the table with fine sandpaper, rounding sharp edges and corners slightly. Then apply an enamel undercoat followed by two coats of semi-gloss enamel.

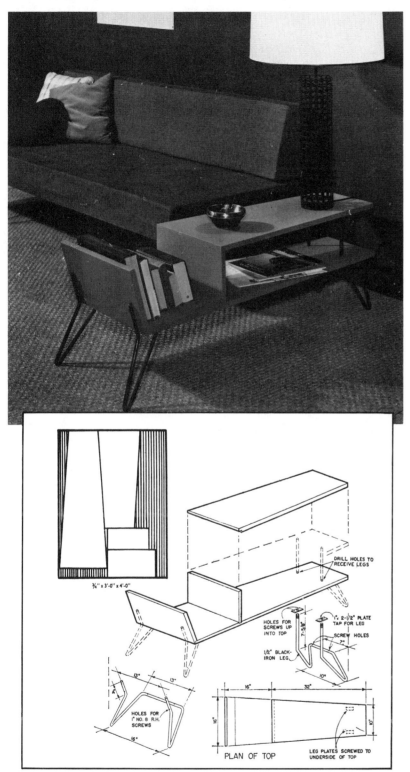

¾" x 3'-0" x 4'-0"

DRILL HOLES TO RECEIVE LEGS

HOLES FOR SCREWS UP INTO TOP

1"x 2-½" PLATE TAP FOR LEG

SCREW HOLES

½" BLACK-IRON LEG.

HOLES FOR 1" NO. 8 R.H. SCREWS

LEG PLATES SCREWED TO UNDERSIDE OF TOP

PLAN OF TOP

BILL OF MATERIALS

Quantity	Size and Description		Purpose
1	¾"	16"x44¾" interior plywood	bottom shelf
1	¾"	16"x32" interior plywood	top shelf
1	¾"	7¼"x14" interior plywood	divider
1	¾"	8½"x16" interior plywood	end
as needed	1"	#8 round head screws	

NOTE: Also need wrought iron legs, leg plates, 6d finishing nails, glue and enamel.

COMPACT PICNIC GROUP

An ideal project for families with small children, this outdoor set of furniture can be easily built in hours with just the aid of hand tools

Here is a compact picnic group that is not only easy to move and set up, but which also takes up no more space than a conventional size table of its type. It is particularly suited for families with small children, because there are no benches for youngsters to overturn.

By following the simplified construction plans (see drawings) you can build this outdoor set of furniture with ordinary hand tools and standard materials available at any

local lumber yard. Clear redwood lumber was used to construct this group but you can also use a less expensive heart redwood grade for a more rustic look, if you wish. There were approximately one-hundred weather-resistant three-inch wood screws used for this project, and screw holes should be drilled slightly undersize and counter-sunk so screw heads are below the surface of the wood. A pair of screws are used at all points.

The bench arms and the top cleats are cut to size and end trimmed at a 60° angle, with all leg pieces cut at 75° angles. You should conduct a dry run test to make sure all the parts fit tightly before starting the actual construction.

Begin by assembling the table top, leaving approximately ⅜-in. space between the 2 x 6-in. units. The center cleat is screwed flat and the end 2 x 4-in. parts are positioned on edge 14-in. on center from the end of the table. Next turn the top face down since the unit is easier to assemble in an up-side-down position.

Construct the leg units and attach them to the top and cleats. Although easy to build, the interlocking legs and bench support with the lapped construction of the double 2 x 4-in. legs will result in an exceptionally sturdy bench and table set. Diagonal braces, cut at a 120° angle are then screwed to the center of the leg units. Finally, right the table to its proper position and fasten the pair of 2 x 6-in. bench boards on each side.

When the group is completely assembled, round off the table top and seat corners to a 2-in. radius, then sand the entire picnic unit smoothly to eliminate any danger of splinters. The redwood set may be left unfinished to weather into a soft pewter color or stained and top coated for additional protection and long life.

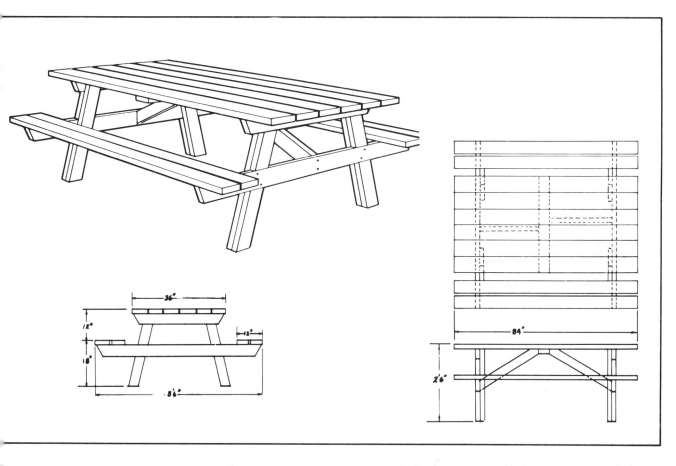

MATERIALS LIST

Note: All lumber indicated is redwood— see text.

Amt. Req.	Size	Length	Use
6	2x6	84″	Top
3	2x4	35″	Cleats
2	2x4	65″	Bench arm
2	2x4	40″	Top & leg braces
4	2x4	34″	Legs
4	2x4	14″	Leg doubles
4	2x4	10″	Leg doubles
4	2x6	84″	Bench seats

Misc.
00 weather-resistant 3″ wood screws

ft, compact picnic table and bench accommodates between eight and ten ults. Right, before beginning actual nstruction on the set, be sure to lay t all the parts to assure a tight fit.

Drop Leaf Secretary

Here's an easy-to-build project that has the look of expensive furniture, but can be built at a low cost

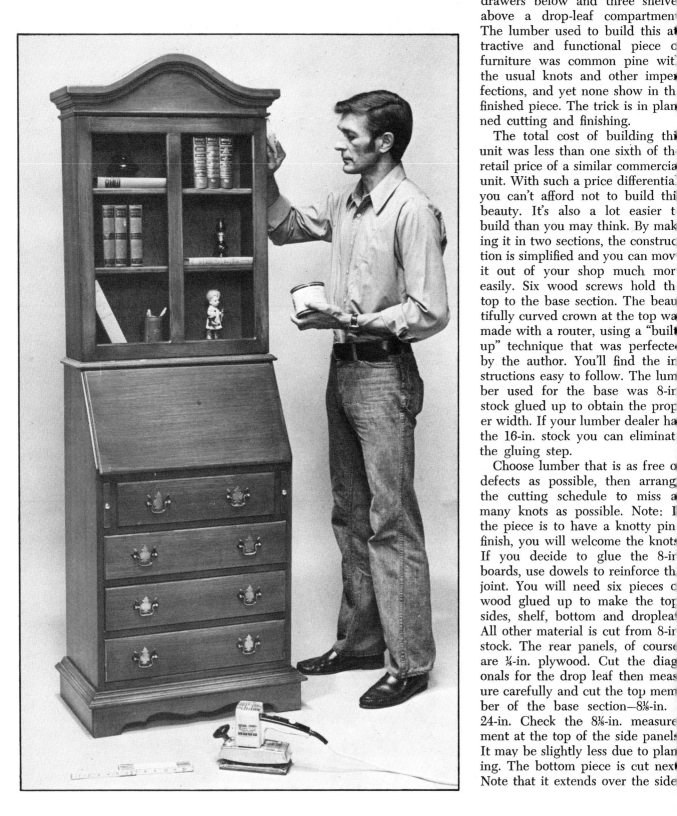

Looking for a place to keep those odds and ends of books, bills, letters, documents and writing materials that always accumulate in average households? Here's a sturdily built Early American design with plenty of storage room to solve that problem. It has four drawers below and three shelves above a drop-leaf compartment. The lumber used to build this attractive and functional piece of furniture was common pine with the usual knots and other imperfections, and yet none show in the finished piece. The trick is in planned cutting and finishing.

The total cost of building this unit was less than one sixth of the retail price of a similar commercial unit. With such a price differential, you can't afford not to build this beauty. It's also a lot easier to build than you may think. By making it in two sections, the construction is simplified and you can move it out of your shop much more easily. Six wood screws hold the top to the base section. The beautifully curved crown at the top was made with a router, using a "built-up" technique that was perfected by the author. You'll find the instructions easy to follow. The lumber used for the base was 8-in. stock glued up to obtain the proper width. If your lumber dealer has the 16-in. stock you can eliminate the gluing step.

Choose lumber that is as free of defects as possible, then arrange the cutting schedule to miss as many knots as possible. Note: If the piece is to have a knotty pine finish, you will welcome the knots. If you decide to glue the 8-in. boards, use dowels to reinforce the joint. You will need six pieces of wood glued up to make the top, sides, shelf, bottom and dropleaf. All other material is cut from 8-in. stock. The rear panels, of course, are ¼-in. plywood. Cut the diagonals for the drop leaf then measure carefully and cut the top member of the base section—8⅛-in. 24-in. Check the 8⅛-in. measurement at the top of the side panels. It may be slightly less due to planing. The bottom piece is cut next. Note that it extends over the sides and front ⅞-in.

Rabbet the rear edges of the sides, top and bottom, then carefully measure the opening (from rabbet to rabbet) and cut the ¼-in. plywood panel to fit. The rear must fit snugly as it will be used to square up the lower section during assembly. Cut the 2-in. strips which will form the drawer dividers. You will need eight pieces each 10¼-in. long and eight pieces each 23-in. Be sure that all the strips are cut from the same thickness stock. Now set up the side panels for dadoing. This can be done with a router or on the table saw using a dado blade. If you decide on the table saw, add an extension to the miter gauge for stability. A piece

of ¾-in. stock about 2½-in. wide and 18-in. long will do. If you use the router use a ¾-in. bit, and set the depth to ¼-in. Use a strip of wood to guide the router. This can be clamped or nailed to the work surface. Since this section is not exposed, and nail holes will not be seen, nailing is recommended. To insure accuracy, work both sections together. To prevent the sections from shifting while routing, run a strip of masking tape along the joint on the opposite side of the boards. Locate the guide strip by measuring the distance from the edge of the bit to the edge of the router base. The drawer support frames are now assembled. Drill dowel holes in all members

as indicated. Use a doweling jig to locate and align holes. Use a dowel center finder to position mating holes then identify each with a letter or number. After the holes are drilled, coat the end grain of the side pieces with thinned down glue. Recoat the pieces, insert dowels and assemble the frames. Check for squareness and adjust if necessary.

The writing surface shelf is made up by gluing two pieces of 8-in. stock. Notch the front edge near the ends to clear the knife hinge. Assemble the drawer divider frames into the side members. Apply glue to the edges of the frames (one edge only) and also to the dadoed grooves. Tap the frames

Cut the side panels of the bottom section trying to avoid as many knots as possible. Smooth the edges with a plane.

When dadoing side panels with a router, use a ¾-in. bit, and set depth to ¼-in. Fix a guide to the work surface.

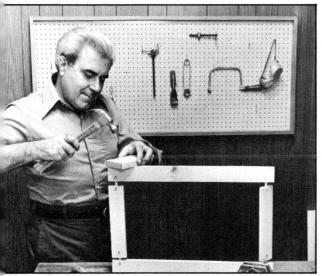

Drawer support frames are assembled with dowels and glue. Use a dowelling jig to locate and align the holes easily.

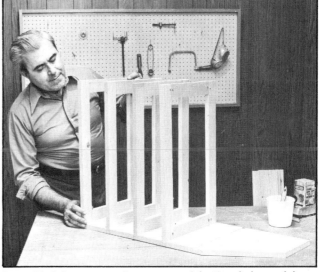

Assembled frames are then arranged in the dadoes of base section side panels. Remaining upper dado is for shelf.

Drop Leaf Secretary

As shown here, make certain that the frame sections are seated firmly into dadoes, by gently tapping them with hammer. Use a block of wood to prevent damage to frame.

gently into place and be sure to line up the front edge of the frames and side pieces. Repeat the procedure for the other side. When assembled, clamp securely until glue sets. Temporarily install the rear panel which was previously cut to square up the assembly. Add the top and bottom pieces. The top fits flush with the sides, but the bottom piece extends ⅞-in. at the sides and front. Assemble with glue and screws. Add the filler strip between the bottom board and the first frame. This will serve as a backup for the molding which will be added later. Cut the drop leaf stop at an angle to match the sloping front of the base. This should be 60°, therefore set the bevel of the table saw blade at 30°. After cutting, smooth the beveled edge and mount with brads and glue. Cut the three base pieces to size then layout and cut the scallop for the front section. Round the scallop edges with a router fitted with rounding cutter then assemble to the bottom board of the base section. Use screws and glue. Cut the drop leaf from a glued up board then rabbet three sides. The top and side rabbets are ½-in. x ⅝-in.

Cut two pieces of ¾-in. stock for the sides of the slide channel. Edge glue a 1½-in. piece of ¾-in. wood to the edge grain. Use glue and nails. Cut the slots into each of the side pieces then install with nails and glue. There should be a slight space between the side pieces and the outer walls to allow the slide to move freely. A piece of match book cardboard taped to one side of the slide will give the proper spacing. A 1½-in. #12 RH screw serves as a stop for the pull-out slide. Place the screw ¾-in. in from the rear edge of the slide and center it top to bottom. Install brass pulls at the center of each slide. The moldings around the base are installed now. Miter the corners and check the fit carefully, before mounting permanently. The drop

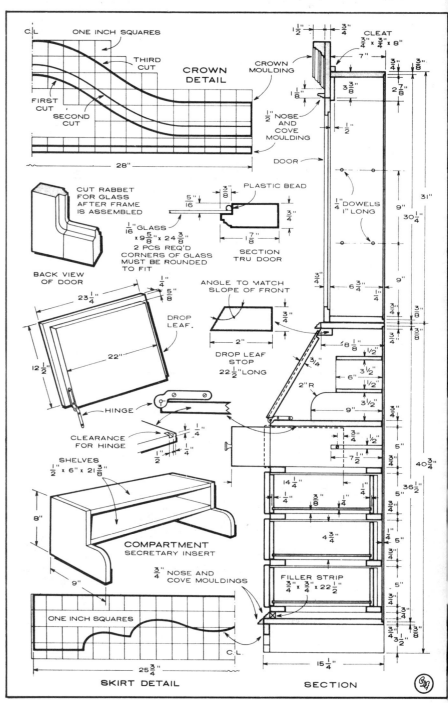

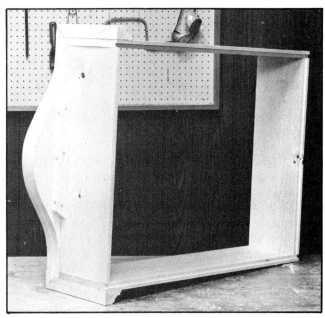

This view shows the drop leaf supports extended. The screw serves as a stop so they won't come out all of the way.

This rear view of the top section laid on its side shows how the crown piece is reinforced with cleat and screws.

Sections of the crown are built up in layers. Each of the three sections is same curved shape set back each layer.

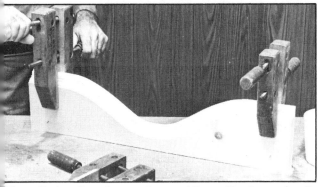

After mitering the edges and assembling with glue and nails, add clamps to ensure a solid bond between the sections.

The completed layered "sandwich" is then cut out. You can use either a band saw, as shown here, or else a saber saw.

BILL OF MATERIALS		
Base Section		
Use	No. Req'd.	Size and Description
Sides	2	¾"x14½"x35¾" pine
Bottom	1	¾"x15⅜"x25¾" pine
Top	1	¾"x8⅛"x24" pine
Shelf	1	¾"x14¼"x23" pine
Drop leaf	1	¾"x12½"x23¼" pine
Filler	1	¾"x¾"x22½" pine
Base side	2	¾"x3½"x14¾" pine
Base front	1	¾"x3½"x25¾" pine
Divider cleats	8	¾"x2"x23" pine
Divider cleats	8	¾"x2"x10¼" pine
Slide	2	¾"x4⅞"x14¼" pine
Slide divider	2	¾"x5"x14¼" pine
Rear panel	1	¼"x23¼"x36½" plywood
Drop leaf stop	1	¾"x2"x22½" pine
Insert side	2	½"x8"x9" pine
Insert shelf 2	2	½"x6"x21⅜" pine
Side	2	Top Section
Top	1	¾"x7"x31" pine
Bottom	1	¾"x7"x22" pine
Shelf	2	¾"x7"x22" pine
Crown	1	¾"x6½"x21⅞" pine
Crown	1	½"x5½"x28" pine
Crown	1	¾"x5"x28" pine
Crown side	2	¾"x7"x28" pine
Crown side	2	½"x2"x10"
Door frame	2	¾"x1½"x10"
Door frame	1	¾"x1⅞"x19¾"
Door frame	2	¾"x1⅞"x23⅞"
Front	3	¾"x1⅞"x27⅝"
Front	1	
Sub front	3	Drawers
Sub front	1	¾"4⅞"x22¼" pine
Rear	3	¾"x4⅞"x19"¼ pine
Rear	1	½"x4¾"x21⅛"
Side	8	½"x4¾"x18⅛"
Bottom	1	½"x4⅛"x21⅛" pine
Bottom	3	½"x4⅛"x18⅛" pine
¾" Nose & cove molding 12′		½"x4¾"x12¾" pine
⅝" Nose & cove molding 6′		¼"x12½"x21¼"
½" Nose & cove molding 6′		¼"x12½"x18¼"
Hinges		
Pulls		
Magnetic catch		
Nails		
Screws		
Glue		

Drop Leaf Secretary

leaf hardware may be installed now. Position the hinge so that the center of the hinge pin is centered over the top edge of the shelf.

The top frame consists of a rectangle with rabbeted edges at the rear to take the back panel. Assemble with nails and glue then set aside. Install the rear panel temporarily to insure squareness. The shaped crown is made next. Draw the curved shape of the top onto a piece of kraft paper on a thin sheet of cardboard. Note that three curved lines are required. Cut the bottom line with a sharp knife or razor and trace onto a piece of wood measuring ½-in. x 5½-in. x 28-in. Align the top edge of the pattern with the top edge of the board. Center the pattern from left to right. Trace out the curved shape then cut with sabre saw or jig saw. Now place a suitable cutter in the router and shape the curved edge as shown. Next, cut the second line on the pattern then follow the same procedure as above. This time the wood should measure ¾-in. x 5-in. x 28-in. Again use a suitable cutter in the router to shape the bottom edge of this second piece of wood. Cut the third and last line remaining on the pattern. Now take a piece of wood ¾-in. x 7-in. x 28-in. and aligning the top edges of the two previously cut and routed pieces, glue all three together. Place the nails where they won't show. Use clamps to hold the pieces firmly. When the glue has set, align the remaining pattern with the top edge of the combined pieces and trace the outline. This line represents the top of the shaped crown. Next carefully measure and miter the built-up pieces, setting the table saw at 45°. Inside of the miter should be the same width as the frame (23½-in.). Now trace the remaining pattern which represents the top line at the crown. Cut out with sabre saw then mount onto cabinet frame. Make a straight length of the shaped molding to be used for the sides of the cabinet. Miter the ends then install. Make up the door frame and mount with cabinet hinges. The drawers are of simple construction. Note that the top drawer is narrower than the rest. Cut all sections to size then assemble with nails and glue. Be sure to drill the clearance holes for the screw heads before mounting the drawer fronts to the sub-fronts. Round the drawer front edges. Install the moldings near the top just below the crown molding and drill clearance holes for the size 1½-in. screws which are used to join the top and base sections. Make and add shelves, fill nail holes, and sand entire cabinet until smooth and apply finish.

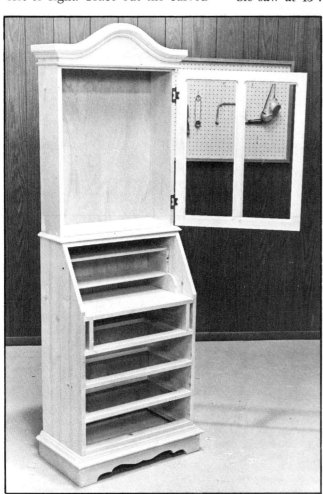

Above is the cabinet nearly completed and ready for the installation of top shelves, drawers, drop leaf and hardware.

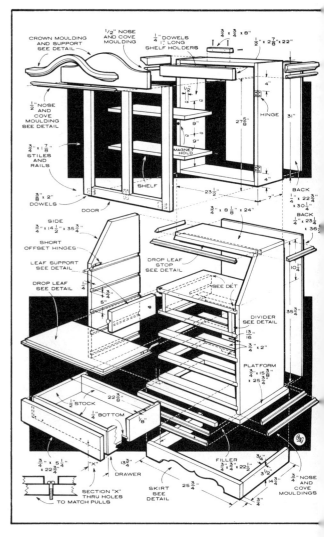

DOUGH BOX END TABLE

A popular and quaint piece any beginner can tackle

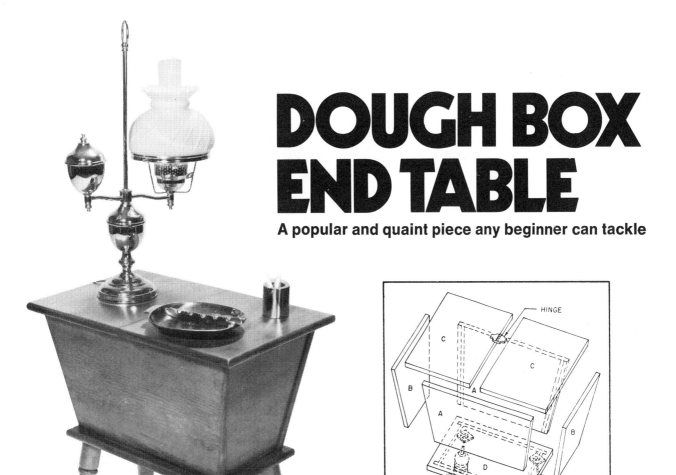

One of the most popular and versatile of Early American creations is the quaint, old-fashioned dough box. It makes an ideal end and lamp table and, since the top is hinged, it provides a roomy storage area for all sorts of miscellaneous items . . . a perfect place for knitting and sewing supplies.

Here is a project that any novice can undertake with success, and it can be completed without an elaborate set of tools. You trace full-size patterns on wood, then saw out and assemble the pieces.

You can order the patterns as shown at the end of this article, or enlarge the plans here to full size.

Cut out the two top panels and the bottom piece to the dimensions given on the plans. The two side pieces "B" are each 11½" high, 12½" long at the top, tapering to 8½" at the bottom. The front and back pieces "A" are also 11¾" high, and are 20" long at the top and 16" long at the bottom. Round the top edges of the front, side and back panels.

Glue and nail the end pieces

between the front and back panels. Use 3-penny finishing nails and countersink the heads. Fasten the bottom in place as shown, in the same manner.

Round the outside edges of the two top pieces. Butt these together and install the butterfly hinge in the center. Carefully position the entire top so that it overlaps evenly the front, back and side pieces, then nail just one section in place.

The legs and their brackets are available at almost all hardware,

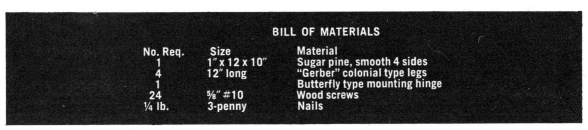

BILL OF MATERIALS			
No. Req.	Size	Material	
1	1" x 12 x 10"	Sugar pine, smooth 4 sides	
4	12" long	"Gerber" colonial type legs	
1		Butterfly type mounting hinge	
24	⅝" #10	Wood screws	
¼ lb.	3-penny	Nails	

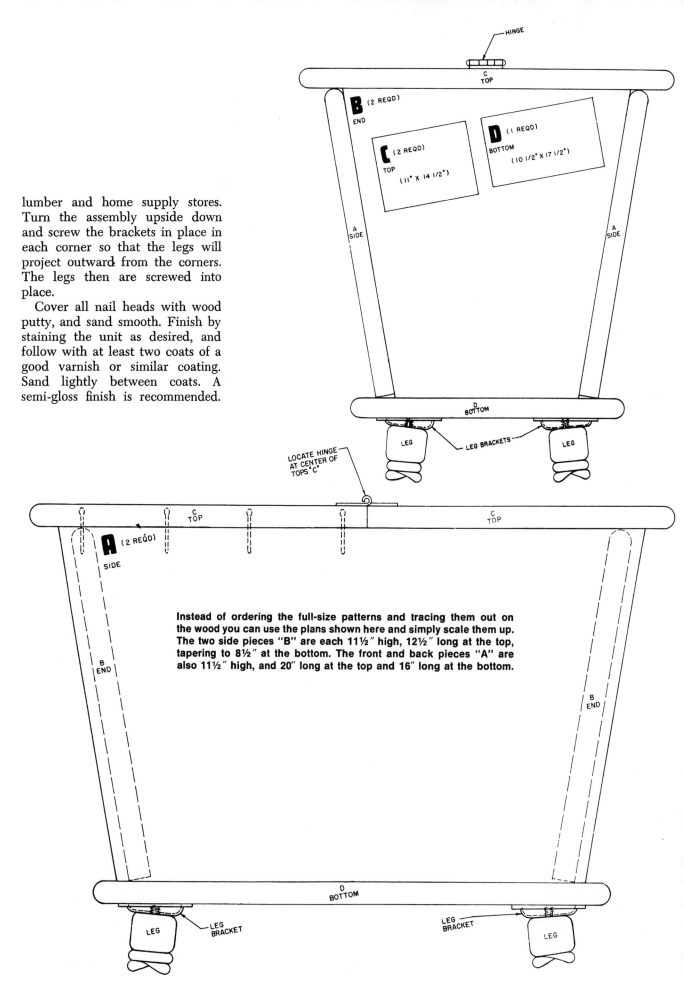

HINGE

C
TOP

B (2 REQD)
END

C (2 REQD)
TOP
(11" X 14 1/2")

D (1 REQD)
BOTTOM
(10 1/2" X 17 1/2")

A
SIDE

A
SIDE

D
BOTTOM

LEG

LEG BRACKETS

LEG

LOCATE HINGE
AT CENTER OF
TOPS "C"

C
TOP

C
TOP

A (2 REQD)
SIDE

B
END

B
END

D
BOTTOM

LEG

LEG
BRACKET

LEG
BRACKET

LEG

lumber and home supply stores. Turn the assembly upside down and screw the brackets in place in each corner so that the legs will project outward from the corners. The legs then are screwed into place.

Cover all nail heads with wood putty, and sand smooth. Finish by staining the unit as desired, and follow with at least two coats of a good varnish or similar coating. Sand lightly between coats. A semi-gloss finish is recommended.

Instead of ordering the full-size patterns and tracing them out on the wood you can use the plans shown here and simply scale them up. The two side pieces "B" are each 11½" high, 12½" long at the top, tapering to 8½" at the bottom. The front and back pieces "A" are also 11½" high, and 20″ long at the top and 16″ long at the bottom.

Grandfather Clock

Material cost is kept low by using veneer plywood. It stands 75″ high

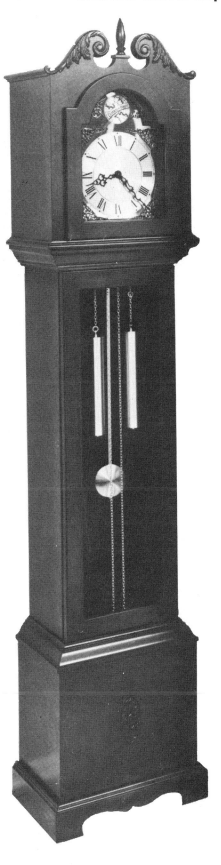

IF YOU HAVE wanted a grandfather's clock, but have been deterred from buying one because of the expense, try building one yourself. This design can be executed for much less than a comparable store model. It has all of the traditional styling of a grand father's clock and yet is designed with economy and simplicity of construction in mind.

You can choose almost any kind of wood for this clock, either solid lumber or birch, maple, pine, or mahogany plywood. The moldings are stock items found in lumber yards everywhere.

Construction is much simpler than it might seem from the appearance of the finished item. The major tool used is a table saw, but a router is helpful if you have one.

Start with the back panel, which can be considered the backbone of the clock. It is a simple rectangle that measures 10½ inches by 69 inches and it is cut from ¾-inch stock. Attach the top and bottom back panel tabs as shown in the drawing. Use finishing nails, and coat the mating surfaces with glue. Be sure to sink nail heads below the surface.

Cut out the lower shelf and lower sides, and nail and glue them in place, then install the floor, floor cleats, and base sides. With the exception of the lower shelf, these are all simple rectangles. Be sure all mating parts are square with each other as you go along.

Make up the front panel, rabbeting the edges as shown in the drawing. Next cut out the base front, mortise its edges, and glue and nail it in place. Install the nosing molding, using miter joints at the corner. This completes the lower section of the clock.

Next cut out and install both the waist sides. Use screws to attach the waist sides to the back panel, and to the lower shelf. Glue, of course, is used on all mating surfaces. Cut out and install the upper sides and upper shelf. The roof cleats can be glued and nailed in place at this time. Note that the side roof cleats do not extend to the forward edges of the upper side panels. Cut out and install the upper and lower waist headers.

The upper front is cut out next. Trace the opening from a full-size pattern, or use the dial itself as a guide. Since there are slight variations in carvings, use the pediment carvings themselves to establish your cutting line. When the front has been cut out and sanded smooth, glue the carvings to the front. Be sure to allow the outer edges of the carvings to extend beyond the sides slightly, so they will blend with the upper nosing molding when it is installed.

Now you can mount the front of the clock, nailing it and gluing it in place. Upper and lower crown molding are installed next, and the finial at the top of the clock. These corners must be mitered at a 45 degree angle. With the addition of the upper nosing molding, the basic clock structure is complete. At this time, however, you can add shelves, if you are using an electric clock movement.

Now make up the dial board. Be sure the hole for the hands is centered exactly. Glue the dial itself on the front of the panel, and mount the movement on the back. The dial board is slipped into place from the top of the clock, and fastened in place with four 1½-inch screws. The roof can now be fastened in place. Use screws, and do not use glue, since this will be the only access to the clock works.

The dial and waist doors are made up next. These can be of ¾-inch stock, with the inner edges rabbeted as shown in the detail drawing or with two layers of ⅜-inch stock. If you use the latter

Grandfather Clock

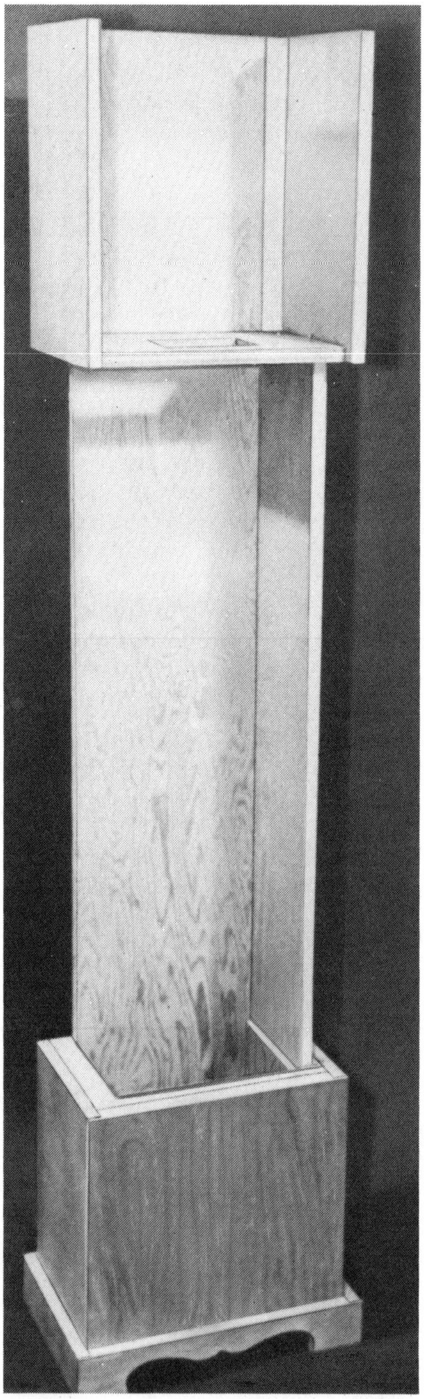

The back panel is the backbone on which the other sections are built. Note the deep rabbeting of the lower front panel.

method, cut one piece to full size for each door. For the waist door, cut the second piece to the full outside dimension, but ¼-inch narrower around the inside. For the dial door, the second piece should be cut so that it fits easily inside the upper front panel, and its inner cutout should be ¼-inch narrower than the first door piece.

When the two pieces of each door are glued together, you wil have a ¼-inch lip running arounc the inside edge against which th door glass rests. It is recommendec that you have the glass cut to th proper shape by a glass dealer unless you are experienced in thi type of work. When the glass i installed, use ¼-inch quarter-rounc stock to hold it in place.

Next, mortise for the hinges, anc

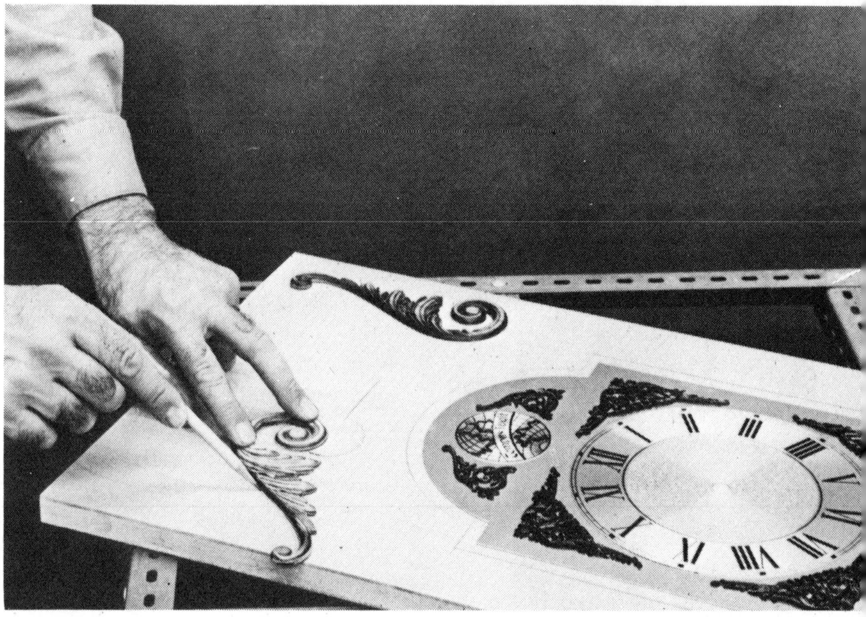

You can use the dial plate itself to trace the cutting line for the opening. Becaus of slight variations in carvings, trace the form of the top from pediment carvings

BILL OF MATERIALS

Quantity	Size and Description		Purpose
1	¾"	10½"x69" lumber of your choice	back panel
2	¾"	1¼"x15¾" lumber of your choice	upper back panel tabs
2	¾"	1¼"x15" lumber of your choice	lower back panel tabs
2	¾"	2⅝"x10¹¹⁄₁₆" lumber of your choice	base sides
1	¾"	2⅝"x16" lumber of your choice	base front
2	¾"	9¹⁵⁄₁₆"x15" lumber of your choice	lower sides
1	¾"	14½"x15" lumber of your choice	lower front
1	¾"	14½"x19⁹⁄₁₆" lumber of your choice	upper front
2	¾"	9¹⁵⁄₁₆"x15¾" lumber of your choice	upper sides
2	¾"	8"x38¼" lumber of your choice	waist sides
2	¾"	2¹⁄₁₆"x12" lumber of your choice	waist headers
4	¾"	8½"x13" lumber of your choice	shelves, roof and floor
2	¾"	1½"x5¾" cleats	roof side
1	¾"	1½"x13" cleats	roof rear
2	¾"	¾"x14¼" cleats	dial board
1	¾"	1½"x13" cleats	floor, rear
2	¾"	1½"x7¾" cleats	floor, side
1	⅜"	12⅞"x14¼" lumber of your choice	dial board
1	¾"	12"x15" lumber of your choice	dial door
1	¾"	12"x34" lumber of your choice	waist door
1	⅛"	9⅛"x12⅜" glass	dial door
1	⅛"	9⅛"x31⅛" glass	waist door
as needed	2½"x7' crown molding		
as needed	¾"x9' nosing molding		
	1" dia.x3½" finial		
	¼"x1"x1⅝" finial base		
	10"x13" dial		

NOTE: Also need: clock movement, pediment carvings, base carving, hardware, glue, etc.

install the doors so they fit flush against the waist and upper front.

Finally, check all the joints, and set any nail heads that protrude. Fill the depressions with wood putty, and you are ready to apply the finish. If you have an open-grained wood, use a paste wood filler before staining. Your local paint dealer is your best source on fillers, stains, and coatings.

All of the pieces making up the lower section are simple rectangles, except for the lower shelf, which is a U-shape. Front piece is rabbeted, the rest are butt jointed.

Dial board with clock mechanism is slipped into place from top of clock. This movement is operated by weights, although an electric movement will work equally well.

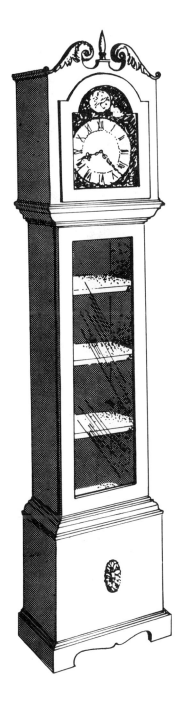

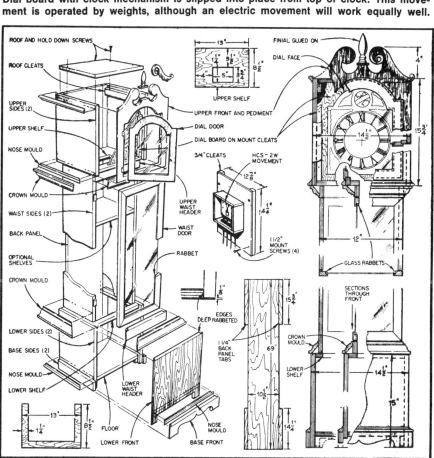

DECORATIVE BOOKSHELF TABLE

Monotonous tasks of sanding, staining, rubbing and waxing are eliminated from this weekend project through the use of pre-finished Java walnut panels. There's also special construction with cleats to speed the assembly process.

SIMPLE IN DESIGN and construction, this unique bookshelf-table in brightly finished walnut is made of prefinished wall panels and molding. This eliminates one of the biggest headaches in furniture making—finishing. Not only is that tedious operation bypassed, but sanding is eliminated since all exposed edges and surfaces are prefinished.

To most craftsmen, the finishing operation is a necessary evil. And this is especially true when working with open-grained woods which must be filled, sealed, stained, lacquered, rubbed and waxed. But this is all done before you even start this project, and it's no ordinary finish either. Scientifically applied, the finishes of better panels are similar to those found only in the top grades of furniture. So with half the battle over, you should have no trouble building this attractive contemporary piece.

Costs will vary depending on the

panels and molding used. The table shown was built for about $25 using a panel of Java walnut with a birch inlay. The panel is grooved, with 16 inches between grooves. The birch strip is only one inch wide so little is wasted when ripping the panels. The top is made by joining two sections with a butt joint. If care is used, the joint will be almost invisible. If a one-piece top is desired, a Weldwood flush panel may be substituted. Such panels are higher in price, however. Manufacturers offer a choice of woods.

The prefinished panels are only ¼-inch thick so they must be supported by a heavier wood such as ½-inch fir plywood. This is ideal as the total thickness of ¾-inch is compatible with the stock molding.

To simplify construction, cleats are used throughout the assembly. This eliminates the need for dadoes and rabbets. It also cuts down on the tools needed. A saw, drill, and

screwdriver are sufficient.

Start the construction with ripping of the prefinished panel. Cut away the grooves, then set the panels aside while you cut the ½-inch plywood to the sizes shown for the top and bottom. Note that the top panel is larger than the bottom as it overhangs the sides slightly. The shape of these pieces is octagonal (see detail).

When taking measurements and cutting pieces bear in mind that the thickness of the material is ¾-inches and not ¼ or ½. This can be confusing to the unwary.

With the top and bottom cut, make the strips for the base and decorative panels. Cut these sections slightly oversize allowing for trimming after laminating. The best way to treat the panels is to cut the ½-inch part in one piece, adding the ¼-inch facing around the perimeter. The ¼-inch stock is mitered first and then laminated. This procedure makes for a struc-

Using cleats throughout the assembly of the unit not only eliminates the need for rabbets and dadoes, but also cuts down on the number of tools required in the construction.

In this view, the top section is lying upside down and a strip of cove molding has been attached to one of the octagonal sides. The ends of the molding are cut at 45° angles.

Because there are so many pieces which look alike, it's a good idea to write an identifying number on the various sections to be joined together, thereby avoiding confusion.

Here the panels are shown in various stages of assembly. The ¼-inch pre-finished stock is laminated to the ½-inch plywood backing before the octagonal opening is cut out.

A radial arm saw can greatly simplify the work of trimming and bevel cutting. Use a sharp blade and be sure to check bevels on scrap wood before cutting the pre-finished work.

An easy way to hold the moldings in place while the glue sets is to use masking tape, as shown. It's a good idea to first check the fit of all parts before applying the glue.

Partially assembled unit is shown here. Note how diagonals are squared off on the inside. Paint interiors flat black.

turally sound panel and saves material on the more expensive ¼-inch panel. Use white glue when laminating and for all assembly work.

The radial arm saw greatly simplifies the work of trimming and bevel cutting. Use a sharp blade and be sure to check bevels on scrap wood before cutting the work. When trimming the molding cut the longest pieces first; thus if you make a mistake, you can re-cut for the next smaller size. An easy way to hold the moldings in place while the glue sets is to use masking tape, as shown.

It is helpful to install the metal grille before attaching the molding as it serves as a backstop for the molding and assures perfect line-up. The grille is held with screws and washers. Normally, if the wood needed finishing it would be necessary to remove the grille. Not so here, as no finishing is required.

Before closing off the grilled section paint the interior flat black. This will contrast nicely with the polished brass of the grille. Use screws and glue in the final assembly.

Maintenance is the same as for any fine piece of furniture. Use a good grade of furniture wax to clean the surface. Avoid abrasive cleaners which may scratch the finish.

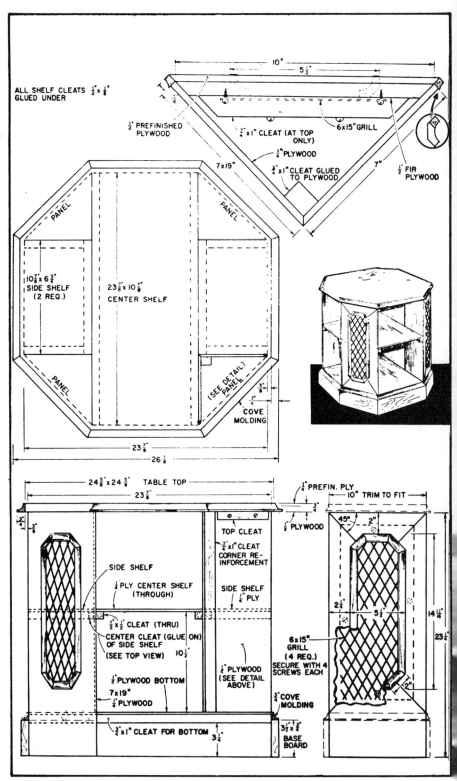

BILL OF MATERIALS

Quantity	Size and Description	Purpose
1	¼" 4'x8" prefinished plywood	outer surfaces
1	½" 4'x4' fir plywood	inner surfaces
	¾"x30' cove molding	
	¾" 1"x12' cleats	
4	6"x15" polished brass grille	
as needed	1¼" round head screws	
as needed	½" round head screws	
NOTE: Also need, white glue and washers.		

END TABLE CELLARETTE

This practical piece has a concealed compartment which holds your favorite libations

THIS ELEGANT end table made of cherry lumber features a compartment for storing your favorite refreshment complete with glasses. At first glance, this piece looks like an ordinary table with three drawers. However, a tug at the decorative pull on the side reveals the hidden compartment. The door drops down in drop leaf fashion so it can be used as a serving surface. The three drawers are reduced in width to make room for the compartment. Full-width drawer fronts help conceal the subterfuge.

The cabinet shown is right-handed. If you want to make a pair of tables for use at both ends of a sofa or chair, simply reverse the dimensions and assembly, mirror fashion. The cabinet is made of solid cherry. This is an ideal cabinet wood because it handles well and is easy to finish. It should be noted that hardwoods are generally thicker than softwoods. For example, one-inch cherry has a dressed or actual size of 13/16″. A piece of one-inch pine however has a dressed or actual size of ¾″. To add to the confusion, a piece of ½″ hard or softwood measures ½″. We point this out because some readers may want to substitute softwoods, thus the dimensions would have to be altered accordingly.

In constructing a piece of furniture such as this, it is important that all fastenings should be invisible. A study of the drawings shows how this is accomplished. You will also note that a considerable amount of dowels are used. This is necessary to assure strong tight joints. Wide boards are hard to come by and even if available, they can seldom be used because of cupping. They would have to be cut into 3- or 4-inch widths then glued to make up the wide boards. All framing members are also doweled.

Gluing the boards takes place after you have decided where to use the various grain patterns. For example, you should use the most attractive pattern for the top, the least attractive for the rear or side that is not exposed. When gluing

END TABLE

boards, make the lengths and widths slightly larger than the finish size. Leave some stock for trimming. The dowels used should be the spiral type, preferably oak. They have a good gripping surface and the spiral groove allows air to escape as the dowel is driven. Dowels used are ⅜" x 2". The doweling jig is indispensible in this type of project. The tool shown automatically centers on the board to assure perfect alignment. The jig can be used with a portable drill or on the drill press. It works equally well on both.

The glue used should be one of the fast setting non-staining types. When gluing hardwood, allow the glue to air dry a few moments before joining the pieces. When wide boards are required, alternate the growth rings as shown. This will eliminate cupping.

Glue-up the necessary pieces to make the top then clamp and allow the glue to set. Trim to size, then shape the edge as desired. The shaping can be done with a router or shaper. Before shaping the edges, sand the top surface so it is flat and smooth. A belt sander is ideal for this operation. Sand with the grain of the wood. Finish sanding can be left until all the parts are completed. When shaping, do the end grain first, then follow with the longer sides.

The left side is dadoed to accept the front frame as well as the drawer guides. The dadoes are blind. They are cut to stop short of the rear edge of the panel. The dado can be cut on the table or radial arm saw fitted with a dado

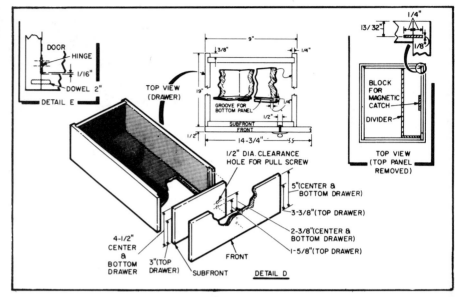

blade. Otherwise, you can use the router. If the router is used, tack a guide strip onto the work surface. Cut the dado so the parts will fit snug. In addition to the dadoes, the side piece will require two grooves; one for a splined joint at the rear and one for the top fasteners. These can be cut best on the table saw. Use a regular saw blade for the ⅛" groove at the top. For the spline, you can use a dado blade or make several passes with the regular blade. When making the spline groove, check the fit on scrap wood before cutting the actual workpiece. Scrap paneling makes good spline stock.

Note: the grooves for the spline and fasteners should be left until the rear and right panel are made. The reason is that these grooves must be cut with the saw at the same setting. Set the fence and blade height to correspond to the dimensions shown on the drawing. For the spline cut, pass the rear panel through the blade with the

work held vertically. The sides are passed through horizontally.

The right side panel must be the same overall size as the left one after trimming. However, it must be cut as indicated. Glue the piece so it is slightly oversize. After glue sets, make cuts 1 and 2 as indicated by the dotted lines in the drawing. Set the two narrow strips aside and from the large piece make cuts 3 and 4. Retain the center piece for the door and glue up parts A, B, C and D to make up the side frame. Be sure to match up the grain patterns in the four narrow pieces and the door. Dowel the frame members and glue up. Use one dowel at each joint. After the glue sets, trim the frame so length and width match the left side panel. Also, trim the door so there will be a clearance of 1/16-inch all around it and the frame opening.

The compartment divider or partition is made with a frontal piece of ½" stock. This piece serves to

A large number of dowels are used in the construction for greater strength. Dowelling jig, above, assures accurate holes.

Cut dadoes in left side piece to accept front frame and drawer guides. Wood strip, right, tacked to board guides router.

The four front frame members are the last of sides to be glued in final assembly. Use clamps with protective strips.

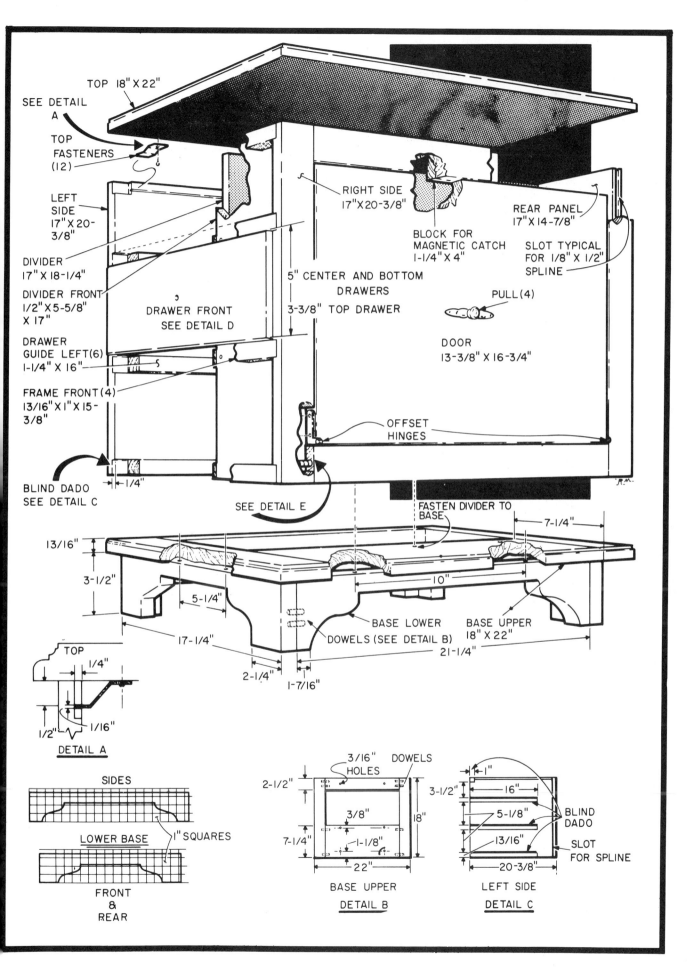

TOP 18" X 22"

SEE DETAIL A

TOP FASTENERS (12)

LEFT SIDE 17" X 20-3/8"

DIVIDER 17" X 18-1/4"

DIVIDER FRONT 1/2" X 5-5/8" X 17"

DRAWER GUIDE LEFT(6) 1-1/4" X 16"

FRAME FRONT(4) 13/16" X 1" X 15-3/8"

BLIND DADO SEE DETAIL C

1/4"

RIGHT SIDE 17" X 20-3/8"

BLOCK FOR MAGNETIC CATCH 1-1/4" X 4"

REAR PANEL 17" X 14-7/8"

SLOT TYPICAL FOR 1/8" X 1/2" SPLINE

5" CENTER AND BOTTOM DRAWERS
3-3/8" TOP DRAWER

DRAWER FRONT SEE DETAIL D

PULL(4)

DOOR 13-3/8" X 16-3/4"

OFFSET HINGES

SEE DETAIL E

FASTEN DIVIDER TO BASE

7-1/4"

13/16"

3-1/2"

5-1/4"

10"

17-1/4"

BASE LOWER

BASE UPPER 18" X 22"

DOWELS (SEE DETAIL B)

21-1/4"

2-1/4"

1-7/16"

TOP

1/4"

1/2"   1/16"

DETAIL A

SIDES

LOWER BASE

1" SQUARES

FRONT & REAR

3/16" HOLES   DOWELS

2-1/2"

3/8"

18"

7-1/4"   1-1/8"

22"

BASE UPPER
DETAIL B

1"

16"

3-1/2"

5-1/8"   BLIND DADO

13/16"

20-3/8"   SLOT FOR SPLINE

LEFT SIDE
DETAIL C

This view shows the partition. Note that screws in the front panel are placed so they will be hidden by front framework.

Nearly completed cabinet is ready for installation of hardware like hinges and chain. Note dummy extension drawer front.

Above photo shows drawer construction. Glides are placed on the drawer guides to allow drawer to open and close smoothly.

END TABLE

close off the compartment and also provides a neat appearance behind the dummy part of the drawers. The dadoes on the divider can be cut full length as shown. When joining the front piece to the divider, place the screws so they will be concealed by the front frame pieces. Install the drawer guides into the dadoes with glue. Cut the front framing members at this time, then set aside.

The base consists of two parts, upper and lower. The upper base is made with one side wider than the other. The wider section serves as the bottom of the compartment. Layout the pieces as shown and glue up with dowels. After glue sets, surface the joints if necessary then shape the edges. Follow the same procedure as for the top. Drill the mounting holes as shown. The lower base is made with splined joints. Cut the pieces to exact size then groove for the spline. Trace the outline for the cutout and cut with a saber saw. Use a router to round off the edges of the cutout. Before gluing the pieces, drill the two mounting holes in each piece. Countersink the holes so the flat head screws will lay flush.

Before final assembly, sand all exposed surfaces. Sand until all surfaces are as smooth as glass. Cut splines and check fit before applying glue. Work on a flat surface and install the splines into the rear panel. Apply the glue to the glue line and fasten the sides. Use strips

of wood under the clamps to distribute the pressure and to prevent marring the cabinet surfaces. Next apply glue and add the front frame members. Check that the assembly is square. Adjust if necessary. When glue has set, insert the partition then turn the unit upside down and install the top. Use top fasteners. These are designed to pull the top down tight when the screws are tightened. With the unit still unside down, install the two screws into the bottom of the divider. Follow with the upper base then the lower base. It is not necessary to use glue at these joints.

The door is hinged to the lower part of the frame opening. Use offset hinges to locate them so the door will be centered in the opening. A chain is used to contain the door. Also, a magnetic catch is installed at the top of the frame.

The top drawer is not as tall as the other two, but all the parts are cut for the larger drawers. After rabbeting and dadoing, the upper drawer can be trimmed to size. Drill the screw clearance hole in the subfronts before assembly. Note that this is off center so it coincides with the center of the drawer front. When fastening the subfront to the front, raise the front about 1/16". Use a shim to assure accuracy.

Since cherry wood is close grained, finishing is simple. Stain as desired, then apply several top coats of clear lacquer or varnish.

BILL OF MATERIALS NOTE: Except where noted, all lumber is 13/16" cherry.

Use	No. Req.	Size		No. Req.	Size
top	1	18"x22"	drawer front	1	½"x3⅜"x14¾"
left side	1	17"x20⅜"	drawer side	2	½"x3"x19"
rear	1	17"x14⅞"	drawer subfront	1	½"x2½"x8½"
right side	1	17"x20⅜"	drawer rear	1	½"x5"x14¾"
door	1	13⅜"x16¾"	drawer front	1	½"x4½"x8½"
divider	1	17"x18¼"	drawer side	2	½"x4½"x8½"
divider front	1	½"x5⅝"x17"	drawer subfront	2	
			drawer rear	2	½"x4"x8½"
frame front	4	13⁄16"x1"x15⅜"	darwer bottom	3	¼"x8½"x18⅜"
drawer guide left	6	1¼"x16"	spline	1	¼"x½"x48"
base upper front	1	2½"x18"	screws	18	1¾-8 FH
base upper rear	1	2½"x18"	screws	12	½"-8-RH
base upper left	1	2½"x17"	top fasteners	12	
base upper right	1	7¼"x17"	chain 24"		
base lower front	1	3½"x17¼"	offset hinges	2	
base lower rear	1	3½"x17¼"	magnetic catch (PM)	1	
base lower side	2	3"½x19⅝"	pulls	4	

FOLDAWAY
BED/STORAGE UNIT

The material used is mostly ¾-inch pine plywood

Do you need an extra bed or bookcase? Build this unit and you'll have both—a handsome storage unit and a comfortable bed. This is a modern version of the Murphy bed which was very popular at one time. The Murphy beds folded into a wall when not in use, and you may still see them occasionally on TV reruns of the old Laurel and Hardy films, with one comedian being accidentally slammed into the wall while still asleep.

With living space at a premium today, this unit should find wide acceptance among apartment dwellers and home owners alike. Because of its ease of operation, it takes little effort to convert from books to bed. Simply roll out the bottom section and tilt. It's a great idea for a small guest room. It occupies little space either open or closed, and it's attractive as well as useful.

The unit shown was made of pine plywood, but solid pine or other woods may be substituted. Construction has been simplified so that even the novice woodworker should have no problem in making

the piece. No tricky cuts are involved, and butt joints are used throughout.

The piece consists of three parts: upper shelves, lower bed compartment, and the bed itself. The dummy doors and drawers are actually the base of the bed. The bed rides on specially designed non-swivelling casters. These are necessary because they insure that the bed will roll in and out in a straight line. If conventional casters are used, it becomes very difficult to withdraw and replace the bed without striking the compartment sides.

In order to keep the knobs and pulls clear of the floor when the bed is in use, the edges of the front panel are thickened by the use of appropriate moldings.

The bed consists of a framework supported by four uprights. Cross pieces support a panel which, in turn, supports a camper-type mattress. The camper mattress is ideal since it is only three inches thick and measures 26½″ x 70″. It remains in place even when the bed is closed or in the upright position. It

is held with a pair of straps. A piece of foam of equal thickness may be substituted. Before starting construction be sure to have the mattress on hand so that you can fit the parts to it. If the mattress you use differs in size, be sure to change the dimensions shown on the drawings accordingly. Although the area below the bed is open, it can be made with closed sides and bottom to provide additional storage space for blankets, sheets, pillows and the like.

Lower Compartment. If you choose to use solid boards, the top and side members may have to be glued up, unless you use pine, which is usually available in widths over 12 inches. Since the plywood panels measure 4 x 8-feet, you won't have to do any gluing. Assuming that you are using plywood, lay out and cut the top and side pieces of the compartment either on the table saw or with a portable saw. If you use the portable saw, be sure to use a guide strip to assure a straight cut. The strip should be fastened to the board with clamps, one at each end. The thick-

BED/STORAGE UNIT

ness of the strip is governed by the clearance under the saw. Except for some of the smaller trim saws, the guide strip can usually be of ¾-inch stock. After the three pieces are cut, prepare the two cleats which will be used to fasten the top and side members. Cut the cleats two-inches wide and drill three 3/16″ diameter holes for the screws in each face. Install the cleats along the top edge of the side members. Use glue and 2″ FH screws.

The two side pieces will now have cleats at one end. Put them aside and, while the glue sets, cut the rear panel. This should be ¼-inch plywood. However, since it doesn't show (except when the bed is in use) a less expensive wood, such as fir, can be used. This will help keep costs down. After cutting the panel to size, sand all edges and break the sharp corners. Use a piece of sandpaper wrapped around a block, or a power sander.

The sides are now fastened to the top. Position the sides so the top overhangs equally at both ends. Apply white glue to the joints then assemble with 1¼-inch screws. Before the glue sets, tip the "U"-shaped assembly forward so the rear edge is upright. Install the rear panel, noting that the lower edge is flush with the lower edge of the sides. The upper edge of the panel should be set back ⅜″ at the top. The panel is also set back at the sides, but only by ⅛-inch. Provided that the setbacks are equal at the sides, the assembly will be perfectly square because the rear panel acts like a large square. Fasten the panel with one-inch panel nails. These are the nails used to install prefinished wall paneling: They are made with annular grooves and have excellent holding power. (Try removing one and you'll see how well they hold). Use glue at all joints.

Upper Compartment. This is made as a separate unit which fastens to the base piece. The top, sides, shelf and dividers are of equal width. Set the fence of the table saw to 7⅜-inches and rip the required pieces, then cut them to the lengths shown in the Bill of

The cleats used to fasten side members are 2″ wide and receive 3/16″ dia. holes.

Assembling the side to shelf: Push drill is handy for making the screw pilot holes.

To locate position for dividers, set two doors side by side, make a mark on shelf edge even with door, another mark 3/16″ from first indicates inside edge of divider.

When installing the rear panel, use a temporary spacer to keep the top board from sagging. When nailed in place, the rear panel will prevent the top from sagging.

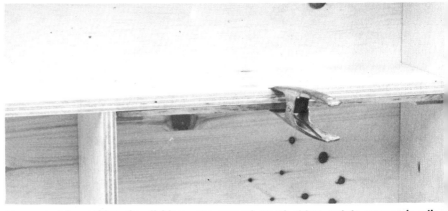

To accurately position the dividers, use several wood strips, cut to proper length, to provide the correct spacing. Use a clamp to hold wood strip against the top.

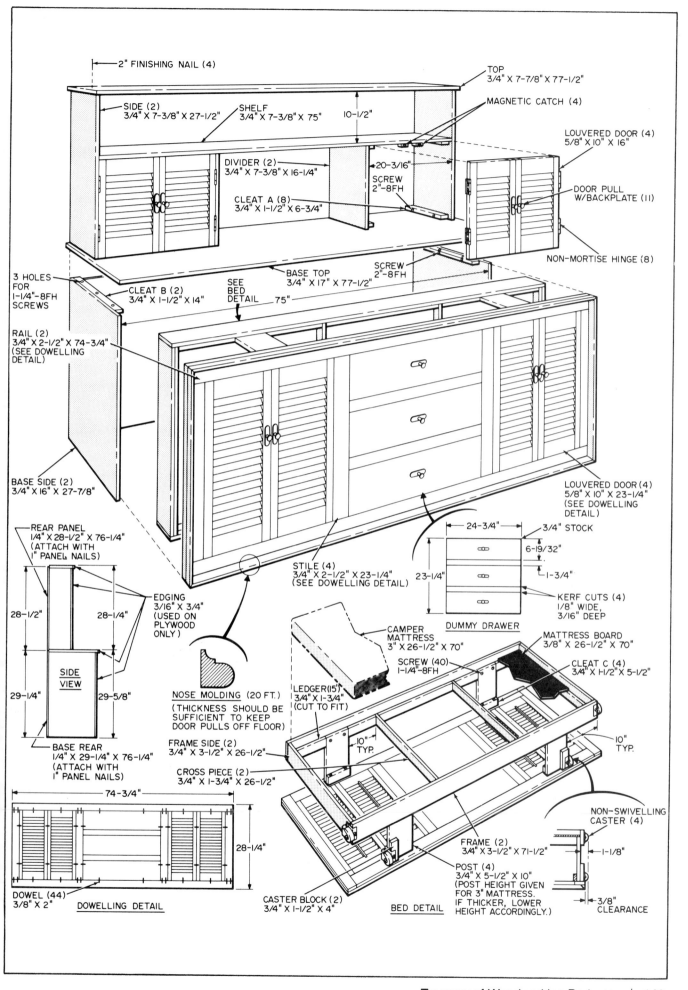

2" FINISHING NAIL (4)

TOP
3/4" X 7-7/8" X 77-1/2"

MAGNETIC CATCH (4)

SIDE (2)
3/4" X 7-3/8" X 27-1/2"

SHELF
3/4" X 7-3/8" X 75"

10-1/2"

LOUVERED DOOR (4)
5/8" X 10" X 16"

DIVIDER (2)
3/4" X 7-3/8" X 16-1/4"

20-3/16"

DOOR PULL
W/BACKPLATE (11)

SCREW
2"-8FH

CLEAT A (8)
3/4" X 1-1/2" X 6-3/4"

NON-MORTISE HINGE (8)

SCREW
2"-8FH

BASE TOP
3/4" X 17" X 77-1/2"

3 HOLES
FOR
1-1/4"-8FH
SCREWS

CLEAT B (2)
3/4" X 1-1/2" X 14"

SEE
BED
DETAIL

75"

RAIL (2)
3/4" X 2-1/2" X 74-3/4"
(SEE DOWELLING
DETAIL)

BASE SIDE (2)
3/4" X 16" X 27-7/8"

LOUVERED DOOR (4)
5/8" X 10" X 23-1/4"
(SEE DOWELLING
DETAIL)

REAR PANEL
1/4" X 28-1/2" X 76-1/4"
(ATTACH WITH
1" PANEL NAILS)

28-1/2"

28-1/4"

EDGING
3/16" X 3/4"
(USED ON
PLYWOOD
ONLY)

SIDE
VIEW

29-1/4"

29-5/8"

STILE (4)
3/4" X 2-1/2" X 23-1/4"
(SEE DOWELLING DETAIL)

24-3/4"

3/4" STOCK

6-19/32"

23-1/4"

1-3/4"

KERF CUTS (4)
1/8" WIDE,
3/16" DEEP

DUMMY DRAWER

NOSE MOLDING (20 FT.)
(THICKNESS SHOULD BE
SUFFICIENT TO KEEP
DOOR PULLS OFF FLOOR)

CAMPER
MATTRESS
3" X 26-1/2" X 70"

MATTRESS BOARD
3/8" X 26-1/2" X 70"

SCREW (40)
1-1/4"-8FH

CLEAT C (4)
3/4" X 1-1/2" X 5-1/2"

BASE REAR
1/4" X 29-1/4" X 76-1/4"
(ATTACH WITH
1" PANEL NAILS)

LEDGER (15)
3/4" X 1-3/4"
(CUT TO FIT)

FRAME SIDE (2)
3/4" X 3-1/2" X 26-1/2"

10"
TYP.

10"
TYP.

CROSS PIECE (2)
3/4" X 1-3/4" X 26-1/2"

74-3/4"

28-1/4"

NON-SWIVELLING
CASTER (4)

DOWEL (44)
3/8" X 2"

DOWELLING DETAIL

CASTER BLOCK (2)
3/4" X 1-1/2" X 4"

BED DETAIL

FRAME (2)
3/4" X 3-1/2" X 71-1/2"

POST (4)
3/4" X 5-1/2" X 10"
(POST HEIGHT GIVEN
FOR 3" MATTRESS.
IF THICKER, LOWER
HEIGHT ACCORDINGLY.)

1-1/8"

3/8"
CLEARANCE

BED/STORAGE UNIT

Materials. Cut the eight cleats to size and, as before, drill the screw clearance holes.

Install the cleats to the side pieces. Position them carefully, especially the upper ones which hold the shelf. The lower ones are fastened flush at the bottom. The cleats for the dividers are mounted flush at top and bottom. Install the side pieces to the shelf first. Lay the shelf and ends on their backs and be sure to work on a flat surface. Apply glue to the joint, then screw the cleats firmly. To assure that the assembly remains square, fasten a diagonal cleat to the back side as shown. Repeat the procedure for the opposite end. The top piece is added next. Center it so the overhang is equal at both ends and at the front.

To locate the position for the dividers, place two louvered doors side by side without space, as shown in the photo. Place a mark on the shelf edge in line with the door farthest from the side panel. Place another mark 3/16-inches

Parts of the lower front section are installed with doweled joints. Two dowels are sufficient to hold louvered sections.

Front panel consists of four louvered doors and center panel simulating three drawers. Add stiles, clamp entire assembly.

The top of the bed post must be flush with the ledge strips. A 5½" cleat is used to mount the posts to the front panel.

Two of the casters attach to the bed frame. The other two casters attach to the posts by means of 1½-in. x 4-in. blocks.

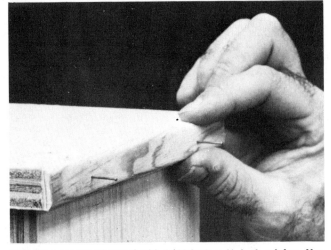

Finishing off the plywood with 3/16-inch x ¾-inch edging. Use glue and brads. For best results, try mitering the corners.

Completed unit is now ready for sanding and finishing. Ours was stained and lacquered, but paint will work just as well.

from the first. This will indicate the inside edge of the divider. Cut and install the rear panel, then fasten the upper section to the lower.

Install the divider next. To simplify the installation, cut four strips of wood making the length equal to the width of the opening. Place two strips at the top and two at the bottom of the opening between the end panel and the divider. Mark the screw hole locations, apply glue and screw the pieces securely in place.

The doors are hung with non-mortise hinges. These are quickly installed since they do not require a gain to be cut in the door or side panel. The specially designed hinge automatically gives the proper clearance allowance between door and frame. Fasten the hinges to the door, then place into the opening, resting the bottom of the doors on a strip of ⅛-inch wood. Mark the position of the hinges on the frame (side panel and divider), then use an awl to pierce the center marks for the screws. Fasten the rest of the hinges and repeat for the other set of doors. Drill a 3/16-inch diameter hole in the center stiles of each door for the pulls. Also mount the magnetic catches to the underside of the shelf. Use·one catch for each door.

Bed Construction. The front panel for the bed is made with louvered doors and a center panel simulating three drawers. Make the center panel first. This should be equal in height to the doors. After cutting the panel to size, cut the double set of grooves representing the rails in between the drawers. Cut the grooves 3/16-inch deep. Drill the 3/16-inch holes for the pulls, then set the piece aside temporarily. Trim ¾-inch from the door bottoms so they will measure 23¼-inch long.

Cut the rails and stiles to size, then lay them on a flat surface with the doors and dummy drawers in place. Be sure that the tops of the doors are oriented (Louvered doors have a top and bottom). With all the pieces aligned, mark a light gauging line on the face of each piece to indicate the dowel locations. Identify each stile with its adjacent part, for example, A-A, B-B, C-C, etc. If you don't, you'll have quite a job trying to match the various parts later on. Drill ⅜-inch diameter holes 1" deep

for the dowels. A doweling jig is most useful for this operation. It will assure straight holes perfectly centered and aligned. If you do not use a doweling jig, be sure that the holes are drilled exactly in the center of each piece.

When assembling the front panel install all of the stiles to the doors and drawer panel sides. If you use snug fitting spiral dowels, you won't need to clamp the assembly. Likewise, you need not clamp the top and bottom rails. The width of the piece was assembled without clamps, because 80-inch clamps are hard to come by. If you have the clamps, use them, but in this instance they are not essential.

Bed Frame. The bed is made with a 3½-inch frame formed into a rectangle as shown. Butt joints glued and screwed make up the outer frame. A ledger strip is added to the inner wall of the frame. This, together with the cross pieces, support the mattress board. The four legs are cut to size and installed with the upper edge aligned with the top of the ledger strips. Cleats are used to attach the legs to the front panel. Two spacer blocks are added to the lower legs in order to align the casters.

To keep the pulls clear of the floor when the front panel is tilted downward, a nose molding is applied around the perimeter of the front section. Be sure the molding is deep enough to keep the knobs off the floor.

The cleats should be glued and screwed to the front panel. However, before applying glue, it is advisable to mount the bed without the glue at first as you test the fit between the bed unit and the lower compartment. Make sure that the clearances are okay and that the bed rides in and out freely. If okay, apply glue and secure permanently.

Add the plywood edging, then sand all surfaces and finish as desired. The unit shown was stained and lacquered, but a two-tone painted finish would be another possibility. The unit could also be left natural with several coats of varnish or lacquer.

The hardware and casters should be available locally.

BILL OF MATERIALS
Except where noted, all lumber is ¾″ pine plywood.

Quantity	Size and Description	Purpose
2	16″ x 28⅞″	Base side
1	17″ x 77½″	Base top
1	¼″ x 29¼″ x 76¼″ plywood	Base rear
8	¾″ x 1½″ x 14″ solid pine	Cleat B
4	⅝″ x 10″ x 16″ louvered	Door
1	7⅞″ x 77½″	Top
1	7⅜″ x 75″	Shelf
2	7⅜″ x 27½″	Side
2	7⅜″ x 16¼″	Divider
2	¾″ x 1½″ x 6¾″ solid pine	Cleat A
4	⅝″ x 10″ x 24″ louvered	Door
40 feet	³⁄₁₆″ x ¾″	Edging
1	1¼″ x 29¼″ x 76¼″ plywood	Rear panel
4	2½″ x 23¼″	Stile
2	2½″ x 74¾″	Rail
1	23¼″ x 24¾	Dummy drawer
20 feet	1-inch	Nose molding
2	3½″ x 26½″	Frame side
2	3½″ x 71½″	Frame
4	5½″ x 10″	Post
4	1½″ x 5½″ solid pine	Cleat C
15 feet	¾″ x 1¾″ pine	Ledger
2	¾″ x 1¾″ x 26½″ pine	Cross piece
2	¾″ x 1½″ x 4″	Caster block
1	⅜″ x 26½″ x 70″	Mattress board
4		Casters
11		Door pull with backplate
4		Magnetic catch
8		Non-mortise hinge
40	⅜″ x 2″	Dowel
24	2″—8 FH	Screw
40	1¼″—8 FH	Screw
36	1″	Panel nails
4	2″ finishing (for top panel)	Nails

NOTE: Also need white glue, sandpaper, and finishing materials.

Mobile Server

Constructed of pine plywood and pine, this handsome piece gives you cabinet, drawer and shelf storage plus a 64-inch surface with the drop leaves extended

This mobile server is small and compact but when its drop leaves are extended, it measures a full 64 in. A closed compartment, three drawers and two shelves provide ample storage. And rails on the lower shelf add a decorative touch.

Except for the trim which is solid lumber, the entire cart is made of pine plywood, thus eliminating the need for gluing up boards. Another advantage in using plywood is the fact that it is stable and not subject to expansion and contraction due to weather conditions. Of course, other species of wood may be substituted for pine, such as birch, oak and walnut. To keep construction simple, we have used butt joints throughout. But you can make rabbeted and dadoed joints instead. If you do, be sure to alter measurements accordingly.

Start construction with the cabinet frame. Cut the sides and top choosing the best grain and knot patterns for the outer surfaces. Before cutting any pieces, check your equipment to make sure all cuts will be straight and square. You may find it easier to have the lumber dealer rip the 4 x 8 panel into the necessary working sizes. If you do so, have them cut the pieces slightly oversize so you can trim them to exact size in your shop.

To conserve lumber and cut down on the weight, a web frame is used to support the drawers. In solid lumber construction the long front and rear sections would be splined or doweled to the shorter end pieces. Since we are using plywood, the frame is made by dropping out the center of the panel and using it for one of the doors. Layout the frame size on the panel, then drill a ¼ in. diameter hole at each corner and drop the center using a saber saw.

To asure alignment of the various sections during assembly, temporarily tack blocks of scrap to the sides of the various panels. Locate these pieces carefully, as the accuracy of the entire assembly depends on their placement. In effect, they act as temporary dadoes and rabbets. If you should decide to use dado and rabbet construction, this step would be unnecessary, Fasten the sections with glue, nails and screws. The nails are used to speed up assembly, but screws are needed for they provide greater holding power than nails. Sink the nail heads and countersink the screw heads only where they will show. The nail heads are filled, but the screws are plugged.

The drawer compartments and guides are made by attaching narrow strips to the underside of the dividers. The strips are cut just long enough to fit within the web frame. The dividers are installed with screws driven from the top. This is necessary especially for the divider placed over the partition. Countersink the screw holes and use 2-in. screws to fasten them to the web frame.

The sub-top pieces, front and rear are fastened at the ends with screws. Likewise, they are fastened to the tops of the two drawer compartments with screws. Again, nails are used first to align the parts, but screws are needed. Glue all joints.

The top is made in three sections. The end flaps are fastened to the center section with strip (piano) hinges. After cutting the three pieces to size, cut and add the edge strips to both ends of the center piece and to the mating ends of the flaps. Do this before installing the hinges. The edging is ripped from solid stock. Make the strips ⅛-in. thick and install with glue and brads.

Lay the top face down onto a flat surface, then install the hinges. Also add the cleats near each end of the center section. Position the cleats so their outer edges will align with the cabinet side panels. The nose and cove trim molding may be added now or later when the rest of the trim is added.

The drop leaf brackets we used are the hinged type which fold flat against the side panels when the

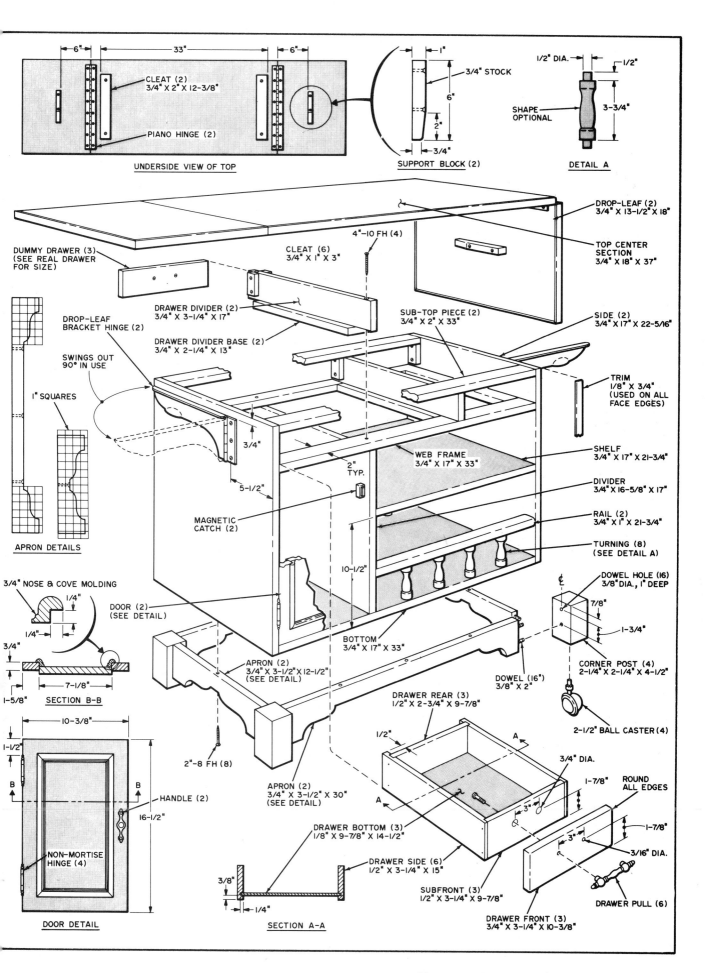

UNDERSIDE VIEW OF TOP

CLEAT (2)
3/4" X 2" X 12-3/8"

PIANO HINGE (2)

SUPPORT BLOCK (2)

3/4" STOCK

DETAIL A

1/2" DIA.

SHAPE OPTIONAL

3-3/4"

DROP-LEAF (2)
3/4" X 13-1/2" X 18"

TOP CENTER SECTION
3/4" X 18" X 37"

DUMMY DRAWER (3)
(SEE REAL DRAWER FOR SIZE)

CLEAT (6)
3/4" X 1" X 3"

4"-10 FH (4)

SIDE (2)
3/4" X 17" X 22-5/16"

DRAWER DIVIDER (2)
3/4" X 3-1/4" X 17"

SUB-TOP PIECE (2)
3/4" X 2" X 33"

DROP-LEAF
BRACKET HINGE (2)

DRAWER DIVIDER BASE (2)
3/4" X 2-1/4" X 13"

SWINGS OUT
90° IN USE

TRIM
1/8" X 3/4"
(USED ON ALL FACE EDGES)

1" SQUARES

3/4"

WEB FRAME
3/4" X 17" X 33"

SHELF
3/4" X 17" X 21-3/4"

2"
TYP.

DIVIDER
3/4" X 16-5/8" X 17"

5-1/2"

MAGNETIC CATCH (2)

APRON DETAILS

RAIL (2)
3/4" X 1" X 21-3/4"

TURNING (8)
(SEE DETAIL A)

10-1/2"

DOWEL HOLE (16)
3/8" DIA., 1" DEEP

7/8"

3/4" NOSE & COVE MOLDING

1/4"

1/4"

DOOR (2)
(SEE DETAIL)

1-3/4"

CORNER POST (4)
2-1/4" X 2-1/4" X 4-1/2"

3/4"

BOTTOM
3/4" X 17" X 33"

DOWEL (16")
3/8" X 2"

2-1/2" BALL CASTER (4)

7-1/8"

1-5/8"

SECTION B-B

APRON (2)
3/4" X 3-1/2" X 12-1/2"
(SEE DETAIL)

10-3/8"

1-1/2"

2"-8 FH (8)

APRON (2)
3/4" X 3-1/2" X 30"
(SEE DETAIL)

DRAWER REAR (3)
1/2" X 2-3/4" X 9-7/8"

1/2"

3/4" DIA.

1-7/8"

ROUND ALL EDGES

B

B

HANDLE (2)

16-1/2"

3"

NON-MORTISE HINGE (4)

DRAWER BOTTOM (3)
1/8" X 9-7/8" X 14-1/2"

DRAWER SIDE (6)
1/2" X 3-1/4" X 15"

1-7/8"

3/16" DIA.

3/8"

1/4"

SUBFRONT (3)
1/2" X 3-1/4" X 9-7/8"

DRAWER PULL (6)

DOOR DETAIL

SECTION A-A

DRAWER FRONT (3)
3/4" X 3-1/4" X 10-3/8"

Mobile Server

flaps are down. In order to clear the strip hinge, they are located ¾-in. below the underside of the top. A support block is fastened to the underside of the flap to compensate for the lowered position of the bracket.

The base consists of four corner posts and a decorative apron. Dowels are used to fasten the assembly. Cut the corners from solid stock. The scalloped design is cut with a saber saw. The long straight section on the front and rear pieces can be made on the circular saw by blind cutting. Such cutting requires that the cut starts and stops short of the ends. To make the cut, the workpiece is carefully positioned against the fence with the saw blade lowered below the table surface. While holding the work firmly with one hand, slowly raise the blade with the other. As the blade breaks through the surface, continue raising until the kerf reaches the forward limit of the cut. Now start feeding the work and stop just a trifle before the scallop starts. Stop the machine and when the blade stops rotating, lift the work away from the blade. Cut the scallops and drop the waste. You will note a slight undercut at each end of the scallop on the rear side of the work. This will not show in the finished piece. If you like, you can cut a sliver of wood to fit the kerf and glue it into place.

When all the pieces have been cut, mark the locations of the dowel and caster holes and bore with a ⅜-in. bit. If you have a dowel jig, use it to bore the holes in the apron ends. Bore the holes one-inch deep. Use dowel centers to transfer the hole locations onto the corner posts. Be sure to work on a flat surface to assure accurate alignment. Gluing should be done in two stages. First, glue the posts to the long apron pieces. When the glue has set, join the long sections to the shorter ones. If all the holes have been drilled straight and square, the assembly should square up when the clamps are applied,

1. Simplified web frame to support the drawers is made by dropping center panel. You save lumber, eliminate joints.

2. Nails and glue are used to fast sections of the mobile server. Dropp panel of frame will become cabinet do

5. Assembly must be perfectly square. If necessary, use diagonal braces to keep it that way until the glue sets.

6. Drawer dividers are made to fit w frame. Bottom strip serves as draw slide. Study preceding drawing carefu

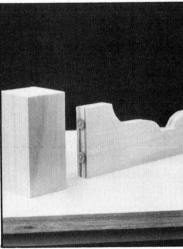

9. Underside of top. Hinged-type drop leaf bracket must clear strip hinge. Block compensates for lower position.

10. Corner post and decorative apron server's base. Dowel centers are be used to mark locations on corner pc

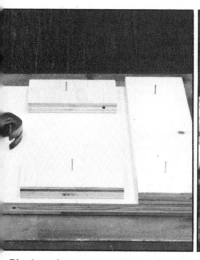

Blocks of scrap wood, temporarily ∎cked to sides of the panels, assures ⸍gnment of sections during assembly.

4. Shelf is attached to partition before end panel is installed. Glue, nails and screws are used to fasten sections.

Dividers are fastened with screws at ∎ch end as demonstrated in this photo. ⸍e temporary spacer assures accuracy.

8. Narrow strips attached to underside of the dividers with nails and screws form drawer compartments and guides.

Dowel (and caster) holes are bored ⸍h ⅜-in. bit, 1 in. deep. The long ∎on has already been glued in photo.

12. Bar clamps are used for final gluing. Omitted for clarity here, protective scraps should be under clamp jaws.

but it's a good idea to check the assembly anyway. If necessary, use temporary braces to hold it square.

The doors are made with recessed panels. This is easily accomplished by the use of molding. Ordinary nose and cove molding is rabbeted on the outer rear edge; it is then mitered and dropped into the frame cut into the door panel. The center panel cut from the door is glued to the back side of the molding. A pair of clamps and a scrap piece of wood across the door will hold it firmly while the glue sets. If you use non-mortise type hinges, you won't have to mortise out a gain in the door or frame.

The drawers are made with a false front. The lumber used is solid pine. The rear panel fits into dadoes cut into the side panels. Rabbets are cut at the front end of the sides to take the sub-front panel. A ⅛-in. groove near the bottom of the side and front panels takes a ⅛-in. hardboard bottom piece. Before assembling the parts, drill the necessary holes for the drawer pulls. Make the holes in the subfront large enough to clear the screw heads for the pulls. Assemble the drawer with glue and 1¼-in. finishing nails. Do not glue the bottom panel. Simply nail it into the lower edge of the rear panel.

The three extra drawer fronts are installed at the rear of the cabinet and held to small cleats attached to the compartment sides. The rear door is also a dummy and is also fastened with cleats.

Use a piece of ¾-in. stock for the rail. Drill the four ½-in. dia. holes for the turnings and drill four matching holes in the bottom panel. Round the edges of the rail with a router then sand smooth. The turnings are turned on the lathe. If you lack a lathe, you can substitute straight dowels or you can purchase the turnings readymade. If you make your own, be sure the tenons are exactly ½-in. in diameter. It is not necessary to glue the rails to the cabinet sides. Gluing the tenons into the bottom holes will suffice.

The edging and trim are added to complete the project. If you use plywood edging, you will find it has a slight radius on the outer

Mobile Server

edges. This rounded edge will form a gap where two pieces butt. You can leave the gap and fill with wood putty or you can notch out the cross pieces slightly to eliminate the problem. If you decide on the filler, color the filler to match the stain you intend to use. Some fillers can be colored with earth colors. Check the instructions of the product you are using. Sink and fill all nail heads then sand the entire cabinet. Break all sharp edges. Dust, then stain as desired, followed by several clear topcoats of varnish or lacquer. Add sockets for the ball casters then insert the stem.

The turnings, hinges and brackets, should be available locally.

BILL OF MATERIALS

Quantity	Size and Description	
1	18" x 37"	Top center
2	18" x 13½"	Top end
2	¾" x 2" x 12⅜" pine	Top cleat
2	¾" x 1" x 6" pine	Top lid support
2	17" x 22-5/16"	End
1	17" x 33"	Bottom
1	16⅝" x 17"	Divider
1	17" x 21¾"	Shelf
1	17" x 33"	Web frame
2	¾" x 2" x 33"	Top support
1	3¼" x 17"	Drawer divider
2	2¼" x 13"	Drawer divider base
2	¾" x 1" x 21¾" pine	Rail
8	¾" x 3¾"	Spindle
2	3½" x 12½"	Base end
1	3½" x 30"	Base front
1	3½" x 30"	Base rear
4	2¼" x 2¼" x 4½" pine	Base corner
2	10⅜" x 16½"	Door
6	¾" x 3¼" x 10⅜" pine	Drawer front
3	½" x 3¼" x 9⅞" pine	Drawer subfront
6	½" x 3¼" x 15" pine	Drawer side
3	½" x 2¾" x 9⅞"	Drawer rear
3	⅛" x 9⅞" x 14¾" hardboard	Drawer bottom
6	¾" x 1" x 3"	Dummy drawer front cleat
30	⅝" x ¾"	Nose & cove molding
32	⅛" x ¾"	Plywood edging
2		Lid support bracket
2		Magnetic catch PM
4	2"	Hinge, non-mortise,
8	⅜" x 2"	Dowels
4		Ball casters
2	1½" x 18"	Strip hinge
2		Door pulls
6		Drawer pulls

All lumber is ¾" pine plywood except "pine", which is solid pine.

13. Before applying glue to trim of the mobile server, check fit carefully. This is good procedure on all shop projects.

14. Water putty can be used to fill gap caused by rounded edging. Alternatives: wood putty or notching of cross pieces.

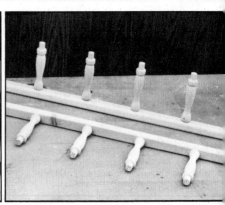

15. Small turnings for rails have ½ tenons at each end. If you make yours be sure tenons are ½ in. in diameter

16. Recessed door for cabinet of the server is made by lowering center panel. The molding has been rabbeted to fit.

17. Moldings are clamped to the frame while glue sets. Scrap block is used under the clamps to prevent marring.

18. Drawers are solid pine with hardwood bottom. Note false front. Rear panel fits dadoes cut into the drawer sides

Library Wall Cabinet

L IBRARY UNITS are always useful, whether they are used singly, in pairs, or to line an entire wall. They are attractive and functional pieces, offering shelves above for books and curios and storage cabinets below. Each unit is easily constructed and butt joints are used throughout. With the exception of the door panels and decorative arched valance, all cutting is straight and simple. Some router work is involved and some ready-made molding is used.

The cost of building the cabinet was kept way down by using common pine and Lauan paneling. The Lauan was used for the rear of the cabinet and also as a backup for the doors. Finished in antique green, the unit couldn't look any better even if it had been made of rock maple.

Start by cutting the sides, top and bottom as indicated. Before assembling the parts, cut the rabbet along one edge. This will form the recess for the back panel. Size

the edge grain of the top and bottom sections by thinning the glue slightly with water. Let the glue dry about fifteen minutes, then apply glue in normal manner and assemble the sections. Use galvanized finishing nails and, if clamps are available, use them. Be sure to work on a level floor and keep the frame square as the glue sets. If necessary, temporarily fasten diagonal cleats to hold the frame plumb.

The shelves can now be cut and installed. Treat the edge grain as outlined above. The front edges of the three upper shelves are rounded after they are installed. The cabinet sides serve as a stop for the router, thus allowing the rounding-off to stop short of the front frame.

Front framing is added next. Attach one vertical first, then the crosspieces followed by the second vertical. This will assure a good tight joint. The door divider can be added at this time. Be sure to center it accurately.

The valance was made by blocking up a piece of 1 x 12-inch stock, although it could have been cut from a single piece of 1 x 18-inch. For economy, it is wiser to block up the ends as shown. Leave the length of the valance oversize and cut it to fit after the blocks have

Library Wall Cabinet

been glued. Use a saber saw to cut the arched curve, then shape the edge with a router.

The main shelf (above the doors) is built out by adding a filler strip and the front overhang. The overhang is cut 1⅛ inches deep to give the shelf a heavy look. Moldings are added now—apply with glue and brads. The small molding at the top shelf is mitered at the inside corners. The top molding (cornice) is mounted at an angle and to support it, small glue blocks are installed.

Doors are of simple construction. Stiles and rails are cut to size and assembled with dowels, using two dowels per corner. Clamps must be used here for a good glue joint. When the frame is glued, shape the inner edges then attach the back board which is cut from a piece of ¼-inch plywood. The center section of the door is glued to the ¼-inch panel. To prevent center from shifting, drive a few small brads into it from rear.

Hinges are set into the door but they are mounted flush on the side panels. Hinge clearance in the doors can be cut in several ways. You can use a chisel, router, or table saw. The table saw method is fast and the results are very good. Measure the thickness of the hinge when closed, then allow the saw blade to protrude ¹⁄₁₆-inch less than the hinge thickness. For example, if the hinge measures ³⁄₁₆-inch thick when closed let the table saw blade protrude ⅛-inch. Mark the hinge positions on the door, and using the miter gauge, make a series of cuts between the marks to clean out the area. Install magnetic door catches or bullet catches as desired.

The rear panel is cut to size, but not installed until after applying the finish material, since it is much easier to work this way. Be sure to sink and fill all nail heads, then sand all surfaces until smooth.

When antiquing a large piece such as this, you may find it easier to work with an antiquing kit which has a latex base material. Latex will dry in a couple of hours

as opposed to the overnight dry required by oil base materials.

Of course, you may want to stain or even leave the wood natural, with several coats of varnish or shellac. This is a matter of taste.

However you finish your library unit, we are sure you will be greatly pleased with it. Its design allows for expansion later if desired, and you can add one or more units to span a whole wall.

BILL OF MATERIALS

Quantity	Size and Description	Purpose
6	¾" 10⅞" x 38" pine	shelves
2	¾" 10⅞" x 83¼" pine	sides
1	¾" 15⅛" x 39½" pine	valance
1	¾" 3" x 39½" pine	base
2	¾" 2¾" x 68⅛" pine	vertical
1	¾" 2⅝" pine	filler
1	¾" 1⅛" x 39½" pine	overhang
1	¾" 4¾" x 34" pine	bottom
1	¾" 1⅛" x 20⅜" pine	door divider
1	¼" 38¾" x 82½" lauan	rear panel
2	¼" 16¼" x 20⅛" lauan	door rear
4	¾" 2¼" x 11¾" pine	door rail
2	¾" 9⅞" x 13½" pine	door panel
1	¾" 1" x 4" pine	catch block
1	¼" 1" x ⅛" lauan	catch block
8	¾" x 8" nose and cove molding	
1	2½" x 39½" decorative molding	

NOTE: Also need: filler, glue, dowels, hardware, and finish coating.

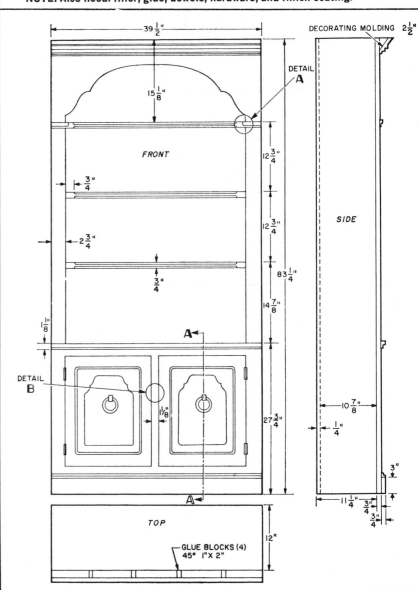

Cabinet frame is assembled with butt joints, which greatly simplifies the construction. Use glue and galvanized nails.

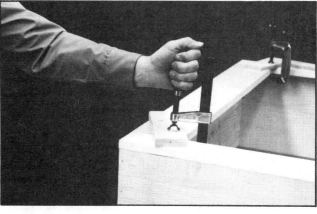

Front framing is also butt jointed with glue and nails. Use clamps for a tight, even fit. Add door divider at this time.

The door stiles and rails are assembled with dowels, then attached to ¼-in. panel along with the raised center piece.

The valance is made by blocking up a piece of 1 x 12 stock. Use a saber saw to cut the curves, shape edge with router.

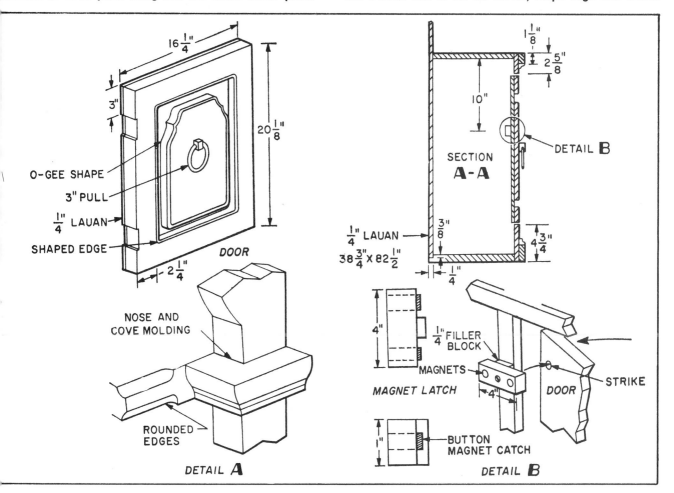

16 ¼"

3"

20 ⅛"

O-GEE SHAPE

3" PULL

¼" LAUAN

SHAPED EDGE

2 ¼"

DOOR

NOSE AND COVE MOLDING

ROUNDED EDGES

DETAIL **A**

1 ⅛"

2 ⅝"

10"

DETAIL **B**

SECTION **A-A**

¼" LAUAN
38 ¾" x 82 ½"

3/8"

4 ¾"

¼"

4"

¼" FILLER BLOCK

MAGNETS

MAGNET LATCH

4"

DOOR

STRIKE

1"

BUTTON MAGNET CATCH

DETAIL **B**

Lightweight Desk

This plan calls for 1 x 12 birch stock, but you can also use plywood

BUILDING THIS handsome desk is a project that any good woodcraftsman can undertake with confidence. The design could be modified, if so desired, by substituting drawers for a cabinet on the pier.

Start construction by edge-gluing one-inch stock birch from the top. Clamp and let dry, then plane all joints and sand to smooth finish. Cut shape of top with bandsaw or saber saw, then sand all edges smooth. Next glue up the stock for the pier section, and sand and plane it. Cut to size, then cut rabbet on bottom edge of sides and back and on back edges of sides. Cut a bottom piece to fit in the rabbet.

Bore upper cleats for #10 1½-inch flat head wood screws, then glue and screw cleats in place, setting them in 1/16-inch from the

edges so that when pieces are assembled they will draw up tight at the joints. Assemble the pier section with glue and screws, squaring assembly and then fastening bottom in place with screws.

Install a shelf in the pier section, and hang the door on butt cabinet hinges, with a magnetic catch and brass knob. Cut the pier base pieces to size, mitering corner joints. Bore for #11 1½-inch flat head screws, apply glue, and assemble with corner blocks, making sure it is square. Now fasten base to pier.

Cut the stock for the leg assembly and stretchers. Bore holes for 7/16-inch dowels 2 inches long. Assemble with glue, clamping until glue has set. Remove clamps and plane and sand all joints flush, then round the front edge of the leg.

Fasten a cleat to the top piece of the leg for fastening to the top.

Bore two holes through the top stretcher for #10 2½-inch flat head screws. Plane and sand stretchers. Bore holes for 7/16-inch dowels in stretchers, pier, and legs, place glue in holes and assemble pier, leg, and stretchers. Clamp square in all directions.

Place the top upside down, then place the leg and pier assembly on the top. Square and fasten all cleats and the upper stretcher to top, then sand again. Stain to the desired shade, apply a coat of sealer, sand lightly, and apply a finish coat of lacquer.

The trim, modern appearance of this desk will make it a welcome piece of furniture as well as a useful accessory in the living room, bedroom, or den.

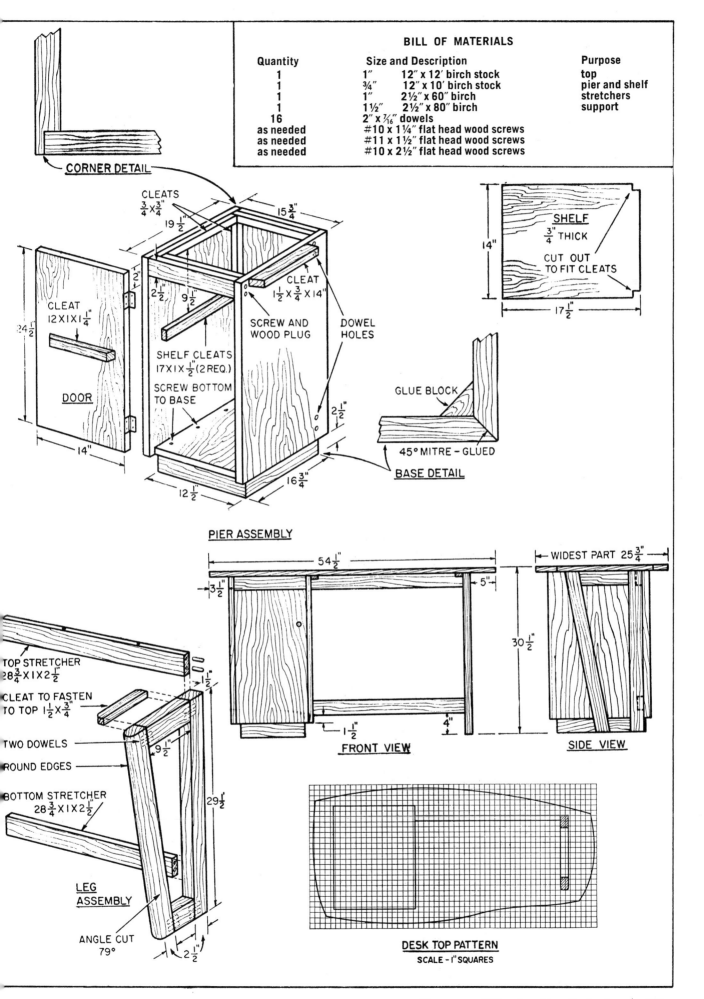

BILL OF MATERIALS

Quantity	Size and Description	Purpose
1	1" 12" x 12' birch stock	top
1	¾" 12" x 10' birch stock	pier and shelf
1	1" 2½" x 60" birch	stretchers
1	1½" 2½" x 80" birch	support
16	2" x ⁷⁄₁₆" dowels	
as needed	#10 x 1¼" flat head wood screws	
as needed	#11 x 1½" flat head wood screws	
as needed	#10 x 2½" flat head wood screws	

CORNER DETAIL

CLEATS ¾ X ¾"

19 ½"

15 ¾"

2"

2 ½"

9 ½"

CLEAT 1½ X ¾ X 14"

SCREW AND WOOD PLUG

DOWEL HOLES

SHELF ¾" THICK

CUT OUT TO FIT CLEATS

14"

17 ½"

CLEAT 12 X I X I¼"

24 ½"

DOOR

14"

SHELF CLEATS 17 X I X ½" (2 REQ.)

SCREW BOTTOM TO BASE

GLUE BLOCK

45° MITRE – GLUED

BASE DETAIL

2 ½"

12 ½"

16 ¾"

PIER ASSEMBLY

54 ½"

3 ½"

5"

WIDEST PART 25 ¾"

30 ½"

1 ½"

4"

FRONT VIEW

SIDE VIEW

TOP STRETCHER 28¾ X I X 2½"

CLEAT TO FASTEN TO TOP 1½ X ¾"

TWO DOWELS

ROUND EDGES

BOTTOM STRETCHER 28¾ X I X 2½"

9 ½"

1 ½"

29 ½"

LEG ASSEMBLY

ANGLE CUT 79°

2 ½"

DESK TOP PATTERN

SCALE – 1" SQUARES

Treasury of Woodworking Projects / 161

3-in-1 Sports Gear Cabinet

WHETHER YOU ENJOY hunting, fishing, camping, tennis, golf or skiing you can adapt this basic cabinet design to hold your gear—or you can build a row of them, each with a different interior arrangement to suit your own needs.

To build the hunting cabinet, first lay out the parts on three sheets of plywood as shown on the plans. True the edges with 1/0 sandpaper on a block and rabbet one end of each side panel for the top.

Assemble the cabinet on its back on the floor with resin glue and finishing nails. Use your square frequently to assure accurate work.

While the glue is setting, glue and nail the door framing strips and the door panel together, following clearance all around as indicated.

When the glue of the cabinet has

set, build the interior shelves and drawers as shown on the plans. Use glue and finishing nails to join the parts to each other and to the cabinet.

Cutouts for the gun stock and barrel racks are made as shown in the plans. The surest way to establish the correct height for each (so the weapons will fit in the case) is by trial and error.. With your guns in the cabinet, try them at various heights. When the correct height is reached, hold the rack in place and mark the position. When the position of each rack is marked, remove the guns and glue and nail the racks in place. Install a hinged bar and a lock on front of the upper rack.

Next, build the shelves and facings in the door. The facing should be flush with the framing strips. Note how quarter-round molding is

used to strengthen the inside corners of the facing.

Smooth all joints and slightly round the corners with 3/0 sandpaper. Fill any nail holes and exposed plywood edge grain with wood filler, smooth the entire cabinet with 3/0 sandpaper.

Place the cabinet on its back and attach the door to the cabinet with four pin-hinges. The door may be hinged at either side. Install a suitable catch or lock.

Give the whole cabinet a coat of primer and then finish it with two coats of semi gloss enamel. Install any lining material you feel is appropriate and any fixtures or hardware needed to accommodate your gear.

The camping cabinet and the ski, golf and tennis cabinet are made in the same way as the hunting and fishing cabinet with different arrangements for the interior shelving as shown on the plans.

In addition, using the basic design for the cabinet shell and door, you can easily improvise your own interior design to accommodate almost anything.

For indoor uses, such as in these cabinets, plywood can be joined with resin glue (white glue) and nails. Use 6d finishing nails for ¾ and ⅝-inch plywood, 3d or 4d nails for ⅜-inch and 1-inch brads for ¼-inch plywood.

HUNTING-FISHING CABINET

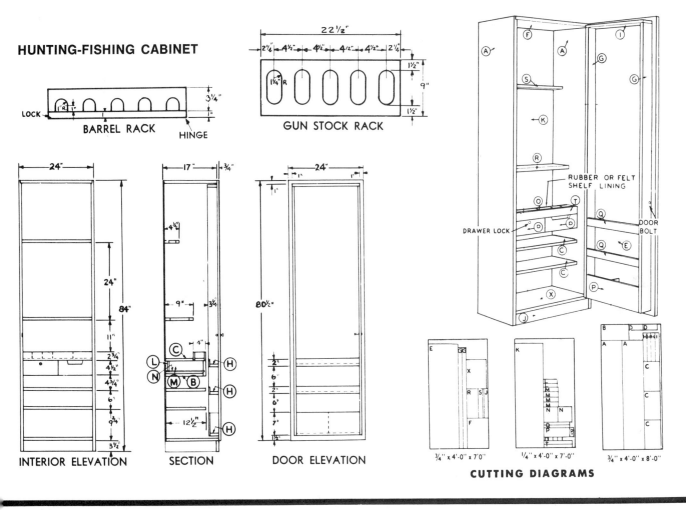

BARREL RACK

LOCK

HINGE

GUN STOCK RACK

22½"

2¼" 4½" 4½" 4½" 4½" 2¼"

1¼"R

1½" 9" 1½"

3¼"

1"R

24"

24" 84"

11"

2¾"
4½"
4¾"

6"

9¼"

3½"

INTERIOR ELEVATION

17" ¾"

4½"

9" 3½"

4"

12½"

SECTION

24" 1" 1"

1"

80½"

2"
6"
2"
6"
7"
½"

DOOR ELEVATION

RUBBER OR FELT
SHELF LINING

DRAWER LOCK

DOOR
BOLT

¾" x 4'-0" x 7'-0"   ¼" x 4'-0" x 7'-0"   ¾" x 4'-0" x 8'-0"

CUTTING DIAGRAMS

SKI, GOLF AND TENNIS CABINET

NOTE: Bill of Materials is on following page

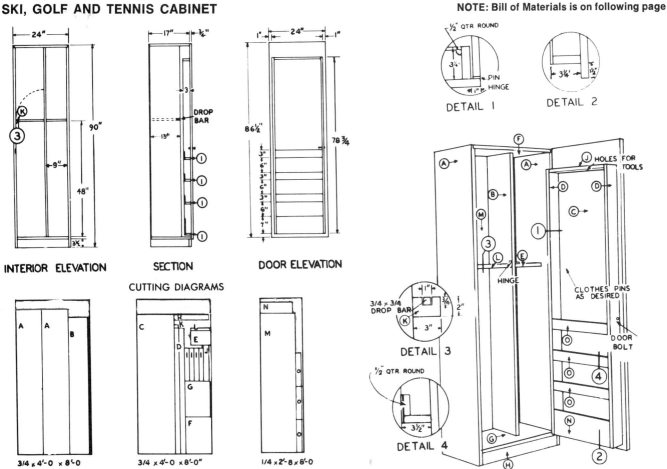

24"

90"

9"

48"

3½"

INTERIOR ELEVATION

17" ¾"

3

DROP
BAR

13"

SECTION

1" 24" 1"

86½" 78¾"

3"
6"
3"
6"
3"
6"
7"

DOOR ELEVATION

CUTTING DIAGRAMS

3/4 x 4'-0 x 8'-0   3/4 x 4'-0 x 8'-0"   1/4 x 2'-8 x 8'-0

½" QTR. ROUND

3¼"

PIN
HINGE
1"

DETAIL 1

3¼"

DETAIL 2

HOLES FOR
TOOLS

HINGE

CLOTHES PINS
AS DESIRED

DOOR
BOLT

3/4 x 3/4
DROP BAR

1"
2"
3"

DETAIL 3

½" QTR. ROUND

3½"

DETAIL 4

Sports Cabinet

CAMP, HIKE AND CLIMB VERSION

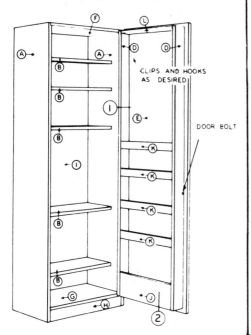

CLIPS AND HOOKS AS DESIRED

DOOR BOLT

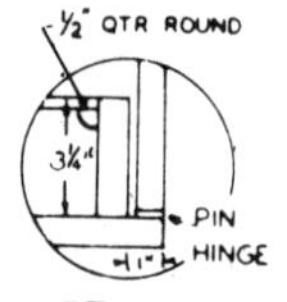

½" QTR ROUND

3¾"

PIN HINGE

DETAIL 1

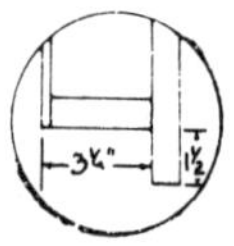

3¾"

DETAIL 2

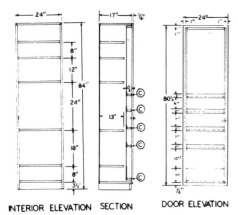

24"

17"

¼"

8"

12"

84"

24"

13"

18"

8"

3¼"

80½"

24"

INTERIOR ELEVATION   SECTION   DOOR ELEVATION

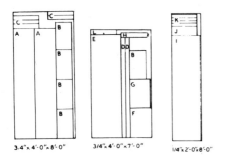

3.4" x 4'-0" x 8'-0"   3/4" x 4'-0" x 7'-0"   ¼" x 2'-0" x 8'-0"

CUTTING DIAGRAMS

MATERIALS LIST—Hunting and Fishing Cabinet

Quantity	Size and Description	Purpose
2	¾" 17"x84" A-D interior plywood	sides
1	¾" 12"x22½" A-D interior plywood	drawer shelf
3	¾" 12½"x22½" A-D interior plywood	shelves
2	¾" 4½"x11¼" A-D interior plywood	drawer fronts
1	¾" 24"x80½" A-D interior plywood	door
1	¾" 17"x23¼" A-D interior plywood	top
2	¾" 3¼"x77¼" A-D interior plywood	door frame
3	¾" 3"x20½" A-D interior plywood	door shelves
1	¾" 3½"x22½" A-D interior plywood	base
1	¾" 3¼"x22" A-D interior plywood	door top shelf
1	¾" 9"x22½" A-D interior plywood	gun stock rack
1	¾" 4¼"x22½" A-D interior plywood	barrel rack
1	¾" 16¾"x22½" A-D interior plywood	bottom shelf
1	¼" 23¼"x80⅛" A-D interior plywood	back
2	¼" 3"x11" A-D interior plywood	drawer backs
4	¼" 3¾"x12⅛" A-D interior plywood	drawer sides
2	¼" 10¾"x12⅛" A-D interior plywood	drawer bottoms
4	¼" 2"x3½" A-D interior plywood	dividers
1	¼" 7"x20½" A-D interior plywood	door shelf fascia
1	¼" 3"x6¼" A-D interior plywood	door shelf divider
2	¼" 2"x20½" A-D interior plywood	door shelf fascia
1	¼" 2¾"x22½" A-D interior plywood	gun shelf face
1	¼" 2⅜"x22½" A-D interior plywood	gun shelf face
1	¼" 20½"x56" cork	backing
	9"x22½" rubber or felt	lining

NOTE: Also need rack hinge and lock, drawer lock, door bolt, pin hinges, 4d and 6d finishing nails, glue, clips and finishing materials.

MATERIALS LIST—Camping and Hiking Cabinet

Quantity	Size and Description	Purpose
2	¾" 17"x84" A-D interior plywood	sides
5	¾" 13"x22½" A-D interior plywood	shelves
5	¾" 3"x20½" A-D interior plywood	door shelves
2	¾" 3¼"x78" A-D interior plywood	door side frame
1	¾" 3¼"x20½" A-D interior plywood	door top frame
1	¾" 24"x80½" A-D interior plywood	door
1	¾" 17"x23¼" A-D interior plywood	top
1	¾" 17"x22½" A-D interior plywood	bottom shelf
1	¾" 3½"x22½" A-D interior plywood	base
1	¼" 23¼"x80⅛" A-D interior plywood	back
1	¼" 7"x20½" A-D interior plywood	door shelf fascia
4	¼" 2"x20½" A-D interior plywood	door shelf fascia
1	¼" ¼"x30" quarter round molding	

NOTE: Also need pin hinges, door bolt, 4d and 6d finishing nails, glue, clips, hooks and finishing materials.

MATERIALS LIST—Ski, Golf and Tennis Cabinet

Quantity	Size and Description	Purpose
2	¾" 9"x13" A-D interior plywood	sides
1	¾" 17"x23¼" A-D interior plywood	standard
1	¾" 16¾"x22½" A-D interior plywood	door
2	¾" 3½"x22½" A-D interior plywood	door side frame
1	¾" 3"x20½" A-D interior plywood	shelf
1	¾" 3¼"x20½" A-D interior plywood	top
1	¾" 2"x3" A-D interior plywood	bottom shelf
1	¾" ¾"x12¾" A-D interior plywood	base
4	¼" 23¼"x86⅛" A-D interior plywood	door shelves
1	¼" 7"x20½" A-D interior plywood	top door tool shelf
1	¼" 3"x20½" A-D interior plywood	drop bar catch
1	½" ½"x30" quarter round molding	drop bar
1	¾" 17"x90" A-D interior plywood	back
1	¾" 13"x85" A-D interior plywood	door shelf fascia
3	¾" 24"x86½" A-D interior plywood	door shelf fascia
1	¾" 3¼"x78¾" A-D interior plywood	

NOTE: Also need hinge for drop bar, door bolt, pin hinges, 4d and 6d finishing nails, glue and finishing materials.

MAGAZINE TABLE

You can easily build this fine piece of furniture in your spare time using either pine or the wood of your choice

Y OU DON'T NEED any fancy equipment to build this fine magazine end table. The Italian provincial legs look difficult to build but indeed they are not. A glance at the drawing reveals that they are built-up using a technique called post blocking. This eliminates the almost impossible task of accurately cutting the narrow section between posts with conventional home shop equipment. A simple method of fluting the legs is also utilized to further enhance the project.

Lumber used was pine, but any suitable wood will do. For a stained or natural finish, you may want to try mahogany, cherry or maple. Walnut may also be used—if you can get it. This fine cabinet wood is becoming rare.

Start construction with the legs. These are cut from 2-inch stock. Set the table saw fence for a 1⅝-in. cut then rip the stock to produce a block 1⅝-in. square. After cutting, sand the surfaces or, if you have a jointer, run a pass on each surface to eliminate the kerf marks of the saw. If the jointer is to be used, make the saw cut a trifle more than 1⅝-in. to allow for stock removal on the jointer. After ripping and smoothing the surface, cut the legs to size and taper the lower ends.

The best way to taper the legs is to use a jig on the table saw. The jig consists of a piece of plywood notched out to hold a leg. The notch is positioned at an angle so that when the jig with a leg in

place is fed through the saw, a thin wedge section is ripped off the end of the leg. This operation is repeated on all four sides to produce the tapered leg. The angle of the notch determines the amount of taper. This set-up can be used for other projects where numerous tapered cuts are required.

The next step is the fluting of the legs. Here again a jig is used for both accuracy and simplicity. The router is mounted to a wooden platform which converts it to a mini-shaper. The cutter is made to protrude through the top of the platform to which a fence has been attached. The work is simply held against the fence and fed through the cutter resulting in a flute (or flutes) being cut.

All routers have a removable base plate. The plate is usually held with four screws. Carefully remove these and set aside. Place the plate on a piece of plywood and use a pencil to locate the mounting holes as well as the center opening. Drill the holes for the screws countersinking the heads. The center hole should be large enough to clear the cutter being used. See the drawing for clarification. Make the legs of the platform tall enough so that the bottom of the router will clear the workbench.

Mount the flute cutter in the router then, using the four screws removed from the router base previously, mount the router in place. Position the fence so that the flute will fall exactly in the center of the leg. Although only one fence is shown for clarity in the photograph, a double fence is recommended to keep the workpiece from swaying.

Some routers are not made with lock-on switches—especially the pistol grip type. If you have one of these, you will have to have an assistant turn on the power as needed, or you can improvise by taping the switch "on" with masking tape. You can then operate the machine by using the plug as a switch. If you use this method, be sure to remove the tape as soon as the job is done.

Since the flutes are "blind" (they do not run off the edge of the

MAGAZINE TABLE

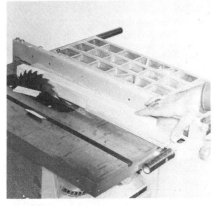

To taper leg ends, use a table saw jig. Jig is positioned so that the saw blade cuts the leg block at a slight angle.

To produce leg fluting, mount router on a frame. Lower work onto cutter, using marks to show where to start and stop.

Blocks which will be used to build up legs are ripped from a piece of ¾-in. stick. Cut or sand ends to 45° angle.

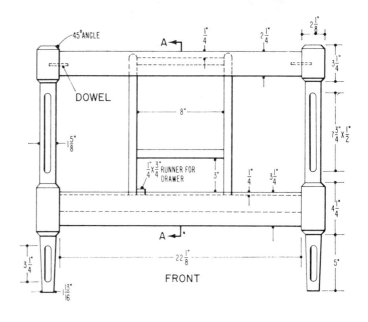

FRONT

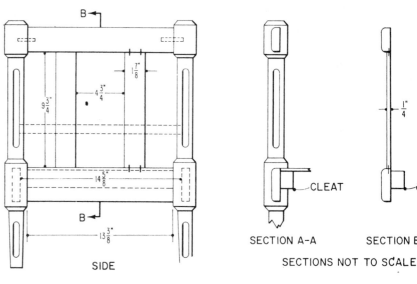

SIDE

SECTION A-A   SECTION B-B

SECTIONS NOT TO SCALE

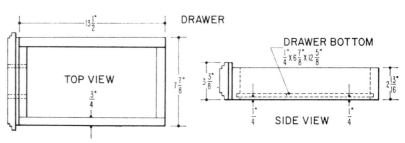

DRAWER

TOP VIEW

DRAWER BOTTOM

SIDE VIEW

work), you will have to lower the work onto the cutter and likewise lift it off at the end of the cut. Do this by placing "start" and "stop" marks on the jig. Determine the location of these by making trial cuts in scrap wood the same length as the legs.

Blocking is the next step. Saw ¼-in. wide strips from suitable stock, then rip two widths. Half the pieces will be ripped 1⅝-in. wide

and the rest 2⅛-in. wide. Cut the lengths to size as indicated then bevel the edges on the sander. Set the table for a 45° bevel then just touch the work to the disc to produce the bevel. If you do not have a sander, use the table saw to make the bevel.

Glue the strips to the legs as shown. The narrow pieces are installed first. To keep the pieces from shifting, snip the ends of 18

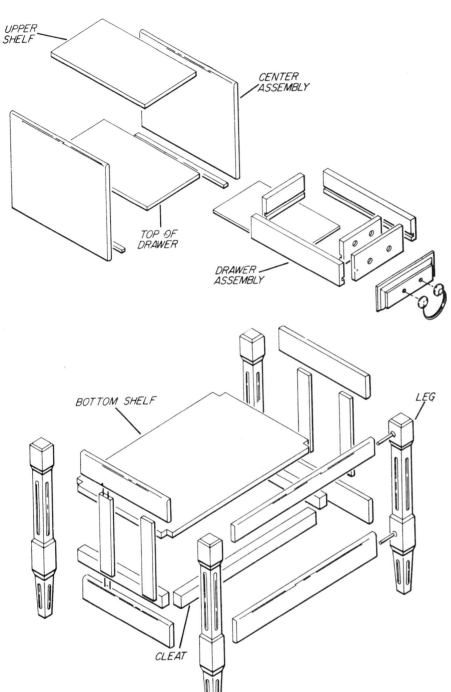

UPPER SHELF

CENTER ASSEMBLY

TOP OF DRAWER

DRAWER ASSEMBLY

BOTTOM SHELF

LEG

CLEAT

The legs are built up by attaching the cut and beveled pieces. To attach, use glue, and then clamp for a good bond.

The apron pieces are joined to the legs with dowels. Use dowel locating pins to accurately transfer the hole positions.

The next step is to cut the lower shelf and then install using cleats on underside. Attach it with dowels to legs.

gauge brads so the pointed end is about ¼-in. long. Use a plier to drive the blunt end into the leg leaving just the point protruding. Use two brads per section and hold the pieces with clamps while the glue sets. The wide strips are installed last.

When all the legs have been glued, use a knife or chisel to bevel the square corners of the blocks.

Cut the upper and lower apron pieces to size then round off the edges with the router fitted with a rounding cutter. Note that three edges are rounded on the upper pieces and only two on the lower.

Cut the four slats to size and round off the edges. Again using the blind brad technique, install the

MAGAZINE TABLE

slats to the upper and lower apron ends. This time make the brads longer (about ½-in.) and allow them to protrude about ¼-in. Apply glue and working on a flat surface, bring the parts together. Clamp until the glue sets.

The apron pieces are joined to the legs with dowels. One dowel in each section will suffice. Use dowel locating pins to accurately position the dowels. A dowel drilling jig is first used on the apron ends. Hole positions are then transferred to the legs by means of the pins. (See photo). Next cut the shelf and install it using cleats on the underside.

The drawer and top shelf compartment is made as a unit and installed separately. Set the lower shelf down about ¼-in. and likewise the upper shelf is set down from the top the same amount.

Make the drawer with a double front as shown and be sure to make screw clearance holes on the sub-front so that the hardware can be installed after the finishing operation is completed.

The front edge of the drawer is shaped with a beading cutter.

Sanding and finishing operations complete the project. To facilitate the finishing, the compartment may be lifted out and installed after the finishing is completed.

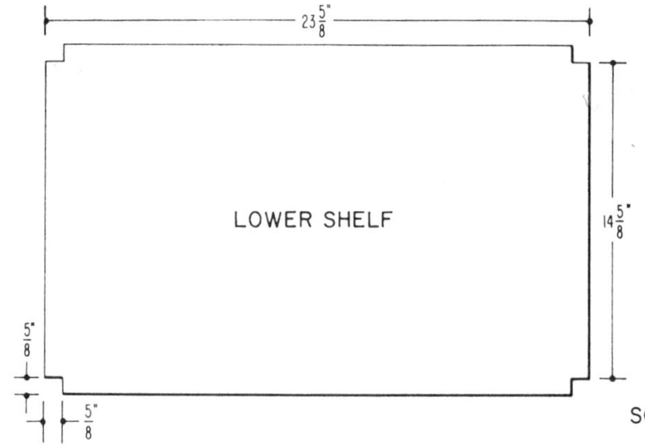

23 5/8"
LOWER SHELF
14 5/8"
5/8"
5/8"

SCALE: 1/4" = 1"

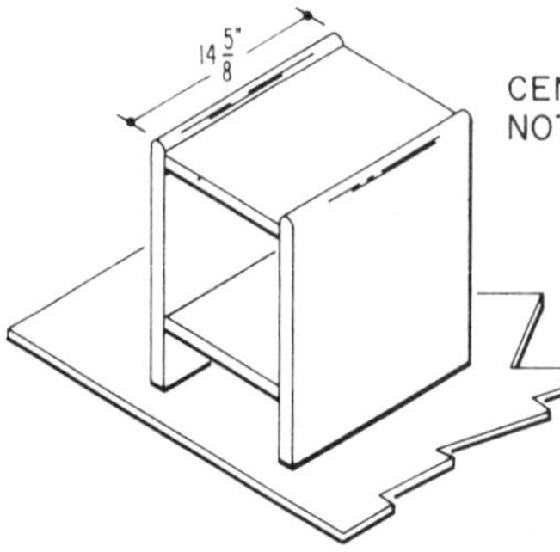

14 5/8"

CENTER ASSEMBLY
NOT TO SCALE

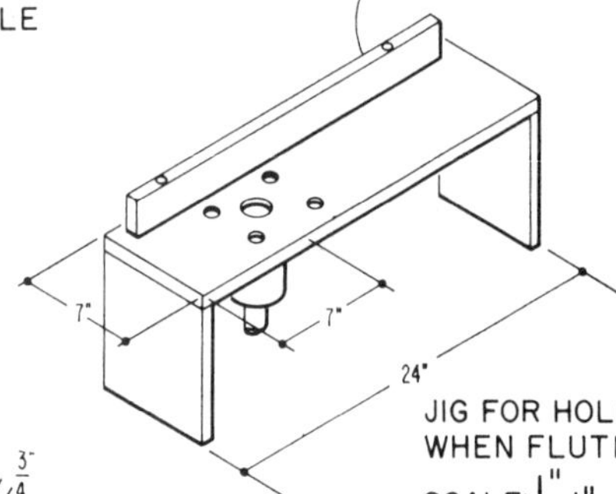

FENCE (USE 2)
7"
7"
24"

JIG FOR HOLDING
WHEN FLUTING
SCALE: 1/8" = 1"

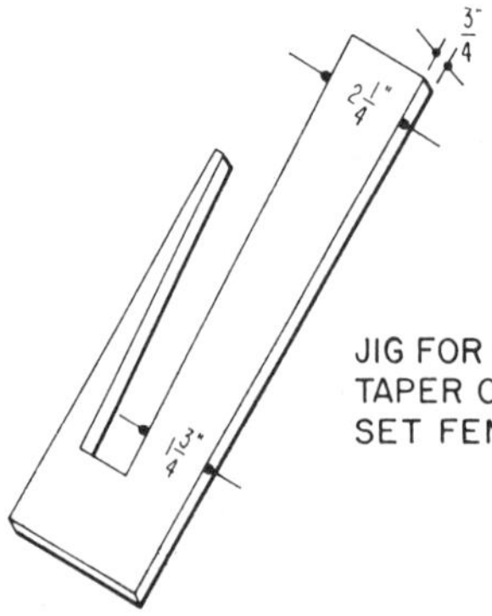

3/4"
2 1/4"
1 3/4"

JIG FOR CUTTING
TAPER ON TABLE SAW
SET FENCE 4" FROM BLADE

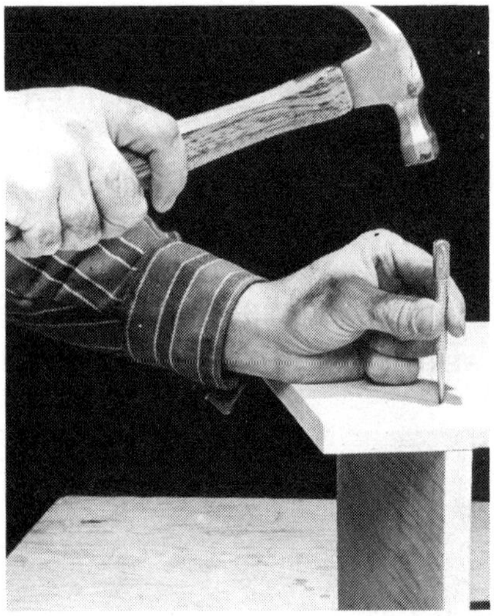

Drawer and top shelf section is built as a unit and installed separately. Assemble with nails, sinking the heads.

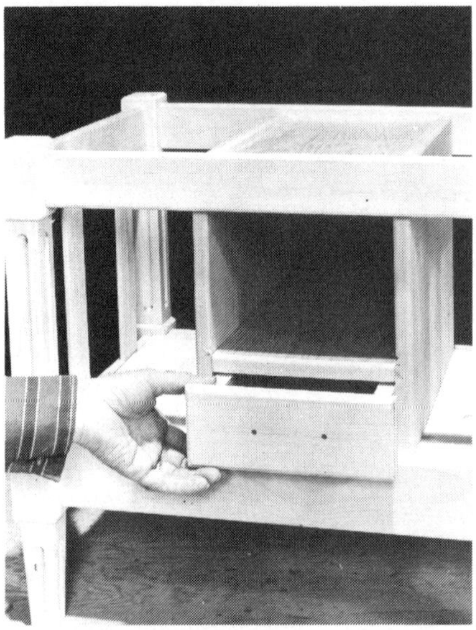

Make drawer with a double front and be sure to make screw clearance holes in sub front so hardware can be installed.

BILL OF MATERIALS

All lumber used is pine (except where noted).

Use	Size	No. Req.
Lower shelf	¾"x14⅝"x23⅜"	1
Cleats	¾"x1"x12"	2
Cleats	¾"x1"x21"	2
Apron lower	¾"x3¼"x22⅛"	2
End apron lower	¾"x3¼"x13⅜"	2
Apron upper	¾"x2¼"x22⅛	2
End apron upper	¾"x2¼"x13⅜"	2
Legs	1⅝"x1⅝"x21½"	4
Blocks	¼"x1⅝"x3¼"	8
Blocks	¼"x2⅛"x3¼"	8
Blocks	¼"x1⅝"x4¼"	8
Blocks	¼"x2⅛"x4¼"	8
Slats	¼"x1⅞"x9¾"	4
Compartment slides	¾"x12"x14⅝"	2
Upper shelf	¾"x8"x14⅝"	1
Drawer roof	¾"x8"x14⅝"	1
Drawer sides	¾"x2 13/16"x13½"	2
Drawer ends	¾"x2 13/16"x6⅜"	2
Drawer front	¾"x3⅜"x8¾"	1
Drawer bottom	¼"x6⅞"x12⅝"	plywood
Dowels	⅜"x2"	16
Pull	3" centers	

Bedside Table

A functional and attractive addition to any bedroom, this table is made from birch plywood and is easy to build

Why must a bedside table be boring? They always look alike. Simple and square, often useful, but never interesting.

This table, however, would be an unusual addition to any bedroom. Its made with a handsome curve that's painted a bright color, and includes plenty of table-top space for phone or bedside lamp. There's also a convenient drawer and even a bin ideally suited for tucking away your telephone directory where it can be found when needed. Drawer and fronts are naturally finished wood, a nice accent to the rest of this colorful table.

It's all made from ¾-in. birch plywood (except for the drawer bottom and slides). See the adjacent Materials listing.

To begin construction, cut out the top, bottom, sides and back as shown in the exploded assembly drawing. Take the sides, and lay out the cut-out. This can be cut with a hole saw for the curve and a table saw for the straight cuts. Or use a saber saw or a band saw for everything. Now, assemble the top, bottom, back and sides with glue and No. 4 finish nails.

The drawer and front are made next, so they fit exactly to the dimensions of the main body of the table. Cut out the drawer pieces as shown in the drawing. Assemble the drawer with No. 4 finish nails through the sides into the front and back of the drawer and glue.

Cut the drawer slides out of a piece of scrap pine and attach them to the inside of the table with glue and No. 17 brads. Use the drawer that you have made to determine the exact position of the slides.

Next, attach the front with glue and No. 4 finish nails through the sides.

To finish the table start by covering all exposed plywood edges with veneer tape. Set all nails and apply wood putty. Sand unit with No. 80, then with No. 120 sandpaper until smooth enough for finishing.

The drawer and front were finished with a fine natural stain made from 60 percent boiled linseed oil and 40 percent turpentine. The main body of the table was finished with four coats of high gloss latex enamel. Each coat was brushed on and sanded with No. 220 paper between coats.

BILL OF MATERIALS

¾" Birch Plywood cut to be the following sizes:
- 3 pieces 18"x18"   1 piece 4⅜"x16⅜"
- 1 piece 17¼"x16½"   1 piece 4⅜"x15"
- 1 piece 16½"x16½"   2 pieces 4⅜"x16⅞"
- 1 piece 5½"x16½"
- 1 piece ¼" Masonite, 15½"x16¼"
- 2 pieces Pine board ¼"x¾"x16½"
- 1 box No. 4 Finish Nails 1½"
- 1 box No. 17 Finish Nails ¾"
- 15' Veneer Tape
- Contact Cement
- White Glue

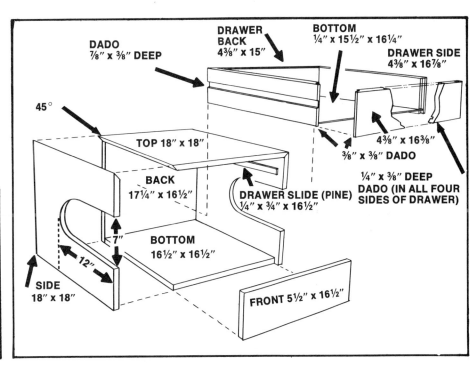

Functional Occasional Table

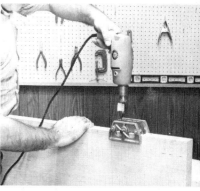

Top is made by joining two or more boards to obtain the necessary width. A dowel jig can help assure accuracy.

Dowel centers help transfer hole locations. Insert them into drilled holes, then align boards. Centers mark the holes.

Both beginners and advanced craftsmen can build this sturdy, all-around table which should be an asset to any home

ALTHOUGH classified here as an "occasional" table, you'll find yourself relying more and more on this as an all-around utility table, continually in use rather than occasionally. Because of its solid construction and sturdiness it will withstand daily use and abuse effortlessly. It can be appropriately used as a coffee table, magazine table, lamp table, or whatever. It is ruggedly built of 1¾-in. pine and has three handy storage drawers. The finished table measures 20-in. x 44-in. and stands 16½-in. high.

The construction is simple and this project is recommended for all classes of woodworkers, from beginners to advanced.

Start with the construction of the top which is made of 1¾-in. stock. Chances are that you won't be able to get a 20-in. board, so you'll probably have to glue up two or more narrower pieces. True up the edges to be glued and if necessary, resaw to eliminate any bumps or dents at the edges. If you have a jointer or power plane, these will do fine. Drill a series of holes to accept the dowels—six holes should do the trick. Use a dowel drilling jig to accurately center the holes. Use dowel centers to transfer the holes to the mating edge. Drill the holes 1-1/16-in. deep, then apply

glue to spiral dowels and insert into the drilled holes. Apply glue to both mating surfaces as well as the projecting dowels, then bring the boards together and clamp until the glue sets.

Make the legs next. Use 3-in. x 3-in. stock or if not available, you can glue up thinner material to make up the 2½-in. squares needed. If you have a jointer, clean the surfaces of the squares taking just a light cut. Trim the ends to size so each piece measures 14½-in. long.

The apron is cut next from 1¾-in. stock. The end and rear aprons are solid but the front is made up in the form of a web so it can accept the drawers. Cut the pieces to size and before assembling the web, drill diagonal screw holes through the top piece (three holes) and one each through the ends of the lower part of the front framework or web. Diagonal screw holes are also drilled into the other three apron pieces. You can do this by hand with an electric drill or on the drill press. Use a 7/32-in. drill bit to make the clearance holes to take the #10 screws. After the frame is glued up, sand the surface flat and it would be a good idea to also sand the surface of the end and rear apron before assembly to table top and legs. Break the sharp cor-

Use spiral dowels for best results. Apply gule to both surfaces, join sections. Below, scrape glued board to make surface become smooth, even.

Surface rough leg stock on a jointer. A jack plane can be used instead if a jointer is not readily available for your use.

Sections are joined with aid of screws and glue. Be sure to work on a flat surface during the assembly.

In this step the shelf cleat is screwed to the leg as shown. Note the solid, snug fit of the notched corners.

The drawers are of simple butt-joint construction. The bottom panel fits into groove on three sides, is nailed at rear. View at right shows the drawers when they're set in place with the corresponding kickers in top panel.

ners of the legs and bottom of the apron pieces. Use a file, sandpaper or router fitted with a rounding-off cutter. When assembling the frame, use nails and glue and if possible clamp the work until the glue sets. Note that when you drive the nails at the bottom ends of the frame, you will have to clear the diagonal screw. See photo.

The table top glue joint should be dry at this point. Trim the top to size and sand the edges. Break all sharp corners with a router.

Next, assemble the apron and legs, working on a flat surface. Apply glue to the ends of the side aprons, then attach to the legs. A clamp should be used to hold the pieces while driving screws. Repeat this procedure until the entire base is assembled.

The drawer guides are made of ¾-in. pine. Note that the two center guides are made differently than the end pieces. Use glue and nails to join the sections, then assemble to the apron using glue and screws driven diagonally. Be sure to space the guides accurately. They must be parallel from side to side to assure that drawers will slide freely.

Drawers are made of ½-in. pine, with butt joints. The fronts are doubled up to eliminate the need for fancy joinery. Cut the sections to size. Then, using the table saw, make the grooves at the lower portion of the side and sub-front pieces. The groove is cut to accommodate the drawer bottoms which are of ¼-in. plywood. You can use either a dado blade or you can make several passes with a regular blade. Check the width of the groove with a piece of the plywood to be sure of the fit. The plywood should slide freely in the groove, but it must not be a sloppy fit. Before assembly, drill the ½-in. screw head clearance hole in the subfront panels. Assemble the drawers with the 1½-in. finishing nails and glue. Drill a 3/16-in. hole in the center of the three drawer fronts before assembling them to the drawers. Use glue and ¾-in. brads, driving the brads from the inside.

Kickers are added to the underside of the table top. These are strips of wood used to prevent the drawers from tipping when opened. Space these so they are in alignment with the drawer sides.

The bottom shelf is made next using three pieces of 1⅛-in. stock 36-in. long. Round the edges and ends of the wood, then join the three with cleats at both ends. The cleats are cut to fit between the legs. Use screws only without glue at this time. Place the shelf on a flat surface, then place the table in position on top of it. Center the table carefully, then with a sharp pencil, outline the area to be notched so the shelf will clear the legs at the corners. Disassemble the three pieces, cut the notches, then reassemble with glue and screws. Before gluing, it might be a good idea to reassemble again without glue just to check the fit. If okay, apply glue and assemble. The shelf is held to the legs by driving screws diagonally from the underside of the cleats.

Give the entire table a good sanding, then finish as desired. Finish used on the unit shown was avocado green antique by Arvon Products. It consists of two base coats of latex, followed by a urethane glaze. The glaze is applied after the base has dried, using either a brush or cheesecloth, making wiped or streaked patterns as you go. Add pulls to drawers and the table is ready to serve you. You can obtain pulls from The Armor Co., Box 290, Deer Park, NY 11729. The company has a number of decorative pulls from which to choose.

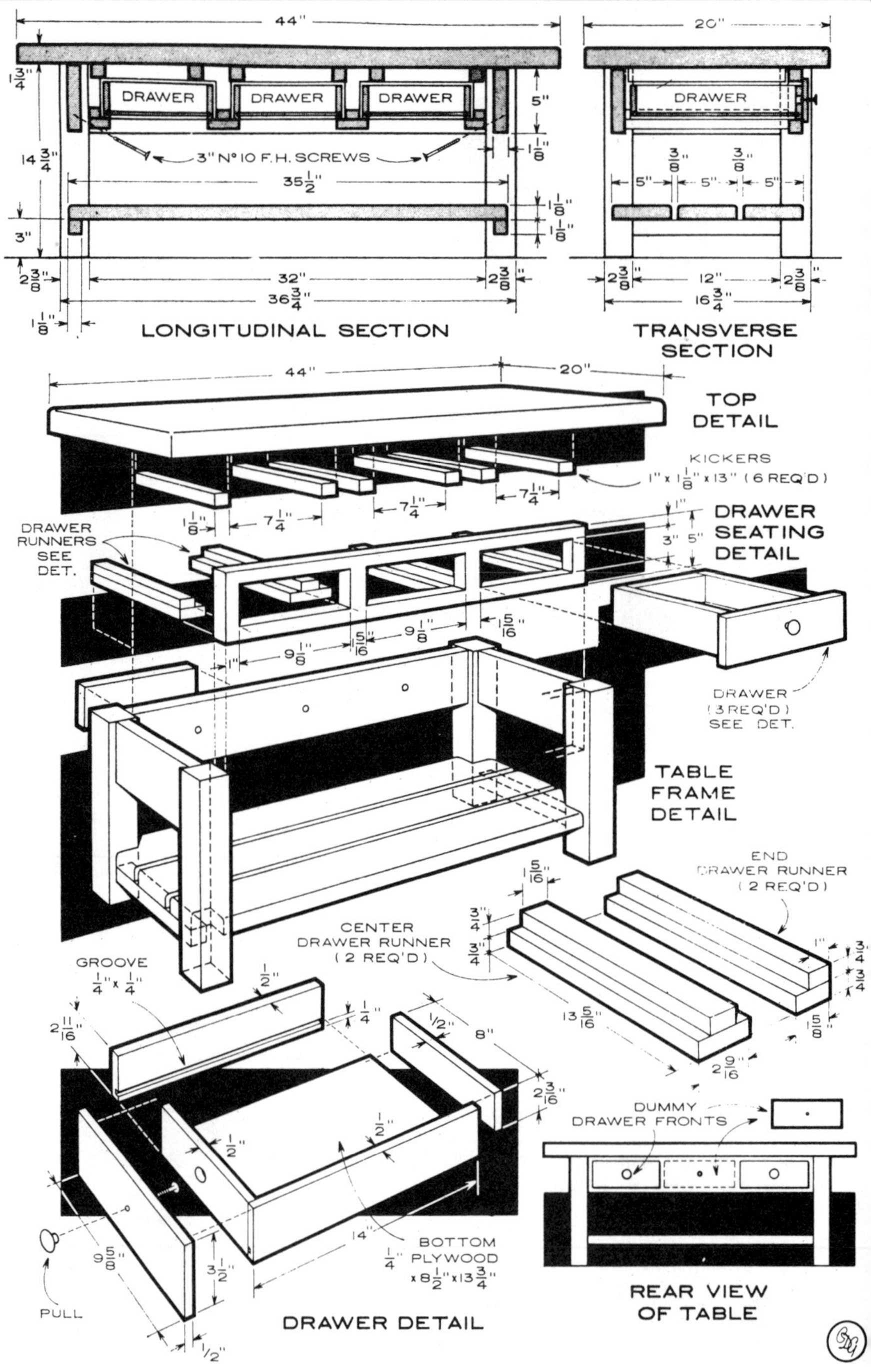

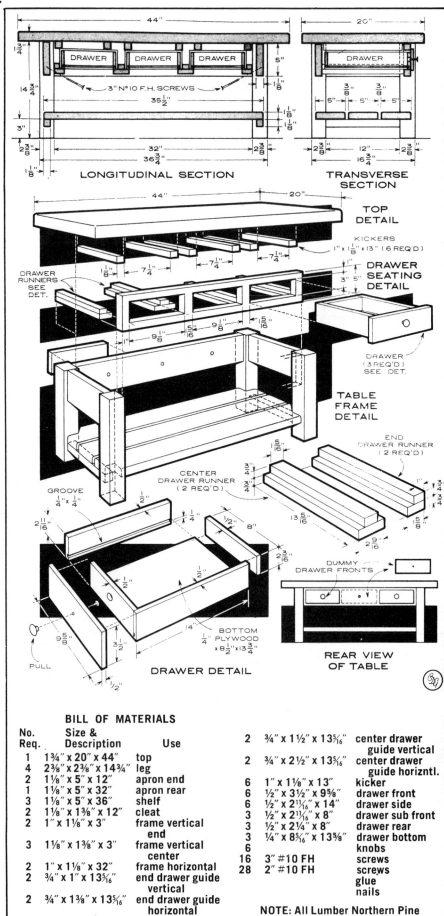

BILL OF MATERIALS

No. Req.	Size & Description	Use
1	1¾″ x 20″ x 44″	top
4	2⅜″ x 2⅜″ x 14¾″	leg
2	1⅛″ x 5″ x 12″	apron end
1	1⅛″ x 5″ x 32″	apron rear
3	1⅛″ x 5″ x 36″	shelf
2	1⅛″ x 1⅜″ x 12″	cleat
2	1″ x 1⅛″ x 3″	frame vertical end
3	1⅛″ x 1⅜″ x 3″	frame vertical center
2	1″ x 1⅛″ x 32″	frame horizontal
2	¾″ x 1″ x 13 5/16″	end drawer guide vertical
2	¾″ x 1⅜″ x 13 5/16″	end drawer guide horizontal
2	¾″ x 1½″ x 13 5/16″	center drawer guide vertical
2	¾″ x 2½″ x 13 5/16″	center drawer guide horizntl.
6	1″ x 1⅛″ x 13″	kicker
6	½″ x 3½″ x 9⅝″	drawer front
6	½″ x 2 11/16″ x 14″	drawer side
3	½″ x 2 11/16″ x 8″	drawer sub front
3	½″ x 2¼″ x 8″	drawer rear
3	¼″ x 8 5/16″ x 13⅝″	drawer bottom
6		knobs
16	3″ #10 FH	screws
28	2″ #10 FH	screws
		glue
		nails

NOTE: All Lumber Northern Pine

Corner Bookcase-Desk

This dual-purpose piece of furniture is easy-to-build from pine, using ordinary tools and ready-made turnings

CORNERS usually present a problem when decorating a room. Here's an ideal piece of furniture that will fit neatly into that wasted corner and serves as a combination desk and bookcase. The desk top provides ample writing space and storage for stationery, bills, pens, clips, etc. The two bottom shelves hold a stack of your favorite books within easy reach.

The desk is very easy to make as it utilizes ready-made turnings which are available at lumber dealers and home improvement centers throughout the nation. It is made of common pine and only a few basic tools are needed. A drill and sabre saw are essential. A router is needed only if you want to shape the edges of the desk top and drawer front. These could be rounded off with a hand plane instead.

The desk measures 30¼-in. high by 40-in. wide by 25-in. deep. The top provides a writing area of more than three square feet.

Unless you use plywood, the top and shelves must be glued up to obtain the proper width. The top involves straight or parallel gluing. The shelves, however, must be mitered. This looks tricky but it can be done easily by using cleats and clamps as shown. Select flat boards and arrange them so that knots will not fall on the cutting lines. Lay out the shelves and draw the 45-degree lines for the miter cuts. The cuts can be made in several ways. The table saw, portable saw or sabre saw may be used. Regardless of the saw used, the cut edges must be perfectly square and smooth. After cutting, a router can be used to true up the edge. This is done with a flush trimmer bit. A guide strip of ¾-in. stock is nailed to the bottom of the shelf. Set the strip exactly at 45-degrees using a miter square as a guide. Set the strip so that it is just a trifle in from the edge. About 1/32-in. will do. Adjust the cutter so that the bearing will ride on the strip. Take a cut and check the edge. It should be smooth and straight. Incidentally, the edge will be as straight as the guide strip so be sure to choose a good straight piece for the guide.

Mark the location of the dowels. These should be placed as shown so they will clear the post holes and the curved edge which will be cut later on. A dowel drilling guide

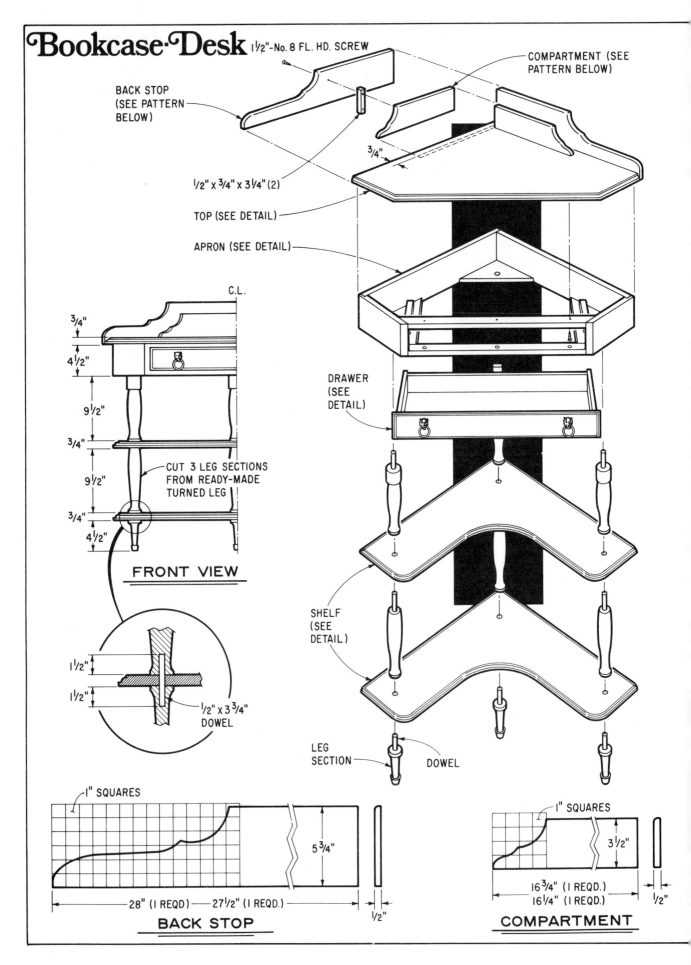

Bookcase·Desk

1½"-No. 8 FL. HD. SCREW

BACK STOP
(SEE PATTERN
BELOW)

COMPARTMENT (SEE
PATTERN BELOW)

3/4"

½" x ¾" x 3¼" (2)

TOP (SEE DETAIL)

APRON (SEE DETAIL)

C.L.

3/4"

4½"

9½"

3/4"

9½"

3/4"

4½"

CUT 3 LEG SECTIONS
FROM READY-MADE
TURNED LEG

FRONT VIEW

DRAWER
(SEE
DETAIL)

1½"

1½"

½" x 3¾"
DOWEL

SHELF
(SEE
DETAIL)

LEG
SECTION

DOWEL

1" SQUARES

5¾"

28" (1 REQD) — 27½" (1 REQD.)

½"

BACK STOP

1" SQUARES

3½"

16¾" (1 REQD.)
16¼" (1 REQD.)

½"

COMPARTMENT

The miter is cut with a saber saw. Be sure to use fine blade, and cut slowly.

Guide strip's nailed to the underside of shelf. It should be set in from edge.

Insert dowel centers into holes; the sharp point transfers center to mating board.

is used for the next operation. Several types are available. The units are self-centering and assure straight accurate holes. Drill ⅜-in. diameter holes 1¼-in. deep to accept the 2-in. spiral dowels. Dowel centers are used to locate matching holes in the mating pieces. Insert three dowel centers in the holes drilled into the first piece. Align the two boards then press together. The hole centers will be transferred to the second piece. Drill these holes to the same depth as the first piece.

Because the end grain is porous, it will be necessary to size the edge with a thin coat of glue. Apply a bead of glue then spread and allow to dry. Apply some glue to the dowels and insert. Tap with a hammer until the dowels are halfway into the holes. To obtain a good tight joint, attach clamping blocks as shown. Apply more glue to the edges and to the dowels then join

the pieces and clamp tightly. The clamping blocks should be 2 x 3 or 2 x 4 lumber. Draw the pieces together until the glue starts to ooze out of joint. Be sure the boards are flat. Use clamps on both sides.

The top is also glued with dowels. Follow the same procedure to make the holes then clamp using glue strips on the edges. To save lumber for the top piece, you can step the sections as shown.

Set the shelves and top aside allowing the glue to set thoroughly. In the meantime, you can cut the pieces for the apron and front frame. The rear edges of the side pieces are rabbeted to accept the back panels. Do this with a table saw or use a back saw and finish off with a chisel.

The bevel cut for the front edge of the sides and the ends of the two strips are cut at a 45-degree angle. After cutting the pieces to size, assemble with screws and

glue. After the apron is assembled, invert the top then position the apron as shown. Strips of wood tacked to the front and sides will keep the sections aligned while drilling the screw pilot holes. The holes are drilled diagonally. Use care not to drill through the surface of the top. A guide marked on the drill bit is recommended.

The crosspiece is treated differently. Here the three screws are installed straight. Screwdriver clearance holes are made in the lower piece. The parts are then assembled as indicated. Be sure to use glue at all joints.

The legs are cut from ready-made turnings. (If you have a lathe, you will probably want to turn your own). Choose a suitable turning and cut apart to make up the various lengths as shown. The cutting can be done with a hand saw or on the radial arm saw. Be sure the lengths are uniform and all

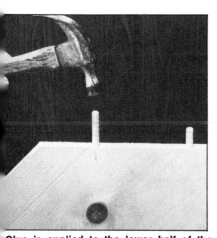

Glue is applied to the lower half of the dowel. Hammer blows drive them home.

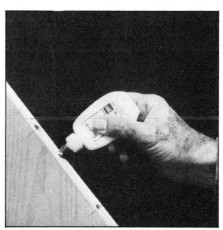

Apply glue to edge grain to size it. Apply second coat before joining the parts.

A yardstick adapted with pivot point is used to draw the radius for the shelf.

Bookcase-Desk

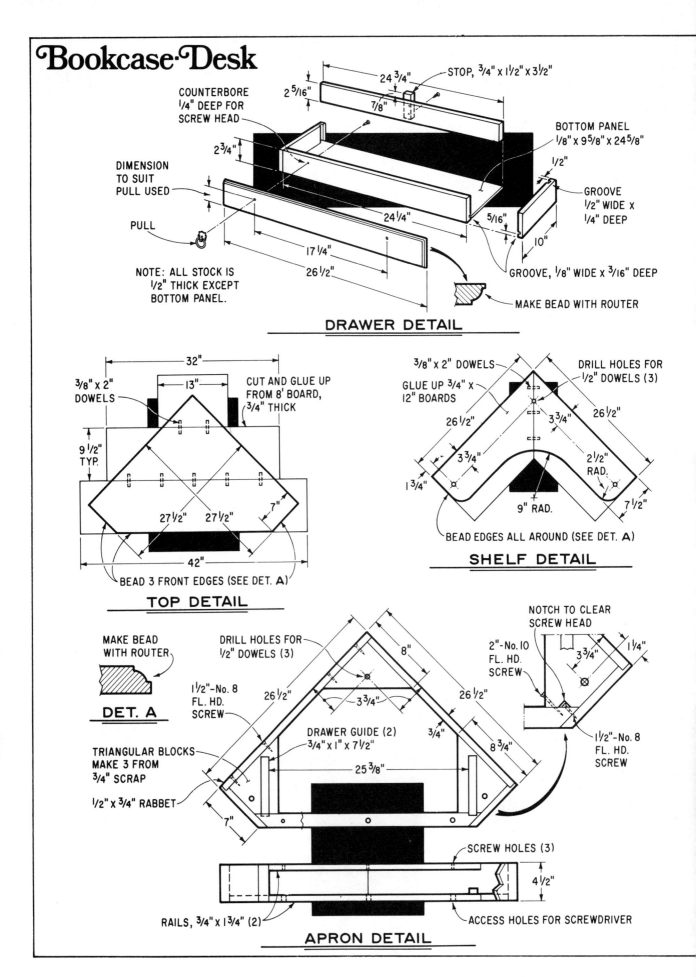

DRAWER DETAIL

STOP, 3/4" x 1 1/2" x 3 1/2"

24 3/4"

2 5/16"

7/8"

COUNTERBORE 1/4" DEEP FOR SCREW HEAD

BOTTOM PANEL 1/8" x 9 5/8" x 24 5/8"

2 3/4"

1/2"

DIMENSION TO SUIT PULL USED

GROOVE 1/2" WIDE x 1/4" DEEP

24 1/4"

5/16"

10"

PULL

17 1/4"

26 1/2"

GROOVE, 1/8" WIDE x 3/16" DEEP

NOTE: ALL STOCK IS 1/2" THICK EXCEPT BOTTOM PANEL.

MAKE BEAD WITH ROUTER

TOP DETAIL

32"

13"

3/8" x 2" DOWELS

CUT AND GLUE UP FROM 8' BOARD, 3/4" THICK

9 1/2" TYP.

27 1/2"   27 1/2"

7"

42"

BEAD 3 FRONT EDGES (SEE DET. A)

SHELF DETAIL

3/8" x 2" DOWELS

DRILL HOLES FOR 1/2" DOWELS (3)

GLUE UP 3/4" x 12" BOARDS

26 1/2"

3 3/4"

26 1/2"

3 3/4"

1 3/4"

2 1/2" RAD.

9" RAD.

7 1/2"

BEAD EDGES ALL AROUND (SEE DET. A)

DET. A

MAKE BEAD WITH ROUTER

DRILL HOLES FOR 1/2" DOWELS (3)

8"

NOTCH TO CLEAR SCREW HEAD

2"-No. 10 FL. HD. SCREW

3 3/4"

1/4"

1 1/2"-No. 8 FL. HD. SCREW

26 1/2"

3 3/4"

26 1/2"

3/4"

DRAWER GUIDE (2) 3/4" x 1" x 7 1/2"

8 3/4"

TRIANGULAR BLOCKS MAKE 3 FROM 3/4" SCRAP

25 3/8"

1 1/2"-No. 8 FL. HD. SCREW

1/2" x 3/4" RABBET

7"

SCREW HOLES (3)

4 1/2"

RAILS, 3/4" x 1 3/4" (2)

ACCESS HOLES FOR SCREWDRIVER

APRON DETAIL

cuts are square. If done by hand, a miter box should be used. The turnings we used are colonial style 28-in. long. They are manufactured by Michael-Reagan of California and we understand they are available throughout the country.

After cutting the turnings apart, drill the centers to take ½-in. dowels. Make the holes 1½-in. deep and be sure to center them. Drill corresponding holes ½-in. diameter in the two shelves to correspond to the holes previously made in the lower part of the top section. Also shape the edges at this time. Assemble the parts, starting with the lower shelf first. Cut the dowels to length, then add to the lower turnings (feet). Groove or crimp dowel so that trapped air can be eliminated from the hole. Failure to do so may cause the wood to split.

Add the second shelf in the same manner. Cut the back stops from ½-in. pine and install with screws from the rear. The compartment is also made and added at this time. Screws are driven from the rear where the heads won't show. The drawer is of simple construction. It is made with an overlapping front. Two pieces of ½-in. lumber are used to make up the front panel. Before assembling the front, shape the edge as desired. We used a bead cutter the same shape as that used for the top, only of smaller size. The side guides are installed with about 1/16-in. clearance between the drawer sides. A small block of wood at the rear of the drawer serves as a kicker and prevents the drawer from tipping when fully extended. It also serves as a stop. It is installed from the bottom opening after the drawer is in place. The pulls are added to complete construction.

Finish the unit with stain and shellac or you may want to try an antique finish. We used a red latex base topped with a dark brown glaze.

BILL OF MATERIALS— CORNER BOOKCASE-DESK

Use	Size & Description		No. Req.
Top	¾" x 11¼" x 8"	pine	1
Back stop	½" x 5¾" x 28"	pine	2
Compartment	½" x 3½" x 16¾"	pine	2
Compartment blocks	½" x ¾" x 3"	pine	2
Rail	¾" x 1¹¹⁄₁₆" x 29"	pine	2
Sides	¾" x 4½" x 8"	pine	2
Corner blocks	¾" x 7" x 10"	pine	3
Shelf (half)	¾" x 11¼" x 27"	pine	4
Turnings	1¾" diameter x 28"	pine	3
Kicker	¾" x 1½" x 3¼"	pine	1
Drawer side	½" x 2¾" x 10"	pine	2
Drawer rear	½" x 2⁵⁄₁₆" x 24¾"	pine	1
Drawer subfront	½" x 2¾" x 24¼"	pine	1
Drawer front	½" x 3¼" x 26½"	pine	1
Drawer bottom	⅛" x 9⅝" x 24⅝"	plywood	1

NOTE: Top is cut into three lengths and glued as shown.

Screws
1½" finishing nails

Lion head pulls	2
⅜" x 2" spiral dowel	13
½" x 36" dowel	1

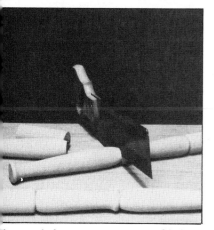

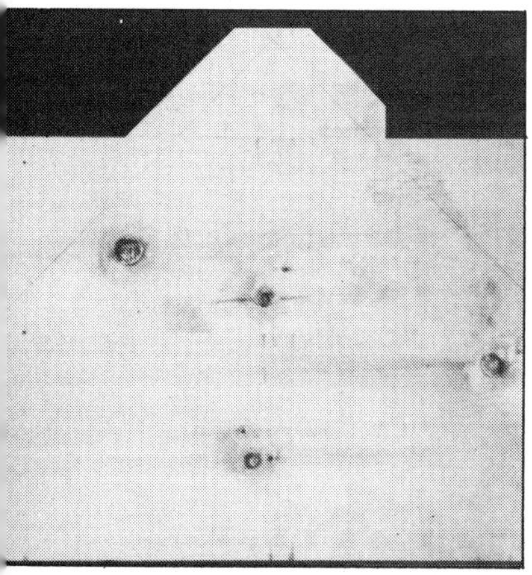

Desk top is glued up in order to conserve wood. The knots should be sound.

The desk sides are assembled with glue, screws. Predrilled holes are for the legs.

Clearance holes are drilled through the crosspiece to allow screwdriver to enter.

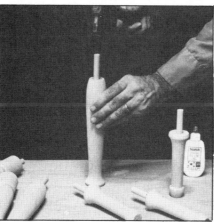

The stock legs are cut apart with back saw. A radial arm saw can also be used.

Dowels are driven into the upper section of leg. Be sure to groove dowel.

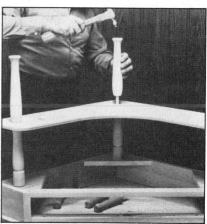

Assembling the desk is simple. Add the shelves and legs to the inverted unit.

CEDAR-LINED HOPE CHEST

With ample storage space and the pleasant fragrance of cedar, this beautiful project will be a welcome addition to any home—and will certainly become an heirloom

THIS ATTRACTIVE HOPE CHEST is lined inside with aromatic red cedar and is the perfect piece for storing linens, blankets, curtains and similar items. In addition, the chest lid is topped with a nice soft cushion which adds to its appearance and is functional as well. This piece can also be used as a toy chest. The drawers and doors are dummies and serve only to enhance the appearance of this lovely piece.

Made mostly of 1″ pine (¾″ actual size) boards, the chest is rather easy to build. Some joints are doweled and others are dadoed and rabbeted. The table saw and router are the main tools needed for this project.

The inside of the cabinet has been lined with cedar, but this can be eliminated if so desired. The cushioned lid is fitted with four tension hinges. These permit the lid to be raised and lowered with ease. The hinges are fitted with springs which can be tensioned to equalize the load.

Construction. The materials list shows the sizes required for each piece; however when gluing up boards for the front, rear and end panels, you should make the pieces longer and wider than shown. These pieces are then trimmed to size after gluing. Because of the width required, these panels should be made by gluing two or three narrow boards to make up

the needed size.

The joints for the glued up boards can be tongued-and-grooved or butted with dowels. Of the two choices, the doweled method is perhaps the easiest. The dowels should be ⅜″ × 2″ and the holes for them should be drilled 1¹⁄₃₂″ deep in each board. This will assure that the joints will close good and tight. To prevent cupping of the panels, the annular rings in adjoining pieces should be reversed as shown in the drawing.

Apply glue to the dowels and to all mating surfaces then clamp securely. When applying clamping pressure, do not overdo. Excessive pressure can cause too much glue to squeeze out, resulting in a weak joint. After the glue has set and clamps are removed, the boards should be surfaced to eliminate any irregularities at the joints. Use a plane followed with a good sanding. The belt sander can be used instead of the plane. Start with 80 grit paper then finish off with 120 grit. For final sanding use a finishing sander with 220 grit paper.

The front, rear and end pieces are joined with tongue-and-groove joints. These are made on any of the following machines: shaper, table saw, radial arm saw or router. We used the table saw fitted with a Rockwell adjustable dado blade. If you lack the dado blade, you can get by just using

the regular saw blade. Simply take several cuts adjusting the fence after each pass. The groove near the bottom is made ½″ wide to take the ½″ plywood panel.

Assembly. The front, rear and end panels are assembled with the bottom panel in place. Before assembly, be sure to drill the screw holes along the lower part of each member.

To insure a good strong joint, glue size the end grain of the front and rear panels. Do this by thinning some glue and brushing it onto the ends of each board. When dry, about 20 minutes time, sand lightly then apply glue full strength and join the pieces. Clamp and allow to set. Use cauls under the clamps to protect the wood. Since the bottom panel is already in place, the assembly should glue up square but check it anyway as it could go off.

Base. The four base pieces are joined with doweled butt joints. Lay out the decorative shapes at the bottom of the front and end pieces then drill the holes for the dowels. There are two dowels at each joint. Before gluing and assembling the base, glue size the end grain of both end pieces as outlined previously. Glue, clamp, then set aside.

The filler strip is prepared next. It is used to fill the space between the front of the main assembly and the front base piece. The bottom

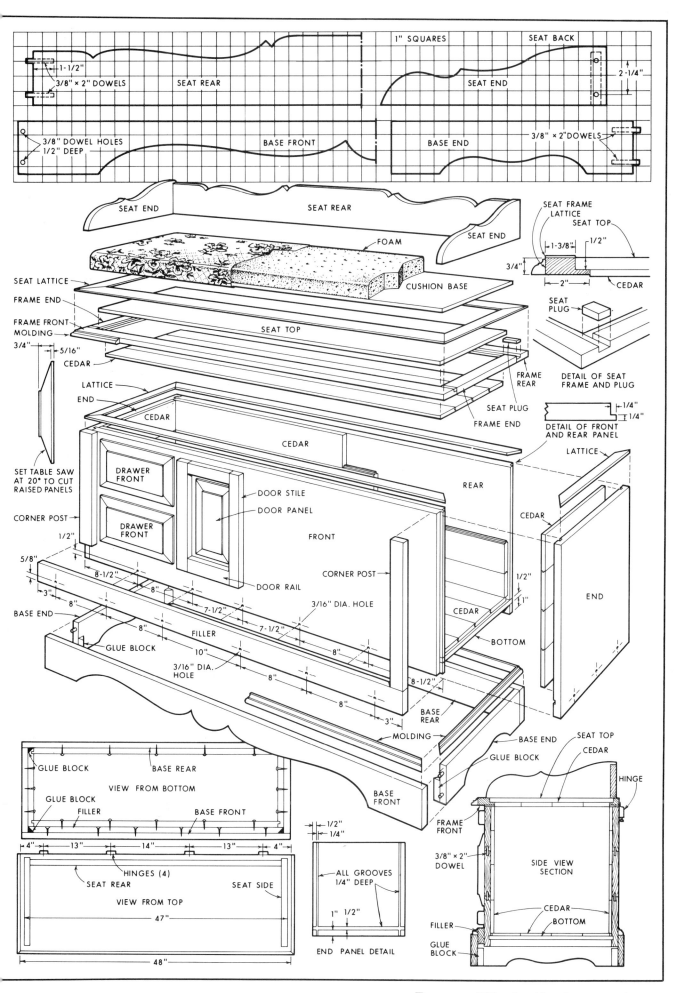

1" SQUARES

SEAT BACK

SEAT REAR

1-1/2"

3/8" × 2" DOWELS

SEAT END

SEAT END

2-1/4"

3/8" DOWEL HOLES
1/2" DEEP

BASE FRONT

BASE END

3/8" × 2" DOWELS

SEAT END

SEAT REAR

SEAT END

FOAM

SEAT FRAME
LATTICE

SEAT TOP

1-3/8"

1/2"

3/4"

2"

CEDAR

CUSHION BASE

SEAT LATTICE

FRAME END

FRAME FRONT
MOLDING

3/4"

5/16"

CEDAR

SEAT TOP

SEAT PLUG

DETAIL OF SEAT
FRAME AND PLUG

LATTICE

END

CEDAR

CEDAR

FRAME REAR

SEAT PLUG

FRAME END

1/4"

1/4"

DETAIL OF FRONT
AND REAR PANEL

SET TABLE SAW
AT 20° TO CUT
RAISED PANELS

DRAWER
FRONT

DRAWER
FRONT

DOOR STILE

DOOR PANEL

FRONT

REAR

LATTICE

CEDAR

CORNER POST

1/2"

5/8"

3"

8-1/2"

8"

DOOR RAIL

CORNER POST

1/2"

1"

CEDAR

END

BASE END

GLUE BLOCK

FILLER

8"

10"

3/16" DIA.
HOLE

7-1/2"

7-1/2"

3/16" DIA. HOLE

8"

8"

BOTTOM

8-1/2"

8"

8"

3"

BASE REAR

MOLDING

BASE FRONT

BASE END

GLUE BLOCK

SEAT TOP

CEDAR

HINGE

FRAME
FRONT

3/8" × 2"
DOWEL

SIDE VIEW
SECTION

FILLER

GLUE
BLOCK

CEDAR

BOTTOM

GLUE BLOCK

BASE REAR

VIEW FROM BOTTOM

GLUE BLOCK

FILLER

BASE FRONT

4"

13"

14"

13"

4"

HINGES (4)

SEAT REAR

SEAT SIDE

VIEW FROM TOP

47"

48"

1/2"

1/4"

ALL GROOVES
1/4" DEEP

1"

1/2"

END PANEL DETAIL

HOPE CHEST

view drawing shows how the filler strip is fastened to the front base piece with 1¼" flat head screws. With the filler strip in place, the base assembly can now be fastened to the chest case. Screws are driven through the previously drilled holes.

Door and Door Fronts. The dummy doors are made of pine strips ripped to 1½" widths. Cut the lengths for the rails and stiles then assemble with butt joints. You can use dowels at the joints if desired, but they are not necessary as the doors are non-working and they will be glued to the backboard (front panel).

The raised panels for doors and drawers are made on the table saw. Do this by tilting the saw blade 20 degrees, then adjust the fence and blade height to produce the raised panel effect. The blade should project 1¹⁄₁₆" above the table. The saw blade should be sharp for this operation. Hold the work firmly and feed it through the blade using the fence as a guide.

After the panels are cut, they will have to be run through the saw to remove the slight angle left by the edge of the saw blade. Do this by returning the saw blade to 90-degrees and let it project about ³⁄₃₂" above the table. Make test cuts on the extra panel and when you are satisfied with the results, cut the panels. Drill the pull holes as indicated then mount the panels and door frames to the front panel. Before doing this however, add the two corner posts.

Applying Cedar. The aromatic cedar is sold by the bundle in random lengths. Each piece is 3½" wide with tongue-and-groove. Start by applying the strips to the floor of the chest. Choose any length and place the first piece at the upper left corner as shown, but ¼" away from the rear panel. Continue along the floor to the right end. Trim the piece to fit. Hold each piece in place with two ¾" brads.

Start the second row in the same manner but stagger the joints. Do this by choosing a strip which is longer or shorter than the first piece in the first row. Continue the successive rows with staggered joints. The final row will fit back to front

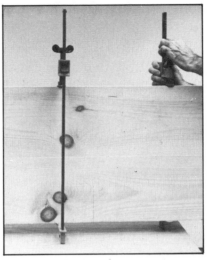

Gluing up boards for the rear panel. If you can find large enough boards that are fairly flat, use 2; otherwise 3 or 4.

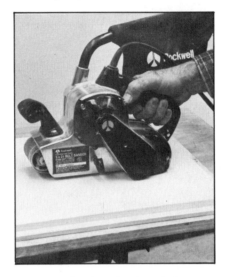

After the glued up pine boards have set, even them up with a belt sander. Then follow up with a finishing sander.

The router guide strip is fastened to a crosspiece to simplify mounting and clamping. Taped stick assures a stop.

Grooves, dadoes and rabbets can be made with a router or on a table saw, as shown. Three passes are made.

When cutting the rabbet on the end of the front panel, use a guide with your router to assure a straight, even cut.

It's important that the corner posts are perfectly perpendicular to the base of the unit. Check accuracy with a square.

Here the router, fitted with a sanding disc, is being used to round off all exposed corners for a smoother look.

A simple jig for gluing up the door frames consists of two 1 × 2s nailed to a board. You should space the two about 9½ inches apart. Next, apply glue to the joints and place the piece between the 1 × 2s. A double wedge is taped into place to tighten the assembly.

Trimming the corners of the raised panels is shown here. Check the cut on a scrap panel before cutting good work.

Two brads placed in each cedar panel is sufficient as the interlocking tongues and grooves hold the pieces securely.

View looking down into the chest, without cedar sides. Two cuts in end panel were made to flatten it.

This is a bottom view of the chest showing how the base pieces are fastened to the unit with screws.

with a ¼″ space.

The back vertical row of cedar is installed next. Start at the lower left and work across to the right. Start the strips with the groove down. The top row will have to be trimmed flush with the panel sides and ends. The top edge of the chest is trimmed with ¼″ lattice to conceal the two dissimilar woods (⅜″ cedar and ¾″ pine). The lattice is mitered at each corner. Fasten with glue and brads.

The nose and cove molding will be added next, but before doing so the corners of the base pieces must be rounded. Use a router with 1/4″ rounding bit for this. The molding is then added to the top of the base pieces. Miter all corners. Fasten with glue and brads.

Chest Top. The top consists of a piece of plywood edged with a pine frame. The underside is lined with cedar and the top is covered with an upholstered cushion. Cut the front, rear and end frame sections to length; then, before assembly, rabbet the inner top edge to take the ½″ plywood panel. When assembled, the frame will have gaps where the rabbets were cut. These are filled in with plugs. Glue the frame members without dowels; just plain butt joints. The addition of the plywood top will add sufficient strength to the assembly. When installing the top use glue at the joint and reinforce with brads driven from the underside.

The cedar is added to the underside of the seat using the same procedure used for the chest. The only difference is that the leading edges are trimmed first to remove the grooves. The last row will also be trimmed to fit.

The seat is now turned upright and the lattice added. This is 1/16″ thick and 1⅜″ wide. Cut from a knot-free piece of pine. Miter the corners then install with glue and brads. This lattice will conceal the butt joints as well as the plugs added previously. The seat ends are cut to shape and drilled to take the ⅜″ dowels. Note that the holes in the end pieces are ½″ deep.

Before assembly, round the top corners with a ¼″-rounding bit. Apply glue and clamp securely. Install the assembly with flat head screws driven from the underside of the seat. Finally, add the nose and cove molding to the front and ends.

HOPE CHEST

Fasten the seat to the chest with four lid hinges. Do not set the tension of the springs until the cushion is installed as the weight will be increased slightly. Stain and finish as desired. Do not apply finish to the cedar as it should be left natural.

Cushion. The cushion consists of a bottom board, urethane foam and upholstery material. To make the cushion wrinkle-free proceed as follows: Place the fabric on a flat surface followed by the foam, then the ¼" plywood panel. Cut a board slightly smaller than the plywood and place it on top of the pile. Now, using deep throat clamps, squeeze the sandwich to about one third of its original thickness then staple the fabric all around the perimeter into the ¼" plywood. When stapling is completed, cut away the excess material that has bunched up at the corners.

When the clamps are removed, the sandwich will expand to its original thickness and the edges will be neat and wrinkle-free. The cushion is simply placed in its nook without fastening. However, if you like, you can hold it with several small pieces of Velcro glued to the underside of the cushion and the seat top.

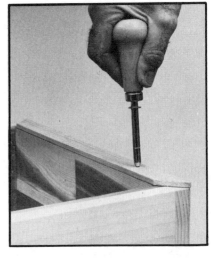

The ¼" lattice is added to the top edge for a pleasing look. Note that all of the corners have been carefully mitered.

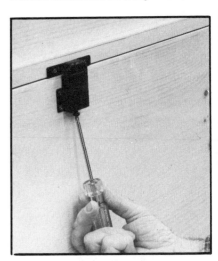

With this particular hardware, the lid support hinges are adjustable. Here, the adjusting screw increases the tension.

MATERIALS LIST

Except as noted, lumber is 1" pine (actual size ¾"). All measurements are in inches.

Use	Size & Description	No. Req'd
CHEST		
front	16 × 47	1
rear	16 × 47	1
end	16 × 16	2
bottom	½ × 15 × 47 fir plywood	1
filler	2 × 48	1
base front	3½ × 49½	1
base rear	3½ × 49½	1
base end	3½ × 16¾	2
corner post	1½ × 14	2
molding	⅝ × ¾, nose & cove	12 ft.
glue block	¾ × ¾ × 2	4
drawer front	5¾ × 12	4
door stile	1½ × 13	4
door rail	1½ × 5½	4
door panel	4½ × 8¾	4
lattice	¼ × 1⅛	12 ft.
SEAT		
frame front	2 × 48	1
frame rear	2 × 48	1
frame end	2 × 12¾	2
seat top	½ × 14 × 45¼ fir plywood	1
seat plug	½ × ⅝ × 2	4
seat molding	⅝ × ¾ nose & cove	8 ft.
seat lattice	1/16 × 1⅜	8 ft.
seat end	4 × 15½	2
seat rear	4¹³/16 × 45½	1
Aromatic Red Cedar	⅜ × 3½ (random lengths)	30 sq.ft.
cushion base	¼ × 14¾ × 45¼, plywood	1
*foam	2 × 14¾ × 45¼	1
fabric		1½ yds.
MISCELLANEOUS		
drawer pull	2½" centers (CH)	4
door pull	tear drop (TDP)	2
screw	1¼ 8 RH	16
screw	1¼ 8 FH	6
staple	¼"	1 box
hinge	adjustable tension (ATL)	4
dowel	⅜ × 2	36

Here is a peek into the completed chest revealing the beautiful and aromatic red cedar lining. Stain outside to liking.

COLONIAL DESK WITH BOOK RACK

In assembling Colonial Desk, cleats are used extensively as in most fine furniture construction. Attach with glue and nails.

Exception to above is temporary cleat in base of cabinet; attach with nails only. It comes off when bottom panel is installed.

Drilling for book rack boards (1⅛ in. lumber). Screws and dowels will be used, with dowels protruding to accept fake tenons.

Installing bottom board. Note two blocks that are aids to positioning. They will be removed after nailing in proper position.

THIS ATTRACTIVE DESK will enhance any room in your home. The single pedestal is an offshoot of the more common double pedestal which was very popular in colonial days. It has four roomy drawers, with the largest one at the bottom made to hold lettersize folders. The pedestal support serves as a book rack to hold a good supply of reading materials.

If you study the drawing you will note that cleats are used extensively. They greatly simplify construction and assembly, as well as eliminating the need to drive nails or screws through the top surface of the desk. Some nails are driven through the side members, but these can be eliminated too by driving nails or screws from the inside of the cabinet.

The pedestal and book rack are cut from 1⅛-in. white pine. We used common lumber as it costs about one half as much as clear. Colonial furniture should have knots, but by carefully selecting your lumber you can eliminate the really bad ones.

You will note that fake tenons are used on the book shelf members. The final effect looks like the real thing, but construction-wise the fake method shown is easier and perhaps a little stronger.

The tools required for this project are a table saw, saber saw, router and drill. In addition you will need the usual hand tools such as hammer, screwdriver and wrench.

Select flat boards for the top and sides. Cut the pieces to size and shape the bottom edges as shown in the

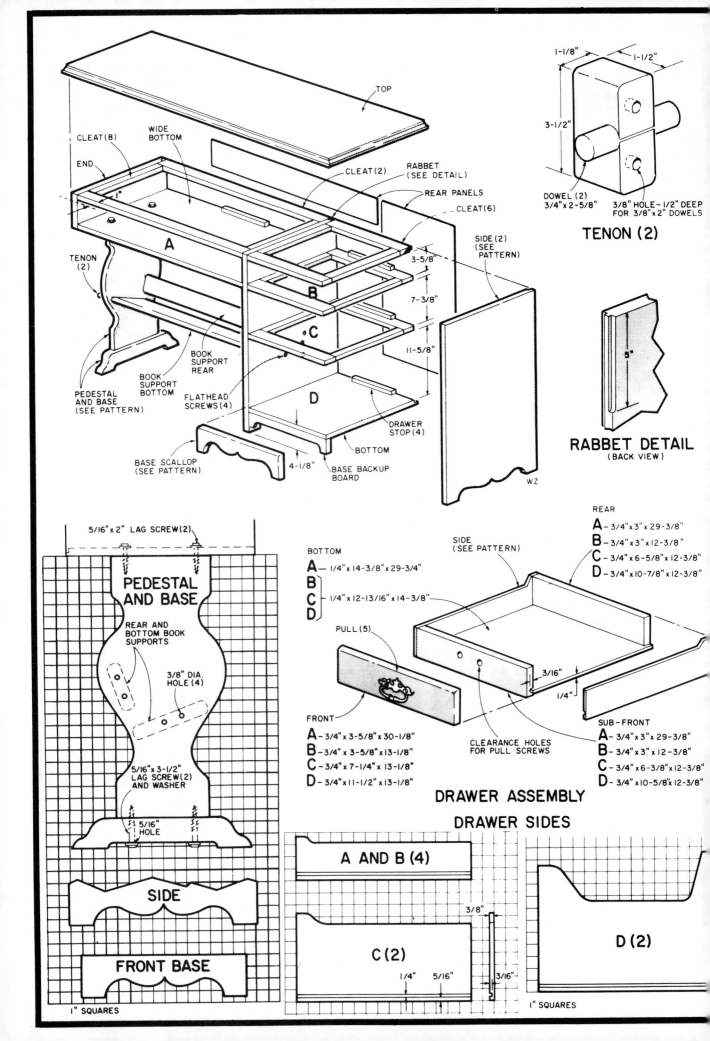

TOP

CLEAT(8)

WIDE BOTTOM

END

CLEAT(2)

RABBET
(SEE DETAIL)

REAR PANELS

CLEAT(6)

A

TENON
(2)

B

3-5/8"

SIDE(2)
(SEE PATTERN)

7-3/8"

C

11-5/8"

BOOK
SUPPORT
REAR

BOOK
SUPPORT
BOTTOM

FLATHEAD
SCREWS(4)

D

PEDESTAL
AND BASE
(SEE PATTERN)

DRAWER
STOP(4)

BASE SCALLOP
(SEE PATTERN)

4-1/8"

BOTTOM

BASE BACKUP
BOARD

WZ

TENON (2)

1-1/8"   1-1/2"

3-1/2"

DOWEL (2)
3/4"x 2-5/8"

3/8" HOLE-1/2" DEEP
FOR 3/8"x2" DOWELS

5"

RABBET DETAIL
(BACK VIEW)

5/16"x 2" LAG SCREW(2)

PEDESTAL
AND BASE

REAR AND
BOTTOM BOOK
SUPPORTS

3/8" DIA.
HOLE (4)

5/16"x 3-1/2"
LAG SCREW(2)
AND WASHER

5/16"
HOLE

SIDE

FRONT BASE

1" SQUARES

BOTTOM

A — 1/4" x 14-3/8" x 29-3/4"
B
C — 1/4" x 12-13/16" x 14-3/8"
D

PULL (5)

FRONT

A — 3/4" x 3-5/8" x 30-1/8"
B — 3/4" x 3-5/8" x 13-1/8"
C — 3/4" x 7-1/4" x 13-1/8"
D — 3/4" x 11-1/2" x 13-1/8"

CLEARANCE HOLES
FOR PULL SCREWS

REAR

A — 3/4"x3"x 29-3/8"
B — 3/4"x3"x 12-3/8"
C — 3/4"x 6-5/8"x 12-3/8"
D — 3/4"x10-7/8"x 12-3/8"

SIDE
(SEE PATTERN)

3/16"

1/4"

SUB-FRONT

A — 3/4"x3"x 29-3/8"
B — 3/4"x3"x 12-3/8"
C — 3/4"x 6-3/8"x12-3/8"
D — 3/4"x10-5/8"x 12-3/8"

DRAWER ASSEMBLY

DRAWER SIDES

A AND B (4)

3/8"

C (2)

1/4"   5/16"

3/16"

D (2)

1" SQUARES

DESK WITH BOOK RACK

Use lag screws to join shaped pedestal and base sections, as well as top section to pedestal. Use washers under screw heads.

Attaching scalloped base to backup board at front of desk. Glue with nails only at the sides. Refer to pattern and exploded view.

A router with its beading cutter is used to trim top edge of the Colonial Desk. Do only front and sides; don't trim the back.

Drawer stops are nailed and glued to rear of each compartment. Place so drawer fronts protrude ⅜". Drawings show details.

drawing. After cutting the scallop design, run a router with rounding off cutter to round off the outside face of the cut. Do not rout the inside face.

Place the top board face down onto a flat surface. (The top of a table saw is ideal because it is exceptionally flat). Next cut and install the cleats as indicated, using glue and 1¼-in. brads. The rear cleats are rabbeted to accept the ¼-in. back panel. Make the rabbet either on the table saw or with the router. Note that the front cleat is placed 1-in. in from the front. Side cleats are placed 1¾-in. in from the edge.

Side panels are prepared next. Rabbet the rear edge of both, but note that the left upright is rabbeted at two places near the top. The smaller rabbet is to accept the rear panel of the wide drawer compartment.

To assure proper alignment in assembly, make up a couple of temporary cleats; at this time also cut the bottom panel for the drawer compartment. Install the temporary cleats so that the bottom panel rests on them as shown. Glue up the section and nail it in place, using a square to make sure the sections are perpendicular. If necessary, nail a diagonal to hold the sections while the glue sets. Add the drawer compartment cleats and install the single drawer compartment, using a temporary spacer block to support the bottom board while nailing.

The 1⅛-in. lumber for the book rack section is cut to size and edges are rounded with the router. This time both sides are done to obtain a half-round effect.

The base piece for the upright is made by gluing up two pieces of ¾-in. stock. After shaping, assemble to upright with two 3-in. lag screws.

To align the shelves, drill the dowel holes in the end piece and place it right up to the center upright. Center it and then transfer the hole centers, using a pencil. Next locate and drill matching holes in the shelves, then assemble using dowels and screws as indicated. Drive the dowels so they protrude ½-in. from the outside.

Make up two fake tenons and assemble with glue.

Drawers are made with double fronts. Sides are ⅜-in. plywood, fronts and rear are ¾-in. pine, bottoms are ¼-in. plywood. In order to keep drawers level when they are extended, the side panels are made to rise at the rear.

Cut the drawer sections to size then dado the bottoms to accept the ¼-in. bottom panels. Drill clearance holes in the sub-front panels and assemble the section with nails and glue. Do not install the front yet. Sand the edges of the ¼-in. bottom panels and slide into place. A little glue in the groove will keep the bottom from rattling.

To install the fronts, center the front over the drawer from side to side, raising the front 1/16-in. above the bottom of the drawer. This 1/16-in. offset at the bottom will center the front panel in the compartment opening.

Before permanently mounting the panel, tack it into place with a couple of nails and check the fit. If it is okay, apply glue and mount permanently.

The unit shown was finished in antique olive using a prepared kit. The process is simple. A base color is applied to the work. After drying, a glaze coat is brushed on and then wiped off. Wiping can be done with paper, cheesecloth, or even a dry brush. Highlights can be added to give the piece an authentic antique appearance.

BILL OF MATERIALS

Top	¾x17¼x48"	pine ...1 req'd.	Drawer, side	⅜x7¼x15"	plywood....2 req'd.
Side	¾x16⅛x29¼"	pine ...2 req'd.	Drawer, side	⅜x11½x15"	plywood....2 req'd.
End	¾x5¼x16⅛"	pine ...1 req'd.	Drawer, bottom	¼x14⅞x29¾"	plywood....1 req'd.
Bottom	¾x13¼x16⅛"	pine ...1 req'd.	Drawer, bottom	¼x12¹³⁄₁₆x14¾"	plywood....3 req'd.
Wide bottom	¾x16⅛x30¼"	pine ...1 req'd.	Drawer, stop	⅜x¾x8"	pine ...4 req'd.
Base scallop	¾x3½x14¼"	pine ...1 req'd.	Rear panel	¼x4½x30¾"	plywood....1 req'd.
Base backup board	¾x3x13¼"	pine ...1 req'd.	Rear panel	¼x14¾x25"	plywood....1 req'd.
Cleat	¾x1x11⅞"	pine ..8 req'd.	Pedestal	1⅛x10¾x21⅝"	pine....1 req'd.
Cleat	¾x2x13¼"	pine ..6 req'd.	Pedestal base	1¾x2½x15⅞"	pine....1 req'd.
Cleat	¾x2x30¼"	pine ..2 req'd.	Book support,	1⅛x4x27⅜"	pine....1 req'd.
Drawer, front	¾x3⅝x30⅛"	pine ...1 req'd.	rear		
Drawer, front	¾x3⅝x13⅛"	pine ...1 req'd.	Book support,	1⅛x6¾x27⅜"	pine....1 req'd.
Drawer, front	¾x7¼x13⅛"	pine ...1 req'd.	bottom		
Drawer, front	¾x11½x13⅛"	pine ...1 req'd.	Tenon	1⅛x1½x3½"	pine ...2 req'd.
Drawer, sub-front	¾x3x29⅜"	pine ...1 req'd.	Tenon dowel	¾x2⅝"	maple ...2 req'd.
Drawer, sub-front	¾x3x12⅜"	pine ...1 req'd.	Lag screws	⅝x3½"	2 req'd.
Drawer, sub-front	¾x6⅜x12⅜"	pine ...1 req'd.	Lag screws	⁵⁄₁₆x2"	2 req'd.
Drawer, sub-front	¾x10⅝x12⅜"	pine ...1 req'd.	Flat washers for screws		4 req'd.
Drawer, rear	¾x3x29⅜"	pine ...1 req'd.	Dowels	⅜x2"	4 req'd.
Drawer, rear	¾x3x12⅜"	pine ...1 req'd.	FH screws #8 x 2½"		4 req'd.
Drawer, rear	¾x6⅝x12⅜"	pine ...1 req'd.	Pulls 3" centers		5 req'd.
Drawer, rear	¾x10⅝x12⅜"	pine ...1 req'd.			
	⅜x3⅝x15"	plywood....4 req'd.			

Hutch Bookcase

This hardwood piece uses pre-turned legs. It's designed for quick and easy assembly

Tᴴɪs ᴇʟᴇɢᴀɴᴛ bookcase is easily made with ordinary tools. No lathe is needed, since the two gracefully turned legs are store bought. The unit shown is made of ash wood, but any wood may be substituted. Ash is similar to oak. Both are hardwoods and take a beautiful finish.

The base and upper hutch top are made as two separate pieces. This facilitates construction and makes the piece more mobile. The front apron is not a drawer; the pull is merely decorative.

Start with the base piece. Cut the boards for the top and lower shelf. These must be glued up to obtain the necessary width. If you have a shaper, you can use a glue joint cutter to form the sections, otherwise use butt joints and dowels. Reverse every other piece to prevent warping of the large flat surfaces. If dowels are used, they should be the spiral grooved type 2-inches long.

Use a good furniture glue and clamp the parts securely until the glue sets. The lower shelf is cut with square edges. The upper piece is shaped on three edges with a router. Before shaping, however, the surface should be sanded to remove any unevenness at the glue line. A belt sander is ideal for this operation. If hardwood is used start with a medium grit paper then finish with a fine grit. If you are working with a softwood such as pine, use care not to gouge out the surface. Raise and lower the

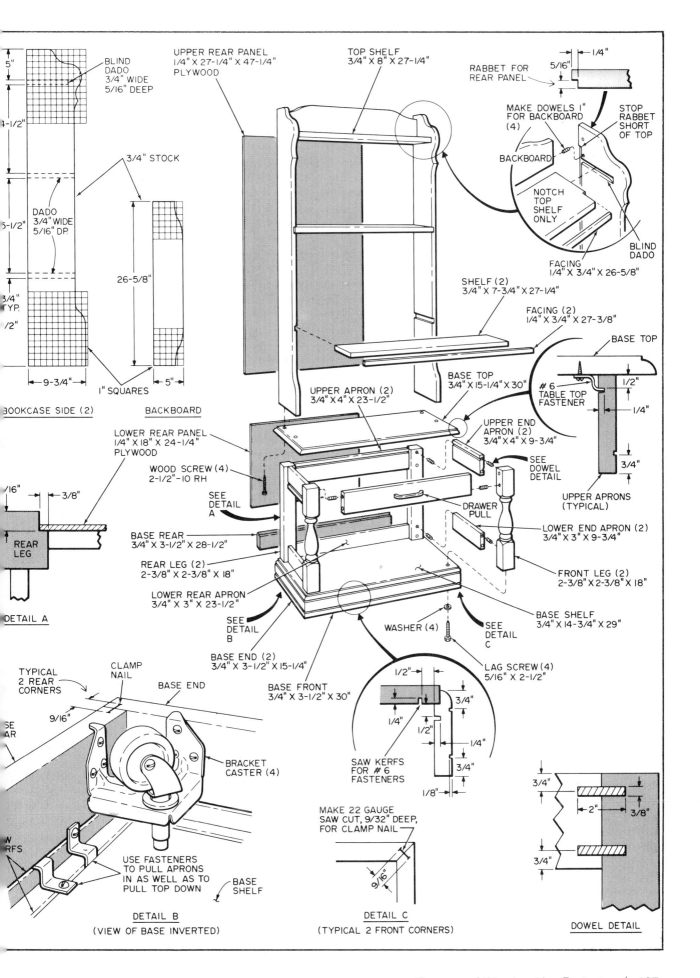

BLIND DADO
3/4" WIDE
5/16" DEEP

3/4" STOCK

DADO
3/4" WIDE
5/16" DP.

26-5/8"

9-3/4"

1" SQUARES

5"

BOOKCASE SIDE (2)

BACKBOARD

UPPER REAR PANEL
1/4" X 27-1/4" X 47-1/4"
PLYWOOD

TOP SHELF
3/4" X 8" X 27-1/4"

RABBET FOR
REAR PANEL

1/4"

5/16"

MAKE DOWELS 1"
FOR BACKBOARD
(4)

STOP
RABBET
SHORT
OF TOP

BACKBOARD

NOTCH
TOP
SHELF
ONLY

FACING
1/4" X 3/4" X 26-5/8"

BLIND
DADO

SHELF (2)
3/4" X 7-3/4" X 27-1/4"

FACING (2)
1/4" X 3/4" X 27-3/8"

BASE TOP

BASE TOP
3/4" X 15-1/4" X 30"

6
TABLE TOP
FASTENER

1/2"

1/4"

3/4"

UPPER APRON (2)
3/4" X 4" X 23-1/2"

UPPER END
APRON (2)
3/4" X 4" X 9-3/4"

SEE
DOWEL
DETAIL

UPPER APRONS
(TYPICAL)

LOWER REAR PANEL
1/4" X 18" X 24-1/4"
PLYWOOD

WOOD SCREW (4)
2-1/2"-10 RH

SEE
DETAIL
A

DRAWER
PULL

LOWER END APRON (2)
3/4" X 3" X 9-3/4"

FRONT LEG (2)
2-3/8" X 2-3/8" X 18"

3/8"

REAR
LEG

DETAIL A

BASE REAR
3/4" X 3-1/2" X 28-1/2"

REAR LEG (2)
2-3/8" X 2-3/8" X 18"

LOWER REAR APRON
3/4" X 3" X 23-1/2"

SEE
DETAIL
B

BASE END (2)
3/4" X 3-1/2" X 15-1/4"

BASE FRONT
3/4" X 3-1/2" X 30"

WASHER (4)

SEE
DETAIL
C

BASE SHELF
3/4" X 14-3/4" X 29"

LAG SCREW (4)
5/16" X 2-1/2"

TYPICAL
2 REAR
CORNERS

CLAMP
NAIL

BASE END

9/16"

BRACKET
CASTER (4)

USE FASTENERS
TO PULL APRONS
IN AS WELL AS TO
PULL TOP DOWN

BASE
SHELF

DETAIL B
(VIEW OF BASE INVERTED)

1/2"

3/4"

1/4"

1/2"

1/4"

3/4"

1/8"

SAW KERFS
FOR # 6
FASTENERS

MAKE 22 GAUGE
SAW CUT, 9/32" DEEP,
FOR CLAMP NAIL

9/16"

DETAIL C
(TYPICAL 2 FRONT CORNERS)

3/4"

2"

3/8"

3/4"

DOWEL DETAIL

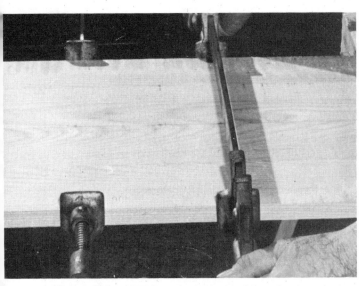

If your lumber isn't wide enough for the sides, glue two or more boards together: Drill accurate dowel holes, apply glue to dowels and insert, clamp boards until glue sets. Alternate the clamps.

The two front corners of the base require miter joints. Use clamp nails, which will close the joint tightly. The clamp nail is hammer driven into the 22-gauge saw-cut slot which is 9/32-inch deep.

With the base and post assembly upside down, drill the lag screw holes through base and into post ends. Then insert lag screws and, with socket wrench, screw lower shelf tight to corner posts.

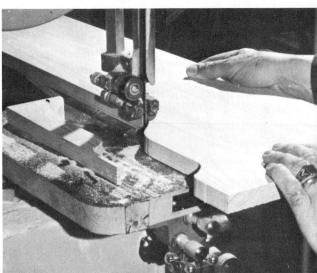

The top and bottom of the bookshelf side have curves which are traced from kraft paper with a grid of 1" squares (see diagram). You can use either a band saw or saber saw to make these cuts.

The blind dados in the bookcase sides can be made with either a router or a table saw with cutter head. If you use a table saw, lower the work onto the revolving blade, tilting board as shown.

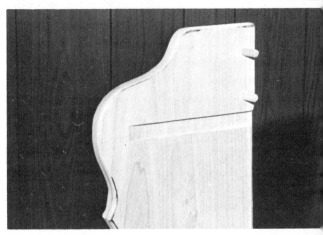

Detail of blind dado: If you use a router, make the cut with several passes, instead of attempting the full cut in one pass. The two spiral dowels will join the bookshelf side to the backboard.

Hutch Bookcase

tool squarely.

Cut the apron pieces next. These are grooved as shown. The groove can be cut square by using the table saw. Set the blade to protrude ⅛-in. above the table and adjust the fence ¾-in. from the blade. If the router is used, use the router fence to locate the groove. Use a "V"-cutter.

The lower front aprons are mitered at the corners. There are several ways to join the miters. The spline is the most practical, and can be steel or wood. Wood splines can be cut from a piece of ⅛-in. plywood. Steel splines called clamp nails are readily available. They are driven into 22-gauge kerf cuts. They are designed to tightly close the joint since they are driven with a hammer. Clamps are not required.

After the lower apron pieces have been mitered, cut the rabbet along the top inner edge. This will support the lower shelf. The rabbet can be made with a router or by making two passes on the table saw. Either method works well.

The shelf is fastened to the apron using table top fasteners. These are "Z" shaped steel brackets which pull the joints tightly because they are screwed into place. They simply rest in a groove cut ½-in. from the apron edge. Normally they are used to pull the top down tightly. However, in this instance, they are also used to draw the rabbet joint tightly against the edge of the shelf. To accomplish this, a second groove is cut on the underside of the top. (See sketch.)

Assemble the lower apron first, using dowels at the rear and clamp nails at the front on the mitered corners. Apply glue into the rabbet cut, then lower the shelf into place. Install the fasteners and draw them tight with round head screws.

Now cut the legs. The turned legs are made of 3-in. stock. If you purchase them ready-made, be sure to use 24-in. lengths. These have sufficient blocks at the ends which can be trimmed. The rear legs are made from square or glued-up blocks. One corner in each block

is rabbeted to take the ¼-in. rear panel. Cut the turned legs so there will be 5 inches at the top block and 5 inches at the lower end.

Drill ⅜-in. dia. holes into the ends of all the apron pieces. Drill corresponding holes into the legs. This is easily done by the use of dowel centers. Drill the corresponding holes into the legs. Join the legs to the short aprons. Use a block of wood under the hammer to protect the surface of the leg. Use ⅜-in. x 2-in. spiral dowels. Clamp till the glue sets, then repeat for the longer apron pieces. Fasten the top with the "Z" brackets. The lower shelf is fastened to the legs with 2-in. lag screws using a washer under each lag screw head. Sand the assembly.

The bookcase is made from solid stock. If you cannot obtain good flat lumber of sufficient width, glue up two or more pieces. Layout the outline for the shape at the top and bottom, then cut with a band saw or saber saw. Use a router to round off the outer edges, and follow with the dado cuts. The two lower dados are cut full length, while the top dados are blind cut. The dados can be made on the table saw fitted with a dado blade or you can use a router. If a router is used, do not attempt to cut the full depth of the dado in one pass. Take several shallow cuts until the full depth is achieved. You will have

to use side guides to keep the router "on course."

If a table saw is used, cut the blind dado by lowering the work on the revolving blade. Tilt the board as shown. Make several trial cuts on scrap pieces to determine where to start the cut.

When all the dados have been cut, make the shelf pieces and install them by gluing. The backboard is doweled and installed also at this time. While the glue sets, clamp the assembly, making certain that it is perfectly aligned. Check with a square, and add a couple of diagonal cleats at the rear edge to keep it square while glue sets.

The shelves are cut so that they are flush with the sides (except for the top one). After they are in place, add the face strip to each shelf. The two lower strips are made to extend past the length of the shelf, while the top face strip is the same length as the shelf.

Cut the rear panels for the upper and lower sections and install with panelling nails, which are ring grooved and will hold tightly.

If you wish to make the unit mobile, add concealed casters with shelf-locating corner brackets. If a prefinished panel is used for the rear, apply finish material to the pieces before installing the rear panel. We used Beverly's provincial satin stain and several coats of clear lacquer.

BILL OF MATERIALS

NOTE: All lumber used, except legs, is ash.

Quantity	Size and Description	Purpose
2	¾" x 9¾" x 51½"	Bookcase side
1	¾" x 5" x 26⅝"	Backboard
1	¾" x 8" x 27¼"	Shelf, top
2	¾" x 7¾" x 27¼"	Shelf, center & lower
2	¼" x ¾" x 27¼"	Facing
1	¾" x 15¼" x 30"	Base, top
2	¾" x 4" x 23½"	Apron, upper
2	¾" x 4" x 9¾"	Apron, upper end
2	2⅜" x 2⅜" x 18"	Leg, front
2	2⅜" x 2⅜" x 18"	Leg, rear
1	¾" x 3" x 23½"	Apron, lower rear
2	¾" x 3" x 9¾"	Apron, lower end
1	¾" x 14¾" x 29"	Base shelf
2	¾" x 3½" x 15¼"	Base end
1	¾" x 3½" x 30"	Base front
1	¾" x 3½" x 28½"	Base rear
1	¼" x 27¼" x 47¼" plywood	Rear panel, upper
1	¼" x 18" x 24¼" plywood	Rear panel, lower
4		Clamp nails
4		Bracket casters
44	⅜" x 2"	

MOVABLE SERVER

Designed in the traditional style, this server will provide more than nine square feet of serving area when leaves are raised. And there's plenty of storage space

THIS ELEGANT SERVER measures 48 inches long but stretches to 78 inches when the leaves are extended. There is ample room for any occasion, whether it be a banquet or family gathering.

The three roomy drawers can be used for storage of linens and silver. The two compartments will hold plenty of tableware and appliances and, if necessary, they can be fitted with shelves. The original was made without shelves. Sturdy lid supports fold flat when not in use and the hidden casters are handy allowing the large piece to be moved about with ease.

Construction is basic with butt joints used throughout. The raised panel is easily accomplished on the table saw and the shaped edges are done with a router.

The lumber used is common Idaho pine which is available in most lumberyards in glued up

stock to 24 inches wide. This server requires 18-inch material. Choose flat board and avoid boards with loose knots. The knots are not objectionable, but they should be sound and free of sap.

Since the new lumber sizes have been in effect, you will find that 18-inch stock measures actually 17¼-inch so don't be confused when looking over the materials list. Likewise, one inch stock measures ¾-inch. Therefore, 1-inch x 18-inch really measures ¾-inch x 17¼-inch.

In looking over the drawings, you will note that the top is doubled. This makes for a sturdier piece and it also facilitates assembly. Cleats are eliminated and you won't have to drive nails or screws through the top surface.

Cut the boards to size as per the specifications. If you purchased long boards, it would be best to rough cut them to size with a porta-

ble saw or you may want to use saber saw to part the large sections. It's a little slower, but much safer. If a board sags toward the end of the cut when using a portable, the tool could kick and this could be dangerous. The saber saw will not kick. This doesn't mean that the portable saw should not be used, but use it only when necessary. As a matter of fact, the saw is ideally suited to trim the board after they have been rough cut, you do not have a radial arm saw. If you use the portable saw, clamp a guide strip on your work to assure a smooth straight cut.

If you use the radial arm saw chances are that it will not cut the full width of your boards, but with a little ingenuity you can do it. Set the fence to the rear-most position then make the cut. Draw the arm forward as far as it will travel then if the cut is not completed

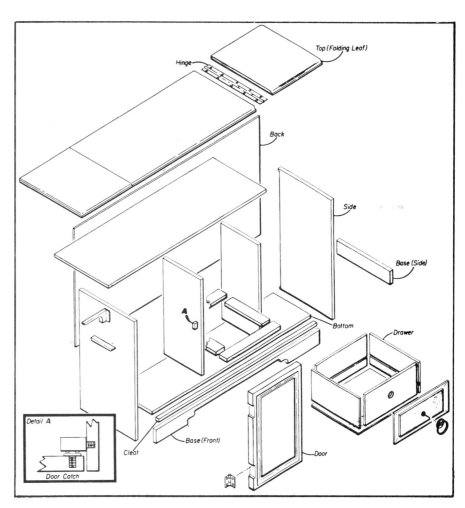

Top (Folding Leaf)

Hinge

Back

Side

Base (Side)

Bottom

Drawer

Detail A

Base (Front)

Cleat

Door

Door Catch

carefully raise the leading edge of the panel up slowly until the board separates. Keep fingers clear of the blade.

After the boards are cut to size, rabbet the rear edges to take the ¼-inch plywood panel. Use a table saw or router. If the table saw is used, set the height of the blade ¼-inch above the table and the fence ⅜-inch away from the blade. Make the first pass holding the work vertically. The second pass with the blade readjusted and the work held horizontally will remove the stock forming the rabbet. Assemble the parts with glue and nails. The nails will be concealed by the drop leaf at the top and the apron at the bottom. Before assembly, it would be wise to cut the rear panel, which can then be used to keep the cabinet case square while the glue sets. Simply insert it temporarily with a few brads, then remove after the glue has set.

The drawer compartments are built up as a separate modular unit, then inserted into the previously assembled case. Be sure to keep the unit square during assembly. Bar clamps are useful to hold the parts but not essential. If you use nails to hold the sections, try cement-coated finishing nails. They hold very well and will not work loose. The best combination, however, is the use of screws and glue, especially if you lack the bar clamps.

Install the drawer compartment centering it within the main case. Use glue on all joints and again, fasten with nails or screws.

The apron at the base of the cabinet is now added. Use a saber saw or jig saw to cut the scallop in the front piece. When the two side pieces and front have been cut and before installation, run a router fitted with a rounding cutter over the edges to break the sharp corners.

DROP LEAF MOVABLE SERVER

Here door frames are rabbeted after they are assembled. The rabbet groove is made deep enough so that the back of raised panel will fit flush with the back of the door frame

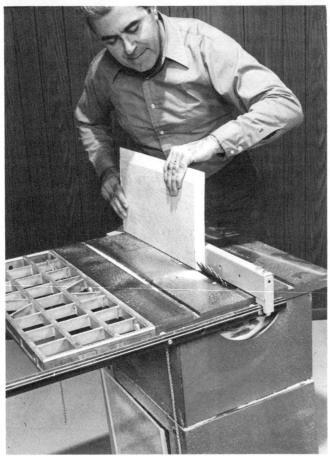

The panel raising is done by setting the saw blade at 15 degrees, and then feeding the work slowly and carefully. The saw blade must be given plenty of time to make the cut.

The panels are then fitted to the door frames from the rear. The corners of the panels can be rounded to match rabbeted corners, or else you can chisel the frame corners square

Assemble the side pieces by driving screws from the inside of the side panels. The front apron is fastened by means of a cleat, as shown.

The top board and drop leaves should be cut from the same board, if possible. This will assure continuity in the grain pattern and is especially important if the unit is to be stained. Cut the parts, then shape the edge with a suitable router cutter, followed by a good sanding especially at the square edges where the leaves and top meet.

To apply the piano hinges, place the top and leaf sections upside down on a clean flat surface. Pull sections together and mark the location of the screw holes. Install a few screws and check the fit. If okay, add the rest of the screws. Now add the wood spacer to the underside of each leaf, then fasten the top to cabinet. The drop leaf hinges are now installed. With leaf in open position and the leaf up, locate the mounting holes for the

hinge. Drill pilot holes, then install the hinge. Repeat for other side. Note that the drop leaf hinges come in a set—one left and one right one.

The doors are simple in construction. Cut the frame pieces and assemble with dowels and glue. Use one dowel per corner and be sure to keep the surfaces flat when gluing. When the glue has set, rabbet the backside of the frame to take the raised panel. Perhaps it would be best to wait until the panels are cut before proceeding with this step.

The door panels are cut to size then the saw blade is tilted 15° and raised 1¼-inch. Set the fence so that the saw leaves a 1/16-inch step on the surface of the board (see drawing). To assure proper fit, cut a trial piece on scrap wood before cutting the doors. When the panels have been cut, rabbet the door frame so that the back of the panel is flush with the door frame.

The rabbeting of the frame will

leave a radius at each corner. This can be left as is and the raised panels rounded to match, or the rounded corners can be cut square with a chisel. Apply a bead of glue in the rabbet, then insert the panel and clamp.

Mortise the doors to accept the full depth of the hinges. The hinges are then flush mounted on the side panels.

The drawers are made as per drawing. The front panels are raised as were the door pieces. Before adding the front piece to the drawers, drill ½-inch clearance holes to allow clearance for the drawer hardware. Fasten the front with 1-inch round head screws and glue. Place stops at the rear of the drawer compartments to limit the travel of the drawers.

Sand the entire cabinet then add the casters and door catch hardware. Finish as desired. The server shown here was finished with two coats of latex antique base paint

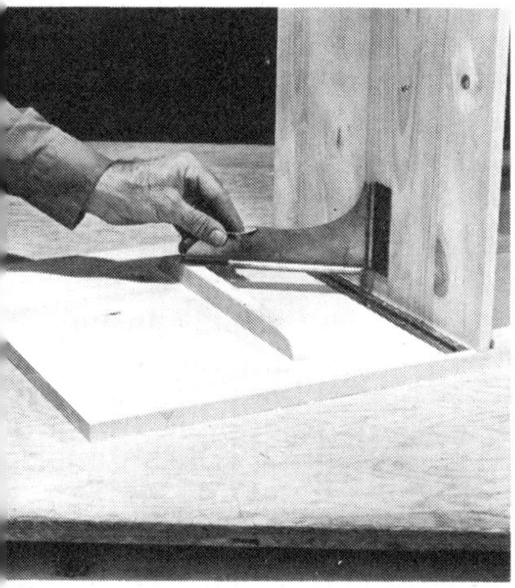

Pictured here is the drop leaf support which is mounted with sufficient space to clear the strip hinge.

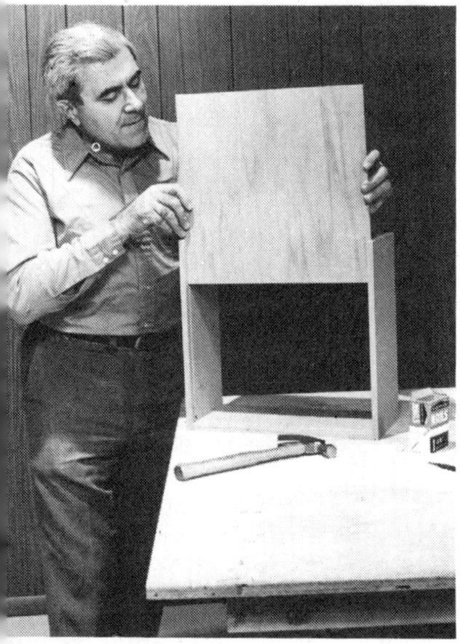

Drawer bottoms of ¼-inch plywood slide into the side panel dadoes. Cut sides from a medium density overlay.

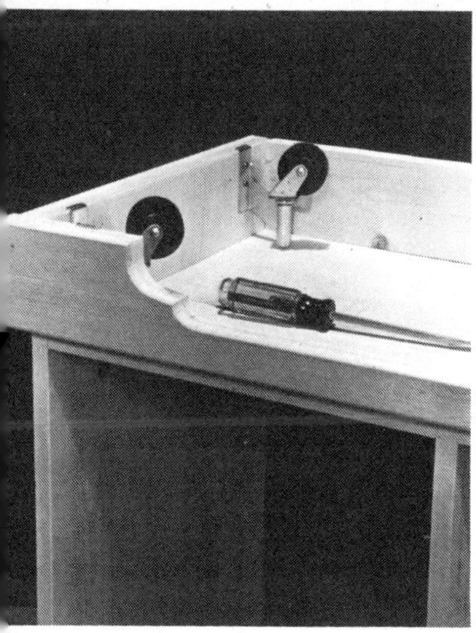

Shown above is the positioning of the self-aligning casters which will give the drop leaf server its mobility.

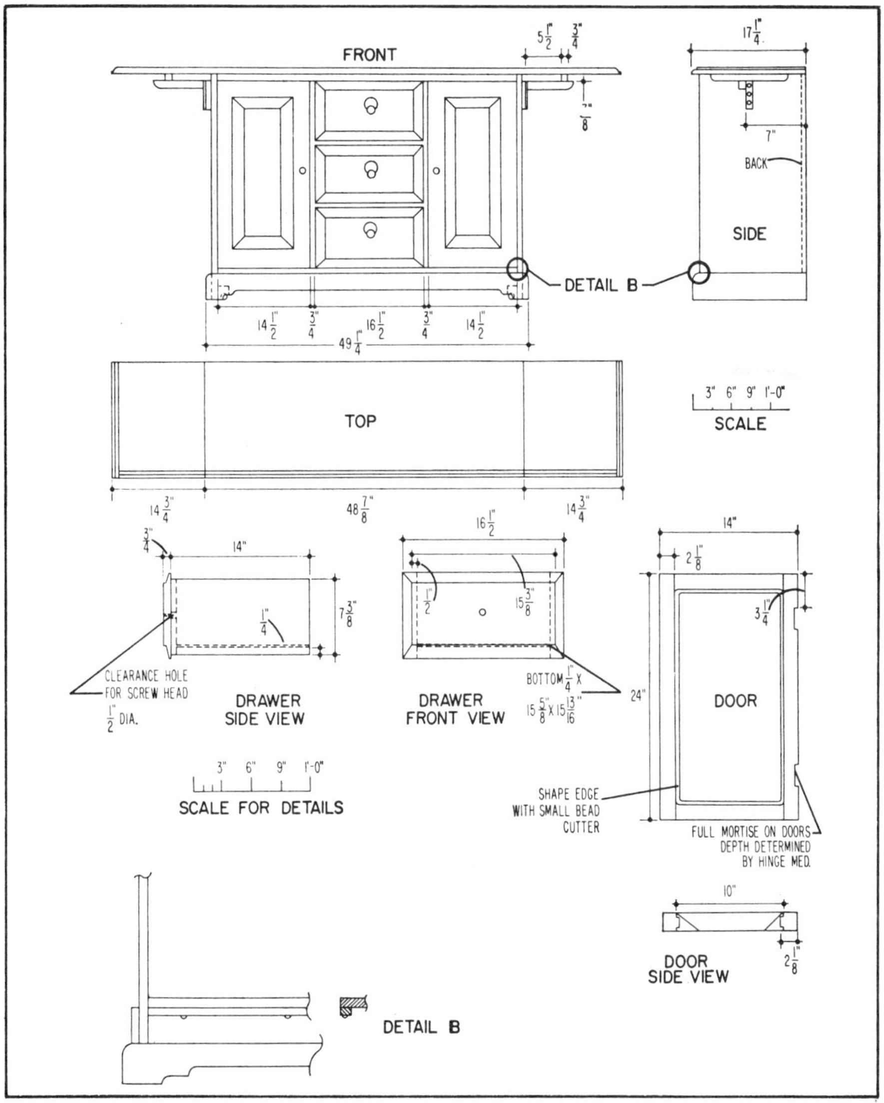

BILL OF MATERIALS

Quantity	Size and	Description	Purpose
2	¾"	16¼"x29¼" pine	Sides
2	¾"	16¼"x46" pine	bottom and sub-top
1	¾"	17¼"x48⅞" pine	top
2	¾"	14¾"x17¼" pine	top ends
2	¾"	16"x24⅛" pine	uprights
4	¾"	2⁵⁄₁₆"x16½ pine	front and rear shelf supports
4	¾"	1⅜"x11⅜" pine	side shelf supports
2	¾"	3¾"x16¼" pine	apron side
1	¾"	3¾"x48¾" pine	apron front
1	¾"	1"x42" pine	apron cleat
1	¼"	24¾"x46⅝" plywood	rear panel
2	¾"	⅞"x11⅝" pine	drop leaf spacer
3	¾"	7⁷⁄₁₆"x16⁷⁄₁₆" pine	drawer front
6	½"	7⅜"x15⅜" plywood	drawer sub-front and rear
6	½"	7⅜"x14" plywood	drawer sides
4	¾"	2⅛"x24" pine	door frame sides
4	¾"	2⅛"x9¾" pine	door frame top and bottom
2	¾"	10"x20" pine	door panel
2	1"x16¼"	continuous hinge	
4	1⅜"x2"	door hinge	

NOTE: Also need casters, catches, pulls, knobs, drop leaf brackets and finishing materials.

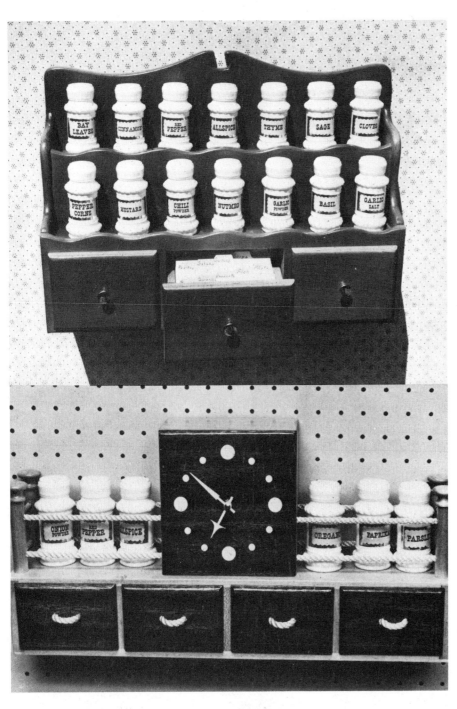

Spice Racks

SPICE racks are often merely functional shelves built onto the insides of cabinet doors. If you have the available wall space, why not bring the spice rack out into the open where it is more accessible, and where it can add a distinctive decorative touch.

Either of these racks will do even more. Both provide drawers for storage of recipe cards and other small items; one also has a clock for timing cooking to perfection.

The rack components can be assembled using conventional joining methods. However, to save time and labor, consider using a Ther-mogrip electric glue gun that utilizes stick glue. This type of adhesive sets in less than a minute, and there is no need to use clamps of any kind; simply apply the hot glue with the gun, then hold the sections together by hand until the bonding material sets. The glue guns are available in most hardware stores.

The Early American style rack is made of pine finished with a warm stain that is in keeping with your colonial kitchen decor. Use a jig-saw, sabre saw, or even a hand coping saw to cut the curved front, end and back sections. The front is preferably cut from a single piece of wood, or it can be assembled from separate pieces glued together. Both front and back pieces lap over the ends, not vice versa.

The rack will look better if you round the curved edges. A shaper does this best, but careful hand-working can also yield a creditable job. Note that the center drawer—used for filing recipe cards—differs from the other two; the sides are shaped so as to permit tilting for installation, and a tab at the rear acts as a drawer stop.

The Nautical style rack, with the clock, is even easier to build since it calls for no curved pieces and needs no face panel. It is more appropriate in a contemporary style kitchen. Use a combination of gum wood and dark mahogany—the latter for the drawer fronts and the clock face.

Note that the lipped drawer fronts simply butt against the compartment framework. Lengths of nylon rope, glued into holes, serve as handles.

The clock box is made separately, and then glued in place as shown. The dial for the clock is made by gluing short lengths of dowel into holes drilled into a ½-inch-thick piece of mahogany along a circle that will bring them close to the tips of the clock hands. Use the hands that come with the clock mechanism. Note that the clock face laps over the edges of the box.

The posts at the top of the cabinet are intended to simulate ship's capstans. The nylon ropes attached to them are anchored in place with bits of melted glue.

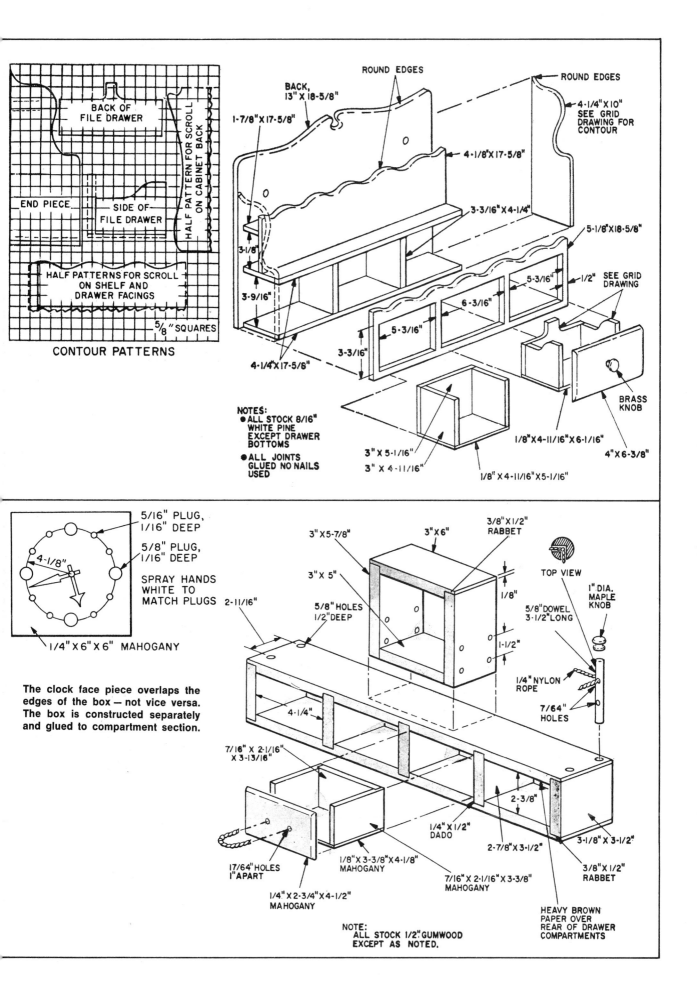

CONTOUR PATTERNS

BACK OF FILE DRAWER

HALF PATTERN FOR SCROLL ON CABINET BACK

END PIECE

SIDE OF FILE DRAWER

HALF PATTERNS FOR SCROLL ON SHELF AND DRAWER FACINGS

5/8" SQUARES

ROUND EDGES

ROUND EDGES

BACK, 13" X 18-5/8"

4-1/4" X 10" SEE GRID DRAWING FOR CONTOUR

1-7/8" X 17-5/8"

4-1/8" X 17-5/8"

3-3/16" X 4-1/4"

5-1/8" X 18-5/8"

3-1/8"

1/2" SEE GRID DRAWING

5-3/16"

3-9/16"

6-3/16"

5-3/16"

5-3/16"

3-3/16"

4-1/4" X 17-5/8"

NOTES:
● ALL STOCK 8/16" WHITE PINE EXCEPT DRAWER BOTTOMS
● ALL JOINTS GLUED NO NAILS USED

3" X 5-1/16"
3" X 4-11/16"

1/8" X 4-11/16" X 5-1/16"

1/8" X 4-11/16" X 6-1/16"

4" X 6-3/8"

BRASS KNOB

5/16" PLUG, 1/16" DEEP

5/8" PLUG, 1/16" DEEP

4-1/8"

SPRAY HANDS WHITE TO MATCH PLUGS

1/4" X 6" X 6" MAHOGANY

The clock face piece overlaps the edges of the box — not vice versa. The box is constructed separately and glued to compartment section.

3" X 5-7/8"

3" X 6"

3/8" X 1/2" RABBET

3" X 5"

2-11/16"

5/8" HOLES 1/2" DEEP

1/8"

TOP VIEW

1" DIA. MAPLE KNOB

5/8" DOWEL 3-1/2" LONG

1/4" NYLON ROPE

7/64" HOLES

1-1/2"

4-1/4"

7/16" X 2-1/16" X 3-13/16"

17/64" HOLES 1" APART

1/8" X 3-3/8" X 4-1/8" MAHOGANY

1/4" X 2-3/4" X 4-1/2" MAHOGANY

7/16" X 2-1/16" X 3-3/8" MAHOGANY

1/4" X 1/2" DADO

2-7/8" X 3-1/2"

2-3/8"

3-1/8" X 3-1/2"

3/8" X 1/2" RABBET

HEAVY BROWN PAPER OVER REAR OF DRAWER COMPARTMENTS

NOTE:
ALL STOCK 1/2" GUMWOOD EXCEPT AS NOTED.

DROP LEAF TABLE

The top opens to provide over 11 square feet of surface area. The two drawers each have over a cubic foot of space

HERE's a neat little table, small in size and price but big in value. Closed, it measures only 19-in. x 38-in. and will fit easily into any nook or available space. It opens to a generous 38-in. x 44-in. to provide ample surface area for dining or working on projects or hobbies such as sewing, painting, etc. It is well-built with full length strip hinges to assure tight level joints and heavy duty supports to hold the leaves with ease. The two full length drawers provide ample storage for table linens, tableware, or hobby materials.

The construction has been simplified and should be easy to build even for the novice. The edging of the top has been done with stock moulding thus eliminating the tedious sanding normally required on the end grain after shaping.

While the table is assembled with screws, none show because of the method of application.

We used lumber core red birch for the top and sub-structure of the table and poplar for the trestle. These woods are not exactly cheap, so if you want to substitute other less expensive materials you can bring the cost down considerably.

Cut the parts to size, then rabbet and dado the side panels to accept the cleats and bottom section. Check the width of the dado on scrap wood. The fit should be snug but not a force fit. Before assembly, drill screwdriver clearance holes through the bottom and cleats as shown. This will allow you to fasten the "box" to the top with ease. You will need an extra long screwdriver for this operation. Be sure the holes are properly aligned.

Assemble the cleats and bottom to the sides with nails and glue. Use 2-in. finshing nails and drive them from the top and bottom where they won't show. The center cleat can be nailed from the outside and the nail heads then sunk and filled.

Working on a clean surface place the three top sections face down, making sure that the grain patterns are aligned. Locate the strip hinges and assemble. Keep the joint tight when locating the screw holes for the hinge. Mount three screws on each side and

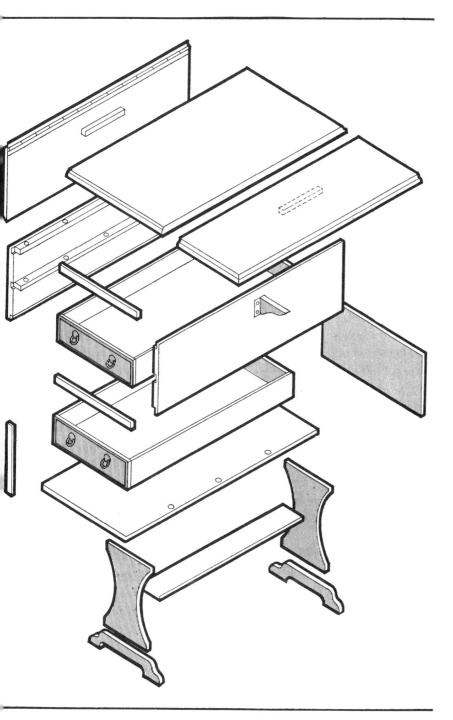

It's a good idea to use a template to get the right curves for base and feet. Trace the pattern on a grid of two-inch squares.

Rabbet and dado the sides to accept the cleats and bottom section. Use glue and 2-in. finishing nails to attach these pieces.

Full length strip hinges assure tight, level joints. Work on a clean surface and keep the joints tight when locating the holes.

check the operation of the hinge. If okay, mount the rest of the screws.

The pedestal base is made next. The feet are cut from 1¾-in. stock and the upright from 1⅛-in. lumber. Make kraft paper patterns from the graph drawing and then trace onto the wood. Cut the parts on the jigsaw or with a sabre saw.

Sand all exposed edges, then round off the corners with a router. The uprights are attached to the crosspiece with flat head screws.

The screws must be countersunk sufficiently so wood plugs can be used to conceal them. An alternate is to drive the screws diagonally from the underside of the cross piece. Either method will work, however if you do not have a plug cutter you may want to use the diagonal method.

The feet are attached to the uprights with glue and lag screws. Use washers under the lag screw heads to keep the heads from digging into the wood.

DROP LEAF TABLE

The upper part of the table can now be mounted to the top using 1¼-in. #12 flathead screws. If you do not use the long screwdriver method, you will have to reach in and drive the screws from the inside. The area is quite cramped, but you can mount the screws this way, using extreme care and patience. You will note that the rear panel of the substructure has not yet been mounted. This is intentional and will be installed later.

You can now mount the drop leaf support hardware. Install the bracket so that it rests on a cleat as shown. The cleat is held with nails and glue. Taper the leading edge of the cleat slightly to allow the bracket to swing into place without binding.

Mount the assembled top to the pedestal using lag screws. You can gain access to the rear screws easily, since the rear panel has not yet been installed. Apply some glue to the top edge of the pedestal before mounting. Do not overtighten the lag screws.

With the table assembled, extend the leaves and cut the moulding to size. Miter the four outside corners and butt all intermediate joints. Apply the mouldings with glue and brads, then sink brad heads and fill.

The drawers are of simple construction. Cut the members to size and dado the lower section of the front and sides to take the ¼-in. plywood bottom panel. Be sure the drawer is square when assembling. The bottom panel is a good guide to use to check for squareness. The back edge should line up evenly with the back piece.

Be sure to drill the screw head clearance for the pulls in the sub-front piece before assembly. The drawer fronts are shaped with an appropriate beading cutter. Attach it to the sub-front with glue and 1¼-in. finishing nails. Drive the nails in from the inside panel.

Install the drawers and let them protrude ⅝-in. from the frame pieces, then install stops at the rear. These stops are small strips of wood measuring ½-in. x ¾-in. x 1½-in. Place them about ½-in. in from the sides on both the center cleats and bottom panel. The rear panel may now be installed. Assemble with finishing nails and glue. Add the ¼-in. x ¾-in. edge strips to complete the project.

Finish the table as desired. We used an antique green finish with dark glaze. To allow the wood grain to show, we applied a thinned down base coat.

The feet are attached to the legs with glue and lag screws. Use washers under heads to keep them from digging in the wood

Before assembling cleats and bottom to sides, drill screwdriver clearance holes. This will permit you to attach top easily.

Mount the drop-leaf support bracket so that it rests on a cleat. Taper leading edge of the cleats slightly to prevent binding.

Mount assembled top to pedestal using lag screws. You can reach rear screw easily by not yet installing the rear pane

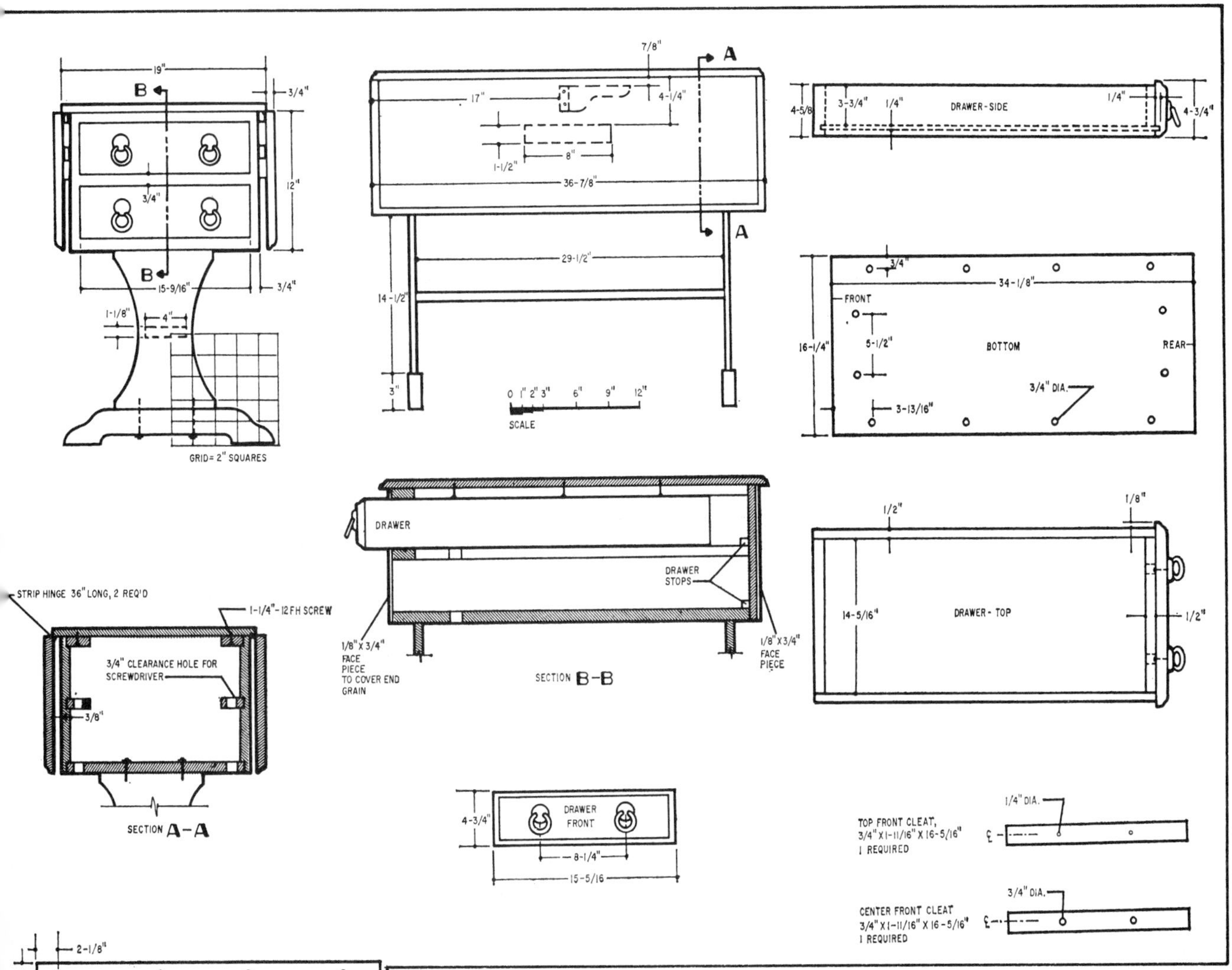

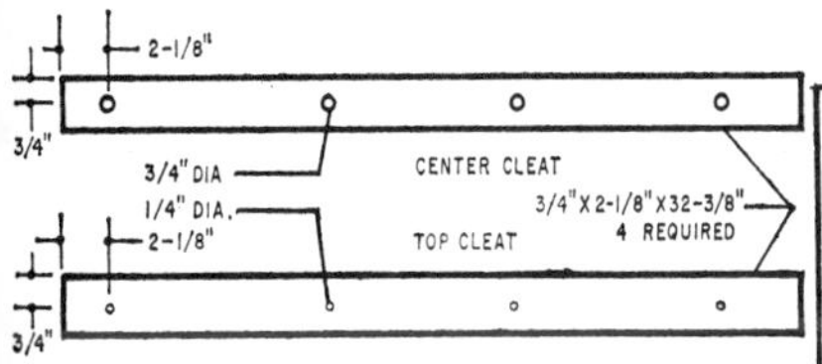

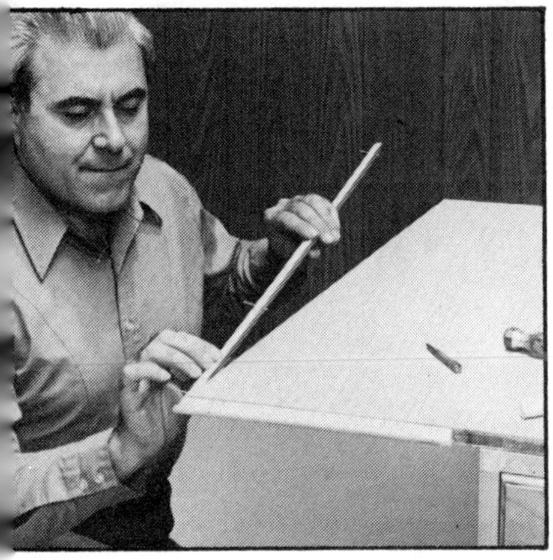

Cut moulding to size and miter outside corners. Butt intermediate joints. Apply with glue and brads, sink heads and fill.

BILL OF MATERIALS

Quantity	Purpose	Size and Description
1	Top	¾" x 19" x 36⅞"*
2	Leaf	¾" x 12" x 36⅞"*
2	Side	¾" x 12" x 34⅞"*
4	Cleat	¾" x 2⅛" x 32⅜"*
2	Cleat	¾" x 1 11/16" x 16 5/16"*
1	Bottom	¾" x 16¼" x 34⅛"*
1	Rear panel	¾" x 12" x 15 5/16"*
2	Upright	1⅛" x 9¼" x 14⅛" poplar
1	Cross-piece	1⅛" x 4" x 29½" poplar
2	Drop leaf cleat	¾" x 1½" x 8"
2	Drawer side	½" x 4⅝"" x 32" pine
2	Drawer front inner	½" x 4⅝" x 14 5/16" pine
2	Drawer front outer	¾" x 4¾" x 15 5/16"*
2	Feet	1¾" x 3" x 20¼" poplar
2	Drawer rear	½" x 3¾" x 14 5/16" pine
1	Drawer bottom	¼" x 14⅝" x 31¾"
	Nose & cove molding	½" x ⅝" x 15'
4	Lag screws	5/16" x 3"
4	Lag screws	5/16" x 2"
10	FH screws	1¼"—12
4	FH screws	2"—12
2	Strip hinge	36"
4	Lion head pulls	
2 Left, 1 Right	Drop leaf bracket	

*¾" lumber core birch plywood

Mini-Office

Small enough to fit most anywhere, you can build it easily in the lumber of your choice

HERE's a compact mini-office that packs a lot of punch. It's small enough to fit most anywhere and yet it holds a typewriter, office supplies and a file drawer for all your important papers. When open, the top measures a full 22-in. x 36-in. The cabinet stands 30¼-in. high and is 22-in. deep and 18-in. wide. The upper compartment serves as the storage area for the typewriter. A pullout shelf supports the typewriter in use. The compartment door and drawers below have matching fronts with raised panels which are easily made on the table saw. The drawers ride on double track hardware which eliminates sticking and insures smooth, quiet operation.

Common pine was used for the prototype, but you can substitute whatever species you desire. Select boards which have a pleasant grain and knot pattern. Unless you use plywood, you will have to glue up boards to make the necessary widths. Use dowels to strengthen the joints. A doweling jig will assure accuracy in locating and drilling the dowel holes. Drill the ⅜-in.

diameter holes 1⅛-in. deep. This will allow sufficient clearance so that the joint will close tightly. Apply glue to half the length of the dowels then drive them into the edge of the board. Apply a thin coat to both mating edges as well as the protruding dowels, then bring the parts together. Clamp securely and allow glue to set. If you cut the boards slightly oversize in width, you won't need blocks under the clamps. Simply

trim to size after removing the clamps.

Cut the rabbets and dadoes next. You can use a router or table saw for this operation. If you decide on the router, you will need to clamp guides on the work piece. Use the widest router bit you have and make successive cuts until the proper depth and width is achieved. For cutting the dadoes and rabbets on the table saw, use a dado blade and bolt a wood strip to the fence.

Above, a doweling jig is used to accurately drill the holes for the dowels. Right, three dowels per board are sufficient for joint. Apply glue, then close joint with hammer blows.

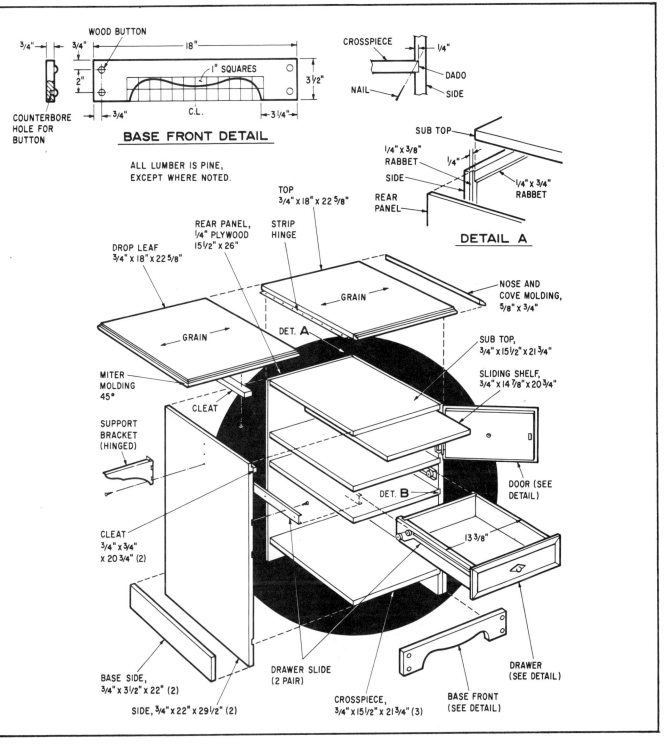

WOOD BUTTON

3/4" 3/4" ⊢──────── 18" ────────⊣

COUNTERBORE
HOLE FOR
BUTTON

2"

1" SQUARES

3 1/2"

3/4" C.L. 3 1/4"

BASE FRONT DETAIL

ALL LUMBER IS PINE,
EXCEPT WHERE NOTED.

CROSSPIECE ─── 1/4"

NAIL ─── DADO

SIDE

SUB TOP

1/4" x 3/8"
RABBET

1/4"

SIDE

1/4" x 3/4"
RABBET

REAR
PANEL

DETAIL A

TOP
3/4" x 18" x 22 5/8"

REAR PANEL,
1/4" PLYWOOD
15 1/2" x 26"

STRIP
HINGE

DROP LEAF
3/4" x 18" x 22 5/8"

GRAIN

GRAIN

DET. A

GRAIN

NOSE AND
COVE MOLDING,
5/8" x 3/4"

SUB TOP,
3/4" x 15 1/2" x 21 3/4"

SLIDING SHELF,
3/4" x 14 7/8" x 20 3/4"

MITER
MOLDING
45°

CLEAT

SUPPORT
BRACKET
(HINGED)

DET. B

DOOR (SEE
DETAIL)

CLEAT
3/4" x 3/4"
x 20 3/4" (2)

13 3/8"

BASE SIDE,
3/4" x 3 1/2" x 22" (2)

SIDE, 3/4" x 22" x 29 1/2" (2)

DRAWER SLIDE
(2 PAIR)

CROSSPIECE,
3/4" x 15 1/2" x 21 3/4" (3)

BASE FRONT
(SEE DETAIL)

DRAWER
(SEE DETAIL)

This will be necessary when cutting the rabbets along the top edge of the side pieces. The wood strip keeps the dado blade safely away from the metal fence. Use a piece of 3/4-in. stock. Most fences are provided with holes for this purpose. Use flat head bolts or round head screws to fasten the board.

Cut the sides to their proper length (assuming you left them slightly oversize when gluing),

then cut the dadoes. Make a trial cut on scrap to check the size. If it is all right, proceed to cut the dadoes. Cut the matching dadoes and rabbets for each fence setting.

Next cut the four horizontal sections. These are also made up of glued stock. Since these won't show, you can use stock of lesser quality. Be sure to cut the pieces square. Plane the front edge of each piece then check the fit with

the dadoes cut in the side panels. If the pieces are badly bowed, it may be necessary to cut a groove through the center to straighten them. Cut the groove on the table saw and make it about 1/2-in. deep. This will weaken the piece until it is assembled but once in place, the groove will have no effect on the strength of the piece. Be sure to keep the groove on the underside. Apply a thin coat of glue to

Mini-Office

the edge grain of the compartment dividers (horizontal pieces) and allow to dry. This will size the absorbent end grain, thus preventing a "dry" joint.

If you have sufficient clamps you can glue up the assembly without nails or screws. Otherwise you can use nails or screws to hold the parts while the glue sets. Drive nails or screws diagonally from the underside of each divider except for the top one which can be fastened through the top as shown.

Make the top by gluing up several pieces of stock chosen for a pleasing grain appearance. Knots are permissible but they should be tight and not too large. The length of the pieces should be at least 38 inches. This will allow you sufficient stock for trimming later. Use dowels as was done with the other sections. If you use a doweling jig be sure to always align the tool from the same side. This will insure perfect alignment and accuracy of the holes even if there is a slight variation in the lumber thickness.

After the top is glued, cut the piece in half then trim the ends so that each piece will be 18-in. wide. Plane or join all edges. Do not mount the top at this time.

Door and drawer fronts are constructed next. These are cut with a raised panel edge. First cut the doors to size, then bevel the edges on the table saw. Set the blade to

a 15-degree tilt then adjust the fence to produce the bevel. Make trial cuts on scrap the same thickness as the fronts. A planer blade is recommended for this cut. It will leave a smooth clean bevel. The saw blade will leave a small triangular edge which should be removed. Do this by recutting the pieces with the blade tilt set to 0-degrees and projecting about ⅛-in. Set the fence as required and trim each piece. Again make trial cuts on the scrap previously cut.

The upper compartment contains a door, the others are drawers. The door has a sub-front to which the hinges are attached. Cut this from ½-in. pine. Drill a clearance hole ½-in. diameter for the pull screw head. Drill the screw body hole (¼-in. dia.) into the front panel. Attach the front and sub-front with glue and brads. Hinges can now be installed. Use 2-in. semi-concealed non-mortise hinges and mount as shown.

Make the drawers next. The sides, rear and sub-front are made of ½-in. pine. The bottoms are ¼-in. plywood. Cut the pieces to size then assemble with glue and finishing nails. The grooves, dadoes and rabbets are made on the table saw or with the router. Drill the screw and clearance holes before assembly as was done with the door.

Add the strip hinge next. Place both halves of the top on a flat surface with the bottom side facing up. Butt the pieces carefully then position the hinge and mark the

hole centers. Install only the four corner and two center screws. Check the fit. If the fit is all right, install the balance of the screws. The top can now be joined to the cabinet. Leave it on the flat surface and carefully place the cabinet in place on it. Center it from side to side. The rear edges of the top and cabinet are mounted flush. Mount the top with glue and screws. A few nails driven first before screwing will assure that the top will not shift during assembly.

The drop leaf support bracket is mounted next. Use three flat head screws. The bracket will be properly positioned if installed with the cabinet upside down on a flat surface. The bracket is made to fold flat when the leaf is down. A bracket support cleat is installed on the bottom side of the lid as shown.

The shelf for the typewriter is made to slide snugly between the underside of the top and two cleats. Stops on the shelf prevent it from being pulled out too far. The stops consist of round head screws installed as shown.

Drawer hardware, pulls and hinges must be removed when applying the finish. (Note: Strip hinge can be left on, but care must be taken not to paint or stain it.)

Seal the wood with a penetrating sealer then apply stain as desired. We used the following: clear Firzite diluted 50% to be used as a sealer. Next, a coat of Ethan Allen dark pine stain. When the stain has dried, follow with a coat of

Below, a wood strip attached to saw fence keeps blade from the fence when rabbeting the ends. When hammering the dowel joints, right, use a piece of scrap wood to avoid marring the edges.

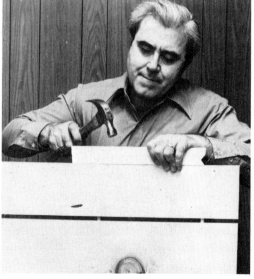

Sapolin dark walnut stain. This combination gives one of the finest pine stain finishes I have ever seen. Follow with two coats of Deft clear satin finish.

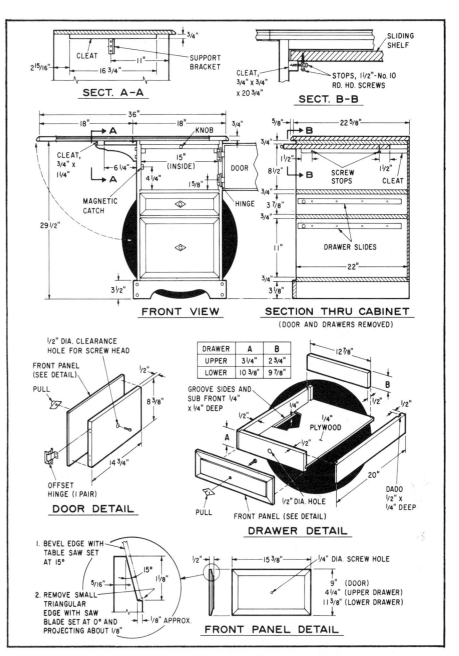

SECT. A–A

SECT. B–B

FRONT VIEW

SECTION THRU CABINET
(DOOR AND DRAWERS REMOVED)

BILL OF MATERIALS

All lumber pine except where noted

Use	Size & Description	No. Req.
Top	¾" x 18" x 18"	2
Sub top	¾" x 15½" x 21¾"	1
Side	¾" x 22" x 29½"	2
Cross piece	¾" x 15½" x 21¾"	3
Base side	¾" x 3½" x 22"	2
Base front	¾" x 3½" x 18"	1
Drop leaf cleat	¾" x 1¼" x 16¾"	1
Nose & cove molding	24"	4 pcs.
Sliding shelf	¾" x 14⅞" x 20¾"	1
Shelf cleat	¾" x ¾" x 20¾"	2
Rear panel	¼" x 15½" x 26" plywood	1
Door front	¾" x 9" x 15⅜"	1
Door sub front	½" x 8⅜" x 14¾"	1
Drawer front	¾" x 4¼" x 15⅜"	1
Drawer sub front	½" x 3¼" x 12⅞"	1
Drawer side	½" x 3¼" x 20"	2
Drawer rear	½" x 2¾" x 12⅞"	1
Drawer front	¾" x 11⅜" x 15⅜"	1
Drawer sub front	½" x 10⅜" x 12⅞"	1
Drawer side	½" x 10⅜" x 20"	2
Drawer rear	½" x 9⅞" x 12⅞"	1
Drawer bottom	¼" x 12⅞" x 19¾" plywood	2
Strip hinge	1" x 22"	1
Buttons		4
Magnetic catch		1
Offset hinges		1 pair
Drawer slides		2 pair
Pulls		3
Knob		1
Screws	1½-10 RH (stops)	4
Screws	1¼-8 FH (cleats)	8

DOOR DETAIL

DRAWER DETAIL

DRAWER	A	B
UPPER	3¼"	2¾"
LOWER	10⅜"	9⅞"

FRONT PANEL DETAIL

1. BEVEL EDGE WITH TABLE SAW SET AT 15°
2. REMOVE SMALL TRIANGULAR EDGE WITH SAW BLADE SET AT 0° AND PROJECTING ABOUT ⅛"

9" (DOOR)
4¼" (UPPER DRAWER)
11⅜" (LOWER DRAWER)

Left, the sub top is nailed into place. It fits into the rabbets in side pieces. The strip hinge is fastened with flat head screws, below. Make the pilot holes with an awl. Right, the drawers are made of ½" stock except for bottoms which are ¼" plywood. Cut pieces to size, assemble with glue, finishing nails. Drill screw and clearance holes before assembly.

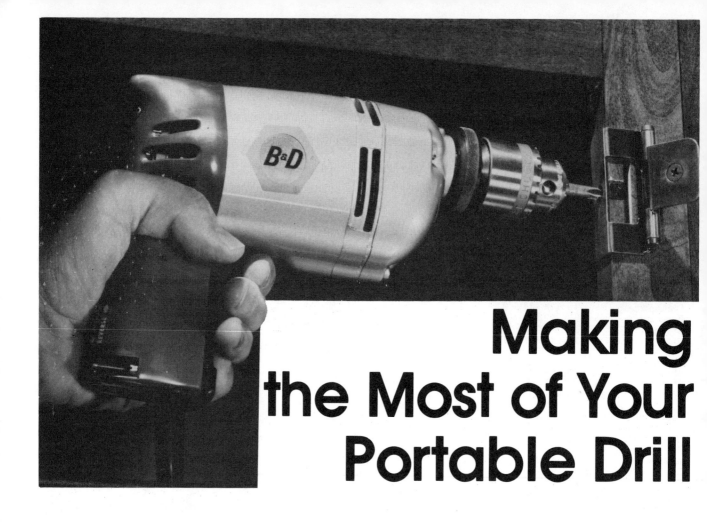

Making the Most of Your Portable Drill

THE PORTABLE ELECTRIC DRILL with the various accessories available is, without a doubt, the most useful and versatile portable power tool there is today. Originally intended as a portable power tool for drilling holes, it has developed into a power pack for operating such attachments as: a circular saw, jigsaw, belt or disc sander, grinder, buffer and polisher, and wood lathe. It even operates an air compressor for paint spraying.

New time and labor saving attachments for the portable electric drill are being developed every day to make it even more useful and versatile.

The size of a portable drill indicates the maximum diameter of drill bit the chuck will take and bore a hole through mild steel. Larger diameter drill bits for boring holes in wood have ¼-inch shanks to fit the popular ¼-inch portable drill. Home workshop electric drills are available in ¼-, ⅜-, and ½-inch chuck sizes and are

duty rated as *light, standard* or *heavy duty*. The price of a drill varies with its duty rating and this rating depends largely on the design of the equipment's motor.

Light duty drills are for intermitent use only. Since their motors are wound with small diameter wire on the field and armature coils, these drills tend to "heat up" if overloaded or used continuously for long periods of time. Overheating eventually breaks down the insulation and the drill motor shorts out. When used intermittently they are entirely satisfactory since the motor has a chance to cool between jobs, thus prolonging the life of the drill.

Standard and heavy duty drill motors are wound with larger diameter or gage wire than the light duty drills, which in turn requires larger aluminum cases to house the motors. Heavy duty drills also have larger ball bearings, hardened gears and shafts, and more rugged construction throughout. All this

adds up to higher cost. The standard duty drill, however, will run continuously under an average load with small temperature rise and take short overloads without harm.

The standard duty drill is probably the most satisfactory for home workshop use because of its construction, price and ability to operate drill attachments for longer periods of time than required to merely drill a hole. The heavy duty drill, although satisfactory for home use, would be uneconomical for occasional use because of its higher price.

The type and speed of the drill chuck must also be considered when purchasing a drill. Choose a geared-type chuck operated by a key if the drill is to be used with attachments. Drill-chuck speeds vary from no-load speeds to 500 rpm for ½-inch drills to 1600 to 2800 rpm for ¼-inch drills. The correct speed for a particular drilling job depends upon the size of the drill bit and the type of material

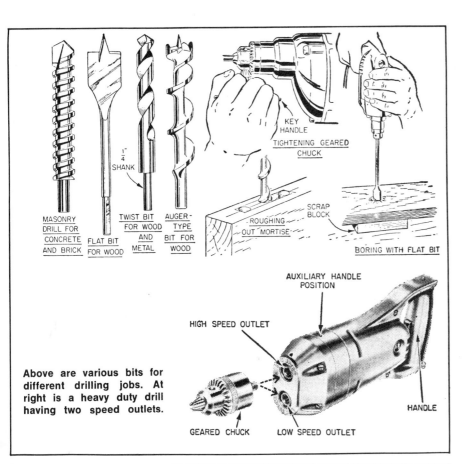

MASONRY DRILL FOR CONCRETE AND BRICK

FLAT BIT FOR WOOD

TWIST BIT FOR WOOD AND METAL

¼ SHANK

AUGER-TYPE BIT FOR WOOD

KEY HANDLE

TIGHTENING GEARED CHUCK

ROUGHING OUT MORTISE

SCRAP BLOCK

BORING WITH FLAT BIT

Above are various bits for different drilling jobs. At right is a heavy duty drill having two speed outlets.

AUXILIARY HANDLE POSITION

HIGH SPEED OUTLET

GEARED CHUCK

LOW SPEED OUTLET

HANDLE

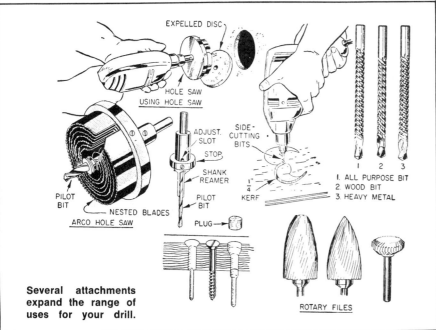

EXPELLED DISC

HOLE SAW USING HOLE SAW

ADJUST. SLOT

STOP

SHANK REAMER

PILOT BIT

PLUG

PILOT BIT

NESTED BLADES

ARCO HOLE SAW

SIDE-CUTTING BITS

¼" KERF

1. ALL PURPOSE BIT
2. WOOD BIT
3. HEAVY METAL

ROTARY FILES

Several attachments expand the range of uses for your drill.

DRILL SPEEDS FOR HIGH SPEED STEEL TWIST DRILL BITS							
	Mild Steel	Tool Steel	Hard Cast Iron	Copper Bronze Brass	Steel Forging	Wood	Masonry Concrete Stone
¹⁄₁₆	6000	3000	4000	8000	3700	12000	
⅛	3000	1500	2200	5000	1800	7000	
³⁄₁₆	2000	1000	1500	4000	1200	4000	
¼	1500	750	1000	3000	900	3000	700
⁵⁄₁₆	1250	600	900	2800	750	2500	600
⅜	1000	500	700	2600	600	2000	500
⁷⁄₁₆	875	425	600	2400	500	1800	400
½	700	400	500	2200	400	1600	300
NOTE: For carbon steel twist drills, reduce speeds by one half.							

being drilled. Most ¼-inch drill attachments operate best at a speed of about 1500 ot 2500 rpm. Drill speed will drop 200 to 300 rpm when a load is placed on the drill bit or attachment.

Since it requires two drills (a ⅜- or ½-inch slow-speed and a ¼-inch high-speed) to handle all the jobs around the house, some manufacturers make a two-speed drill for home workshop use. The drill-speed reducer is another way of making a ¼-inch drill do the work of a large slow-speed drill. Variable-speed drills are also available.

Drill bits are available in a wide variety of types and sizes for boring holes in almost any material. The common twist drill can be used for both wood and metal and is especially useful where there is danger of boring into hidden nails or screws, as frequently occurs in building repair.

Auger-type bits have shanks of a fixed size in a set regardless of hole boring size. These cut fast and clean and can be accurately centered by inserting the points at intersecting lines or in dimples made by indenting the wood with a center punch or awl. Flat bits, also extend the diameter capacity of a drill. To prevent splintering the underside of the wood when the drill bit breaks through, rest or clamp a block of scrap wood under the work piece. Flat bits are excellent for fast rough boring. When drilling holes larger than ¼-inch with a ¼-inch drill, keep the drill-feed pressure light and "nurse" the drill through the material to prevent overheating the motor.

Boring is adaptable to ornamental as well as utilitarian work, where gallery edgings are being made. Clamp two strips of wood together, using the joint for a center line. Various patterns are possible with variation of bit size and spacing. Bore a series of holes with an auger bit to rough out a mortise.

A hole saw saws out discs instead of reducing the material to shavings as a boring bit and makes it possible to cut 2½-inch diameter holes with a portable drill. The nested blades are removable so that the one of the diameter selected can be used alone by inserting it in its groove and locking with a

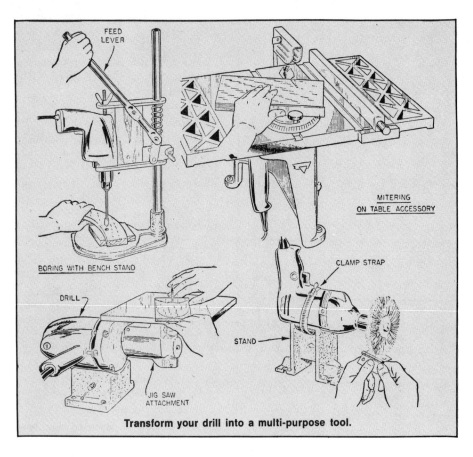

Transform your drill into a multi-purpose tool.

Labels within image: FEED LEVER, BORING WITH BENCH STAND, DRILL, JIG SAW ATTACHMENT, MITERING ON TABLE ACCESSORY, CLAMP STRAP, STAND

screw. The hole saw is guided and held on center with the pilot bit. Apply pressure until the cutter has sawed through the board. As the saw is withdrawn, the center spring ejects the disc.

A side-cutting drill bit converts your power drill into a router-like tool that will cut intricate curves, making a ¼-inch wide kerf. First bore a hole with the side-cutting bit, then force it along the layout line with the bit in the waste wood. Adding a push and pull, or sawing action is helpful, when cutting diagonal to the wood grain. The sides of the hole can be beveled by tilting the bit at the apropriate angle.

First aid to driving screws is the screwdriver bit which bores a pilot hole for the threaded part of the screw, a shank. hole in the piece that is to be screwed down, and countersinks the hole for a flat-headed screw all in one operation. Such a bit may have a stop adjustable for height so that the hole can also be counterbored for a wooden plug, either to be dressed flush to hide the screw, or to appear as a false dowel rising a little above the

surface. To use such bits, tack or clamp the parts together and bore in the usual manner. Bits are available for the various sizes of wood screws. To drive screws rapidly, the speed reducer can be used. Several types and sizes of screwdriver bits are available.

The most generally useful disc sander for portable drills is a flexible rubber back-up disc faced with an abrasive sheet which is held with a screw sunk into the depressed center. Insert the shank of the sanding-disc arbor in the drill check, and sand by pressing a part of the disc against the work while rotating. With the soft backing there is little tendency to gouge in, and the strokes feather off well, leaving no offsets. Cross scratches are removed by finishing with fine sandpaper. On broad work a better job of surfacing is done if the machine is mounted on a sliding base and locked at a slight angle. Stroke toward the raised side of the disc.

A flat sanding disc with a flexible joint is suitable for freehand use with a portable drill because the shank accommodates itself to small variations from the vertical

of the holding position. So used, the gouging is reduced and a flat surface is easily obtained. An oversize sandpaper disc used on the metal tends to reduce sanding laps.

Sanding-disc tables, adjustable for tilt and provided with small miter gages, can be set for accurate sanding of small work, correcting miter joints and hopper cuts. Move the piece across the face of the disc while holding it firmly against the mitergage head to avoid uneven cutting due to the more rapid travel of the sandpaper near the outside of the disc. Vibration-type sanders, with straightline or orbital motion, are also available as attachments for drills. The rapidly moving pad sands smoothly and will work up into corners of panels and other recesses.

Many of the advantages of a drill press are obtained by clamping a portable drill to a bench stand. Held rigidly in the yoke, the drill is raised and lowered with a lever, the drill moving in a vertical line. The depth of boring is regulated by clamping the yoke at the required height, or in some models, by locking a collar below the yoke, on the column, to limit travel. Before drilling, press the switch-lock button to free both hands for holding the work and feeding the machine.

The circular saw attachment has many of the features of a standard portable saw, and is used like it, guiding the indicator along the line, or tacking or clamping a straightedge to the work for the edge of the bottom of the attachment to slide against. By the use of a dado arbor, which has a tilted washer and socket joint arrangement for a wobble saw, a cutting blade is made to sweep from side to side, cutting a wide groove.

Saw tables, complete with rip fence, miter gage, and table extensions, turn the portable drill with its saw accessory into a standard table saw. For this work the miter gage, swiveled to the required angle, guides the work past the blade. When setting the rip fence for cutting a board to width, measure the distance from the fence to a blade tooth which is set toward it.

HOW TO USE A TABLE SAW LIKE A PRO

For each sawing job there's a method to handle it quickly, safely and accurately

THE TABLE SAW is an efficient and effective tool. It saves you a tremendous amount of hard labor. It can turn out work that is straighter and more precisely dimensioned than you could possibly get otherwise. And it can be operated with complete safety year after year.

A table saw (often called a bench saw or circular saw) is a power tool, not a toy. *Caution!* Use the saw correctly. It's an axiom that if you use the tool correctly, you are also using it safely.

Operating a table saw is simple and safe. The entire unit is solidly planted where it belongs. There's just a small blade rotating, most of it under the table and out of the way. Only a very small segment is exposed, usually only about an inch in height. But small as it is, the blade can wreak plenty of havoc when used carelessly or improperly.

Here are the essentials of good woodworking practices:

Have a saw of good quality and of ample size for the work to be done. The larger the table size, the better. Extra side extensions help to stabilize the wood stock as it is fed into the blade. A small table provides only a small area to hold a board steady while it is being cut. The saw fence should be of study construction, with a dependable locking device, and preferably of the self-aligning type so the fence is square with the blade each time it is set.

Have sufficient clearance on all sides of the tool to handle boards without hindrance. If you're running an 8-foot long board through the blade, you need at least 16 feet of clear space, plus the width of the blade and room for yourself. If the space is long and narrow, you can mount the saw on casters to turn it sidewise for crosscutting. An extra table or roller platform at the back of the saw will support the board as it comes through, making it easier and safer to handle.

Keep the shop floor clean, and have ample lighting. Sweep up sawdust and wood chips that might cause you to slip. Lights should be in a non-glare fixture, preferably fluorescent, and cover a large area. Don't let sawdust accumulate under the saw.

Use blade guard and splitter whenever possible. Have a push stick handy at all times for feeding narrow stock. Use only sharp and clean blades; dull blades require excessive pushing and make rough cuts. Keep the saw mandrel properly aligned with the blade so the stock will cut true and won't bind against the fence.

Wear proper clothing—no dangling sleeves or tie. Avoid wearing at the side of blade when running stock, not directly in back of it. And never reach to remove waste pieces of stock when the blade is running.

Possible mishaps. It's best to be informed of possible hazards and prevent them. When something goes wrong it happens instantly—without warning. There's no time to correct errors then. Here is a list of such situations and protective measures.

1. Out-of-line ripping. When feeding a board, it should be kept in contact with the fence until the blade has made a deep cut into the stock. If the board is moving in without side support, an open space between the stock and the fence becomes larger. The board then wobbles so that the cut suddenly swerves out of line. If your fingers are nearby holding down the stock, they may be pulled into the blade. Never rip stock that does not have a straight edge to go against the fence and keep fingers wrapped tightly around the fence top.
2. Kickback. This happens most frequently when ripping and

TABLE SAW

the work is fed too quickly, or binds in the blade. The wood is thrown back with great force. Never stand directly in line with the blade. Hold work down firmly and use the splitter to keep kerf open.

3. Binding. This occurs when crosscutting with a blade that is dull or rusty. If the saw belt is of the right tension, the motor will stall, and it should be shut off instantly.

4. Narrow stock. Always use a push stick to feed narrow stock along the fence. When fingers must be used for holding down the wood, hook the other fingers over the top of the fence, and slide them along as the work goes through the blade.

Each sawing job calls for a special method, which should be followed scrupulously. There will be plenty of times when your inventive talents will be called on to solve special problems. That means planning and setting up jigs that hold the work securely, particularly when you cut tenons, lock miters, bevels, and irregular shapes.

Handling large panels. A common problem is that of cutting large plywood panels. A ¼-inch wallboard panel is light enough, and can be handled on a saw of average size provided you set up a table nearby for extra support, or have a roller-topped extension stand. Even with the ¼-inch stock, it's difficult enough to run the panel through and keep it always firmly against the fence.

A ¾-inch plywood panel is usually beyond the ability of a single person, and it's best to have assistance—to carry it into the workshop as well as to align it properly on the saw.

Your assistant should stand alongside the saw as the panel end approaches the blade, pressing in from the side against the fence. Both persons then slowly guide the panel along until it is halfway through, then the assistant goes to the back and supports the panel as it emerges. In the final stage, the

To make a rabbet, hold board upright against fence for first cut, then lay flat, cut side down, for the second cut.

person feeding moves to the side and continues pressure at the side to hold the panel edge at the fence so the cut is straight and true all the way. The feeder supports the free side of the ripped panel, while the assistant pulls the other part until it clears the blade.

An easier way to handle a full-length ¾-inch panel is to precut it roughly to width with a portable circular saw or jig saw. The straight factory-cut edges on each side are retained to go against the fence for final ripping to precise size. Precutting is also helpful for getting the panel into a basement workshop when the entranceway presents difficulties. Only the large, professional model saws can cut to the center of a 4-foot-wide panel, so usually this must be done with a portable saw.

Methods of ripping. Ripping is cutting in the same direction as the grain, and is always done against the fence. When ripping, always use the blade guard and splitter. The splitter prevents the wood from squeezing together at the saw kerf and thus makes it easier to feed the stock smoothly.

When setting the fence for the cutting width, use a folding ruler to measure the distance from the fence to the inside tip of a saw tooth that is set toward the fence. Thus you have the width that the blade will cut, and avoid including the thickness of the kerf. That is, if the stock you want is on the fence side and the waste stock outside. But it can be reversed; the outside

Beveling is done by tilting the blade to the required angle. The position of the fence will control depth of the cut.

piece can be the desired size. In that case, measure from the outside edge of a saw tooth to the edge of the wood, and the kerf will now be on the waste stock toward the fence.

For ripping duplicate pieces to uniform width, use the fence side of the blade. This will eliminate need for measuring each time, and the dimensions will be uniform.

Adjust the blade height so it is just above the thickness of the wood. Lock the fence, making certain it won't shift. Swing the blade guard into place. Hold the board flat on the table, and advance it towards the blade. As it moves into the blade, place the free hand so that the thumb and forefinger are pressing down on the stock just before the blade, and holding the wood against the fence. The other fingers should be bent around the fence. In that way, if the blade should suddenly cause the wood to veer, the hand will remain safely gripping the fence, out of danger. This should be standard practice, even when the blade guard is used.

When ripping a board that is more than 6 feet long, provide support at the free end of the saw for the stock as it comes through; otherwise, you'll find the free weight pulls it down and makes it difficult to run the last part through smoothly. It is possible to walk around to the back while holding the board in place, and pull the rest of the board from there, but this is clumsy and could cause problems.

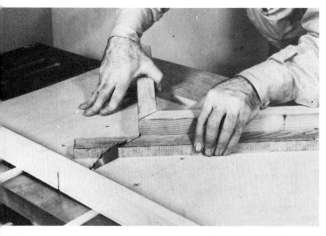

This accurate mitering jig is simply a sliding panel with two tunners that move in the table slots. Work is held against large blocks which have been accurately positioned at 90°.

The quickest method of producing accurate tenons is by using a special tenoning jig. The work is clamped to the jig which slides on a runner. The jig adjusts for various tenon widths.

When ripping narrow stock, with less than 3 inches between the blade and the fence, always use a push stick instead of your fingers to run the wood alongside the blade near the end of the cut. When ripping thin strips at the fence side, stand well away as the strip will suddenly shoot back at your side of the table.

Taper ripping. It is possible to rip a board at an angle to make one end wider than the other. This is done with the aid of a tapering jig, consisting of two hinged boards, with a stock block on the open end of one side. The jig is opened to form an angle that will give the desired taper. It is set against the fence and the stock placed so a corner is at the stop block. The entire unit—jig and stock—is pushed through. Because of the offset formed by the open jig, the blade cuts through the stock at an angle, wider at the front than at the back. Such a jig can prove extremely handy on a wide variety of construction projects.

Miter cutting is normally done with the miter jig, which can be adjusted to any angle by loosening a thumb screw. But there's a tendency for the wood to creep slightly while it is cut, so wherever possible, the work should be held with a C-clamp. Even so, the results may not be perfect on small work. A better method is with a large sliding panel which has two runners that move in the table slots. The work is easily held against large, correctly-positioned blocks set at

90° angles.

Crosscutting to length. The miter gauge is used when sawing work across the grain to obtain the desired length. The miter gauge should be tested occasionally to make sure it is square with the blade. The work is set against the gauge, which is moved towards the blade until the cut is made. In crosscutting, the blade guard may be a hindrance and there's the temptation to remove it entirely. But this should be done only after you have acquired experience.

If the saw table is quite small, situations may arise when you want to cut 12-inch wide stock and there's insufficient clearance for the wood between the front edge of the blade and the miter gauge.

A solution is to lower the blade so the wood can move forward over the blade plate. While holding the stock down, start the motor and raise the blade so it cuts through; then you can push the wood through with the gauge to complete the cut.

If you want to cut a number of pieces to the same length, adjust the stop rods on the miter gauge to correct position. Then each piece is moved against the bent end of this rod and will be cut to the same length.

Another way is to clamp a stop block at the front end of the fence so that the wood can be placed on the gauge in correct position. As the wood passes the stop block, it remains in the same position for cutting. But *never* use the fence it-

self—or a stop block clamped near the blade—as a jig. This will cause the wood to bind and swing around out of your grasp, perhaps pulling your fingers into the blade.

Rabbeting and tenoning. There are many woodworking jobs that require rabbet joints, such as drawer fronts and cabinet doors. This entails setting the blade at precise height for each of two cuts. The first cut is made with the board held vertically against the fence. Then the board is placed flat on the table with the cut end down, edge against the fence, and run through a second time, removing the square strip.

The blade height for each cut should be set first by measurement, but then tested for accuracy by running through a few pieces of waste stock. When vertical and horizontal cuts mate at the precise position to clear the edge stock, the setup is right to go ahead.

Dadoing across the grain, and grooving along the grain, are best done with an adjustable dado cutter, or a set consisting of several blades of different thickness placed together for a cut of the correct width.

Adjust the blade height by making test runs to cut the groove of the desired depth. When running the stock, hold it down firmly over the cutter, as the wood tends to bounce slightly which results in an uneven cut. When using dado blades, the table insert plate must be changed for one that has a slot wide enough for the cutter.

TABLE SAW

For tenoning, a special jig makes the job easier, as the stock usually is long and must be fed into the blade along the narrow edge. Clamps on the jig hold the stock firmly and safely.

Half-lap joints, used for making frames for boxes or screens, bring two parts together, each of which has been cut to half the thickness of the wood so the corners match evenly and flush. The cutting is done against the miter gauge, either with a dado blade or a regular crosscut blade. It is essential that the blade height be precisely at half point. As the dado blade will not be of the correct thickness, the work must be shifted while making several passes across the blade to obtain a sufficient width of cut. Because of this, the use of a regular blade is suggested.

First place the two pieces to be joined so the corners are square to each other. With a pencil, mark lines at the inside edge on each part. After the blade is set to correct height, half the thickness of the work, make the first cut on the inside of the marked line. Then move the stock about ⅛-inch closer to the blade and repeat the pass, thus widening the kerf. Repeated passes, while moving the stock about ⅛-inch each time, will complete the lap cutting.

Repeat this with the other part, and fit the two pieces of stock together. In most cases, the cleared section must be smoothed with the edge of a chisel to clean out loose fibers. The half-lap joint must fit perfectly flush on all sides.

Beveling and chamfering are done by tilting the saw (or the table) to the required angle. Position of the fence will control the depth of the bevel cut. When a full 90° angle is desired, as for a mitered cabinet top, a strip of wood is clamped to the fence to provide a soft facing. Then the tilted saw blade is raised while it is running, until it just begins to bite into the extra fence facing.

If the fence is positioned correctly, the blade just misses the top edge of the board, or the veneer if it is plywood. A few test cuts will be necessary to make the final adjustment in both fence and blade height so the mitered corners will fit precisely.

Getting a straight edge. It's not the fancy cuts that will give you trouble, so much as the ordinary, everyday situations. You may have perfectly good pieces of solid maple stock that would be just right for a desk frame, but have rough, uneven edges. How do you get them straight enough so they can be ripped on the table saw? This is a common problem because many are sold that way.

The solution is easy if you have a jointer—in fact, that's a prime purpose of the jointer. The board is run through the rotary cutters until the sides are perfectly straight and smooth. Another way, but much slower and more difficult, is to plane the board by hand, checking with a square until it is true. Or you might try tacking the maple to another thin, straight board, setting the edge a little distance from the fence, so that as the bottom board moves along, the blade also cuts into the hardwood and forms a new straight edge.

Sawing plastic veneers. When sawing plastic laminate sheeting (Formica, Micarta, etc.) on a table saw, always keep it face up to prevent chipping of the plastic coating at the edges. When cutting the thin plastic itself, feed slowly while holding the stock down close to the blade with a flat piece of wood to prevent bouncing. It is easier to saw when the plastic has already been laminated to a plywood backing.

When cutting plastic with a portable power saw, turn it face down, as this type of saw revolves the opposite way. The saw teeth must cut from the finished side down

When sawing the plastic, or tempered hardboard, use a carbide-tipped blade or special hardened metal-cutting blade. A regular blade can be used, but it will quickly become dull.

Correcting saw troubles. Burning, which scorches the sides of the stock and sometimes causes smoke, is due either to a dull blade or green wood. Some of the hardwoods, particularly birch, are very difficult to cut on small-diameter home saws. If your saw has variable feed pulleys, set the belt for lower rpm. If gum or resins accumulate on the blade and make it sticky, wash it with turpentine or other solvent. Raising the height of the blade about ¾-inch above the thickness of the stock often will make cutting easier.

When the blade binds in the kerf, use the splitter to keep the kerf open. Binding may occur near the end when ripping a long board, because of the weight at the far end or possible twisting as a result of misalignment. Supporting the board with a table will correct this problem.

TABLE AND GAUGE SETTINGS FOR COMPOUND ANGLE CUTS

Work Angle	4-Sided Butt Joint		4-Sided Miter Joint		Hexagonal Joint		Octagonal Joint	
	Blade or Table Tilt	Miter Gauge	Blade or Table Tilt	Miter Gauge	Blade or Table Tilt	Miter Gauge	Blade or Table Tilt	Miter Gauge
5°	½	85	44¾	85	29¾	87½	22¼	88
10°	1½	80¼	44¼	80¼	29½	84½	22	86
15°	3¾	75½	43¼	75½	29	81¾	21¼	84
20°	6¼	71	42	71	28¼	79	21	82
25°	10	67	40	67	27¼	76½	20¼	80
30°	14½	63½	37¾	63½	26	74	19¼	78¼
35°	19½	60¼	35¼	60¼	24½	71¾	18¼	76¾
40°	24½	57¼	33¾	57¼	22¾	69¾	17	75
45°	30	54¾	30	54¾	21	67¾	15¾	73¾
50°	36	52½	27	52½	19	66¼	14¼	72½
55°	42	50¾	24	50¾	16¾	44¾	12¾	71¼
60°	48	49	21	49	14½	63½	11	70¼

Figures are in degrees and are for direct setting to tilt scale and miter gauge. Scale providing tilt starts at 0° and miter gauge at 90° in normal position.

ALL ABOUT PAD SANDERS

When the job calls for finely controlled finishing, it's best to use one of these

THERE ARE MANY good reasons why you should consider the purchase of a finishing pad sander, similar to the one shown here, even if you already own a belt or disk sander. A pad sander does not produce the troublesome swirl marks characteristic of disk sander action; and because it is slower cutting than a belt sander, it can be controlled more easily to produce really fine wood finishing jobs. The pad sander can save you hours of time by making many other around-the-house chores easier to do. It can be used to remove old paint and varnish before refinishing, for smoothing out spackle used to patch holes in walls, buffing the wax applied to the family car or to furniture, and even for polishing small metal and plastic objects.

The most popular type of pad sander features a rotary motor that imparts an orbital motion to the sandpaper attached to the platen of the sander. The orbit may be circular or elliptical, but in either case the orbit is so small that you cannot see it in action. Orbital action removes wood much faster than linear (straight back-and-forth) action that is typical of a second, less expensive breed of pad sander that utilizes a magnetic vibrator to drive the platen. Some deluxe pad sanders provide both orbital and linear sanding at the

flick of a switch. If you are interested in ultra-fine finishing of good furniture, the extra cost of such a combination job may be justified; but for the average homeowner and craftsman, the orbital sander alone is sufficient.

Basic sanding procedures. Although many pad sanders have grips for two-handed operation, do not assume that this is because pressure must be applied. In fact, a pad sander works most efficiently if you apply no more pressure than that provided by the weight of the machine; use your hands simply to guide the machine over the work.

If your sander is double-insulated, it can be safely plugged into any wall socket that provides proper AC voltage. If the sander is not double-insulated, it should have a three conductor cord terminating in a three-pronged grounding plug. Use the grounded plug only in a suitable, properly grounded socket to ensure your personal safety. If you must use a long extension cord, select one having No. 18 A.W.G. (American Wire Gage) or larger conductors for distances up to 100 feet. If the wire is too lightweight, there may be enough of a voltage drop to damage the sander motor.

Most pad sanders utilize strips of sandpaper measuring about 3⅔ x 9 inches which you can obtain by

cutting (don't tear) a conventional sheet of sandpaper into three equal parts. Clips at the front and rear of the platen hold the sandpaper in place, over the sander pad. Stretch the sandpaper as tightly as possible before fastening under the second clip because loosely attached sandpaper will not perform efficiently. Start the sander and let it get up to proper speed before laying it down on your work, move it about slowly and evenly in overlapping arcs, and remove from the work before shutting off the motor.

Actually, no special skill is required to use a pad sander. You will get the hang of it within a minute or two after you first turn it on. But you won't obtain the best possible performance from the sander unless you become familiar with the various types of sandpapers that are available, and what they are used for. No one type or grade of sandpaper can possibly handle all your sanding jobs, and buying all available types and grades would be a waste of money.

Choosing the right sandpaper. You can scratch one type of sandpaper off your list immediately, as far as its use with any mechanical sander is concerned; it's the old-fashioned flint sandpaper having granules of quartz as the abrasive material. Flint sandpaper simply is

PAD SANDERS

not strong enough for machine use. This leaves you with three other basic types of sandpapers: garnet, aluminum oxide and silicon carbide. In many instances their uses overlap, but not necessarily in reverse order. For example, you could use aluminum oxide papers for those jobs that a garnet paper could handle easily, but the garnet paper cannot equally well substitute for the aluminum oxide paper when the job calls for more abrasive toughness than is characteristic of garnet.

Aluminum oxide is a synthetic material that is somewhat harder and tougher than garnet, and significantly tougher than flint. But the slightly higher price of aluminum oxide paper is more than offset by the longer use you will get from it. Aluminum oxide paper is unquestionably the favorite among home craftsmen.

Garnet is superior to flint, but it is losing out to aluminum oxide so you may not even find it in all stores. If you do, and the price is right, it will serve very well for ordinary woodworking.

Silicon carbide is a very hard synthetic mineral (almost as hard as diamond) so it can tackle really tough jobs. It is usually applied to cloth or waterproof paper backings so that it can be wet with water or light oil for final smoothing and polishing operations. You are likely to see silicon carbide papers only in the finer grits. Both silicon carbide and aluminum oxide papers are suitable for working metal as well as wood.

The abrasive characteristics of sandpapers are rated in several different ways, but the two most common systems utilize grit numbers and/or a numerical grading scale. Grit numbers run from about 16 (very coarse) to 400 (very fine). The finer the particle, the larger is the grit number which actually indicates the number of openings per square inch of screening through which the abrasive particles could pass. The numerical system works just the opposite; the smaller the number, the finer the grit size. In

Because a pad sander has slower cutting action than a belt sander, it can be controlled more easily to produce really fine wood finishing jobs like table tops.

fact, the industry soon ran out of real numbers and had to go to a multiple zero numbering system as finer grades of sandpaper were developed. For example, grade 4 paper is very coarse; the coarsest coarse paper is number 2; the coarsest medium paper is 1/2; the coarsest fine paper is 3/0 (an abbreviation of 000); and the coarsest very fine paper is 6/0 while the finest very fine paper is 10/0.

As a general rule, you should use a slightly coarser sandpaper on hardwoods to obtain the same degree of smoothness you could get on softwood with a slightly finer sandpaper. Use the coarsest sandpapers only for roughing which implies the removal of a considerable amount of wood. A medium grit paper should be used for blending which involves some material removal and the imparting of a fairly smooth finish. Fine sandpapers are used primarily to eliminate fine scratches made by coarser sandpapers. Very fine grits are used for final polishing and rubbing actions.

To start, you should try out the effects of the various grades of sandpaper (very coarse, coarse, medium and fine) on both soft and hardwoods. But do not buy every grade within these basic categories until you see a specific need; and you would probably waste your money buying very fine sandpaper unless you are involved in a finishing project that calls for extremely fine finishing. To get you thinking in the right direction, not only in the selection of papers for wood-

working but for other applications such as processing of metals and plastics, here is a summary of the recommendations made by the manufacturer of one of the pad sanders illustrated:

Soft wood and wallboard. Use 2-1 grit garnet cabinet paper for fast material removal, 1/2-2/0 garnet for material removal with fair finish, and 3/0-5/0 garnet finishing paper for fine finish. Aluminum oxide papers of comparable grits can be used, but the toughness of aluminum oxide is not actually required when working with such soft materials.

Plastics. 60-100 grit aluminum oxide for material removal, 120-220 silicon carbide with paper "C" weight for material removal with fair finish, and 240-600 silicon carbide wet paper "A" weight for fine finish.

Hardwoods and hard composition materials. 36-50 grit aluminum oxide for material removal, 60-100 grit aluminum oxide for material removal and fair finish, and 120-180 aluminum oxide finishing paper for fine finish.

Paints and varnishes. 2½-1½ open coat garnet paper for material removal, 240-400 silicon carbide wet paper "A" weight for fine finish.

Fine finishing techniques. If you want the best possible finish on your woodworking projects, you must follow specific surface preparation procedures. Hasty or inexpert use of a sanding machine will lead to disappointment, in which case you should not be too ready to blame

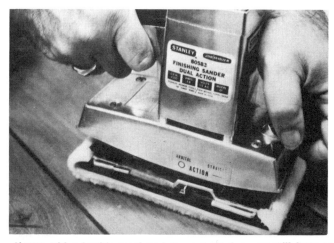

No pressure should be applied with a pad sander. It works best if you use your hands simply to guide machine over the work.

If you add a lamb's wool pad to your sander, you will have a machine to buff and polish many kinds of surfaces and objects.

the equipment. Good finishing, even when using time- and labor-saving machines, requires patience.

The wood should first be sanded down to the smoothest and flattest possible surface using various selected grades of sandpaper. Do not jump from a coarse to a fine sandpaper and expect good results; prepare the surface in stages until you have the kind of smooth finish you want.

When working with hardwoods, you can obtain noticeable improvement in the surface as you go to finer grits, all the way down to a 9/0 paper. But such very fine paper would be wasted on softwood which just won't sand down to a comparable surface. About the finest sandpaper that is practical for softwood is a 6/0 paper. Also, it is rather pointless to work toward an ultra-smooth surface if you plan to apply an enamel coating which would fill in minor pores anyway. A 4/0 or 6/0 paper should be fine enough to prepare a wood surface for enameling.

If you intend to apply a clear type coating, and especially if the wood is to be stained with a water stain, the sanded surface should be wet down with clear, warm water. This makes the wood swell and raises fine surface fibers so that they can be removed with a final sanding, using the finest sandpaper used in the preliminary sanding, *after* the wood has dried thoroughly, preferably by standing overnight. Do not skip this step if you are to use water stains. Some workers go

one step further and apply a coat of thin shellac or a special sanding sealer after the fibers have been raised to harden them before the final sanding; this produces an even smoother final finish. Just be sure not to apply a sealer that might prevent a stain from being absorbed properly by the wood.

These tips provide only the rudiments of good finishing practice, and will be quite adequate for many average wood-finishing jobs. But if you plan to do very exacting finishing, or re-finishing of fine furniture, you should refer to books that deal with such subjects in detail. There are many special tricks and techniques you should learn before attempting serious finishing work.

Other applications. Your pad sander can be used for many purposes other than the basic job of preparing wood for finishing. An orbital sander will do a good job removing old paint and varnish provided that you pick the right kind of sandpaper. Ordinary closed coat sandpapers will soon clog up and become useless; what you need is a special "open coat" abrasive having the grit particles spaced relatively far apart so that they do not clog as easily. It's also important to keep the sander moving constantly with broad, sweeping motions. If you stay in one place too long, the paint or varnish may become soft and gummy because of the frictional heating. If you use a liquid paint or varnish remover to speed the job, let the solvent dry

completely before using your pad sander. In all such removal jobs, the loose paint or varnish should be scraped off with a putty knife before the sander is used, to make the sandpaper last longer.

The taped joints and spackled nail head indentations in a new gypsum wall can be smoothed quickly and easily with your pad sander by using a fine grit, open coat abrasive. Similarly, it's a cinch to repair cracks and nail holes (as from old picture hooks) in existing walls by spackling and then sanding smooth with the pad sander. Caution: plaster dust is very abrasive, so do not let it accumulate on or inside your sander; use compressed air (vacuum cleaner) to blow the dust off frequently.

You will find many other practical uses for your pad sander around the house. Buffing the wax on your car is a cinch if you add a lamb's wool pad to your sander. Mount the sander upside down in a vise and use it to buff and polish all sorts of small objects, such as metal jewelry. Experiment with different types of buffing pads, from thin cloth to scraps of carpeting. The use of buffing compound may help the process. The sander is also excellent for tough rust removal jobs. Just go over that decrepit old saw, or other tool, with your sander after fitting it with fine sandpaper. You may be surprised at the big improvement.

Undoubtedly, you will think of still more uses for this versatile tool if you experiment with it.

How To STAIN AND FINISH FINE WOOD

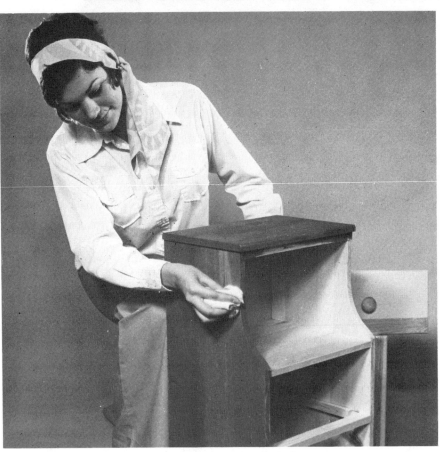

Too often, and in too many places, beautiful pieces of rare woods have lost their exciting identity, with grains suppressed by sullen, opaque stains. It's an easy way to finish wood, but it's not the right way. It is not even tasteful.

Properly finished, the grain of wood becomes an integral part of the furniture, and not every length of wood is worth the time and effort. If the wood you are working with is not worth the trouble, paint it or hide it with cheap stain. But if the wood is rare and the grain exciting, do the job right—let the grain shine through.

There are more ways to hide grain than to bring it out. You can find plenty of pigmented stains, colored varnishes and tinted shellacs. None of these has any important place in furniture finishing. All hide or obscure the grain.

Pigmented stains are the worst offenders. They're compounded with opaque materials which work harder to kill the luster and depth of wood than they do to beautify it. They're helpful in only one case: when it is necessary to fake a grain.

If you want to use these stains, try this idea. Avoid mixing the colorless liquid which rises to the top of the can with the heavier pigments which sink to the bottom. Instead, lift the liquid from the top without mixing. The color is fairly weak, but it works nicely when a light effect is needed.

Oil Stains. Stains can deliver excellent results if you'll take the time to find the clear oil types. In many stores you'll find them under the name "penetrating oil stain." These can be used to tone wood to any shade or color without affecting the grain patterns.

Wipe on a liberal amount of the stain, let it penetrate into the wood for a few seconds, then wipe it off. The longer the stain is left on, the less you remove; the more coats applied, the darker the effect. For light tones, dilute the stain with turpentine or a substitute (it doesn't matter which). Be sure to put a good primer coat over the stain. Shellac is a good material, but if you prefer a commercial sealer use a clear one. The primer-sealer serves one function: It gives a surface on which you can build up final, smooth finish coats.

Clear and penetrating oil stains are available in many tones and shades, but if you buy three—walnut, maple and mahogany—you have enough to mix any tone you may need.

Certain of the better "prepared stains" are worth trying on some woods. One is a nearly clear stain with added plastic compounds which build up a smooth, tough surface. The oil colors the wood only slightly; it is clear enough to let the beauty of the grain come through. On lighter woods, the stain has a slightly yellow coloring —something you may or may not like. On darker woods it's hard to beat.

Aniline dyes darken the wood without affecting the grain. They are available as water-soluble or alcohol-soluble materials. You buy them as a dry powder, mixing a small amount with the proper liquid. Anilines are strong and one or two ounces will handle several large pieces of furniture.

Water-soluble anilines are applied directly to the unprimed wood. Most woods have distinct areas of "dense" grain and "porous" grain—layers grown in the spring and summer and in the fall and winter. The faster-growing spring and summer layers are the most porous. They absorb more color and the fibers can lift. The water-soluble dyes raise these fibers and you'll have to resand the wood after the stain dries even if you've raised the grain several times during sanding.

Resanding is safe and easy if you'll apply a thin coat of shellac after the stain has dried. The shellac will hold the fibers erect. You can smooth the surface without working into the stain—if you sand lightly with a very fine abrasive paper or with steel wool. A 000 or 00000 steel wool is preferred.

Chances are you will have to re-sand even when you prime-coat wood without staining. A brush drawn over wood pulls up tiny fibrils. The primer holds these erect as it dries. The result is a rough surface which can be smoothed by a few light rubs with steel wool. Be sure to thoroughly clean the surface before adding another coat.

Alcohol-soluble stains seldom raise the grain and, if they do, have less effect than a water stain. They can be used over raw wood or mixed with shellac or varnish.

Although anilines are available in a host of colors, you will need only a few. Buy three: walnut, mahogany and maple. From these you can mix any color for any wood.

An example: If you want a mahogany brown, add a small amount of walnut to the maple stain. The result is a rich mahogany stain you can't buy ready-mixed. Want a dark cherry stain? Add a little maple to a mahogany base. For a lighter cherry, add a little mahogany to a maple-walnut base.

Faking wood grains. Some woods are nearly uninteresting in their own grains but become much more interesting when they are stained to look like another wood. The New England whitewood or tulip poplar is one example. It is much more exciting when it has been stained to simulate cherry, mahogany or even birch or cedar.

Here, pigmented stains are helpful. A clear stain can change the grain coloring, but it does not obscure the grain pattern—the one thing necessary in this case. Pigmented stains not only color the wood, but help hide the grain.

In some cases even the opaque pigments may not alter the grain enough. A thinned wood filler may be just what you need.

Mix a standard wood filler—white is best—with turpentine to make a smooth, not-too-thin paste. Tint the paste with stains to the color you want and spread the filler over the wood surface. Wipe off the filler. The amount you leave on the wood will control the amount of grain showing through. A little experimentation will let you simulate

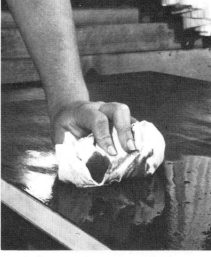

Left, clear oil stains which are available in many tones and shades, will give good tonal qualities without obscuring the fine grain of the wood. The oil stain at the right is allowed to penetrate pores; then it is wiped off evenly with a clean rag.

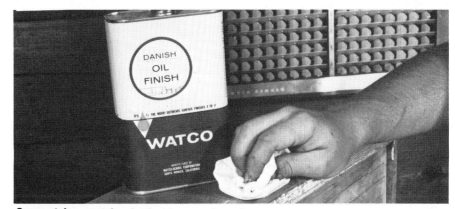

Some stains contain plastic compounds and are worth trying on some woods. They require no other surface care. One nearly clear stain builds up a smooth, tough surface. Oil colors wood only slightly, letting the beauty of the grain come through.

Shown at left is shellac which is an excellent primer of finish coat. It should be thinned only with a wood alcohol. As pictured at the right, it is brushed on, allowed to dry, then it is sanded lightly with a very fine sand paper before second coat is applied.

Left, varnish is a tough, durable finish coat. You should use turpentine or a good substitute to thin—a thinner varnish is less likely to show brush marks. Right, it is applied with brush, thoroughly dried, then rubbed with fine steel wool and waxed.

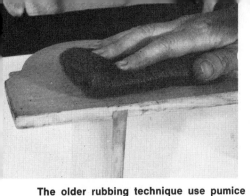
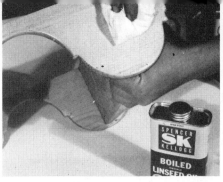

The older rubbing technique use pumice and then rottenstone; using steel wool as shown will give you the same results.

Left, shellac is rubbed with a pad dipped in linseed oil until the shellac is dry and has a smooth surface. Right, in the French method thinned shellac is brushed into the surface. Not used often today, it works well and can be worth time required

both the color and the grain of many woods this way.

Finishing the surface. The type and the amount of stain are dictated by the wood, its coloring and its grain. In some cases no stain at all is dictated. What is required is a simple, protective finish that gives good depth and luster. Early cabinetmakers found the answer in the French polishing method, which can be used on either raw wood or stained wood. It is not often used today, but works well and can be worth the time required.

Use white or clear shellac, about 3- or 4-pound cut (which means that 3 or 4 pounds of shellac gum have been dissolved in one gallon of alcohol). Thin the shellac with wood alcohol and brush it onto the wood, rubbing the wet shellac into the wood after brushing.

Use a rubbing pad made by placing a wadding of cotton inside a soft cotton cloth. Pick up a little linseed oil on the bottom of the pad (the oil is used only as a lubricant during rubbing). Rub the shellac uniformly before it dries. Repeat the brushing and rubbing process 6 to 12 times, making each pass with more shellac and less thinner. Some finishers prefer to make the first coats with a one pound cut, increasing the mix by moving to increased shellac-cut percentages, finishing the final coats with 3- or 4-pound cut shellac. After the first two coats are on and dry, you should sand between each additional coat with a fine grit paper or with fine steel wool.

A plain shellac finish has many uses. It's easier than the French system and gives comparable results. Again, use clear shellac, thinning it with three or more parts wood alcohol. Brush on each coat of shellac, sanding with abrasive or steel wool after the coat has

dried. Cover with three to five light coats, then polish.

Be sure each coat has dried thoroughly before you sand. It may be an overnight procedure. When the finishes are on and rubbed, polish with a good wax.

On warm days you may find the shellac is dry enough to sand in 3 or 4 hours. On humid days, the alcohol in the shellac may draw moisture from the air, creating a white film on the surface. The only solution is to remove the shellac with wood alcohol and start again when there's less humidity.

Varnish is absolutely essential if the wood is to be used around hot places or moisture or if it is to get table-top treatment. It's best to prime the wood with two or three coats of thinned shellac, although a commercial sealer will work as well. Let the primer or sealer coat dry, then rub it lightly with 000 steel wool. Clean the surface with a brush and cover with a layer of quality synthetic varnish. The synthetic varnishes dry faster and give a better surface.

Use a new brush for each varnish job. You'll get best results if you'll varnish with cheap brushes; better than if you've used a good brush which has been cleaned several times. Don't try to save varnish—it is seldom as good the second time around.

When you varnish, try thinning with equal amounts of turpentine or turpentine substitute if it seems hard-flowing. A thinner varnish is less apt to show brush marks. Another trick, often better than thinning is to heat the varnish. Heated varnish will flow easily and dry faster.

Linseed oil finishes are becoming popular again, after a hiatus of many years. Avoid the true linseed oil finish as you would pigmented

stains. Such a finish collects dirt as it is applied, and from then on. The result is a grimy finish that is both without luster and without grain. A far better answer is the *fake linseed oil* finish several wood finishers use.

Coat the raw wood with a mixture of varnish thinned with 2 or 3 parts turpentine. Rub the mix into the wood with your hand, working vigorously for 3 to 5 minutes, until you feel your hand become hot and the varnish become tacky. Wipe off the excess with a clean dry cloth. Let the coat dry, then sand lightly with 00000 or 000000 steel wool. Apply two or three additional coats of varnish, sanding between each coat.

Let the final coat dry thoroughly then sand again lightly. Brush linseed oil over the varnished surface, covering areas not varnished for extra protection. Let the oil soak into the surface for 12 to 15 minutes, then rub clean with a dry cloth. The result is a finish that is clean and durable and that looks like a real linseed oil finish but lacks its obvious drawbacks.

Conditioning finishes. All finishes except the "fake linseed oil" finish can be protected with wax. The linseed oil should not be waxed, but it can be brought back to life from time to time by removing the oil surface and re-surfacing with another round of oil.

The other finishes should be well sanded with super-fine steel wool (0000 or finer), then covered with a good furniture polish or wax. The final result is a finish that has more luster, more depth, more patina than any finish you can get through short-cut methods. And beneath the finish you can see the beautiful, rich, natural grain of the wood. That's the right way to finish wood It's well worth the effort.